CUBA's
RACIAL CRUCIBLE

Locations referenced in this work.

BLACKS IN THE DIASPORA

Herman L. Bennett, Kim D. Butler, Judith A. Byfield, and
Tracy Sharpley-Whiting, editors

(A list of books in the series will be found at the end of this volume)

CUBA's
RACIAL CRUCIBLE

The Sexual Economy of Social Identities, 1750–2000

KAREN Y. MORRISON

INDIANA UNIVERSITY PRESS

Bloomington & Indianapolis

This book is a publication of

INDIANA UNIVERSITY PRESS
Office of Scholarly Publishing
Herman B Wells Library 350
1320 East 10th Street
Bloomington, Indiana 47405 USA

iupress.indiana.edu

∞ The paper used in this publication
meets the minimum requirements of
the American National Standard for
Information Sciences—Permanence of
Paper for Printed Library Materials,
ANSI Z39.48–1992.

Manufactured in the
United States of America

Cataloging information is available from
the Library of Congress.

ISBN 978-0-253-01646-1 (cloth)
ISBN 978-0-253-01654-6 (paperback)
ISBN 978-0-253-01660-7 (ebook)

1 2 3 4 5   20 19 18 17 16 15

Para los que ya no estan
Para los que estan
Y los que vendrán
Especialmente los Cubanos que me permitieron contar sus historias

For those no longer with us,
For those present,
For those yet to come,
Especially the Cubans who allowed me to tell their stories

CONTENTS

ACKNOWLEDGMENTS

WHAT IS TYPICALLY TERMED A SCHOLARLY "MONOGRAPH" IS often anything but. Many hands, minds, and hearts go into the production process. That is especially the case for this project. I am grateful for the assistance and support received at many different levels and in various forms.

My ability to travel to Cuba for primary research was initially supported by a Tinker Foundation graduate student travel grant. The McKnight Foundation Doctoral Fellowship managed by the Florida Education Fund was absolutely vital for the yearlong stay in Cuba needed to access appropriate archival and oral history sources. The Marilyn Yarbough Dissertation/Teaching Fellowship at Kenyon College eased my entry into the combined occupational requirements of publishing and classroom instruction. Faculty development grants at Moravian College and the University of Massachusetts Amherst allowed me to maintain important connections with Cuban colleagues and with historical resources.

Several Cuban research institutions dedicated to the humanities and social science enabled my entrée into those resources: the Instituto de Historia, Centro de Antropologia, Instituto Cultural Juan Marienello,

Biblioteca Nacional José Martí, Archivo Nacional, the parish archives of Espíritu Santo Havana, San Julian of Guines, San José of Colón, and, most significantly, the archives of the Arzobispado de la Habana. In the United States, the impressive holdings of the Special Collections of the George Smathers Libraries of the University of Florida, the Cuban Heritage Collection of the University of Miami, and the Levi Marrero Collection of Florida International University also increased the depth of this project.

At the more personal level, I received valuable professional guidance from my graduate committee at the University of Florida that was chaired by Jeffrey Needell and included Kathryn Burns, David Geggus, and my friend and mentor, the late Helen Safa. Members of the History Department at Moravian College from 2002–2008 also encouraged the evolution of this project, as have my colleagues in the W. E. B. Du Bois Department of the University of Massachusetts Amherst. I am also appreciative of the intellectual exchanges fostered by the Mellon Mutual Mentoring Grants at the University of Massachusetts and the Five Colleges Atlantic Studies Consortium. This project has also benefited from suggestions of the anonymous readers and Herman Bennett.

Additionally, I have been fortunate to have astute, professional friends offer their suggestions for the improvement of various sections. They include Sherry Johnson, Paul Lokken, Lowell Gudmundson, Laura Lovett, Holly Hanson, Mary Renda, Kiran Asher, Laura Briggs, Roberto Márquez, Michele Reid-Vazquez, Erika Edwards, Agustín Lao-Montes, and Rachel O'Toole. Corrective insights were also provided by three trailblazers in Afro-Cuban scholarship, Aisnara Perera Díaz, Maria de Los Angeles Merino Fuentes, and the irrepressible godfather to a generation of scholars, Tomás Fernández Robiana. My profound thanks also goes to José Miguel Rueda and Barbara Danzie León, without whose friendship and knowledge much of my research would not have been possible.

My deepest gratitude and love goes to those people who maintained my sanity and tolerated my moments of insanity: the Maynard family; good friends little Adaline Kariuki, Flavia Araujo, Kelli Morgan, Shannel Grimes, Mona Lisa Williamson, and Mitzie Setalsingh; my "sister"

Kemi; my brothers Wayne and Adrian; my father Wendell "Tony;" and my mother Ouida "Pat." And finally, the Watson family: Linda, Juanita, Aurelio, Yolanda, Lionel, and Cristina Sánchez for creating and maintaining my personal ties with Cuba.

INTRODUCTION

*A Crucible of Race: Historicizing the Sexual
Economy of Cuban Social Identities*

THE INTERVIEW HAD GONE AS PLANNED AND I PREPARED TO
leave Julia's small, but comfortable, Old Havana apartment.[1] With the
self-assurance of her eighty-three years, Julia had thoughtfully told her
family's history by oscillating between recollections of pride, humor,
and pain. As we wrapped up and I turned off the voice recorder, I asked
an impromptu question that deviated from my carefully constructed
questionnaire. I felt somewhat intrusive crossing into such intimate terrain. But after two previous afternoons listening to Julia's very personal
reminiscences, I hoped she would not mind. I ventured, "Y porqué usted
no tuvo hijos con su marido segundo? (Why didn't you have children
with your second husband?)"

"No quise crear confusión racial dentro de mi propia familia (I had not
wanted to create racial confusion in my own family)" was her unhesitat-
ing response.

These words left me momentarily dumbstruck, feeling a totally unexpected mix of amazement and puzzlement. Racial confusion? What
type of racial confusion could have existed if this nearly white, but
African-descended, woman had had children with her Spanish husband? Weren't the informal rules of Cuban racial assignment clear in

xiii

such cases? The pair's offspring could likely have passed as white. Yet, Julia had intentionally avoided that possibility. Why?

I then asked her "Que entiendes por confusión racial? (What do you understand as racial confusion?)" and she responded, "Ya en mi familia teníamos muchos conflictos y competencia entre los mas claros y los más prietos, y yo ya tenía hijos mulatos con mi primer marido. No quise esto dentro mi casa (Already in my family we had many conflicts between the lighter ones and the darker ones. I already had mulatto children with my first husband. I did not want that [type of conflict] in my own home)."[2]

In Julia's situation, race complicates what would otherwise be a simple story of a husband, wife, and children. It reminds us that for Cuba, as with most post-emancipation and post-colonial settings, race-making has been a process occurring just as much in intimate private spaces as in public political discourse. Despite shifts in scholarly interpretations over the last century from an acceptance of the biological basis of race to the promotion of a more socially constructed vision, many of the historical, sexual, and reproductive tendencies that first made race salient still remain.

Race is a biopolitical form linking social power to the material bodies born of sexual practices. For most societies, racially homogeneous mating has been the norm, and by contrast heterogeneity has often been seen either as progressive or "race suicide." Julia's words subtly reveal the tensions in those differing notions of racialized reproduction and represent an entry point for exploring the sexual, reproductive, and family-formation choices that collectively contribute to making race or racial meaning in Cuba. In her concerns, one sees individual choices set within a context of broader societal perceptions and limitations. While Julia's responses are striking in their unconscious rejection of the practice of *blanqueamiento* (whitening) that has been presumed to be a central component of Cuban and Latin American race relations, they should also remind us that in racial heterogeneous societies, even in situations that appear unproblematic or normal, race has been an ever-present factor in reproductive practices.

Taking such visions of racialized reproduction as its point of departure, *Cuba's Racial Crucible* analyzes the historical norms and exceptions in family formation that have contributed to the dynamics of

Cuban racial identities. It draws on a substantial body of archival sources, literary texts, and personal interviews to create an ethno-historical study of the changing notions of racial citizenship in Cuba. It traces the shifts from the colonial exaltation of whiteness to the contemporary multi-racial conceptualizations of the national family. Such shifts have occurred despite racial discrimination and inequality continuing to exist in Cuban life. Popular contemporary sayings such as "Quién no tiene de Congo, tiene de Carabaí" (Who does not descend from the Congo descends from the Carabalí)[3] and "Y tu abuela, dónde está?" (And your [black] grandmother, where is she?)[4] reveal the continuing ideological struggle of positioning African ancestry as essential to Cuban identity. Both sayings are defenses against the rejection of African heritage and oppose any possible equation of white purity and *cubanidad* (Cubanness). The second question, however, is more pointedly ironic than the first. Black and mulatto Cubans often ask it with disdain, in the hope of shaming their lighter-skinned compatriots who attempt to hide or ignore any African background. So while recognition of multi-racial heritage represents an important shift from previous colonial perceptions, it is still contested.

But how have these shifts in ideological notions of racial citizenship occurred? Most analysts have long recognized the insufficient explanatory force of either post-1959 revolutionary change or Fidel Castro's charismatic leadership. Recent scholarship on Cuban race relations also has disavowed dichotomous assessments of aggressive, racist whites, and passive, victimized people of African descent. Instead, these studies highlight Cuba's racial complexity and consider Afro-Cuban historical agency in politics, military actions, and intellectual challenges to eugenic theories.[5] Many scholars now conclude that despite these vigorous efforts, at least since the late nineteenth century, a Cuban nationalist rhetoric of racial inclusion has continued to belie the anti-black discrimination that remains a persistent legacy of colonial slaveholding. Cuba's modern leaders have simultaneously valued a multi-racial nation while maintaining the structures of white privilege, even in revolution.[6] *Cuba's Racial Crucible* builds on this recent scholarship by adopting an original intersectional feminist and social constructionist approach to race that demonstrates how Cuban racial meaning and identities have emerged as much from the reproductive practices of sexual behavior, familial life, and kinship recognition as they have from the political and economic activities typically explored in academic literature.

This study highlights the inextricable links between "family," "race," and "nation" in the competing nationalist visions of Cuba that have existed since the eighteenth century. Each item in this trinity relates to notions of "blood ties," or genealogy, but they differ in scale.[7] The family represents the smallest unit, while nation and race are defined much more expansively. Beyond the non-biological political ideologies that shape modern nations, belief in common heritage has often crept into nationalist discourses. The selective genealogical memory used to foster nationalism is similar to those from which notions of familial and racial identity emerge. All give rise to strongly felt visions that distinguish between "us" and "them." The familial, racial, and national "we"s each derive from dynamic social reproductive processes, with individuals, families, civil institutions, and government policy makers manipulating ideological arguments to create the material conditions most advantageous to the collective identities they value. Thus, while our trinity of family, race, and nation may carry some universal significance, they are quite particular to place and time.

Cuba's Racial Crucible examines the particular Cuban intersections of race, nation, and reproductive sexuality over a *longue durée,* 1750 to 2000.[8] Spanish colonialism, slavery, late nineteenth-century Cuban nationalism, early twentieth-century modernizing nationalism, enduring African-based religions, and revolutionary socialism have each provided distinct racial images of the suitable Cuban family and nation. This study centers the perspectives and actions of African-descended people as it demonstrates that throughout the island's history individual Cuban women and men have generated both new racial definitions and racialized bodies through their racially oriented sexual and family-formation choices.[9] They have acted in conjunction with the regulations created by dominant groups, at times reinforcing prevalent goals and at others disrupting them. For this reason, it is necessary to look beyond the official race-making qualities of laws such as *partus sequitur ventrem* (lit. "that which is brought forth follows the womb") by

La Familia revoluncionaria (mixed-media assemblage) by Leandro Soto, 1988.
Courtesy of Leandro Soto.

which children in New World slave societies inherited the servile status of their mothers; *limpieza de sangre* (purity of [Catholic] blood) requirements; or the Spanish royal Pragmatic Sanction of 1776, which restricted inter-racial marriage, to the alternatives forged both consciously and unwittingly by individuals.

A reformulation of Frantz Fanon's theory of a *sexual economy of race* exposes the individual agency at work in reproductive race-making practices and places these practices in conversation with the social-stratification concerns found in African Diaspora, Latin Americanist, feminist, and post-colonial scholarship. Revising Fanon, I posit that a society's sexual economy of race is the historicizing of the racialized social judgments and reproductive outcomes that surround the material acts of biological mating.[10] For racially heterogeneous societies such as Cuba, the local sexual economy of race changes to reflect often submerged conflicts over the generational continuity of the nation and the social identities that comprise it. It is a site from which one can explore how central collective identities, such as race and class, are valued and how they manipulate local material conditions to survive through social and biological reproduction. The sexual economy of race combines the production of the material and discursive elements that structure racial meaning through a series of essential race-making behaviors, in a process which involves four steps:

(1) It begins with the social categorization of sexual actors according to the race, class, gender, etc.
(2) It continues through the classification of the sexual relationships with evaluative descriptors, such as marriage, consensual union, or rape.
(3) It then marks the resulting offspring with the racial and other social labels.
(4) Finally, each successive generation remembers, or forgets, these earlier stages in either a normative or counter-hegemonic fashion.

Through this dynamic sexual economy, all human bodies are ascribed with racial meaning and disallowed social neutrality based on selectivity in both real procreative choices and their genealogical memory. In the modern Cuban context, a multi-racial nationalism is built in a contested manner upon everyone's potential for "Congo or Carabalí" ancestry.

The notion of a sexual economy of race rests on the premise that, in addition to their material determinants and political expediencies, races exist because people have historically chosen or, one could argue, have been forced, to reproduce in racially determined ways.[11] Fanon initially outlined the sexual economy of race as the recognition of racially differentiated value accruing to bodies in a colonial, sexual encounter. With his psychiatrist's sensibility, he noted that there often exists a popularly accepted calculus of racialized sexual expectations, with black intra-racial mating the least valued and white exclusivity the most appreciated. He then explored the pathology of the colonized subject's desire to couple with the white body, to claim it and become validated through it.[12] For Fanon, such sexual values were fixed and permanent results of colonialism's psychological violence. He envisioned oppositional violence by colonialized subjects as the only truly counter-hegemonic possibility and unfortunately minimized other forms of ideological anti-colonialism associated with sexuality and family formation.[13]

In order to move beyond Fanon's static conception of the sexual economy of race, one which emphasizes momentary, and often racially self-debasing, sexual practice, it is necessary to adopt a more dynamic, long-term approach to sexual choices and procreative practices, and to explain the tensions between normative and divergent visions of race engendered by these practices.[14] Just as recent Cuban race relations literature has reduced the previous emphasis on Afro-Cuban victimization, and just as feminist analysis has often challenged the false naturalness assumed for nuclear patriarchal families and begun to reveal the ways in which family existed as another site for the unequal exercise of power, this study marks a similar analytical shift in reading racial and colonial power relations with its redefinition of Fanon's sexual economy of race. Whereas Fanon highlighted colonialism's reshaping of sexual desire and procreative goals to establish and perpetuate racial hierarchies, I demonstrate how colonial and post-colonial Cubans also used multi-generational reproductive structures to disrupt oppressive racial forms and create alternatives. I argue that the emergence of Cuba's current multi-racial nationalism was not solely a product of twentieth-century revolutionary agendas; nor did it emerge exclusively from political acts. Rather, as I demonstrate in the following chapters, it was also born out of Cuba's reproductive and familial past, Cuba's uniquely evolving sexual economy of race.

This methodological focus on the local dynamics of the sexual economy of race makes explicit the ways in which the biological has always been interpreted through the social. For example, a recent analysis of Cuba's human genetic heritage found that "the Native-American contribution to present-day Cubans accounted for 33% of the maternal lineages, whereas Africa and Eurasia contributed 45% and 22% of the lineages, respectively," and in terms of the paternal lineages, "strikingly, no Native American lineages were found for the Y-chromosome, for which the Eurasian and African contributions were around 80% and 20%, respectively."[15] The 2012 Cuban population census, meanwhile, lists the population proportion by "skin color" as 64.1 percent white, 26.6 percent mulatto, and 9.3 percent black.[16] The differences in the data sets speak to the social construction of identity. The latter set reflects the continuing narrative weight of white male genealogy and the minimization of the gendered contributions of Cuba's African and indigenous populations. This study attempts an objective examination of the reproductive interactions of these groups by positioning often-ignored narratives of self-segregated racial reproduction told by African-descended people alongside claims of more fluid genealogies. The discursive modes of Afro-Cuban social survival have been largely untold, but have nevertheless been key processes in the construction of Cuban national identity.

The various forms of black racial existentialism articulated by Afro-Cuban politicians, intellectuals, and civic organizers were not just political acts.[17] They had social reproductive value and promoted the continuation of a racially distinct community. This existentialism was also not the exclusive practice of an intellectual class. Many common Afro-Cubans, like Julia above, engaged in existential choices. These choices, which ranged widely between submitting to dominant racial notions and creating alternatives, were highly personal and intimate ones, often limited to an individual and her family. However, those intimate practices also shaped collective popular thought. Again, for example, the racial confidence evident in the expression of an undeniable "Congo or Carabalí" past extends the personal and the genealogical beyond the circle of the immediate family to create a vision of Cuban commonality.

This book stands in conversation with the literature on racial formations most saliently described by the American sociologists Michael Omi and Howard Winant in *Racial Formation in the United States* (1994). They define racial formation as "the sociohistorical process by which racial categories are created, inhabited, transformed, and destroyed."[18] However, whereas their historical analysis emphasizes changes in racial meaning brought about through public politics, again this study highlights the mechanisms of social reproduction central to racialization processes such as family formation and selective genealogical memory. Drawing on intersectional approaches to the study of identity outlined by black feminist scholars such as Patricia Hill Collins, my project places the sphere of domestic reproductive behaviors in equal relation to public politics in shaping race and race relations. It presents the family as social tool for mediating the interactions between the state, community, and the individual with respect to the creation of racialized citizenship. This approach represents a departure from a social scientific emphasis on individual negotiation of racial identity. Instead it highlights the multi-generational familial practices of racial classification and socialization that are both informed by state and other institutional racial ideologies and generative of subaltern alternatives. Gender-specific state, ecclesiastic, and community policies associated with family formation are important considerations in this regard. This study's feminist perspective reveals how Cuban men and women historically have had different sexual and reproductive options and have therefore made gender-distinct contributions to local racialization.

Cuba's Racial Crucible explores the interaction between four areas of the sexual economy of race: individual reproductive behaviors; family memory or genealogy; the legal regulatory structures of state and Church regarding the family; and public intellectual discourse that idealized family as fundamental to the nation. Key sources are colonial-era baptismal and marriage records, paternity recognition petitions, major works of nationalist literature, and the genealogical memories recovered through personal interviews. In these, I do not read "family" simply as the nuclear husband, wife, and child unit. Instead, this study takes a discursive and ethnographic approach to family, allowing Cubans to define for themselves complex, multi-layered connections of long-term affinity and publicly recognized biological descent.

The use of family for interpreting national identity has its roots in the anthropological study of cultural difference. In attempting to classify cultural groups, nineteenth-century anthropologists described the elaborate systems of kinship that conferred community membership. However, they unfortunately utilized Eurocentric, evolutionary schemes—with the Western nuclear family placed at its zenith—to create negative assessments of non-European peoples. More recent anthropological scholarship has found these methods problematic and instead posited culturally relativist views of kinship and family that eliminate external standards when gauging kinship systems' value. These scholars acknowledged that social-group membership could be constructed in a variety of forms that did not align with common European perceptions.[19]

In contrast to anthropology's focus on cultural difference, within the academic discipline of history, studies of the family began as a means to explain radically new population-settlement and other demographic patterns associated with capitalism's consolidation in Western societies, particularly as related to the growth of the working class. For example, the analysis of links between nineteenth-century industrialization and proletarianization of labor required an understanding of earlier norms of domestic production. Pre-industrial households and the families that built them were critical, especially for Marxist scholars.[20] Within American and Caribbean historiography, family studies took on a racial dimension that was initially narrowly focused on the degrees of post-emancipation, African American assimilation into the dominant society.[21] With the patriarchal European family implicitly positioned as the norm, scholars of these regions often have stressed the exceptional quality of African American behaviors. Issues of familial matrifocality and male marginality have been debated as to their ability to demonstrate African American difference. Afro-Latin American populations have not received the same scholarly attention. Examination of their historical experiences of family has often been lost due to the greater focus on white elites. Here again the patriarchal family has been presented as the point of departure, and those not conforming to it largely dismissed as insignificant social agents.[22] This dismissal extends to women of all categories who were expected to remain subordinate to the reproductive interests of white men.

This has been the case for Cuban society. It has been officially imagined in terms of patriarchal whiteness, despite a large population of color. The white family was elevated to a level of political importance, while all others were initially ignored or only recognized for their economic value of supplying labor.[23] However, we cannot allow this story to rest there. This book builds upon the valuable work of historian Verena Stolke (formerly Martínez-Alier) that demonstrated the racial tensions between the social regulatory practices of the Catholic Church and the Spanish colonial state and the reproductive actions of individual Cubans. Stolke's *Marriage, Class, and Colour in Nineteenth-Century Cuba* (1974) presents an empirical history that pre-dates the English-language engagement with Michel Foucault's more theoretical concerns about social regulation of sexuality. She describes how racially restrictive marriage policies were essential to the maintenance of white supremacy during Cuba's colonial period. For much of the nineteenth century, government officials supported white families' efforts to prevent marriages between "unequal" partners, especially those of African descent. Such people were marginalized in even the most intimate aspects of their lives, in addition to suffering the material deprivations associated with slavery. With these findings, Stolke challenged earlier scholarly assertions of the exceptional, benign quality of Latin American race relations.

Although her research did not include the twentieth century, Stolke explicitly accepted that the 1959 Cuban Revolution provided a necessary corrective to the lasting effects of earlier discriminatory measures. In her estimation, the revolution resolved Cuban racism by attending not only to issues of economic equality and political access, but

La actualidad palpitante

PRECAUCIONES DE DON JEREMIAS

"Don Jeremias's Dilemma": "Let's not speak of that [portrait] right now, because, if by any chance the Evarista Party triumphs, it will be convenient to have her for an ancestor."[24] Source: *La Politica Cómica* (1912), republished in Bronfman, *Measures of Equality,* 80, with her translation.

also to racial questions in family life, such as the status of illegitimate children.[25] More recent analyses of Cuba's racial history challenge Stolke's direct extension of colonial problematics into the revolutionary era by noting subtle transformations in race's role in politics, labor relations, and wealth distribution during the late nineteenth and early twentieth centuries. Many conclude that Cuba's mulattoes and blacks were not as marginalized as Stolke argued. They were important historical actors in all aspects of Cuba's evolution.[26] Moreover, whereas Stolke concentrated on the study of marriage and attended less thoroughly to the range of reproductive behaviors that occur outside its bounds, I consider social reproduction more broadly as a complex interaction of individual mating choices (within and outside of marriage), the socialization of offspring, institutional regulation of the family, and the discursive projections of reproductive ideals.[27]

For African Diaspora scholars and Latin Americanists, *Cuba's Racial Crucible* contributes to the comparative literature on race relations in slave and post-emancipation societies in the Americas. Central questions in this domain are whether the meaning of "blackness" is fundamentally similar throughout these societies or whether specific local practices generate significant differences in racialized forms of citizenship. Recent projects such as George Reid Andrews's *Afro-Latin Americans* have highlighted regional similarity. Others describe a notable dissimilarity and reject a generalizable Latin American model of race relations.[28] Despite emerging from the same context of Iberian colonial law and labor demands, Cuban experiences have important differences from those found in other Latin American countries. Not even Brazil, with its similarly large African-descended population, has experienced such high levels of public engagement in the racial meaning of citizenship and policies of racialized reproduction. This study cautions against the once-popular commentaries on Latin American racial views that saw them as preferable to U.S. ones, and also against those interpretations suggesting a convergence of these views, as prompted by the increase of race mixture in the United States. This study clearly demonstrates in the Cuban case that miscegenation alone is not a corrective to racism and racial inequity. In fact, both have often been reinforced when whitening is stated as a goal. On the other hand, inter-racial family formation holds the potential for decreasing the social distance associated with racism when all elements of cultural and biological ancestry are equally esteemed. This study highlights the importance of such moments in Cuban life.

Finally, *Cuba's Racial Crucible* also speaks to post-colonial studies issues. It considers how formerly colonized people have negotiated the Eurocentric legacy of colonialism, the universalist claims of Western liberal democracy, and the unitary vision of rational modernity. In the Cuban situation under study, race relations are not presented as a terrain solely of resistance and opposition. Natural syncretisms in cultural, political, and social forms appear as individuals seek the best immediate social outcomes for their family members. And despite the dominance of whiteness, Cubans have created space outside it, sometimes borrowing from African knowledge systems and sometimes forging local innovation. Long-standing convergences of African and pre-Enlightenment Western valuing of ancestry and genealogy are made public in the hybrid post-colonial context, especially in the presence of Cuban revolutionary denunciations of cultural imperialism. Within the context of global racializing forces, the reproductive and familial behaviors of Cuban women and men gave "race" local life and meaning. Their stories are recovered and retold here.

CUBA's
RACIAL CRUCIBLE

1

Ascendant Capitalism and White Intellectual Re-Assessments of Afro-Cuban Social Value to 1820

HIMNO DEL DESTERRADO
José María Heredia (1825)

THE EXILE'S HYMN

¡Dulce Cuba!, en su seno se miran
en el grado más alto y profundo,
las bellezas del físico mundo,
los horrores del mundo moral.
Te hizo el cielo la flor de la tierra;
mas, tu fuerza y destinos ignoras,
y de España en el déspota adoras
al demonio sangriento del mal.

Sweet Cuba! We see at your breast
the most exalted and profound
delights of the natural world
and the greatest moral horrors.
The Heavens graced you as the earth's flower;
but you remain ignorant of your destiny and power,
And in Spain, with its despotism, you adore
evil's bloody terror.

¿Ya qué importa que al cielo te tienda
De verdura perenne vestida,
Y la frente de palmas ceñida
Á los besos ofrezcas del mar,
Si el clamor del tirano insolente,
Del esclavo el gemir lastimoso,
Y el crugir del azote horroroso
Se hoye sólo en tus campos sonar? . . .

Does it still matter if the Heavens bless
you with a perennially verdant dress
and adorn you with luscious palms
like kisses that you blow to the tide,
if the clamor of insolent tyranny,
the slave's lamentful cries, and
the slashes of the angry whip
are the only sounds heard in your countryside? . . .

¿A la sangre teméis . . . ? En las lides
Vale más derramarla á raudales,
Que arrastrarla en sus torpes canales

So you fear patriotic blood . . . ? In the battle,
it is better to shed it by torrential floods,
than to let it waste slowly from the veins,

Entre vicios, angustias y horror.	in sin, agony, and pain.
¿Qué tenéis? Ni aun sepulcro seguro	Cuban—you do not even have
En el suelo infelice cubano.	a safe grave on your own repressed terrain.
¿Nuestra sangre no sirve al tirano	Doesn't our blood only serve to fertilize
Para abono del suelo español?	Spain's tyrannical domain?

INTRODUCTION

In "Himno del desterrado," the early Cuban nationalist poet José María Heredia imagines a new and distinctive Cuban blood, one born with "insolent tyranny" in relation to imperial Spain.[1] He deploys imagery common in Western modernity, using blood as a metaphor for a united, nationalist past and for a similarly cohesive future. But his indignation at the "slave's lamentful cries" under the "slashes of the angry whip" expresses an ambiguity with respect to the inclusion of African heritage in a unified Cuba. Were African-descended people to be only slaves for Cuba's economic development or were they to be freed to act as compatriots in creating the nation? Such considerations were part of the many conflicts apparent in Cuba from the middle of the eighteenth century to which Heredia was giving voice. Capitalism, liberalism, monarchy, and slavery vied with each other to shape the colony's future. By the middle of the eighteenth century Cuban capitalists were gaining ground in what had been a long-standing struggle against more seigniorial forces and the absolutist tendencies of the Spanish state. These conflicts continued until the 1810s, by which time Cuba's leading merchants and export agriculturalists had won significant concessions from a metropolitan government much weakened by Napoleonic military intervention. But this politically ascendant group then had to face Spain's new liberal nationalist politics that sought to constrain autonomist possibilities for the remaining Caribbean colonies after the mass defection of continental Latin American territories. In the evolution of these processes, Cubans of different ideological stripes were positioned against an evolving Spanish monarchy that remained very consistent in its primary goals of self-preservation and the lucrative management of its empire.

"It is of little importance to the state that the inhabitants of Cuba be white or black; it only matters that they work greatly and are loyal."[2]

This statement by one of Cuba's earliest historians, Nicolás Joseph Ribera (1724–1775), is an important, but often unacknowledged, assessment of the role of race in Cuba's early colonial history. It confers upon Spanish monarchs a utilitarian approach to the social differences marked by race and suggests a de-emphasis on slavery, and perhaps even capitalism, in favor of a larger set of imperial objectives. An implication of this assessment is that modern versions of anti-black racism do not equate to earlier forms. While the Roman legal doctrine *partus sequitur ventrem,* where a child's initial servile status equaled that of the mother, was the pre-eminent determinant of social identity throughout slaveholding regions in the Americas, in Spanish territories it was also qualified by other considerations.[3] Prior to the 1810s, Spanish colonial visions of blackness could acknowledge social worth beyond economic or labor value. One's political loyalty often took priority over racial identity as a strong remnant of a feudal perspective on the management of empire that by the early nineteenth century had still not been erased by capitalism's emphasis on profit and its economic reading of social relations. But this outlook was not immutable. In a continually contested ideological terrain, capitalist priorities would gain the upper hand, but never fully silence pre-existing alternatives. The interpretations of racialized reproduction presented in this chapter take a long-run view of these ideological struggles, following them over the course of the eighteenth century, up to the 1820 criminalization of Cuba's slave trade. This chapter outlines the institutional framework of state, church, and military practices in which Cuba's free and enslaved African-descended people moved and created social identities for themselves and their families.

When Philippe de Bourbon assumed the Spanish monarchy in 1700 as Philip V his objectives were not unlike those of the Hapsburg kings who preceded him. Their most pressing aims had been to maintain unquestioned dynastic control over government, ensure the empire's profitability, and prevent the encroachment of rival European nations on existing Spanish territory. It was within this context that the new policies that historians have designated the "Bourbon reforms" began during Philip V's reign and were developed further by subsequent Bourbon monarchs, enduring until the crisis of Spanish imperial governance occasioned by Napoleon's 1808 imprisonment of Ferdinand VII. Especially during the reign of the second Bourbon king, Charles III, and in the wake of the 1762 British occupation of Havana, these reforms not only impacted the economics and politics of the empire; they also stimulated important, if unintended, social outcomes specific to Cuba. In Cuba, these reforms, their reception, and their contestation reshaped the social reproduction of race at the local level. All aspects of Bourbon colonial governance, from the control of religious orders to the reconfiguration of economic relations, transformed the constitutive elements of race, and especially of blackness. Caught between ascendant colonial capitalism and other imperial concerns, such as the economic and social upheaval occasioned by the Haitian Revolution, the varying white notions of the racialized reproduction surrounding Cuba's African-descended people reflected these ideological and material struggles. And the race-making practices generated in the process became fundamental to the emergence of Cuban national identity. These Bourbon policies culminated in 1817, when shortly before conceding to British pressure and criminalizing the slave trade, Spain's newly restored absolutist government issued a royal order concerning the need to whiten the island's population and to shift away from imported African labor.[4] With this, the tacit, existential and racist threats that Cuba's mulattoes and blacks had previously faced became codified as imperial policy.

While recent scholarly literature has challenged previous beliefs in the Bourbon reforms' internal coherence and the novelty of their final objectives, these reforms were created within an era defined by two new and related major forces: the solidification of a capitalist political economy and the insertion of Enlightenment philosophies into Spanish imperial statecraft. As notions of meritocracy gained currency in the bureaucratic administration of empire, at the grander social level patriarchal hierarchy and seigniorial order remained important operating frameworks. The Spanish Crown continued to attend to all its vassal subjects by grouping them into recognizable corporate units, despite the fact that fluid colonial social realities (especially of origin, class, and race) complicated these categories.[5] Cuban-born whites were imagined as distinct from their peninsular cousins; wealth increasingly challenged noble birth as a determinant of elite status; and the variety of colors and castes found within colonial Cuba often defied neat classification. Nonetheless, the Crown's corporatist approach largely distinguished five major social units within Cuba: Catholic clerics; secular economic leaders and titled nobility; white commoners; African-descended free people; and enslaved people. Bourbon policies intended to manage one of these groups often generated unexpected outcomes for the others. We will see below that the reforms that had the most profound effect on the meaning of race on the island were those that limited the scope of Catholic institutions, reorganized the military, restricted the open selection of marriage partners, promoted agricultural exports, and directly addressed living conditions for enslaved people.

EARLY AFRO-CUBAN CATHOLICISM

Bourbon reconsideration of religious authority impacted the long-standing Catholic acculturation processes that had been essential to building even the limited degree of social respectability that African-descended individuals could achieve in the early colonial period. Since the fifteenth century, Spanish monarchs had repeatedly stressed the need to indoctrinate African ethnics as good Catholics.[6] This policy rested on an assumption equating Catholicism with loyalty to Spain, in contrast to the dangers posed by Jewish and Islamic "infidels." With the rise of Protestantism, this distinction was extended to a lesser degree to nationals of other European nations. A combination of religious and imperial goals was at play when Africans and their children (both free and enslaved) were baptized and confirmed as co-religious Catholics alongside Hispanic whites. These groups often worshiped in the same parishes and integrated lay religious brotherhoods, although social inequality and segregation persisted.[7] In many cases, black intimate unions were blessed by Catholic marriage, and their offspring given the social honor of legitimacy. These practices stand in well-noted comparison to the religious exclusion of enslaved people commonly experienced in English-speaking regions of the Americas. A generation of U.S. historians used this contrast to compare the oppressive intensity of slave systems and to describe national generalizations in racial meaning.[8] While these debates have ebbed, I suggest that temporal shifts in these two distinct issues require deeper examination. The views on race and slavery of the Spanish government, Church, and people did not remain stagnant over the nearly 400 years of colonial rule in Cuba.

The existing Cuban historiography on the depth of Afro-Cuban Catholicism during the colonial period divides almost neatly along political and institutional lines. State-sponsored Cuban historians writing since the 1959 revolution tend to discount early Catholic socialization among Afro-Cubans. Writers in this vein instead emphasize the close social and economic association between Cuba's elite and Catholic clerics, which occurred especially in the nineteenth century. Such scholars suggest that these groups prioritized white creole education over missionary activity among African ethnics and their Cuban-born descendants.[9] By contrast, Catholic authors such as Monsignor Ramón Suárez Polcari describe a more inclusive, though still racially discriminatory, early colonial Church that at the diocesan level even ordained black and mulatto priests, despite some white resistance. Polcari documents a 1685 complaint by the island's lieutenant governor to the Spanish Crown about "the number of priests who were the sons and grandsons of mulattoes and even worse, the case of one Juan del Rosario, the son of an African slave woman. He is not only a mulatto, but [his] color is so dark as to cause irreverence."[10]

Similarly, the inter-racial educational institutions managed by local religious orders offered a limited degree of mobility to young men of color. Surviving records offer the example of pardo carpenter and militia battalion commander Antonio Flores educating his son Joseph Ignacio at Havana's Jesuit school during the 1750s. In the 1760s, another pardo, Miguel Aviles, trained in medicine under the Catholic clerics of San Juan de Dios Hospital.[11] In using such records to distinguish eighteenth-century experiences of black social mobility associated with the Church from the more pronounced discrimination that emerged later, Polcari acknowledges, but does not explain, an increased racial boundary against the admission of Afro-Cuban men to the priesthood and other learned careers that developed in the nineteenth century. This increased institutional discrimination paralleled other social transformations of racial meaning brought about by the rise of Cuban capitalism. We will return to this point later in the chapter.

Distinctions existed between colonial Cuba's two types of Catholic lay brotherhoods (*cofrádias* and *cabildos de nación*). Unlike cofrádias, with their devotional focus on particular Catholic saints, Afro-Cuban cabildos de nación were often organized by the approximate regional origins or linguistic commonalities of African ethnics. Cabildos of this type were reported in Cuba as early as 1535 for Santiago and 1568 for Havana.[12] The ostensive public aim of many of these brotherhoods was to promote Catholic education and socialization. Both the Spanish state and Cuba's Catholic authorities supported this mission. For example, in 1755 the bishop of Cuba, Pedro Agustín Morel de Santa Cruz, wrote to the Spanish monarch Charles III, celebrating the successful spiritual work that had been done within Havana's twenty-one African-descended cabildos. The bishop also claimed hopefully that such religious indoctrination would lessen the "auspicious disorder" that originated in these groups.[13]

The bishop was right to have such concerns. Black cabildos were one of the important sites for the New World reproduction and reformation of African ethnic identity. For all their outward Catholicism, specific African ethnic cosmologies remained unifying points among members. They restructured as best they could particular African ethnic forms of authority, relying frequently on the personages of cabildo "kings" and "queens" to do so. They were disconnected from their original biological lineages, but rebuilt and modified the spiritual lineages that were central to African forms of self-identification.[14] As this current study will discuss in later chapters, these spiritual lineages would subsequently combine with social perceptions of biological kinship to influence Cuban racial meaning. A basic understanding of the social importance of African spiritual lineages begins with an awareness of how many traditional African cosmologies held veneration of one's ancestors and of the supernatural powers personified as various gods to be critical to success and survival in the earthly realm. One was not truly a person without continued recognition of spiritual ancestry. For many non-Islamic African peoples, the beneficence, neutrality, or malevolence of spiritual beings, who were thought to move in both visible and invisible forms among the living, depended on a host of factors. The management of these factors often rested with trained specialists. Priestesses and priests proficient in local African mysteries of communicating with the spiritual realm educated those who sought their guidance, initiated them as spiritual children (in a manner that eventually conformed to the language of Catholic godparentage), and led them in the proper modes of acknowledging their reverence of the spirits. A common demonstration of such reverence was to "feed" or propitiate one's gods and ancestors with offerings of those experiences or objects they had most needed or enjoyed in life.[15] Intentionally opening oneself up to short-term spirit possession by these spirits was just one of many methods of appeasing their desires and demonstrating loyalty to them.

Adherents to Hispanic norms perceived such African practices as barbaric and criminalized them under the general label of *brujeria* (witchcraft). Such dismissal and denigration forced secrecy upon African-derived beliefs, and guaranteed their appearance in historical documents only as bizarre behavior and criminal activity. In colonial Cuba, many African ethnics and their Cuban descendants sought refuge from direct Hispanic repression of their worldviews and rituals by shielding them under a Catholic cloak. In this way, the strong non-biological, spiritual kinship established among the initiates of the same Afro-Cuban priest or priestess was hidden from public view. During the colonial era, few contemporary outsiders would have been aware that cabildo members continued African-derived religious and social views to strongly identify themselves as collectively belonging to spiritual lineages that descended from preceding generations of priests and their initiates. Few direct articulations of these redefined "familial" ties, such as the 1829 statement by María de Belén Álvares, queen of the Carabalí Bogre cabildo, that she was responsible for the materials of "this family," survive in the general historical record.[16] These bonds received scholarly recognition only in the late twentieth century,[17] but, as we will see, such extended spiritual genealogies have been key sites for Cuban interpretations of race, and especially of blackness.

One clear effect of Bourbon policies toward Catholic institutions was to direct educational responsibilities for black indoctrination and socialization away from the regular, monastic orders (especially Jesuits, Dominicans, and Franciscans) toward parish-level diocesan priests. The first catechism guide for Africans in Cuba only appeared in the latter part of the eighteenth century and was intended for use by such parish priests.[18] This reflected the increased favor that non-monastic clerics had gained as the Spanish Crown attempted to recapture some of the local authority perceived to have been lost to the papacy through the monastic orders. Monastics were distinct from standard, diocesan parish priests in that they answered to the pope and not to the Spanish king. As such, "regular" orders were "supra-national" entities that often did not adhere to the Crown's nationalist goals. At the end of the seventeenth century monastic friars were a large component of Cuba's clerical population. A 1689 survey indicated that of the 529 total, 225 were parish priests and the remaining 304 belonged to the orders (including 100 cloistered nuns).[19] Additionally, these orders also represented a particular worry for eighteenth-century Spanish mercantile capitalist thought, based on their extensive economic activities. Some received substantial financial support from the monarchy, while others held significant independent properties in land and slaves. These situations further complicated long-standing monarchial concerns over their potential challenge to its power. When the new "enlightened" bureaucracy surrounding the Bourbon kings sought greater financial returns from the empire, they looked to Catholic institutional properties as a cache of untapped wealth. Catholic-managed production was reconceived as archaic and incompatible with economic progress.

The changing fortunes of the Jesuits under eighteenth-century Bourbon reforms within Cuba exemplify how the strain in Church and state relations impacted black life. The Jesuit order was founded in the sixteenth century in militant reaction against the Protestant Reformation, and for much of the next three centuries its members were fervently allied to the pope, instead of to European monarchs, including those of Spain. In the Americas, the Jesuits were primarily dedicated to the Catholic indoctrination of indigenous people, and for this reason their presence in the Caribbean was fleeting through the middle of the seventeenth century. However, Jesuits established themselves in Havana in 1721 and quickly received considerable support from local benefactors, many of whom made large testamentary bequeaths that added to the order's local wealth.[20] As an institution, the order became one of the island's largest slaveholders, possessing 423 enslaved people in 1767.[21]

Also by that time, through purchase and donation, the Jesuits also owned significant land in provincial Havana and the central town of Puerto Principe, including three sizable sugar plantations. One of these plantations, Rio Blanco, was the largest of its time and also was exceptional in comparison with the typical private holdings—for the religious instruction given to the enslaved, for its attention to the slave sex ratio, and for its encouragement of legitimate marital families among them. Of the sixty-three slave women held there, only one was unmarried. Pro-marital and natalist policies ensured that most of the children born on the plantation were the offspring of these legitimate relationships.[22] In these ways, the Jesuits encouraged black family formation patterns that paralleled those of whites and did not allow slaves' economic utility to deny their value as social contributors to the Catholic community. Nevertheless, the racial limits of slavery ensured that these legitimate families possessed a unique and segregated degree of social respectability. While their children did not suffer the stigmatization of illegitimacy, the social prestige of legitimacy remained insufficient to earn freedom. Slavery and Catholicism were in close association. But putative Catholicism was a necessary requirement for enslaved people in order to start on a legal path to freedom.

The Spanish monarchy did not take the social importance of these practices into consideration when it expelled the Jesuits from all its Spanish American territories in 1767 and subsequently sold their properties, including enslaved people, to private purchasers. The Catholic indoctrination and Hispanic socialization that the Jesuits had provided to their bondspeople was eliminated. Other orders, such as the Bethlemites, continued similar work on their plantations (such as San Cristobal de Baracoa, which was reported to have 500 "married" slaves in 1801), until their properties were also confiscated by Spain's new liberal government in the 1840s.[23] The absence of these slaveholding and instructional orders, especially ones with such extensive holding as the Jesuits, slowed black and mulatto acculturation to the Hispanic aspects of colonial Cuban life at a time when the tendency to perceive race as an indicator of permanent cultural difference increased. Socialization and religious education were left to individual slave owners and parish priests. These priests had neither the communal organization nor institutional strength of the orders. The results were haphazard, and dependent on the individual character and talents of each cleric. Although little record of priestly efforts with Cuba's African-descended people survives, it is likely that while some were deficient in this process, others were effective on a small scale. As chapter 2 discusses more fully, this diminished institutional interaction was one contributor in the decline in Afro-Cuban legitimacy rates and other outward signs of the acceptance of Hispanic social norms. As a result, the social markers of racial difference increased and were subsequently used by some to further justify discrimination.

BLACK AND PARDO MILITIAS: RACIALIZED HONOR

The racial ambiguities inherent in reforms of Catholic institutions were also present in the Bourbon reorganization of the colonial military. Adjusting to changing eighteenth-century strategic considerations, Spain's rulers sought better ways for their American colonies to defend themselves against imperial rivals. These reforms impacted the entire Afro-Cuban population through the mulatto and black men who served in empire's military units. In terms of social reproduction, a subtle debate exists within Cuban historical scholarship about the extent to which their military service offered a path to Afro-Cuban upward mobility and social respectability.[24] Central to this debate is the fact that such service not only impacted the lives of individual men, but also brought changes for Afro-Cuban communities, especially when the wives and children of militiamen shared in their material and social situations. This was a period in which social mobility and respectability were generally understood in familial terms. Individual men socially advanced or declined alongside their families. Overall, the military participation, like Catholic acculturation, presented opportunities for socio-economic gains for the African-descended population, but these were set within a countercurrent of an emerging capitalist and racist order that fostered increasing segregation. The racial limits experienced by members of this community are more easily seen in relation to the social corporatism long practiced by the Spanish Crown. As it had done since the earliest colonial moments, the Crown continued to manage its vassal

subjects in racialized categories, but its privileging of whiteness increased in the late eighteenth century.

Bourbon military reforms arose in response to Spain's pressing defensive needs of the period and its engagement in a series of global wars
fought in Europe and in its colonies: the War of Spanish Succession
(1701–1713), the War of Austrian Succession (1739–1748), and the Seven
Years' War (1756–1763). Bourbon monarchs confronted ongoing European hostilities and strengthened the empire's military capabilities with
a two-pronged approach that concentrated on the distinct mobiliza-
tions of, first, the permanent army and navy corps, and then the voluntary local militias. Both groups were professionalized and their person-
nel substantially increased during the century. However, there were
important racial and ethnic distinctions between the two types of military units. As a legacy of Spain's medieval Reconquest mentality, the
staffing of the standing army and navy was largely limited to peninsular
Spaniards; these professional units did not knowingly admit non-whites.
In the Americas, as a check on their revolutionary potential or as an indictment of their presumed racial purity, even white creole participation was restricted: it could not be greater than 20 percent.[25]

Social inequality, especially of race and color, also mattered in the local militias, but not in terms of the exclusion of African-descended men,
as was the case with the professional military. Instead, despite appre-
hension about the political loyalties of such men, throughout Spanish
America many racially integrated local units were founded in the late
sixteenth century. However, beginning in the seventeenth century, these
militia units became increasingly segregated, with distinct battalions for
whites, pardos, and blacks. Some integrated forces continued in Spanish
American rural regions, but in diverse urban environments throughout
colonial Spanish America and in sizable Cuban towns, manpower was
sufficiently available to staff segregated units. Moreover, the urban commercial guilds that often sponsored these units extended their long-
standing, exclusion of African-descended men into this area of defensive
local service. However, given that the need for imperial defense out-
weighed and outranked white creole racism, the Spanish government
created a parallel structure of non-white voluntary militias in these urban settings.[26] By 1765, this process had even resulted in the creation of

a unit of enslaved men in Havana, the Compañia de Morenos Esclavos (Company of Black Slaves), in response to the desperate manpower crisis associated with the Seven Years' War. By 1770, African-descended troops comprised 42 percent of Cuba's militias and 29 percent of the total of its military force.[27] In the years between 1763 and the start of the Haitian Revolution, pardo and black militias were highly esteemed. They were essential defensive support against British threats. In this period, African-descended identity achieved a greater association with notions of military and social honor than it had in earlier points in Spanish American history.

Despite these impressive participation statistics, the social advancement resulting from militia participation was not distributed evenly within the Afro-Cuban community. As with all forms of military service, the costs and benefits accruing to these men and their families often differed according to rank. Non-commissioned enlisted men and their families are traditionally under-compensated for the loss of life, physical abilities, and income associated with war. For this reason, although black and mulatto participation rates were very high in the middle of the eighteenth century—with two-thirds of free men of color serving in Havana's militias in 1778—it is important not to read these rates as an indication of ultimate social or economic advantage achieved by these men and their families.[28] This is especially true given the compulsory nature of militia service, the racism that limited alternatives for men of color, and Spain's long history of forcing both free and enslaved African-descended men to labor in public works projects. Even differences in the names of white units and those of African descent speak of racial power. The 1769 royal instructions on militia management labeled white units as *regimientos voluntarios* (voluntary regiments), but omitted that voluntary marker for Afro-Cuban units: Batallones de Pardos Libres (Battalions of Free Mulattoes) and Batallones de Morenos Libres (Battalions of Free Blacks).[29]

Among free Afro-Cubans, the officer corps and their families received the greatest benefit from the Bourbon military reforms. In the period before the Haitian Revolution's successful slave insurrection and its subsequent destruction of French colonial wealth, Bourbon military expansion and professionalization contributed to the men's sense of prestige within colonial Cuban society. Officers were often drawn from free artisans of color and given a great deal of autonomy in unit command. For example, during Spain's participation in the North American independence struggle against Britain between 1779 and 1783, moreno Manuel Blanco and pardo Joseph Sanchez gained the rank of captain in companies that they personally created, and for which they named their subordinate officers and gained the beneficial *fuero militar* (special legal privileges conferred on military men).[30] With the Haitian Revolution, this type of autonomy subsequently decreased, and white suspicions of mulatto and black servicemen increased, even for officers.

At the other end of the social spectrum, non-commissioned militia service was often offered to Afro-Cuban enlistees as an alternate to criminal punishment and other forms of repressive control. Once in the militia, the compensation enlisted men received was well below that of officers. For many free men of color, the loss of everyday income in favor of their low militia pay when on active campaign meant hardship for their families. Although Lucas Gutiérrez was a captain in Havana's black militia, his 1662 letter to the Spanish Crown was an early Afro-Cuban protest about racist treatment in these units. Specifically, Gutiérrez expressed his discontent that black and mulatto militiamen were made to clean Havana's streets instead of earning a living for their families.[31] Discriminatory practices created further status distinctions between mulattoes and blacks. In comparison with other color categories, black soldiers were the lowest paid, despite their high participation rates. Such pay discrepancies reveal the effort by the Spanish Crown and colonial authorities to forge and solidify status differences of race and color in a manner similar to its corporatist approach of the general population. Those experiencing such discrimination could hardly ignore its reality. In 1714, one attempt to eliminate such restrictive practices called on the Spanish king for redress. A different Joseph Sanchez, who also was a captain in a free pardo militia company, requested royal protection from the racial insults he and his troops experienced. "Some people call us dogs and mulattoes, in hatred and anger . . . we want to be called by our names, or as pardos." Through the Council of the Indies, the Crown's response was only to "recommend" fair treatment.[32] Race continued to matter, and even the most senior black and mulatto officers had to bow their heads to the lowest-ranked white enlisted man.[33]

Despite continued racial discrimination, some men of color advanced socially through their involvement with the militia. For example, when the communities of Spanish Florida were resettled into Cuba after the territory's loss to the British in 1763, all of the free black or mulatto families who received land on which to re-establish themselves were those whose fathers or husbands had been active in the militia. Among them was the Mandingo Francisco Menendez, who had become the militia captain at Fort Moses where Spanish authorities encouraged the settlement of runaways from British North American slavery.[34] Social mobility through the militia was also experienced by other Africans. Such was the case of Antonio del Rey from "Guinea" and his wife Rosalia Sabiona from "Kongo." Antonio's 1796 will indicated that he was both a former royal slave and a veteran of the moreno militia. The will also tells of the considerable assets the couple held when he named her as his heir. In addition to the wattle and daub house they owned within the walls of Havana and their two slaves, Rosalia would continue to receive the military pension guaranteed by his possession of the fuero militar.[35]

What social meaning did militia service under Bourbon monarchs have for Afro-Cubans? The Crown continued long-standing feudal corporatist practices of hierarchal vassalage, and the social realities of the Americas allowed this corporatism to have a more racialized focus. Spanish kings tied black and mulatto militia men to imperial status by extending honor and privilege to individual soldiers and their families. These groups gained a sense of social and political purpose with the acknowledgment of their importance in protecting the Spanish empire. The esteem granted them as soldiers enabled them to address the monarch about personal and community concerns. Despite these advantages, militia service also brought disruption of personal lives and greater immediate interaction with often problematic white authority. The explicit racial structure of the militia offered no protection against discrimination and only allowed for mobility within the boundaries of races. While most of these men and their families were not subject to the direct repression of slavery, they did not enjoy racial equality. For this reason, an unintended consequence of segregated militia units was the institutional structure they provided for combined racial and anti-racist organizing. The anti-racist rebellion led by former militia soldier José Antonio Aponte in 1812 was an example of utilizing the social space created by segregated Afro-Cuban military units to demand non-discriminatory reforms from the state. Militia involvement also did not mitigate against other forms of creating and maintaining specifically Afro-Cuban identities and cultural practices. For example, in the middle of the eighteenth century, while black militia captain Manuel Blanco possessed his own personal wealth, social standing, and the fuero militar, he was also a well-regarded leader of a Lucumí cabildo and strongly identified with a very specific African community and its culture.[36] As much as "it only mattered that they worked greatly and were loyal" (to paraphrase Ribera's quote from above), the loyalties of many colonial Afro-Cuban militia men remained divided. Race, color, and culture were constantly at play. Militia units were just one site for the evolving social reproduction of difference in colonial Cuba.

BOURBON MARITAL REGULATIONS

Perhaps the policy reconfigurations that brought the most obvious transformations of racialized reproduction and exposed the continuing tensions between the Spanish state's feudal and liberal social goals were those prompted by Bourbon marriage reforms. Despite their dramatic racial impact, these reforms were not directly motivated by the goal of heightening racial distinction between Europeans and African-descended people. The earliest of these reforms were prompted by a desire to maintain status distinctions between peninsular Spanish and white creoles within the professional military and were modeled on the long-standing prohibition of peninsular administrators marrying into creole families that date back to 1575. Similarly, a 1632 royal cedula required that all military men obtain royal permission before publicly announcing their intentions to marry. The concern here was to prevent the transfer of political loyalty away from a unified Spanish empire toward the potentially separatist ambitions of Spanish American colonists. Importantly, few mandates of this type were explicitly racialized. One exception was a 1687 royal response to complaints by officials in

Santo Domingo that too many white soldiers were marrying mulatta women. The Crown indicated that soldiers were free to marry anyone they chose, but their professional advancement could be compromised by inappropriate selection.[37]

Deferring censure of inter-racial families away from marriage choice and toward male career advancement was an approach that followed well-established policy that again built upon Spanish medieval concerns about the social and political dangers potentially stemming from unwarranted fraternization with infidels and other enemies.[38] Under Spain's sixteenth- and seventeenth-century Habsburg monarchs, concern about racialized reproduction was not managed through marriage regulations. Marriage in this period was thought to express a sense of the sacramental equality of all Catholics and remained subject almost exclusively to ecclesiastical oversight, with little interference from the Spanish Crown. Racial restrictions on reproduction were instead imposed through bureaucratic requirements to prove *limpieza de sangre* (purity of blood) in the occupational domain, where the Crown's decisions were not subject to the Church's doctrinal and theological contestation. Candidates for university admissions, bureaucratic posts, and state-managed inquisitorial positions had to prove their "Old Christian" descent. Interestingly, within continental Spanish America pure indigenous descent or indigenous and European admixture was also acceptable as proof of "good" descent. Genealogical impurity was limited to traditional "infidels" (Jews and Muslims), descendants of Christian heretics, and all African-descended people, where such heritage was known to any degree of public memory. All of these were potential enemies of the state, while the loyalty of Old Christian Spaniards was subject to much less suspicion.[39] In this way, genealogy, religious culture, and patriotism were conflated with the social policy of the early modern Spanish state. Non-Christians and subsequent generations of their converted offspring retained the aura of national disloyalty.[40]

After the Council of Trent (1545–1563), the Catholic Church held exclusive control of the legal records of Christian ancestry. Its marital and baptismal records were used to certify or disqualify one's genealogical claims to Old Christian identity. Good Catholic marriage into genealogically sound families was all-important for individuals who hoped to retain elite status or those who were upwardly mobile within the traditional social frame. However, by the mid-eighteenth century, new Enlightenment views were fostering alternative legal perspectives on the relationship between the individual, the state, and the Church with regard to marriage. Enlightened philosophers and jurists saw the power of the Church as excessive and non-progressive. Policy makers began to seek ways to limit the Church's non-spiritual operations.[41] At the same time, the increasing number of marriages of socially unequal people tolerated and even encouraged by Spanish American clergy was seen as disruptive to the well-ordered imperial hierarchy and to the compartmentalization of distinct estates that had been integral to the Spanish monarchy's social management. Enlightened theorists attempted to restrict Church authority in marriage policy without indiscriminately transferring power to individuals, who could be equally threatening to the state. Only select persons or families were worthy of such political confidence, and those were white, Catholic, or Old Christian patriarchs. Guided by such Enlightened thought, Charles III's Pragmatic Sanction of 1776 created the Spanish state's first general policy on marriage since Alfonso X's thirteenth-century feudal laws. Those older civil laws had been combined with Trentine religious dictates to define the legal dimensions of early modern Spanish marriage, and they did so with little regard for race. Although stabilizing the boundaries of long-standing medieval estates and the emerging capitalist classes was the more immediate motive behind the pragmatic, the new mandate added an official vigor to colonial attempts to maintain racial authority and symbolic power in the hands of Catholic Spaniards.

Comparable to the manner in which the Council of Trent had shifted social power from individuals toward the Church, the pragmatic was a secularizing force that renewed the Spanish state's authority over family formation practices. Prior to the Council of Trent, various methods existed for formalizing marriage, and many involved verbal contracts between individual men and women. Trent invalidated personal contracts and required priestly consecration for marital legitimacy. By contrast, the pragmatic reasserted the jurisdiction of two secular forces in the legitimation of marriage: civil representatives of the state and senior family members (especially patriarchs). The pragmatic expressly forbade minors younger than twenty-five years of age to wed without parental consent. And in all cases, objecting parents or other family elders could seek the intervention of state officials in preventing marriages that might threaten the collective honor of individual families. Faced with increasing class mobility within his empire, the mid-eighteenth-century monarch Carlos III identified the impetus of this new legislation as the desire "to contain in a healthy manner the disorder that has been growing over time . . . as the abuse of *unequal* marriage has become so frequent . . . These practices cause disruption to the good order of the state and lasting discord and prejudices within families, exist against the good intentions and pious spirit of the Church . . . and are opposed to the honor, respect, and obedience children owe to their parents."[42]

The pragmatic left the exact meaning of "unequal" unspecified. Various characteristics could have been contained within its purview. It is on this point that both historical experiences and their related historiographies differ for Spain and Latin America. The pragmatic was written to combat tacitly the perceived social disruptions associated with the advance of Spanish capitalism against older feudal social forms, and its reach extended "from the highest classes of the state, without exception to the most common of the nation."[43] Yet historians of eighteenth- and nineteenth-century Spain have engaged very little with the legislation's local impact, noting that it was largely ignored or bypassed as marriages based on emotions of love and affection further displaced material and collective family considerations.[44]

The Spanish American experience was very distinct, and inherently more racialized. The transfer of the pragmatic to the region by royal order in 1778 was accompanied by several important modifications that reflected the Crown's corporatist social management style. The first distinction was the *exclusion* of "mulattoes, blacks, *coyotes* [black and indigenous admixture], and persons of similar castes or races . . . except for those who serve me as officials in the militias, or those who have distinguished themselves by other means." This statement was an implicit re-articulation of the exclusion of African-descended peoples from the Hispanic notions of honor and civility that had initially justified slavery. Yet an exception was made for black and mulatto militia officers whose service to the state had earned them a partial recognition of social honor. The Spanish American Pragmatic of 1778 also explicitly prohibited Catholic clerics from providing marriage licenses for *unequal* couples in which one was a minor. This requirement was absent in the continental version. Practices specific to other racial categories were also present in the Spanish American order, but the general honor associated with white and indigenous populations was not questioned. The retention of family honor was the rationale by which members of these groups contested potentially threatening marriages before government officials.[45]

Spanish America witnessed a much greater adherence to the pragmatic by colonial officials and elite and upwardly mobile families. In 1780, Bishop Santiago de Hechavarria, Cuba's ecclesiastical chief, responded to the pragmatic with unequivocal support and even went beyond the stated requirements. He ordered that even those older than twenty-five years of age had to seek either parental approval or license from the colonial courts.[46] This requirement had a chilling effect on reproductive mobility by class and race in colonial Cuba. But the background racist ideologies of Spanish-American colonists were not new with the pragmatic's transfer into the region. Contemporary Mexican examples cited by historian María Elena Martínez indicate that the pragmatic did not create but rather re-enforced the pre-existing white creole racial anxiety for retaining a sense of Old Christian purity amidst perceptions of thoroughgoing racial contamination.[47] Throughout the colonial period elite families constantly sought official certification of their racial purity. Although historical records similar to the colonial Mexican genealogical certifications have not been examined for Cuba, one must imagine that the racial anxiety of white creoles in Cuba was similar to that found in Mexico, despite critical differences in the racial composition of these colonies.

In Mexico three racial groups had predominated throughout the colonial period. A small minority of whites politically subjugated the other racial categories and had a limited degree of success in the imposition of their cultural norms. African-descended people were important in urban labor and mining. Indigenous populations were numerically superior in rural areas, but were increasingly migrating to the cities.

In terms of racial reproduction, while white intermixture with persons of African descent was discouraged in both official and popular domains, intermixture between whites and Indians and to a lesser extent between Indians and Africans was not. This ability of indigenous people to be acceptable mating partners for both whites and blacks created a multi-racial situation in which disparaged African ancestry could enter into the familial and genealogical space of the best Old Christian families through racially acceptable, indigenous intermediaries.

This same tripartite phenomenon of inter-racial reproduction occurred in Cuba and the Spanish Caribbean generally, but with a different time-frame and intensity. The Caribbean's indigenous population had been either decimated or reproductively absorbed into founding Spanish families by the end of the sixteenth century, well before the region's African slave trade brought consistent numbers. While there were incidences of incorporation of African-descended people into elite white families, they were likely much fewer than in the Mexican case, given the much smaller proportions of facilitating indigenous population. As a result, Cuba was much whiter than Mexico. But it was also much blacker, though the boundary between the two was under constant strain.

Each group's demographic representation is less significant than the ideological and political forces that upheld or challenged each identity. Bishop Hechavarria's response to the pragmatic set the tone for the way in which the Cuban Church utilized its power over racial reproduction. The Church did more to uphold whiteness than even the Spanish Crown had asked and its interpretation endured for more than a generation. However, an 1803 royal order reaffirmed the rights of men above age twenty-five and women above twenty-three to marry without parental consent or governmental license, although as potential husbands, colonial officials and soldiers still required such licenses.[48] Nevertheless, another clarification to the pragmatic in 1805 unintentionally opened room for greater racial restrictions. It stated, "those persons of known nobility *and* known purity of blood who, having attained their majority, intended to marry a member of the said castes [negroes, mulattoes, and others] must resort to the Viceroys, Presidents and Audiencias of the Dominions who will grant or deny the corresponding license, without which marriage of persons of known nobility and purity of blood with negroes, mulattos and the other castes may not be contracted, even if both are of age." More strident observers of racial boundaries inter-preted the mandate's definitional *"and"* to cover all whites, even those who were not members of the nobility. Especially from the 1830s on, ra-cial inequality was considered a civil impediment to marriage for which dispensation was required.[49]

Although these laws were intended for all of the Spanish empire, they effectively had an impact only in Cuba and Puerto Rico. By the 1820s, independence efforts had succeeded in continental Spanish America and in the Caribbean colony of Santo Domingo. In these areas, the Crown's racial restrictions on marriage did not last as long as they did in Cuba and Puerto Rico. For the remaining Spanish Caribbean, the repro-ductive value of whiteness increased for many. By the mid-nineteenth-century one observer noted, "The island of Cuba is the Spanish colony where the most exaggerated aristocracy exists . . . the whites there are the ones who fill government ministries with requests for titles of Cas-tile, privileges, and honors, which they base on grandfathers who may or may not really exist."[50] Genealogical memory of whiteness was ac-tively advanced by certain families, and structurally supported by both the Spanish Crown and leading elements of the Catholic Church. How-ever, as we will see in chapter 4, not everyone accepted these practical and ideological limits of race.

ECONOMIC LIBERALISM, SLAVE SOCIETY, AND THE NEGATIVE CONTRACTION OF BLACKNESS

The economic policies of Spain's Bourbon kings made little direct refer-ence to race and racial reproduction, despite the significant and perhaps unintended impact they had on these issues. It is an undebated point of Cuban history that the Bourbon economic reforms negatively trans-formed the experiences of African and African-descended people while simultaneously fostering an economic dynamism for the colony as a whole. In the process, a high price was paid in black and mulatto lives for the increased profits reaped by Cuba's small entrepreneurial class that maintained significant political and social connections to Spanish power. The cautious alliance between colonial oligarchs and metropolitan authorities brought an ideological shift in racial meaning that threatened Afro-Cubans' survival, narrowed the very sense of their humanity, and justified further physical mistreatment and violence toward them. Between 1789 and 1820, the newly liberalized slave trade advocated by capitalist forces coincided with an increased rhetoric of white control over presumed uncivilized Africans and their descendants. Additionally, by the 1830s a new liberal constitutionalism that ended the absolutist authority of the Spanish monarchy also enhanced the private property rights of slaveholders. New and evolving notions of citizenship eliminated the royal vassalage previously accepted by all Spanish subjects, including the enslaved people held in the remaining Spanish American territories. Yet these dehumanizing processes were not inevitable, complete, or accepted without challenge. Space existed for the creation of both inter-racial and black intra-racial solidarity in politics and social life. Local and international Catholic voices continued to defend the spiritual potential of the enslaved.

In the first half of the eighteenth century, economic considerations remained secondary in Bourbon policies toward Cuba. The first priority remained defense, and imperial decision makers sought strategies that would make the colony self-sustaining with respect to military and administrative costs. Again, although in doing so they paid little direct attention to race, many of their strategies had an adverse impact on both free people of color and the enslaved. The reforms tightened the economic possibilities of free blacks and mulattoes and limited much of the concern for slave humanity seen in earlier periods. New patterns of racial meaning in both the labor and social domains were created as Spain's Bourbon monarchs moved beyond their previous belief that Cuba's military and economic value to the empire could be developed largely with Spanish labor and with highly restricted importations of enslaved Africans.

Spanish economic reform in Cuba began slowly during the first decade of the eighteenth century, with a key moment being the British slave asiento of 1713. This contract between the British and Spanish governments gave exclusive rights to sell enslaved Africans in Spanish America to the British South Seas Company for a period of thirty

years. This treaty represented at once both a triumph and loss for imperial mercantilism. On the one hand, a monopoly of British capitalists
had gained unprecedented and almost unlimited access to most Spanish ports. On the other hand, the imperial boundaries that theoretically
undergirded Spanish mercantilism were explicitly undermined by a
diplomatic expediency that acknowledged the reality of contraband,
corruption, and lack of local manufactures that had made earlier Spanish efforts to tightly control trade to Cuba impractical.

Beyond the British asiento's importance to the evolution of global
capitalism, it also represented a previously unrecognized reshaping of
racialized reproduction throughout Spanish America in general, and
Cuba in particular. The asiento all but eliminated the insistence on Catholic indoctrination that had prevented any earlier assignment of slaving
contracts to so-called heretical nations, such as the British or the Dutch.
On this point it is important to examine the tensions surrounding the
asiento contract briefly given to the Cadíz-based Dutch banker Balthasar
Coymans from 1683 to 1687. Support of several members of Spain's
Council of the Indies allowed Coymans to bypass the standard opposition to non-Catholic slave traders. However, his well-placed adversaries
would not rest. The matter was even brought before an inquisitorial
court. Coymans's contract went forward only with the unusual stipula-
tion that ten Capuchin monks had to be part of the African and ship-
board conversion of the captives. The concern was that without the mediating presence of these Catholic friars, Dutch agents could indoctrinate
captive African ethnics to Protestantism and in selling them into the
untested new Catholic slave populations of Spanish America would
create an environment for the spread of unacceptable and disruptive
theologies.[51] Most historical assessments of the Coymans contract have
minimized the value of this clause, seeing it as a thinly veiled strategy
for preventing Dutch acquisition of Spanish slave-trading wealth. Such
strong economic determinism denies the profound Catholic sensibili-
ties that also informed Spanish governmental decisions of the period.

No other slave-trading contract was extended to non-Catholics before the 1713 British asiento, and in it the only Spanish restriction related to religion appears as a slight request: "with the condition that the
persons who shall go to the West-Indies to take care of the concerns of

the assiento shall avoid giving any offence, . . . Care being taken that neither the commanders of those ships employed by the assientists, nor the mariners do give any offence or cause any scandal to the exercise of the Roman Catholic Religion."[52] Although this was an implicit warning against Protestant evangelizing, it lacked the mandate for Catholic instruction of the enslaved that had been imposed on Coymans.

The other significant transformation in social reproductive policy associated with the British asiento was the removal of previously required gender proportions for Spanish American slave imports. Whereas earlier contacts had stipulated that either one-quarter or one-third of slave shipments were to be female, the language of the British asiento was vague on this point. It only required that the shipments "included both male and female."[53] Although we have no evidence that previous gender ratio requirements were enforced, for the few sixteenth- and seventeenth-century ships reporting such statistics, gender ratios often approached the indicated proportions.[54] By the middle of the eighteenth century, however, slave-trade gender ratios had dropped dramatically after the precedent set by the British asiento. Subsequently, intra-racial reproductive possibilities for African-descended people declined dramatically throughout Spanish America, including Cuba. In this way, capitalist concerns again compromised the Spanish monarchy's earlier appreciation of Catholic black families. More specifically, the reproductive capacity of African-descended men was increasingly disregarded, at the same time that Hispanic valuing of the productive labor capacity of African-descended women lagged behind its acceptance in other parts of the Americas.

In opening a greater number of Spanish American ports to international trade in both goods and people, the British asiento was the first step toward liberalized trade in the colonial Spanish American world. However, it also remained consistent with the cautious non-materialist social engineering that previous Spanish monarchs practiced in the Americas, with its limit of 4,000 slave imports per year for the entire region. This number fell well short of the production demands of colonists from Puerto Rico to Peru. As they witnessed the slave-based economic success of Barbados, Jamaica, and Virginia, Spanish American colonists clamored for a leveling of labor costs that they believed higher investments in slavery could provide. Colonial profit seeking was pitted against the government's concern about its loyalty to the empire and its concern that at such great distances from Spain and given sufficient African manpower the colonists could become new territorial lords.[55] These contests were observed in the late seventeenth century when the British governor of Jamaica's 1684 commented on Spanish American promotion of slave-based labor, by noting that "particular Spaniards may be in their senses, but the Government is out of it."[56]

In addition to the impact on the reproductive potential of the enslaved, Bourbon economic policies also had a deleterious effect on Cuba's free people of color. This began with Philip V's significant revisions to Spain's existing mercantilist trade system. From the start of the colonial period, Spain's trade regulatory agency, the Casa de Contratación, had entrusted the Sevillian merchant guild, the Consulado de Sevilla, to manage the day-to-day operations of trade between the metropole and the colonies. This system tightly constrained Latin American goods into a single market. At the beginning of the eighteenth century, Philip V was motivated by a desire for greater trade efficiency to replace the Sevillian monopoly with one based in Cádiz and create other smaller trading units. One of these was the Royal Tobacco Company, established in Cuba in 1717 as a monopoly that was allowed to set a uniform crop price that severely disadvantaged most small producers. The importance of this to the history of Cuba's racialized reproduction is that, contrary to an enduring Cuban historical myth perpetuated by the anthropologist Fernando Ortiz, small-scale tobacco farming was not the exclusive domain of white families. Through the middle of the nineteenth century, a good proportion of its growers were free mulattoes and blacks who held modest plots. The unprofitable price set by the tobacco monopoly tested the viability of many of these ventures. In response, in several armed uprisings between 1717 and 1723, multi-racial groups of small tobacco growers rebelled against the state's new trade restrictions. These revolts, though not nationalist, were among the earliest to draw political distinction between Cubans (conceiving themselves as a unique territorial group) and the Spanish government. However, the memory of the multi-racial character of these rebellions was lost after they were crushed by the Spanish colonial army. The resulting land loss furthered the proletarianization of non-elite free Cubans, of both African and European descent. But, as free people of color had fewer options for economic independence, they felt a greater impact, one that threatened their very survival.[57]

The practices detrimental to small-scale producers were expanded even further with the establishment of the Royal Havana Company in 1740 and its control over a variety of Cuban exports. At its inception, the company was led by Spanish merchants and large-scale Cuban planters who were especially active in promoting the sugar trade. Company policies disadvantaged small producers and led to further elite *latifundia* (land concentration). In 1758, the company won a new tax policy that reduced the rate paid by its sugar manufacturers to only 5 percent of sales.[58] This was substantially less than the taxes paid by most other, independent farmers. The company also expected to benefit from shifts in the Crown's slave-trade policy. In 1753 King Ferdinand VI authorized direct importation of enslaved Africans by Spanish merchants, in contrast to the previous use of foreign intermediaries. However, the rates of slave arrivals did not change substantially. Despite a privileged market position, the scarcity of labor prevented the company from stimulating the Cuban economy in any profound way. Capitalist reorganization stimulated growth, but the effects were incremental and not very dynamic.[59]

The British occupation of Havana between 1762 and 1763 motivated the Spanish government under Charles III to speed the implementation of the economic reforms that had been very cautiously attempted earlier during the reigns of Philip V and Ferdinand VI. British-held Havana experienced unprecedented economic activity. British manufactures and enslaved Africans were sold against the promise of future Cuban produce. Estimates range between 3,500 and 10,000 for the number of enslaved people brought to Havana under the ten-month occupation.[60] After the reacquisition of Havana, the Spanish monarchy could not ignore the economic boost that liberal trade had generated, and a 1765 trade law opened Cuban exports to several Spanish ports beyond the previous restriction to Cadíz.[61] The displacement of small, rural producers of color begun under Phillip V continued with greater force as wealthy Cubans with access to merchant capital guided subsequent

Spanish monarchs toward economic development policies based on the efficiencies of large export-oriented plantations. Additionally, with the anti-colonial struggle of the British North American colonies and the newly won independence of the United States in 1783, a massive new market opened for Cuban sugar. Few other Cuban products were adequately financed so as to capitalize on this opportunity, however. In 1760, Cuba exported 5,500 tons of sugar, but by 1791 that quantity had tripled to 16,731 tons.[62]

In 1789 a royal order opened the Spanish Caribbean slave trade to all European purveyors, regardless of nationality, and, as a result, Cuba experienced an unprecedented mass importation of African ethnics. An important reproductive aspect of this order was that it again stipulated the one-third proportion of African women that had been removed with the 1713 asiento.[63] The Crown's promotion of natural reproduction among the enslaved is implicit in this mandate. However, oversight for it has not been documented. Slave traders and buyers pursued their preference for male labor. The slave population faced the continued demographic challenge to reproduce itself, in addition to the labor conditions and violence it already endured.[64] Almost simultaneously, Cuba's creole oligarchy demonstrated its increasing political strength by successfully lobbying against the 1789 royal regulations that would have instituted the first empire-wide safeguards to slave welfare. The powerful slaveholders displayed a unified will and demonstrated that they were not docile royal subjects. They effectively reduced the feudal structures of vassalage that previously had the power to intervene against their private property rights as slaveholders.[65]

By the early 1790s, Cuba's wealthy creoles received the support of the colonial administration in establishing civil institutions such as La Sociedad Económica de Amigos del País (the Havana Economic Development Society), the Real Consulado de Agricultura y Comercio (an agricultural and commercial guild), which combined the functions of a commercial tribunal and chamber of commerce), and the local newspaper of record, the *Papel Periódico*. These were utilized by landed patricians, clerical and secular intellectuals, and liberal professionals to guide local economic and social reform, while initially leaving long-standing governmental structures unchallenged.[66] These agents sought the ex-

pansion of Cuba's export economy, especially in relation to sugar. The
Cuban planter class also benefited spectacularly from the loss of world-
leading sugar production in the French colony of Saint Domingue, as
the slave revolts there eventually led to the creation of the nation of Haiti.
For all the caution that that volatile situation provoked in Cuba, slave
importation continued to have its fervent defenders, such as the lead
spokesperson for the Cuban plantocracy, Francisco Arango. The importation of African ethnics continued in an unrestricted manner between
1789 and 1820. During this period, Cuba was transformed by the liberalized slave trade and the racial controls placed upon African ethnics and
their creole descendants from a society with slaves to a slave society.[67]

SLAVES, VASSALS, OR CITIZENS?: AFRO-CUBAN IDENTITY AND EARLY POLITICAL LIBERALISM

The economic liberalism that created important reforms within Cuba
was also paralleled by similar philosophical and political transformations. All fostered new racial meanings that extended beyond public
politics to impact basic issues of social identity. Cuban liberal philosophies developed in the hands of white male intellectuals and redefined
the boundaries of the politically permissible for Afro-Cubans. They experienced the era's tensions between feudal vassalage, slavery, and liberal citizenship in unique ways. For example, the ability they once held
as either free or enslaved individuals to appeal to the Crown was curtailed at the same time that they were initially excluded from emerging
notions of the citizen. Previous appeals to the Crown were noted earlier
in this chapter for Afro-Cuban university applicants and militia men.
A late eighteenth-century successful appeal to royal mercy also has
been documented in the collective freedom petition of the community
of royal slaves at the important copper mines outside of Santiago.[68] Examples from elsewhere in the Spanish Empire include maroon petitions
and peace settlements founding free black towns in colonial Mexico
during the seventeenth and eighteenth century.[69] Against this back-
drop of monarchical political authority, new liberal conversations about
race and rights were contentious, with many different constituencies
striving to promote themselves at the cost of their opponents. Despite

the simple dichotomies of peninsular vs. creole, planter vs. laborer, royalist vs. patriot, or black vs. white with which Cuba's nineteenth-century political struggles are often told, the reality was much more complex, shifting, and informed by international political philosophies.

Cuba was unique for the way in which its early liberal political thought developed both alongside the expansion of slavery and in the presence of a sizable and widely settled free black and mulatto population. This was in some ways comparable to the U.S. experience at the turn of the nineteenth century. However, capitalism arrived there fully embedded in earlier British colonialism, unlike its slower evolution in the Spanish colonial case. Also for the United States, an expanding slavery and a significant free mulatto and black population were separated by region: one found in the South, the other in the North. The federalist liberalism that developed in the United States neutralized the early challenges free people of color had directed against its inherent racism.[70] Instead, U.S. political liberalism effectively defended slavery and hid discriminatory politics under the mantle of "states' rights."

Cuban liberal politics emerged out of the Spanish Enlightenment and are often attributed to anti-scholasticism and the emphasis on rational objectivity found in the early eighteenth-century writing of Benedictine friar Benito Feijoo. Yet the open engagement with these new forms of thought was delayed in Cuba until the last quarter of that century. Inquisitorial vigilance and lack of printing presses curtailed the circulation of new ideas. Moreover, the near constant wars of the eighteenth century drained much of the island's energies that could have been directed toward intellectual innovation. Although few direct articulations of liberal political thought have been found for Cuba before the crisis in Spanish governance occasioned by Napoleon's imprisonment of Ferdinand VII in 1808, both Cuban intellectuals and common free people were actively exposed to these new ideas by the 1770s. Some of this exposure occurred as Cuban troops served as military auxiliaries to U.S. patriots in their independence struggle against Britain. When the Cubans returned home, they did so imbued with a guarded respect for republican government that remained hidden until the rise of liberal politics within metropolitan Spain.[71]

Similar to how they united to promote economic development, the better placed members of late eighteenth-century Cuban society joined to express their unique local concerns in the same civil institutions such as La Sociedad Económica de Amigos del País, Havana's Real Consulado de Agricultura y Comercio, and the newspaper *Papel Periódico* that are often cited as fonts of proto-nationalist beliefs.[72] But before 1808, the rhetoric of universal rights and full citizenship seen among many of liberalism's northern European and Anglo-American proponents (even if exclusive to white men) was absent from Cuban public discourse. Cuban liberal thought was utilitarian and geared toward the immediate pragmatics of the country's economic progress, without engaging in extended discussions of individual rights. Notions of rights and honor that defined one's place in the social collective diverged only slightly from their pre-existing feudal definitions. Late eighteenth-century reformists consciously framed each proposal or appeal to the Spanish Crown by describing themselves as "loyal vassals."[73]

Francisco Arango (1765–1837) was the most prominent spokesperson for the Cuban creole reformist spirit from the late 1780s through the three decades of the nineteenth century. His writings reveal the evolution of political thought of Cuba's most vocal economic sector of the period—sugar producers and merchants. He famously outlined a fundamental program for Cuban progress that was dependent on enlightened white male leadership and enslaved black labor, and therefore was highly concerned with racialized population dynamics. His proposed management of these population dynamics evolved through three unique stages that each attempted to balance capitalist labor needs against changing perceptions of potential black violence. In his first phase of writing about Cuba's social and economic development that lasted to the middle 1790s, before the full extent of the scope of the Haitian Revolution became apparent, Arango advocated the unrestricted importation of enslaved Africans into Cuba. He expressed no doubt about the Spanish empire's ability to control a black population that would presumably exceed the number of the island's white residents. Arango's proposals completely objectify African ethnics into a subhuman workforce. Gone was the earlier rhetoric of African incorporation into Hispanic society as converted Catholic souls and royal vassals, which had been part of early-colonial requests for slave labor. In emphasizing the potential success of the select class of planters and merchants, Arango made no reference to the free mulatto and black population and ignored the economic contributions of their small landowners, domestics, teachers, day laborers, and independent artisans. The early news of violent revolts in Saint Domingue, however, prompted Arango to briefly acknowledge the humanity of enslaved people. He noted that "slaves have aspired to civil liberty prompted by the example of their owners."[74] But this was a extremely rare for Arango in this period. A continuous supply of newly enslaved Africans was needed to replace older workers as they died off. Consideration of slave social reproduction was missing within the planter class that Arango represented. In their hands the definition of blackness contracted to lose the sense of social contribution permissible under the feudal objectives of the previous absolutist monarchy. It came to represent solely a material input in capitalist productivity and, alternatively, a threat to the liberal white social order when considered through the prism of Haiti.

By the middle 1790s Arango's advocacy of planter interests was increasingly influenced by the events in Saint Domingue. His writings from this period express greater fear about Cuba's large free black and mulatto population and their potential to act against whites. Although Arango stressed that Cuban enslaved and free people of color were distinguished from their counterparts in Saint Domingue by the good treatment they received, he also acknowledged that Cuba's racial solidarities were politically determinant. He could not imagine free people of color aligning themselves more with whites than with enslaved people:

> Some speak of a distinction between free people of color and slaves, separated by their different interests, which would create a social divide that is important to us. But they are all blacks; they more or less have the same complaint and a reason to feel disgust toward us. General opinion and global sentiments have condemned them to live in misery, dependent on whites. And for this reason, they will never conform themselves to their fate, but will be disposed to destroy the creators of their debasement. We must prevent this situation and even though we remain dependent on the labor of these men—for they are the only ones suitable for labor in this difficult climate—we must be careful to consider the right political and military actions.[75]

Arango called for Cuba's whites to protect themselves from this potential racial threat by undertaking two distinct actions with regard to
the resident African descended population: the disbanding of the militias of color and the implementation of additional measures to improve
slave welfare. The first of these proposals hoped to calm white fears by
sharpening racial distinctions and stripping men of color of both access
to government-supplied arms and of the honor associated with militia
service. Arango could not envision them as eventual compatriots who
shared similar interests; they existed for him only as a group to be sub-
ordinated to white economic interests. "Nothing will be done to promote
Cuban development if one does not guard against seditious movements
of blacks and mulattos."[76] That concern over potential violence from
the free population of color extended into fear about their reproduction
rates. There was a negative implication behind Arango's 1811 observation that, especially in Havana, "for the past two years the number of
baptisms of color were almost twice those of whites."[77]

While subordination was obvious for slaves, Arango did not want that
condition to foster inappropriate violence from individual slave owners.
His second proposal attempted to lessen this motive for slave revolts.
He maintained that the right conditions would make enslaved men and
women amenable to their status and allow them to serve their owners
well. The appointment of a special *fiscal* (magistrate) with oversight responsibilities would limit what Arango defined as atypical slave-owner
cruelty. He trusted that most Cuban slave owners would not be troubled by such new regulations, for they were already generous in the
treatment of their charges.[78] Importantly, in this period of unrestricted
slave trading into Cuba, Arango's proposal made no mention of slave
reproduction. It was an irrelevant element in relation to local labor needs
that were adequately met by the trade. Arango did not stop to compare
costs and benefits of natalist policy at this time as he later did, after 1820
and the Spanish Crown's criminalization of Cuba's slave trade.

With the 1808 Napoleonic destabilization of the Spanish monarchy
and the subsequent rise of liberal government within Spain, new debates arose about the continuation of the slave trade, about creating new
boundaries of citizenship, and about the politics of republican representation. The conversations forced Arango to again reconsider the racial

dynamics of Cuba's economic development. He approved of the new U.S. political model, with its race-based exclusion of the African-descended population. Although he was unaware of the state-level determination of U.S. voting rights, he was fascinated by what he perceived there as

> the political advantages that should consider as equal the free African and the light-skinned quadroon, although he could be the son or grandson of meritorious free people; there prevails the concept that one drop of African blood corrupts the white until the most remote degree, in terms that even when our senses nor memory can detect this history, we return to the testaments of the dead or moth-eaten parchments to find such evidence and forestall any close identification between ourselves and our slaves.

However, while Arango claimed to desire an eventual move away from these strictures and toward more open political access "for the natural progression toward the magnificent work of national unity," he accepted that the provincial government that the Spanish constitutional convention was attempting to define for Cuba and the rest of Latin America was not yet ready for such racial inclusion. "The best evidence suggests that no good can be done with respect to our people of color, if law and public opinion do not first reject the barbarity of slavery and disregard the shame that now stains the descendants of that disgraceful tree."[79] Here Arango's faint reference to slavery's abolition was decidedly insincere, given its central economic value for both Spain and Cuba itself. His position was intentionally unachievable at that historical moment. Cuban whites would not accept mulattoes and blacks as equal citizens as long as slavery existed, and Arango was gambling that neither would members of the Spanish constituent assembly be willing to cut their own economic throats by abolishing slavery in the Latin American provinces.

Arango acted less assuredly with respect to the Spanish constituent assembly's position on the slave trade. With the examples of French, Dutch, and British abolition before it, the assembly debated several serious proposals for the trade's immediate or gradual termination in the entire Spanish empire. In challenging these legislative thrusts, Arango again turned to economic expedience and argued that the continuation of the slave trade was a necessary evil that benefited all Spaniards, and that its immediate end would be their ruin. Unlike the British, Cubans had not made the anticipatory investment in slave reproduction. Arango noted with a degree of cynicism that slave owners were justified in previously discouraging slave reproduction because of the cost of unproductive slave children and the "inhumanity" they would have experienced due to a lack of slave-owner care.[80] By his calculations Cuba would need a slave trade for many years before a reproductive program could be successful. A trade that was more focused on the importation of African women was needed to rectify this problem.

Arango was in fact suggesting that his slave-owning compatriots would have to shift to pro-natalist practices if they were to maintain their dependence on slave labor. Cuban slave owners might not have been able to control their fate with respect to governmental intervention in the slave trade, but they were able to initiate policies that would determine the size and racial composition of their labor force. After the criminalization of the Spanish slave trade in 1820, Arango actively encouraged slave reproduction on his own plantation, La Ninfa. However, promoting the reproduction of the already significant free black and mulatto labor force remained outside Arango's vision of his country's future. He firmly retained dichotomous notions of black servile labor and white citizenship. Cuba's economic success relied on increasing the population of both: one to work and the other to protect and rule.[81]

Despite the dominance of Arango's views within Cuba's early nineteenth-century political community, important fissures and alternatives existed. A range of political voices offered very different approaches to issues of racialized citizenship within Cuba. Many of these alternative voices were found among Cuba's leading Catholic clerics, who took a more holistic view of the country's progress and looked beyond the narrow focus on capitalist development and profits articulated by Arango. Enlightenment philosophy had expanded their pre-existing Catholic notions of human perfectability to combine both the spiritual and the secular in the quest for the greatest social good. Community, country, and nation were to be created by and for all of their participants, not just the agricultural capitalists or the international merchants.

One of the earliest instances of this Catholic reformist politics was expressed by the bishop of Santiago, Navarre-born Joaquín de Osés y

Alzúa (1755–1823), who headed this important Cuban diocese for a thirty-year period from 1793 until his death. Bishop Osés was concerned about the concentration of wealth among the merchants and large planters of Havana. He rejected the development proposals emanating from Arango and the Consulado of Havana, which ignored small farmers and urban artisans.

> Although a complete equality of wealth is not possible for all the families of a country, it is very possible to create good proportions, that is to say that not all should exist in a few hands, in a way that leaves the rest of society indigent. Two classes of citizens compose the island's current situation: those who lack the necessities and those who are drenched with too much, expressed in leisure to corrupt tradition.[82]

When Osés spoke of that second class of citizens, he was expanding the concept of citizens to free men of color. He had worked behind the scenes for four years in assisting 1,065 royal slave miners and their families to gain their freedom in 1799.[83] His vision of Cuba's future was one in which the working class was comprised of both whites and African-descended people, who shared some of the island's wealth with the elite.

The bishop of Havana, Juan José Díaz de Espada y Fernández de Landa (1756–1832), acted similarly to Bishop Osés in contesting the capitalist priorities of early nineteenth-century Cuban politics. He too envisioned a more integrated and equitable society. This Navarre-born Spaniard drew on his academic and philosophical training under the second generation of the Spanish Enlightenment thinkers to forward a more populist notion of progress. From the moment Espada arrived in Cuba to head the Havana diocese in 1800, he was confronted by an ascendant planter oligarchy that attempted to constrain the local Church to their own economic and political interests. Of immediate concern was this class's efforts to escape payment of the centuries-old mandatory 10 percent Church tithe, the *diezmo,* which was the key financial support for local parish operations. To counter negative planter notions of the constraint on economic development created by the diezmo, Espada penned his own economic treatise, *Diezmo reservados* (Tithes Preserved) in 1808. In this Espada took an integrated approach to Cuba's economic future within the Spanish imperial system. He was critical of the mono-cultural tendencies of the planter class and proposed a diversified approach that supported the economic interests of a variety of social sectors, including small farmers and urban workers. He saw slavery as unnecessary and dangerous, as it created a society built around violence and the extermination of a people. He accepted small farmers and wage-earning laborers as the best engines of agricultural development because the former worked their own land and the latter also benefited from a good harvest. Neither had to be motivated by the brutality that enslaved people experienced.

While Espada was profoundly aware of Cuba's racial diversity, he did not perceive it as an intrinsic threat to the island's political progress. His writings ignore the specter of Haiti that was so central to Arango's thoughts and which prompted much greater suspicion and surveillance of free blacks and mulattoes. Espada instead outlined both the Hispanic acculturation of the island's African-descended population and the lessening of white racist discrimination and violence toward this group. He also promoted greater attention to slave reproduction and the expansion of manumission mechanisms as the solutions to the colony's persistent labor shortages. Moreover, he rejected the racial division of labor that was the Cuban norm and argued that both free-white and black laborers could work in similar settings. Espada did not accept the climatic arguments that held whites could not perform manual labor in tropical environments. His future Cuba was one that had greater equality between its European and free African-descended residents. "An intelligent writer should come forward to argue that in America it is by no means convenient to support a law that some creoles desire, which would continue inequality and absolutely criminalize marriages between pure whites and other groups." While Espada looked approvingly upon the republican government of the United States and hoped to adapt it to Spain's empire, and Cuba in particular, he did so without admiration for its racial policies. Instead, Espada used the U.S. example to explicitly challenge the obstacle that slave labor and the continuation of the slave trade posed for Cuba's implementation of a democratic political system.

> Consider that currently in America there is a constitutionally maintained
> system, or if you prefer, an essence, that keeps a large number of men, those
> equivalent to day laborers, but in even worse condition, from aspiring to be
> property owners. Slaves, torn from Africa, prevent landowners from employing
> free men, who by necessity would welcome such work. Such work would allow
> them to eventually acquire their own land, taking wives, and multiplying the
> population and the ranks of property owners. This will not happen because
> slaves bury with their own hands their own future.

By "bury with their own hands their own future," Espada alludes to
both the economic and reproductive potential of enslaved people. Both
were lost in their captivity. He was very direct in his opposition to the
slave trade:

> Already it is a much debated question in Europe about the injustice of the slave
> trade, but it is wasteful to think of it in this way. The Bishop of Havana does
> not want to address the question of justice. Whether it is just or nor, hasn't it
> influenced the population? Is it necessary and useful for agriculture? Experience
> and reason would answer in the negative.

While we may not know the depth of the reception of Bishop Espada's
stance by Havana's faithful Catholics, this group provided a much wider
audience than the narrower planter and commercial classes to which
Arango directed his proposals. It appears that Cuba's clerics were lean-
ing more heavily toward opposing slavery. Although there were a few
exceptions, such as the pro-slavery position taken by the priest Juan
Bernando O'Gavan's 1821 pronouncement that "the slave enjoys comfort and even a certain degree of luxury,"[84] growing numbers accepted
the indictment by University of Havana rector Father José Águstin Caballero that slavery was "a human malice . . . the worst civil atrocity that
men have committed."[85] His student and colleague, Félix Varela, became even more influential in the anti-slavery views he imparted to the
next generation of Cuban political thinkers. Varela's 1821 "Proyecto y
Memoria para la Extinción de la Esclavitud en la isla de Cuba" (Project
and Memorial for the Extinction of Slavery on the Island of Cuba) privately circulated among them. The slow march toward national independence thus began with the realization that slavery and its legacy had
to be addressed if any political progress was to be expected. A growing
number of white Cubans came to imagine African-descended people

not as slaves, but as neighbors, colleagues, and compatriots. Although the expediencies of export capitalism continued to control local politics and uphold the value of slavery through the middle of the nineteenth century, anti-slavery sentiments made important inroads in constructing a vision of a free Cuba and in imagining more inclusive notions of the place of blackness and African-descended people within it.

CONCLUSION

The rise of Cuban nationalist liberalism was not an unproblematic process with respect to notions of blackness. Earlier beliefs about the social utility of both free and enslaved people of color to Spain's Catholic empire were only slowly overtaken by more profit-oriented, capitalist concerns. In this way, while white liberals considered concepts of citizenship for themselves, they increasingly perceived African-descended people almost exclusively as labor. The retention of earlier notions of Catholic and military honor for people of color declined. Yet, these older visions were sustained by blacks and mulattoes themselves, and by some whites, including important Catholic clerics. Afro-Cuban social and demographic reproduction remained contentious issues that co-existed with more racially exclusive visions of Cuban identity that valued little outside of white Hispanic norms. The next chapter explores the efforts of Cuba's African-descended population to reproduce itself and to have a lasting impact on their country's social development.

2

Slavery and Afro-Cuban
Family Formation during Cuba's
Economic Awakening, 1763–1820

The valley well known of Matanzas is nigh,
And trembling, my brother, I gaze on that place,
Where, cold and forgotten, the ashes now lie
Of the parents we clung to in boyhood's embrace.

—From Juan Francisco Manzano,
"The Dream: Addressed to My Younger Brother"

INTRODUCTION: MANZANO'S FAMILIAL VISION AND AFRO-CUBAN REPRODUCTIVE COMMONALITIES

Despite the earnest attempts by white colonials to influence racialized reproduction, Afro-Cuban familial and sexual behaviors retained a degree of independence. This was true even with the extreme limitations of slavery and racial discrimination. Historical family-formation and reproduction processes have been essential in determining Afro-Cuban visions of community and, eventually, of national citizenship. However, Cuban historical studies have not fully explored the pre-nineteenth-century versions of these processes because severe source limitations have made them difficult to access and because of a tendency to imagine the social patterns of this period as fully overturned by the pressures of the capitalist, export-oriented economic boom that followed.

Such dismissal of historical continuity is rarely warranted and suggests the possibility of a more cautious approach to social change. Moreover, though limited, the period's standard social history sources can be read not only for their demographic aspects. They can also attest to Afro-Cuban social agency and intentional selectivity in social reproductive practices.

For these reasons, before this chapter turns to an analysis of general patterns revealed in the pertinent ecclesiastic sources, it is useful to briefly consider the family of the early nineteenth-century writer Juan Francisco Manzano (1797–1854) as an example of the family formation and race-making practices that were open to his contemporaries. Manzano's family and his related commentaries provide insights into the norms, the uncommon moments, and signs of lasting change related to slavery and racial meaning in early colonial Cuba. Beyond a doubt, Manzano was exceptional in the context of Cuban slavery. Although he was born a slave, he achieved what very few of his background were able to: literacy and freedom. Favored in his youth by his owners, he was exposed to the canons of classical and Spanish literature, and he used this foundation to later produce his own powerful prose and poetry. Once his texts became known in Havana's literary circles, one of their luminaries, Don Domingo Delmonte, organized the purchase of Manzano's liberty as a collective humanitarian project for this intellectual elite. A century and a half after his death, Manzano's works remain world treasures for their beauty and for his unique place in Latin American history. He was the only slave from the region to publish. The surviving texts offer an unparalleled literary entry point into Cuban slave society for their mixture of personal and poignant glimpses of pain, survival, and triumph. Family life was central to these.

Manzano's was not a family of relatively recent nineteenth-century African arrivals, upon whom Cuban slavery scholarship has focused. His progenitors were forcibly brought to Cuba before that critical period, perhaps as early as the seventeenth century, into a colonial context that was yet to be fully defined by capitalism. Manzano's eloquent work reminds us of an important continuing quality of Cuban slavery: enslaved people were not solitary beings who existed only in relation to their masters. They lived in a social environment that often centered on familial ties of biological and affinitive kinship. Manzano highlights this reality in explaining some eighteenth-century elements of his background.

> The Senora Doña Beatrice, the wife of Don Juan M., took a pleasure every time she went to her beautiful estate, the Molino, to choose the finest creole children about the age of ten or eleven years, and carry them to town, where she gave them instruction conformable to their new condition. Her house was always filled with these young slaves instructed in everything necessary to her service. One of the favorite young slaves was Maria M, my mother, who was greatly esteemed for her intelligence, and her occupation was to wait on the Senora Marquesa of J. in her advanced age. This lady was accustomed when she was pleased with her attendants, to give them their liberty when they were about to marry; . . . providing them with all things necessary, as if they had been her own children, without depriving them after their marriage of the favor and protection of her house, which extended even to their children and husbands; of which conduct there are many notable examples, amongst those who were not even born in the house. Various changes, however, taking place in the service, Maria became the chief waiting woman of the Marquesa. In this situation she married Toribio de Castro, and in due time, I was ushered into the world.
>
> My mistress took a fancy to me, and it is said I was more in her arms than in those of my mother. She had all the privileges of a slave who had acted as a dry nurse, and also partly as a wet nurse; . . . and having married one of the head slaves of the house, and given a little creole to her mistress, I was called by this lady, "the child of her old age," I was brought up by the side of my mistress without separating from her, except at bed time, and she never went out without taking me in her carriage . . . [I was] treated by my mistress with greater kindness than I deserved, and whom I was accustomed to call "my mother."[1]

In addition to highlighting his biological family, Manzano fondly recalled a fictive inter-racial kinship his owners initially developed with him. To his mistress, he had been "the child of her old age," and he called her "my mother." Despite this intimacy, Manzano's owners took no steps to free him. His emancipation was not even considered as his status progressed from pampered child to trusted servant. What is important here, however, is not what might be perceived as the hypocrisy of the situation. More valuable is the awareness that both biological and affinitive families existed beyond rhetoric. They were real entities with the ability first to shape the lives and opportunities of black and mulatto individuals and then, in a more collective manner, to define Cuban notions of race.

These race-making potentials appear in Manzano's description of his biological family. Manzano's works portray four generations of it, from his grandparents to his own children. In each generation, reproductive and familial choices were made and social categories such as "pardo" or "mother" expressed. All this occurred within the contexts of the society's racial beliefs and limitations. For instance, given that Manzano's parents were enslaved creoles, in some earlier generation their newly enslaved African progenitors had transcended the heavy odds against slave procreation and bore offspring. His father was a "pardo." And although Manzano does not provide a simple identity marker for his mother, she may have been considered "parda" as the daughter of an African woman and a mulatto. His parents had been among the small minority of black and mulatto Cuban children who were fortunate enough to survive into adulthood and who then bore their own offspring. Grandchildren followed later. These eighteenth-century Afro-Cubans achieved not just demographic success; they had ideological relevance to the foundations of general Cuban identity. They were active agents in the society's sexual economy of race, initiating important reproductive and other social outcomes. But were these four generations of Manzano's family the reproductive exception among colonial Afro-Cubans? Or did they mirror the experiences of many others?

This chapter addresses these questions by treating Afro-Cuban social reproduction as a fluid input within the larger processes of Cuba's colonial evolution. This reproductive contribution was not just a material matter of demographics and labor; assessment of this contribution must also consider both the structural constraints on the group's biological viability and the discursive politics of its representation. This material and discursive dualism becomes more salient when we ask how membership in Cuba's various socio-demographic groups was defined, and how the demographic success of these groups was either encouraged or inhibited. In short, how did family formation factor into the material and ideological efforts that created racial meaning and categories in colonial Cuba?

This chapter reviews the reproductive transformations experienced by Cuba's African and African-descended populations over two distinct periods that reveal significant structural differences in Spanish imperial politics and in the nature of Cuba's slave trade: 1763–1789 and 1790–1820. The first period begins after the Spanish recovery of Havana after ten months of British military occupation. It ends with the 1789 liberalization of Cuba's slave trade, which the Spanish Crown previously had regulated very tightly. The second period ends with the criminalization of Cuba's slave trade and the shift to more surreptitious means of acquiring African ethnic laborers. During the previous two and a half centuries of Cuban colonization, the island's economic marginality within Spain's vast empire had set the tone. Cuba's strategic military value often was overshadowed by the natural resources of colonies such as New Spain, New Granada, and Peru. However, Cuba's tenacious early settlers skillfully manipulated every human and material resource available to them in forging their new society. They did so within a world historical context that was slowly transitioning from the last stages of feudalism to the eventual, but not preordained, dominance of capitalism. These colonists made African ethnics and their descendants essential to Cuba's economic growth. However, African ethnics and their descendants insisted on defining themselves, not just as laborers but also as social contributors. Afro-Cuban social reproductive behaviors preserved some semblance of their humanity, while it further distinguished them from whites.

African ethnics and their Cuban-born descendants differentiated themselves socially along several lines, including color and servile status. In addition to these individualized characteristics, the duration of individual family presence in the Americas was a significant social marker. Families such as Manzano's who already had a multi-generational history in Cuba had to adapt to the changes wrought by the massive influx of new African captives. Some within this older cohort sought to reenforce their identification with Hispanic social norms, while others accepted a greater racial and cultural association with the newcomers. The tensions caused by "re-Africanization" and American creolization were profound.[2] Gender and origin were also social determinants; the opportunities open to newly arrived African men, for example, often differed markedly from those open to second-generation mulatta women. Such men all had entered Cuba as slaves, but some managed to obtain freedom. By contrast, servile status was less likely for this mulatta category of Afro-Cuban women, but those who experienced it often had to rely on emancipation strategies similar to those available to their African male counterparts. For all, Afro-Cuban racial unity remained tentative, despite the racial repression that strengthened it. Their family-formation choices reflected this challenge and demonstrated exogamous, hydridizing, and endogamous practices across several social categories. Free and enslaved, black and mulatto, creole and African, men and women interacted with diverse results in their intimate spaces.

1763–1790: ECONOMIC AND SOCIAL REPRODUCTIVE TRANSFORMATIONS

After Spain regained Havana in July 1763 in the wake of a ten-month British occupation, administrative changes generated new cultural and sociological patterns throughout the island. Aggressive new trade policies gradually replaced the previous restrictions. The Conde de Ricla, Cuba's first post-occupation captain general, initially even allowed British traders continued access to Cuban purchasers. Royal mandates also ended the trade monopoly previously granted to the Royal Havana Company and Cádiz merchants. Direct commercial access was opened to eight additional Spanish peninsular ports and new Spanish-controlled slaving activities along the West African coast were encouraged.[3] Between 1763 and 1789, an estimated 41,604 African ethnics were forcibly brought into Cuba.[4] This population dramatically added to the 32,000 enslaved people estimated to have been held on the island on the eve of the British occupation.[5] While the quantity of these imports was later dwarfed by the masses of captives who arrived under the unrestricted slave trade after 1789, the rate of entry in this period was significantly greater than estimates for the previous two and a half centuries. All levels of Cuban society had to adjust to these increases.

By the time of the first semi-reliable census in 1774, in a total population of 171,620 persons, whites numbered 96,440 (56.2 percent), free people of color 30,847 (18.0 percent), and enslaved people 44,333 (25.8 percent) (see table 2.1). By 1792, all these populations had grown rapidly. The number of whites had increased to 133,559, a growth of 48 percent. The free African-descended population stood at 54,152, a 76 percent increase.

Table 2.1. Cuban population increase, 1774–1792

	1774	*1792*	*Percent increase*
White	96,440	133,559	48
Free people of color	30,847	54,152	76
Enslaved	44,333	84,590	91
Total	171,620	272,301	59

Source: Tabulated and calculated from Kiple, *Blacks in Colonial Cuba,* 26 and 28.

But the rise in the slave population was even more dramatic. Their numbers jumped to 84,590, up by over 90 percent.[6] While much of this last increase largely corresponded to the combined input from the legal and contraband slave trades, natural reproduction among enslaved people was also a factor. That this reproductive activity never reached replacement rates does not preclude its sociological significance for the evolution of Cuban creole identities in this period. Reproductive forces similar to those causing a significant natural increase among Cuba's free people of color also impacted enslaved people on a smaller scale. An inverse demographic relation existing between the two groups was the result of manumissions, which augmented the free population and subtracted from the slave population.

One of the greatest factors distinguishing the reproductive potential of Cuba's free mulattoes and blacks from that of the enslaved was the gender ratios in each group (see table 2.2). Free people of color were more likely to have been locally born than enslaved people were, and therefore their gender ratios were much more balanced. By contrast, many of Cuba's export-oriented planters combined their economic goals with gendered notions of labor and purchased greater numbers of male bondspeople. As discussed in chapter 1, the gender ratios within the slave trade were less actively stipulated in the imperial slaving contracts utilized for much of the eighteenth century, up until 1789, and slave owners showed an overwhelming preference for African male laborers. African ethnic women were present in much lesser proportions.

The 1774 census gave the first official glimpse of the significant imbalance in the gender ratio among the enslaved in Cuba. There were nearly two enslaved men for every enslaved woman and this situation

Table 2.2. Cuban black and mulatto gender proportions by year, free and enslaved

Year	Enslaved male (%)	Free black and mulatto male (%)
1774–1775	64.9	52.4
1778	64.2	47.8
1792	56.0	48.3
1817	62.4	58.8
1827	63.9	48.8
1841	64.4	49.5

Source: Marrero, *Cuba,* 9:178 and 181 (using census data).

continued throughout most of nineteenth century, peaking in 1841. The subsequent gradual improvement resulted largely from the eventual curtailment of the contraband slave trade (the legal trade was criminalized as of 1820). Another factor in this leveling may also have been greater interest shown by planters in both the productive and reproductive capacity of enslaved women. The early nineteenth-century spokesperson for the interests of export merchants and large planters we met in chapter 1, Francisco Arango y Parreño, led by example and encouraged child-bearing among the people he held in bondage. He proudly spoke of the nearly balanced gender ratio achieved at his La Ninfa sugar plantation in 1829. One hundred and twenty-eight female laborers worked alongside 154 men. Women represented the majority of cane cutters, with only two men out of a team of seventy. One of these women was even the slave driver for the group. The gender ratio of this plantation offered better opportunities for enslaved people to find sexual partners and bear children. Arango noted some measure of success at slave reproduction, with fifty-eight births of enslaved children.[7] But these types of statistics were rare before the 1820s. In this period, few other planters confessed to such profit-oriented reproductive programs of slave breeding. They accepted the purchasing of Africans as more cost effective while the supply was readily available.

LATE 1760S PARISH-LEVEL AFRO-CUBAN FAMILY DATA

Macro-level demographic data provide useful counts of Cuba's inhabitants in their various social categories, but they cannot reveal the extent to which its African-descended population of both free and enslaved people still controlled much of the sociological dimension of their reproductive lives and gave it meaning. The ecclesiastic vital registries that historians have often been mined for macro-level demographic information can alternately be read in a more discursive manner that highlights social agency. Colonial Spanish-American baptismal records provide some meaningful indicators of the conditions in which children were born, giving attention to the color, ethnicity, and servile condition of the parents. For enslaved people, owner's names were reported. Researchers have often read the presentation of these categories as true representations of unalterable identity. This current study instead acknowledges the flexible assignment of many of these labels and outlines the context in which their meanings varied.

Shifts in the sexual economy of race are observed in these records as efforts to stabilize racial meaning compete with unexpected disruptions. For example, the distinction between legitimacy and illegitimacy in these records has no material meaning. Instead these classifications reveal racial patterns of conformity to Catholic social norms, as well as parents' public recognition of their offspring and acknowledgment of their own sexual relationships. Similarly, in distinguishing between African ethnics and creoles of color, these documents gave implicit cultural meaning to place of birth and provided a short hand for perceived differences in socialization that the recording priests felt compelled to report. Analyzing infant and African adult baptisms from the intermural Havana parish of Espíritu Santo between March 1765 and August 1767 from this discursive perspective highlights Afro-Cuban reproductive choices and compensates for the general absence of direct commentaries on these practices.[8]

One sociological issue that can be gleaned from these registries is social creolization. The set of social processes we define as creolization were not simply the result of one's birth in the Americas. Creolization occurred as Old World practices and beliefs were either selectively adapted to new America settings or disregarded entirely.[9] The ethnic labels found in Spanish American baptismal records are imprecise indicators of creolization. They may be better understood as announcing the beliefs about culture and race held by recording clerics. Their classificatory schemes could either encode imagined links between culture and biological heritage or disrupt these. Differences in labeling African ethnics and their Cuban-born children are telling on this point. In discontinuing the use of African regional labels in baptizing children born to African ethnic parents, priests marked in abbreviated form the presumed impossibility of socializing new African ethnics in the Americas. The priests thus revealed their own presumption that Cuban-born and the African-born shared little culture commonality. The present-day maintenance of African ethnic identities within Afro-Cuban religions demonstrates the limitations of such perspectives. (See chapter 8 for further discussion of this theme.)

A narrow, geographically defined vision of creolization can be inferred from the proportion of African ethnic baptisms relative to the creole infant ones. The black and mulatto baptisms recorded at Espíritu Santo reveal a much greater number of creole births than entries for new African captives. This parish saw 643 infants of color baptized in comparison to only 123 African ethnic "adults." Even if very high infant mortality rates are allowed for, at this moment the demographic connection of the creole black and mulatto population to African ethnic communities was decreasing. The local community grew more from local births than it did from African arrivals. African ethnic adults were only 16 percent of those baptized.

Moreover, two-thirds of mulatto and black children were born to creole women, as opposed to African ethnic mothers (see table 2.3). The general Afro-Cuban experience had become multi-generational, but slavery had not. In this domain, a sharp reproductive distinction existed between the free and the enslaved. While African women accounted for two-thirds of slave mothers, they were only a third of the combined free and enslaved total, as slightly more children were born to free women of color (329) than to enslaved ones (314). This pattern complicates comparisons with other, contemporary racial regimes in the Americas where African-descended reproduction occurred predominantly among the enslaved instead of the free.[10] In addition to those children born of free mothers, a small number were baptized as free despite their mothers' enslavement.[11] The mothers' owners in these cases consented to the children's free status, but there is no indication of whether this freedom

Table 2.3. Parental status in baptisms of children of color, Espíritu Santo Parish, Havana 1765–1767

	Mother						
Father	African slave	Black slave	Parda slave	Free black	Free parda	Free African	Total
African slave	115	22	1	6	2	8	154
No father	70	32	11	21	35	0	169
Black slave	5	22	0	6	0	1	34
Pardo slave	0	4	1	1	4	0	10
Free black	2	8	0	55	13	1	79
Free pardo	0	5	6	9	145	0	165
Free African	8	1	0	3	2	0	14
Spanish	0	0	0	1	7	0	8
Creole (no race listed)	0	1	0	2	7	0	10
Total	200	95	19	104	215	10	643

Note: Baptisms indicate the fathers may be of either marital or non-marital designation.
Source: Archivo de la parroquia Espíritu Santo (hereafter "AES"), *libro 8 de bautismos de pardos y morenos, 1759–1767*, entries 1317–2083.

was purchased or given as a gift. Such acts mediated the standard application of *partus sequitur ventrem,* where children born to enslaved mothers inherited their servile status, and slightly eased the rigid link between African descent and enslavement, at least in this urban setting.

Also with regard to creolization, the gender and age dynamics among African ethnics also speak to the complex process of adapting their prior ethnic norms to their new environment. Of the thirty-eight "adults" baptized at Espíritu Santo in 1765, twenty-two were male and sixteen female. According to the ages recorded for fourteen of the males, these were in fact boys and young men between the ages of eight and eighteen, with an average age of 11.7 years. Ages were also reported for half the female "adults," ranging from twelve to twenty and with an average of 16.6 years.[12] So, at least for this urban parish, the arriving captives were prepubescent boys and teenage girls already of childbearing age. These older girls and young women were more likely than their younger male counterparts to have been knowledgeable of the religio-political practices of the African ethnic communities from which they were taken and more likely to have been initiated as adults into these practices. By virtue of this gendered age difference, these young women were also more likely to adapt the religio-political norms of their homeland to their Cuban captivity.

In 1760, the Havana parish of Espíritu Santo was densely populated, with some 11,000 congregants.[13] The parish had been founded in the early seventeenth century to serve enslaved people, but now contained a mix of all classes and colors. Some of Cuba's leading early nineteenth-century political figures such as the intellectuals José de la Luz y Cabellero (1800–1862) and Antonio Bachiller y Morales (1812–1885) were baptized at its altar.[14] The 643 black and mulatto children baptized there over the twenty-seven-month period between March 1765 and August 1767 seems an exceptionally high number, given the reasonable estimate of the parish's African-descended population of 4,800.[15] If this population had the same birthrate of the more gender-balanced mid-eighteenth-century France at 38.77 per 1,000, then 419 births would have been expected over these twenty-seven months.[16] While this discrepancy remains unexplained, the data provide useful indicators of the social divisions and reproductive racial meaning within this population. These 643 infant baptisms reveal Afro-Cuban social segmentation and the extent to which both marital and non-marital families were formed across the social boundaries of origin, color, and status (see table 2.3). Reproductive endogamy along these lines was the norm, though a measurable level of family formation occurred between persons of distinct social stations. However, there were areas in which the transgression of social boundaries did not occur. Most notably, pardo men and whites acknowledged no amorous interaction with African women, and reproductive conjugal relations between white women and black and mulatto men are not documented.

Distinctive reproductive patterns based on the origin, color, and servile status of the mothers are obvious in the records. Free parda women were the largest category of mothers. As separate groups, enslaved and free black, creole women were less than half as fecund. Yet, if these mothers are grouped solely according to color and origin (excluding

Table 2.4. Gender and racial distributions of the Cuban population, 1775

Social status	Free white	Free pardo	Free black	Black slave	Pardo slave
Male	54,555	10,021	5,959	25,256	3,518
Female	40,864	9,006	5,629	13,356	2,206

Note: According to Kiple, *Blacks in Colonial Cuba,* 26, the 1774 census is more reliable and is therefore used above. However, von Humboldt's figures for the 1775 census provide distinctions by color category not seen in the 1774 data and differ only slightly.
Source: Von Humboldt, *Ensayo político,* 108–109.

status), then black creole, African ethnic, and parda women were present in similar numbers: 199, 210, and 234 respectively.[17] This was in a period in which pardas accounted for 37 percent of the female population of color, island-wide. The general proportional distribution between African and creole women of color in this period is unknown (see table 2.4).

Several possibilities may account for this near equal distribution of births by the mother's origin. First, the term "parda" was only partially an indicator of color, suggesting "brown," and did not have a meaning similar to the English usage of "mulatto" in referring to first generation of inter-racial birth to European-descended and African-descended parents. It instead marked any level of perceived European and African joint genealogy and distance from popular assumptions of pure African ancestry and phenotype. Based on the baptismal evidence, the term could apply equally to someone who was bi-racial as to someone with only one white great-grandparent. In a social context defined by the multi-generational presence of free African-descended people, the pardo/parda category increased faster than others. The slow rate of African importations before the 1789 liberalization of the slave trade and the high mortality of enslaved creole children restrained the growth of these other categories. Second, if one compares the births to free parda women with those in all other categories, then the greater frequency of manumission for these women is also a plausible factor. This phenomenon has been widely documented in other slaveholding regions within Latin America.[18] The low numbers of enslaved parda mothers in the parish records are striking and also may reflect this situation. Pardas outnumbered black women within Cuba's free population of color (see table 2.4) and free women could exercise and control their reproductive potential to a degree that slave women could not. Moreover, a self-determined or cleric-assigned choice of the parda label, as opposed to *negra* (black woman), within the baptismal record may have played a role. Pardo/parda also connoted a cultural distance from perceived African barbarity that priests may have conferred in baptism and some African-descended people claimed it for themselves and their offspring.

An explanation for the relatively equal numbers of African ethnic and black creole mothers in the combined free and enslaved categories is less straightforward. Several factors arise from the ideological baggage surrounding each label, as well as the material conditions of these women's lives. One such factor was the high mortality of enslaved people at all ages in comparison to free blacks and mulattoes.[19] This situation would have reduced the number of African mothers relative to creoles, as African ethnics represented a higher proportion of the slave population than creoles. Another factor was the lower fecundity for enslaved African women compared to their creole counterparts, which has been demonstrated for the British Caribbean.[20] A factor that may have increased the proportional presence of African mothers is the fact that the African girls and women who were brought into Havana in the period were already of reproductive age. Again, the 1765 parish records reveal ages ranging from twelve to twenty-five for newly baptized African ethnic girls and women.[21] Black creoles, by contrast, had to survive childhood before entering this stage.

Fathers also had a significant presence in the baptismal record of Cuba's people of color in this period. Fathers were documented for the majority of the 643 baptisms of Afro-Cuban infants in both the free and enslaved categories. Only in 26.3 percent of the cases were fathers not identified. Within the smaller segment of 310 infants classified as slaves, fathers were reported for 63.6 percent; therefore, the illegitimacy rate for enslaved infants was slightly more than a third.[22] For free children of color, fathers were recorded for an astonishing 83.2 percent of the baptisms. An enslaved child was 2.16 times more likely to be registered without her father's name.

The patterns of paternal presence follow those seen among mothers, according to origin, color, and servile status. Free pardos were the largest category of fathers (25.6 percent), followed by enslaved African ethnics. Enslaved creole black fathers ranked fourth after their free counterparts. It is interesting to note that in this sample, free African women did not baptize their children without a father. Neither free nor enslaved African mothers acknowledged reproductive unions with pardo men. This absence marked the observance of intra-racial, social distinction based on origin among Afro-Cubans. By contrast to the high rate of legitimacy among free African women, the majority of children born to enslaved parda women (57.9 percent) did not have their fathers named. When they did marry, it typically was with free pardo men. Yet, marriages between pardas and African ethnic men were also recorded, indicating that any potential cultural differences between the two groups were not insurmountable.[23] It is also true that the rate of out-of-wedlock births to parda women was higher than for any other group. However, across all categories of infant baptisms to women of color at Espíritu Santo, the parents were listed as legitimately married in no less than 71 percent of the entries.[24]

What accounts for such incredibly high legitimacy figures? Unfortunately, the documentation does not include any material that might suggest an answer, but it does confirm a theory that African and African-derived cultural practices did not reject Catholic marriage. Nor were urban slave owners obstructing these unions. Perhaps they even encouraged them? If one looks closely in the baptismal registry at the example set by Spanish monarch Charles III (r. 1759–1788), all births registered to the mothers he owned were legitimate. Not one of these twenty-nine children of *esclavas del rey* (slaves of the king or royal slaves) was born out of wedlock.[25] This raises the possibility that the Crown discouraged out-of-wedlock birth among its enslaved people, behaving in accordance with Church moral dictates. However, additional sources reveal more material concerns and suggest that Crown promotion of slave marriages and procreation in this era was thought to be made "urgent to prevent flight and compensate for the scarcity noted on the coasts of Guinea."[26] Nevertheless, encouragement of marriage does not necessarily equate to a restriction on out-of-wedlock births. Additional re-

search beyond this current study could seek to differentiate the two interpretations of the Crown's actions and investigate its influence on
other owners. Additional pressure for legitimate family formation among
enslaved Afro-Cubans came from other sources. Again, as described in
the previous chapter, the Jesuit and Bethlemite religious orders also
promoted slave marriages and natural reproduction. These orders also
encouraged other slave owners to learn from these examples.[27]

In the 1765–1767 Espíritu Santo records, slightly more than a quarter
of all children of color were born outside of wedlock. They were simply
recorded as *hijo de* (child of) the mother, with no other annotation of
illegitimacy. Only in seventeen cases did both parents appear when the
child was not recorded as legitimate.[28] In one such case, the baptismal
certificate explicitly stated that an enslaved African father *declaró que
sea su hijo natural* (declared the child as his).[29] This was a rarity. The
term *hijo natural* (natural child) was used only in a few cases where
both parents were listed but unwed. More generally, these children
were simply listed as hijo de both parents. The term "hijo natural" was a
designation that went beyond paternal recognition in the ecclesiastic
registries to have important legal implications. Since the medieval era,
Castilian law had used the label exclusively for children born outside of
marriage where no legal or religious impediment prohibited the union
of the parents. In designating a child as a hijo natural, the father accepted the responsibility and the cost of "subsistence, nurturing, and
education."[30] The child also gained the right to a maximum of one-fifth
of the paternal estate.[31] Although enslaved men might not have had the
unfettered ability to fulfill these obligations, free Afro-Cuban men had
to concern themselves with the legal ramifications.

The unwed fathers who did appear in the registries were generally
free. Only four were enslaved: two Africans and two black creoles. And
in two additional records, the fathers were listed in a way that suggests
they were white.[32] That is, unlike what was typical for pardo and moreno
men, no color or status was registered for these men. The documents
only noted that they were *natural de esta [ciudad]* or *natural de Cartegena* (native of this city or native of Cartegena) respectively. That unmarried white men would have declared themselves as fathers of children born to African-descended women would have been acceptable in

the period. White men were listed as the legitimate husbands of parda women in two cases. This demonstrates that although limited, inter-racial marriage remained acceptable, though for very specific race and gender combinations. Again, no inter-racial reproduction or marriage was seen between African-descended men and white women.

Beyond legitimate children and hijos naturales, another category of children also appeared within the mulatto and black baptismal record, those listed as *de padres no conocidos* (of unknown parents).[33] Seventeen such children were baptized at Espíritu Santo between 1765 and 1767. Half had the additional notation of *al parecer pardo* (appears pardo or brown) in their registration. This comment did not appear for children who at least were recognized by their mothers, nor in cases where the father was reported as white Spaniard. Also, no equivalent comment of black appearance was registered. One is left to wonder what motivated the inclusion of this comment, by which the recording priests implied an important social value for pardo appearance and identity.

Parish records from the period do not give any indication of the situation under which these children de padres no conocidos were brought before the Church. However, they were generally placed in the care of free women of color, for whom any potential biological relation to the children is not usually indicated in the records. It is interesting to speculate what classification as hijos de padres no conocidos meant for children of color in a slave society. Were they simply the abandoned children of free mothers? Or were some the children of enslaved mothers? And, if the latter, was this a mechanism through which their freedom was guaranteed at the price of their further loss of recognized ancestry? Or for that matter, could white women have borne such children without suffering social dishonor? And did their fathers' status play a role in their abandonment? Although the available data do not begin to address these issues, the abandonment of children of color represented an area with great potential for social boundary crossing. In chapter 4 we will discuss how the institution of the Real Casa de la Maternidad (the Royal Maternity Home) functioned as a nineteenth-century site in which the racial classification of abandoned children was frequently obscured.

1790–1820: FAMILY FORMATION IN THE GREATEST
PERIOD OF LEGAL SLAVE IMPORTATION

The period from 1789 to 1820 witnessed the greatest intensity in legal slave trading in Cuban history. Large agricultural producers and import-export traders had collectively organized themselves into a politically powerful unit and won capitalist (free trade) concessions that replaced the previous limitations imposed by the absolutist Spanish monarchy. No action exemplified this victory more than the 1789 royal order permitting both Spanish and foreign slave traders liberal, duty-free access to the Havana market. The Spanish Crown returned to reproductive concerns and commonly expressed in slave trade contracts prior to the eighteenth century that "The negroes had to be of good races and at least one third women."[34] The motive for this reassertion is unknown, nor is the extent to which it was enforced. Demand for slave labor increased dramatically after 1795, as indicated by a sharp rise in slave prices.[35] Between 1790 and 1820, an estimated 325,000 African ethnics arrived on the island.[36] By 1817, the number of slaves stood at 225,121 and had increased to 38.9 percent of the island's population.[37]

The nature of Cuban slavery changed in conjunction with the greater number of imported African ethnics. In anticipation of this accelerated, forced importation, the Spanish government attempted to reformulate the regulations on slave life.[38] These regulations were collected into one document, unofficially known as the Código negro español (the Spanish Black Code), and circulated in Spain by a royal cedula in 1789. It was intended to replace the scattered and inconsistent regulations that had controlled slavery previously. In the new law's preamble, the Spanish Crown stated that it was motivated by concern for the welfare of its enslaved subjects. In fourteen chapters, the Código negro español attempted to set minimal standards for many aspects of slave education, treatment, and labor. Enforcement of the regulations was to be part of the expanded responsibility of the *síndico procurador general* (general public advocate).

The feature of the royal mandate most germane to the topic of reproduction is its recommendation that slave owners purposely hinder the establishment and continuation of illicit sexual relations among enslaved people. However, despite the Crown's reformist intentions, Cuban planters and their counterparts throughout Spanish America solicited and won suspension of the new law's implementation.[39] This suspension marked a significant philosophical shift toward disavowing the humanity of the enslaved. It was another major victory of capitalist interests who were seeking to thoroughly objectify enslaved people solely as tools of economic growth. Real reform would have to wait until 1842, when Spain's new liberal representative government implemented legislation that mandated greater concern for the treatment of the enslaved by their owners.[40] In 1789, Cuba's enslaved people also lost one mechanism for gaining freedom. The practice of *coartación* allowed enslaved people to contract with their owners for installment purchase of freedom. Upon entering the contract and with the first payment, the slave became a *coartado* who could not be easily sold to a new owner. Custom at this time allowed children born to *coartada* mothers to inherit the same status. A royal order in 1789 prohibited the practice and limited reproductive access to freedom.[41]

The expansions of sugar production and the slave trade went hand in hand. Annual sugar exports almost tripled between 1790 and 1820, increasing from 77,895 to 215,953 boxes. The number of Africans transported to Havana increased approximately sixfold in the same period, from 2,534 in 1790 to 15,147 in 1820.[42] Great *ingenios* (sugar mills) developed with large slave labor forces, many numbering more than 200 men, often without the presence of enslaved women. The labor regime for slaves engaged in sugar production became much more intense in comparison to urban labor and other agricultural activities. They worked at clearing forests for new fields and firewood, and planted, harvested, and milled the cane. The processing of the cane often involved dangerous night-time labor in order to make the sugar before fermentation set in. The living arrangements for enslaved people on sugar plantations were changed to facilitate increased productivity. Instead of the earlier reliance on small *bohíos* (huts) housing a few individuals or families, enslaved people increasingly lived in *barracónes* (barracks).[43] But despite the intensified labor regime associated with sugar production, Cuba's utilization of its enslaved population remained diverse. In estimated averages over this period, only one quarter of enslaved

people were confined to sugar production; one quarter worked on coffee plantations; one quarter were involved in other agricultural interests (including tobacco); and the remainder were employed in urban
occupations.[44]

Again, information on the familial experiences of enslaved people in
this period is rather limited. What little data exist indicate that their
gender ratio became increasingly unbalanced. In the registries of Havana's cathedral for the period between 1590 and 1600, 54 percent of the
480 African new arrivals baptized there were male and 46 percent
female.[45] By 1790, other data sets indicate that men accounted for
66.25 percent of African entrants. In 1798, that percentage peaked at
85.73 percent. One group of slave merchants complained bitterly in 1805
that despite having brought 80 African ethnic women for sale in the Cuban market, they could not find any buyers. Purchasers simply preferred
men.[46] However, by 1815 the percentage of male entrants had returned
to 66.14 percent.[47] While the African trade was 68.8 percent male in the
period between 1790 and 1820, the intra-Caribbean slave trade to Cuba
was even more imbalanced at 79.0 percent male.[48] The Cuban preference for male laborers was reflected in the consistently higher prices
paid for male slaves in the early nineteenth century. Manuel Moreno
Fraginals's review of the inventories of fourteen "new-style" sugar plantations existing between 1798 and 1822 revealed an average ratio of six
enslaved men to one enslaved woman.[49] This imbalance would change
only with the end of legal slave imports in 1820.[50] The disproportionate
masculine presence was important for its potential effect on the group's
overall reproductive capacity. The crude birthrate (births per thousand
of the total population) would naturally decrease as the gender imbalance increased.

Some analysts suggest that the slave gender ratio statistics should be
used with caution. David Eltis and Stanley Engerman see the gender-
ratio issue as overblown. After all, slave populations in North America
achieved reproductive success despite similar arriving gender ratios
for Africans. Eltis and Engerman also demonstrate that gender ratios
within the transatlantic slave trade did not differ greatly from that of
the voluntary immigrant groups who came the Americas. For example,
men represented 63.1 percent of the free and non-indentured persons

coming from Britain between 1773 and 1776. For German indentured servants arriving between 1745 and 1831, men represented 67.1 percent of the total.[51] And, as mentioned above, the gender ratio calculated from a small sample of seventeenth-century Cuban sources differed little from a sample of early nineteenth-century sources. This evidence suggests that reproductive success among enslaved populations was more closely bound to mortality rates. While overwhelming anecdotal evidence of high mortality rates exists for men enslaved in Cuba's sugar plantations, less evidence exists for the enslaved women and men laboring in other areas, especially in the urban settings where a quarter of Cuba's slave population worked. Demographic historian Jack Eblen suggests that these factors should lead to a reconsideration of natural increase in Cuba's population of color.[52]

The increased proportion of African ethnics with respect to black creoles within the enslaved population may have had a significant impact on reproduction. Moreno Fraginals calculates that plantation labor was almost 96 percent African in the three decades between 1791 and 1822.[53] These high proportions probably had a sizable negative impact on fertility. In other Caribbean countries, enslaved African women demonstrated much lower fertility rates than creole women due to the trauma of forced adaptation to a new environment, an intense labor regimen, and the contraceptive influence of their traditionally longer practice of infant lactation.[54] These observations support the hypothesis of minimal reproduction on Cuba's sugar plantations in this period. However, such limitations did not forestall the complex familial and reproductive lives that many enslaved people were able to achieve in both rural and urban settings.

Within the last ten years studies have thoroughly overturned Moreno Fraginals's earlier assessment of there having been little family formation among Cuba's enslaved people.[55] John Dumoulin has established that between 1803 and 1820 in Santiago, Cuba's second largest city of the nineteenth century and early colonial capital, marriages for the free and enslaved people of color were 62 percent of total marriages at a time when that population represented the majority of the city's residents.[56] Cuban researchers Aisnara Perera Díaz and Maria de los Angeles Meriño Fuentes have made several studies of the provincial Havana region of Bejucal that demonstrate a significant number of slave marriages, lasting consensual unions, and meaningful paternal links within this rural agricultural setting. For the period between 1792 and 1826, 78.4 percent of enslaved infants in this region were baptized as legitimate. It was only from the 1830s that marriage and legitimacy rates began to fall significantly.[57]

One example of the transformation in family-formation patterns seen among the many multi-generational slave families presented by Perera and Meriño is that of José María Lucumí and María del Rosario Rodríguez Carabalí. Although they were initially enslaved to different owners, these two married in 1795. Despite having separate residences, they had several children together. These children received the maternal "Rodríguez" surname as they were also the property of their mother's owner. To facilitate the couple's marital life, José María's owner, the Marqués de Cárdenas de Monte Hermoso, bought María del Rosario in 1804 and by 1805 she had gained her freedom.[58] Two children subsequently born to the couple were baptized with the Cárdenas surname, which was either an acknowledgment of José María's paternity or of the social importance of his owner. The symbols of social respectability that were legitimacy and freedom were utilized by the family's next generation. Their daughter María Luisa Cardenas, who had been born enslaved, gained her freedom by age twenty. While still laboring as a slave on the same plantation of her father's original owner, María Luisa began a relationship with a free "Kongo" African, Cecilio Hernández. The couple married and subsequently had five free-born daughters. Interestingly, the family's respect for legitimacy seems to have declined rapidly in the next generation. Several of María Luisa's daughters bore children out of wedlock, unlike their parents and grandparents. In this way, the family conformed to the general pattern of increasing illegitimacy among both free and enslaved Afro-Cubans in the nineteenth century.

The multi-generational family of José Belen Cazares and María de Jesús Padrón experienced a similar decrease in legitimacy as did the Cárdenas-Rodriguez family, but without the benefit of achieving freedom. The two married in 1809, while both were enslaved to Jacinto Padrón. Although José Belen had arrived in Cuba from the Carabalí West African ethnic group, he eventually earned his freedom. By contrast,

Table 2.5. Average marriage rates (per 100 adults) by race and region, 1791–1796

	Bahía Honda	Jesús, María y José	Jibacoa	Yaguaramas
Whites	27.3	35.5	34.2	27.6
Free mulattoes	21.4	29.0	29.7	35.2
Free black	20.3	29.5	39.3	30.4
Enslaved	14.8	29.7	22.5	15.9

Source: Calculated from figures reported in Archivo General de Indias, Cuba, leg. 1470.

María de Jesús was Cuban-born and spent her entire life in slavery. The couple had at least ten children, of whom only those born after 1817 are known. Of the daughters, five subsequently baptized children of their own in the same parish and all of these were illegitimate. In reconstructing such families, Perera and Meriño draw a complex picture of Afro-Cuban reproductive possibilities under slavery, where the possibilities of establishing strong familial bonds were seized by many, but deviated from Hispanic, Catholic moral expectations.

Marriage rate data from several regions again provide some comparative indication of the social differences between Cuba's various status groups. The data demonstrate that in many but not all regions marriage rates had begun to differ markedly with respect to color and labor condition (see table 2.5).

For example, between 1792 and 1795, the average marriage rates from the extramural Havana district of Jesús, María y José, a neighborhood adjoining the one served by the parish of Espíritu Santo, were fairly consistent for the respective groups of people of color. Whites from that area demonstrated only slightly higher marriage rates. However, in the tobacco-producing district of Bahía Honda west of Havana, marriage rates for whites were much greater than those for people of color. Moreover, there was much greater variation among the latter groups. The central Cuban cattle-raising district of Yaguaramas reported similar figures. However, in this case, free mulattoes recorded the highest average marriage rate, substantially higher than that of whites. Free blacks in the district of Jibacoa in eastern Havana, which at that time was turning more toward sugar production, surpassed the other groups in their average rate of marriage.[59] In all cases, local production factors left unique social imprints on reproductive behavior. Most obviously, marriage rates for enslaved adults in rural areas were in all cases significantly lower than those of free mulattoes and blacks, whereas parity was reached in urban settings.

By the late 1820s, another set of island-wide data indicated that marriage rates among free people of color had in fact experienced a noticeable slump. The 1827 census demonstrates that in that year one marriage occurred for every 194 Cubans, one for every 166 whites, one for every 236 free mulattoes, one for every 347 free blacks, and one for every 207 slaves.[60] Historian Herbert Klein explains the differing marriage rates between the free people of color and the enslaved with the suggestion that "the high slave marriage rate as contrasted to that of the free colored population is apparently due to the fact that the slave population was accountable to a master, and through him to the local church, and was therefore more completely under the influence of the local parish priest."[61] Franklin Knight refines this interpretation by returning to the contrast between urban and rural experiences of slavery. In his analysis, clerical influence was likely greatest on those enslaved person held by the older urban elite who had not become heavily invested in agricultural production. The concentration of priests in Havana and other cities allowed these owners to exert a religious influence on their enslaved. Those in rural settings did not enjoy such access.[62]

These explanations of decreasing marriage rates among Cuba's people of color can be supplemented by three additional factors: increasingly male gender ratios; the growing proportion of enslaved creole mothers; and increased declarations of hijos naturales.[63] If the above statistics on the number of marriages within a given population are determined by the total size of the specific population categories, then they are useful in the analysis of the social ideologies surrounding racialized reproduction only if the respective gender ratios are comparable. Otherwise, distortion of the gender ratios would leave a significant proportion of these populations without the ability to find marriageable partners (see table 2.6). However, with 53,215 more men than women among people of color, marriage remained impossible for many enslaved men.

Table 2.6. Gender and racial distribution of Cuban population, 1817

Social status	White	Free pardo	Free black	Pardo slave	Black slave
Men	130,519	30,512	28,373	17,803	106,521
Women	109,311	29,170	26,003	14,499	60,322

Source: Ortiz, *Los negros esclavos*, 17.

This was especially true in an era when divorce was not permissible. Nevertheless, high mortality rates among enslaved men and the possibility of relationships outside of marriage increased the potential for pairings over the course of an individual's life.

Returning to the baptismal registries of black and mulatto children from the Havana parish of Espíritu Santo in this period, we can detect other internal social distinctions that impacted marriage rates and that enable several important comparisons with the more rural setting analyzed by Perera and Meriño and with earlier data from the same parish. Consistent with the slave trade transformations, the percentage of African adults baptized increased. In the mid-eighteenth-century, Espíritu Santo records it at 16 percent.[64] This proportion rose to 32 percent and 52.7 percent, for 1800 and 1820 respectively.[65] African ethnic people and beliefs had a greater influence on the parish's social practices.

Samples from 1800 and 1820 also reveal the persistence of endogamous mating patterns but lower legitimacy rates (see tables 2.5 and 2.6). The decline in legitimacy rates in this urban parish paralleled the one described for the more rural communities analyzed by Perera and Meriño. While legitimate baptisms stood at 73 percent in the late 1760s and in 1800, by 1820 they had fallen to 51 percent. As will be discussed in chapter 3, a sample from 1857 reveals less than 30 percent of all mulatto or black children were baptized into legitimate families. However, the nature of the data in this period differs slightly from the mid-eighteenth-century sample. Both early nineteenth-century sets are less precise in noting parental color and status.

Thus three new categories related to maternity were present in 1800: those without mothers listed; free creoles, with no color listed;

Table 2.7. Parental color and status in baptisms of children of color, Espíritu Santo Parish, Havana 1800

Father	Mother									Total
	African slave	Black slave	Parda slave	Slave (no color listed)	Free black	Free parda	Free African	No mother	Creole (no color listed)	
African slave	21	2					1			24
No father	29	20	3	8	6		2	10	1	79
Black slave		2		2					1	5
Pardo slave										
Free black		2	1	2	33	1	1			40
Free pardo	2	2			7	37			3	51
Free African							9		1	10
White		1							1	2
Creole (no race listed)		2	1	4	1		1	2	1	12
African (no status listed)	46	3			2		7	2		60
Moreno (no status listed)	4	6	2		1					13
Pardo (no status listed)	1	2	1		1	1				6
Total	103	42	8	16	51	39	21	14	8	302

Source: AES, Libro 22 de bautismos de pardos y morenos, 1800, entries 1–447.

Table 2.8. Parental color and status of children of color, Espíritu Santo Parish, Havana, 1820

						Mother				
Father	African slave	Black slave	Parda slave	Free black	Free parda	Free African	No mother	Creole (no color listed)	Slave (no color listed)	Total
African slave	16	7	1	1					1	26
No father	65	25	5	11	12	3	3	2	13	139
Black slave	4	7							1	12
Pardo slave								1		1
Free black		3		30	2					35
Free pardo			2	5	30	1				38
Free African						5				5
White				1				1		2
Creole (no race listed)	2	3	1	1	1			1	2	11
African (no status listed)	9	1		2		1			3	16
Moreno (no status listed)	1			1						2
Pardo (no status listed)		1								1
Total	97	47	9	52	45	10	3	5	20	288

Source: AES, Libro 33 de bautismos de pardos y morenos, 1820, entries 334–943.

and slaves with no color listed. In that year's sample, of the 302 mulatto and black infants baptized, 14 were registered without a mother's name. For a slave society in which a mother's status was the main determinant of a child's fate under the legal doctrine of *partus sequitur ventrem,* this type of omission was likely not a casual one. Such omissions were too costly to both people of color and slave owners, with the potential loss of liberty for the former and the potential loss of property for the latter. A century earlier, in a 1704 royal edict, Philip V had demanded the elimination of such omissions, and for the mid-eighteenth century Espíritu Santo sample reviewed above none were reported. For 1820, only three such children were recorded. All were enslaved to the same owner, Don Fernando Perez. That he could make such property claims without proving the mother's status compromised the potential achievement of freedom for all African-descended people. The servile status of fathers was reported less often, leading to a new presence within the registries of African, black creole, and pardo men without labor status markers. The near absence of enslaved pardo fathers from both samples is striking. It is likely that such men were reclassified in these records under other categories and that pardo identity was increasingly disassociated from slavery.

Another noticeable difference between the mid-eighteenth-century data and the early-nineteenth-century ones is the decreased proportion of births to free mothers. In the earlier samples, nearly 50 percent of black and mulatto infants were born to free mothers. By 1800 that proportion had fallen to 44 percent, and by 1820 it was 40 percent. Cuban slavery had increasingly become a multi-generational experience. This change cannot be attributed to a decreased proportion of free African mothers, as one might suspect with the increased slave trade and fewer opportunities to achieve manumission. Their proportions increased. Such women represented 1.5 percent of mothers in the 1765–1767 sample, but 7 percent and 3.5 percent in 1800 and 1820, respectively. The greatest decrease in the free mother category was seen among parda women. Their numbers had fallen from a third of black and mulatta mothers to between 13 percent and 15 percent for 1800 and 1820, respectively. Again, while no unassailable explanation of this decrease is possible, it is likely that a great deal of slippage between parda and blanca categories was occurring, with select parda women reclassified as white.[66]

The proportion of creole mothers among the enslaved also fluctuated. In the eighteenth-century records, it stood at 17.7 percent. The 1800 and 1821 samples reported 16.5 percent and 19.4 percent, respectively. Looking forward to the 1847 baptismal data that we will consider in the next chapter, 27 percent of Afro-Cuban mothers were enslaved creoles. This increase may have contributed to lower marriage and legitimacy rates. Demographic historian Barry Higman has observed for the British Caribbean in the early nineteenth century that parental co-residence among enslaved people declined as the proportion of creoles rose. He attributed this decrease in parental co-residence to the greater geographic range of creole social networks in comparison to the limited ones of Africans, who were initially unfamiliar with the setting of their enslavement. Creole slaves had greater possibilities for meeting mates who did not belong to the same owner and who resided in separate locations. This mobility negatively affected the stability of their amorous unions.[67]

A final possibility for explaining the decrease in Afro-Cuban marriage rates would give additional historical agency directly to people of color. In comparing the mid-eighteenth-century baptismal data with the two early nineteenth-century samples, an increased number of parental declarations of hijos naturales is evident in the later sample. In the 1765–1767 Espíritu Santo records, 2.6 percent of newly baptized mulatto and black infants received this designation. In 1800, the proportion increased to 3.6 percent, and in 1820 it nearly tripled, to 12.1 percent. In all these cases, Afro-Cuban parents were exercising their right to recognize legal paternity even without recourse marriage.

Despite the documentation of Afro-Cuban marital families provided by these records, this information does not speak to co-residence and family stability for either the free or the enslaved. The records offer no indication of the economic hardship and successes of free families of color, nor the full extent of slave-owner intervention in the lives of slave and mixed-status families. The legal statutes of the period continued to offer slave families some protection, but their enforcement remained inconsistent. Spanish legal tradition vested the office of the *síndico pro-*

curador general (general public advocate) with the authority to advance the grievances of the common population, including enslaved people, to the Crown.[68] Although evidence of slaves' utilization of the office exists for other regions in Spanish America in this period, similar evidence is rare for Cuba before the middle of the nineteenth century. In one case from 1689, a recently liberated woman sought the procurador's assistance in securing freedom for her children who had remained in bondage.[69] Despite their limited numbers, such claims distinguished the legal parameters of Spanish-American slavery from those of other regions of the Americas.[70] More discussion of the familial dimension of similar nineteenth-century claims will be presented in chapters 3 and 5.

MANZANO'S FAMILY IN HISTORICAL CONTEXT

Returning to Juan Manzano's description of his family background, we may place it in relation to the collective experiences outlined above in order to distinguish between the exceptional and the commonplace in Cuban racialized reproduction prior the 1820 criminalization of the slave trade. Manzano was born in either 1793 or 1797 on the outskirts of Havana to a married couple, in a period before the full capitalist domination of the social relations of Cuban slavery.[71] Although his parents were both enslaved creoles, Manzano recalled their relatively privileged status with pride. His father, Toribio de Castro, had been trained as a tailor, and his mother, María del Pilar, was a respected lady's maid. Both were owned by the wealthy planter family of the Marquesa Doña Beatriz Justiz de Santa Ana de Manzano. The poet notes that his parents' marriage was not the norm among his mother's cohort of enslaved female domestics. This was not due to its mere existence, but due to its character. The others had married free men of color, gained their freedom, and subsequently moved to the cities of Havana or Matanzas. Manzano suggests that his parents were uncommon for marrying another person owned by the same owner.[72] But the couple was more typical in that it was endogamous for both servile status and color. Both were enslaved pardos.

Manzano was the first of his parents' children. As far as he was aware, his mother had five additional pregnancies after his birth. Two resulted in still births; one sister died in infancy; and a brother and a pair of twins, a boy and girl, survived into adulthood.[73] These numbers reflect both the low birthrate and the high rate of infant mortality typical of Caribbean slave mothers. However, these low numbers and the family's somewhat affectionate relationship with their owner do not align well with any assessment of for-profit slave breeding. In Manzano's view, his owner's encouragement of marriage and legitimacy for the children born to her slaves had more socially generous objectives. Again, Manzano recollected,

> One of the favorite young slaves was Maria M, my mother, who was greatly esteemed for her intelligence, and her occupation was to wait on the Senora Marquesa of J. in her advanced age. This lady was accustomed when she was pleased with her attendants, to give them their liberty when they were about to marry; . . . providing them with all things necessary, as if they had been her own children, without depriving them after their marriage of the favor and protection of her house, which extended even to their children and husbands.[74]

In Manzano's admiring memory, the profit motive behind slave owning and potential slave breeding is absent. He instead highlights his mistress's benevolence and calls attention to the freedom she granted many of his parents' cohorts. Lurking behind his words is the fact of his parents' continued bondage, which did not follow the liberatory pattern he outlines above. They only obtained their freedom much later. However, because of their owner's generosity, Manzano's younger twin siblings were born free. This generosity was also extended to Manzano's parents in a more limited form. Upon Manzano's birth, Doña Beatriz stipulated the price at which they eventually might purchase their freedom: 300 pesos each.[75] In setting this price of *coartación* (self-purchase), separating the couple through sale became legally restricted.[76] However, this status did not extend to the children (Manzano and his brother) who were born before this legal act. Manzano was never guaranteed continued contact with his parents, and with Doña Beatriz's death he was willed to his godmother and separated from his family.

The family's experience was also marked by frequent transitions between rural and urban environments, especially as their owner traveled between her city and plantation homes. Manzano experienced these transitions more deeply than did other members of his family. As he matured, he was frequently ripped from the relative comfort of the city and sent to labor in the fields as punishment for even the slightest transgression. Manzano explained the disturbance to his family caused on one of these occasions:

> A question, a hundred threats, the appearance of the plantation clothing, a sugar mill so dreaded in those days because of its overseer . . . whose name alone caused terror in the house when it was used as a threat—all of that heaped onto my scarce sixteen-year-old shoulders so that I did not know how to respond except to plead and cry . . . they took me to my prison cell. I was there four days and nights, with no end to my arrest in sight . . . During this whole time I ate only what my brother and some other boy slipped under the door. Once outside, I was dressed in my plantation workers' clothes . . . I awaited the moment when we would all be gathered together with all the luggage to set out by sea for Matanzas. From the foot of the stairway, my brother stared at me with teary, red eyes. Under his arm he held one of my old capes and his little straw hat. He had not stopped crying since he found out about my fate. We loved each other so much that he never ate half an orange without my taking the other half. I would do likewise. We used to eat, play, run errands, and sleep together. Thus this union, bound by the indissoluble bonds of fraternal love, was broken. Not just for a few hours as on other occasions, but for much more than I or anyone else dared imagine.[77]

This episode reaffirms just how dependent slave families were on the actions of their owners. Even in death, through their wills, owners could exercise their authority. Owners were free to disrupt these families at any moment. Some sufficiently valued the family unity not to do so, others were not so considerate. Although it is difficult to generalize from one case, Manzano's family experiences are insightful. Their somewhat privileged position within the institution of slavery offered a small degree of solace. Many of the family's members eventually obtained freedom through a variety of legal means. Most of their fellow slaves struggled with even greater difficulties in their effort to maintain united families. Still, free and enslaved Afro-Cubans tenaciously faced this challenge and established their own reproductive and marital patterns. From these behaviors, the status markers attributed to them, such "negra criolla" (black creole woman) or "pardo ingenuo" (free-born brown man), gained social significance of their own making.

CONCLUSION

After 1762, Cuban society experienced an economic awakening. New priorities were placed on territorial defense and the development of commerce. Population growth coincided with these efforts. Yet, the social transformations that accompanied them were not immediate. Instead, they evolved very slowly. With respect to race relations, the importation of enslaved Africans slowly accelerated and these Africans were initially inserted into the pre-existing patterns of the slave system. For the period between 1762 and 1790, they labored in diverse settings. The harsh labor regime of the sugar plantation did not completely dominate their experiences. Indeed, slavery was constructed in such a way that still allowed enslaved people to develop family lives as they entered marriages and bore children. There is some evidence to suggest that the formation of their families even received encouragement from slave owners.

Just as with earlier periods, family formation among people of color was not just that undertaken separately by slaves and free people. Nor was it solely a result of brutal sexual violence perpetuated on women of color by white men. All of these forms were present and marital endogamy remained the norm. However, these forms were also augmented by acts that crossed the normal social boundaries of status and color. Families of color were defined by their varied structure. Most were legitimate. In others, fathers formally acknowledged their offspring. And in a minority, children received no legal recognition of paternity. Beyond color and status, the statistics indicate that these families differed little from their white counterparts.

This situation would change dramatically after 1790 when the importation of enslaved Africans accelerated rapidly. The labor regime to which slaves were subjected also intensified as sugar production experienced a boom. On the whole, this period was marked by declining attention to slave families by Crown and colonial officials. Their attention was increasingly directed toward the suppression of potential separatist efforts and the expansion of agricultural production, especially sugar. The creation of new plantations was a labor-intensive process, involving the difficult tasks of land clearing and infrastructure construction.

Rural slave owners preferred African men for such labor and were less concerned with the conjugal relations of their charges. In the earlier periods, attention toward slave families had derived from two considerations: a belief that family bonds could foster less rebelliousness and a sincere Christian belief in the spiritual importance of marriage. Additionally, in earlier eras the division between town and countryside had not been as great. The traditional gender-ratio imbalance in favor of women in urban domestic occupations and in favor of men in agriculture was less marked. As rural production pushed further into the interior and away from the urban centers, enslaved people had fewer opportunities to establish relations that crossed these distances. Nevertheless, many persisted. They survived, brought children into the world, and either resisted or sought to redefine the racial meaning attributed to their physical bodies.

3

The Illegal Slave Trade and
the Cuban Sexual Economy
of Race, 1820–1867

> I spoke to you about enslaved black women, women who
> while their boyfriends, husbands, fathers, brothers, and other relatives
> slept on a platform, or in the shade of a tree, were busy with all their
> responsibilities, from the young girl who began to sigh under the weight of
> the machete or hoe to the mother who hears the cries of her children.
>
> —Anselmo Suárez y Romero,
> "Los Domingos en los Ingenios," 1840 (Sundays at the Sugar Mills)

ANSELMO SUÁREZ Y ROMERO'S FAMILY-ORIENTED INTERPRE-
tation of Cuba's mid-nineteenth-century enslaved women as daughters,
sisters, and wives is a rare one. And the acknowledgment of their masculine counterparts as fathers, brothers, and husbands is even less frequent. Visions of the socially alienated slave have, until recently, been
the norm within Cuban historical studies. Yet other narratives are
possible. For example, when slavers forcibly brought a young Carabalí
boy to Cuba in 1794 and sold him to work as a captive first in coffee cul-
tivation and then in sugar production, the chances that he would live to
see the birth of grandchildren seemed slim. It is a well-accepted historiographic fact that Cuba's nineteenth-century slave population did not
achieve population replacement rates of reproduction. The harsh labor regime, an unhealthy tropical disease environment, a severely imbalanced

gender ratio, and generally inadequate living conditions all mitigated against Afro-Cuban reproduction and family formation. Yet many African ethnics, such as the boy above, who was baptized with the Spanish name Narciso, eventually managed to raise families with several children, and even grandchildren, who gave rise to today's Afro-Cuban population. Through personal family histories and attention to collective social practices, this chapter retells important, unexplored elements of how they met this challenge during the ultimate, and illegal, period of Cuba's slave trade.

Narciso had labored in Cuba for thirty-one years before he married a young woman who was enslaved on the same plantation, El Recuerdo, in rural Havana province. His wife, Amalia, was from the West African Gangá people and had been kidnapped into Cuba in 1803. After four years of marriage, the first child of the couple for whom documents survive was born, in 1829, and Narciso and Amalia had least six more children before 1855, when the last was baptized. At age eighteen, their oldest daughter, Rufina, gave birth to a son; she then married another Cuban creole slave two years later.

Two other of Narciso and Amalia's daughters married African ethnic men. Although both these men had been forced into slavery illegally (the Atlantic slave trade to Cuba was criminalized in 1820) on the same plantation alongside the growing family as early as 1839, they did not marry into it until 1854 and 1865, respectively. The second-generation Afro-Cuban family formed by Narciso and Amalia's daughter Nemesia and her Lucumí partner Telesforo eventually included at least nine children. Although Amalia died in 1860, after thirty-five years of marriage, and Narciso followed her in 1874, with the birth of their first great-grandchild in 1877 a fourth generation of the family entered into Cuban society. While the work of reconstructing such detailed family genealogies for blacks and mulattoes is just beginning within Cuban historical studies, the vitality of today's Afro-Cuban population implicitly bears witness to the fact that the survival of Narciso's family was not unique. The transformations occurring within Cuban slavery during the period between 1820 and 1868 were extreme challenges for such families, but they were not insurmountable.[1] Theirs were not the stories of passive

"El Abuelo" (The Grandfather), 1890. Source: The Cuban Heritage Collection, University of Miami.

slaves. These were vibrant, active people, some of whom were enslaved and some of whom lived in nominal freedom. Their intimate, reproductive choices went beyond demographic statistics to give meaning to the very social categories in which nineteenth-century Cubans lived.

THE NINETEENTH-CENTURY AFRO-CUBAN POPULATION IN EMPIRICAL PERSPECTIVE

The year 1820 marked an important transition in Cuban slavery. As of May 1820, the Anglo-Spanish Treaty of 1817 terminated the legal importation of enslaved Africans into Cuba. The British, who had already criminalized their own slave trade in 1808, successfully pressured the new re-established absolutist monarchy of Ferdinand VII to move toward wage labor. The treaty's signatories hoped that slavery itself would gradually fade into insignificance without a constant resupply of captive African ethnics. However, the treaty was initially implemented without adequate means of enforcement. Cuban slave imports continued clandestinely, supplying the labor for the expanding and more globally oriented export economy.[2]

An economic boom was driven by ever-increasing sugar production. While there were 400 sugar plantations on the island in 1800, according to an 1857 census that figure had multiplied almost four times, to 1,570.[3] Feeding this growth, the contraband Cuban slave trade had surpassed its pre-1820 levels by 1827, as Cuban owners adjusted to new restrictions and developed secretive methods to bypass the law. One American assistant on a Cuban plantation casually recalled the efforts to secretly obtain African ethnics. In November 1821, he received news of a slave ship off the coast of Matanzas and quickly went to bid on new captives. But by the time he arrived, others had purchased the entire lot.[4] Such events were common. For the period 1811 through 1867, historian David Eltis has calculated that approximately 637,700 Africans were imported into Cuba.[5] In an earlier study, Phillip Curtin estimated that the greatest import volume occurred between 1827 and 1840, with the period between 1851 and 1860 also showing high levels.[6] Eltis refined this timeframe to indicate that the highest import levels occurred immediately after the 1817 treaty to just before its 1820 implementation. The period between 1836 and 1840 also shows another dramatic increase in imports, despite an 1835 treaty that expanded British anti-slaving oversight. A final upswing also occurred between 1856 and 1860. After 1860, and coincidentally after the start of the U.S. Civil War, Cuban import levels experienced a dramatic decline.[7] Before that date, the forced mass importation of African ethnics and the birth of creole slaves combined to increase the enslaved population by 55 percent between 1817 and 1861, from 239,694 to 370,553.[8]

Cuba's slave population was not alone in expanding rapidly, and its numbers were intimately entwined with the island's other social sectors (see table 3.1). Over the same period, the white population grew even faster, by 228 percent, the result of both better reproductive factors and increasing immigration. Although the free black and mulatto population grew by 108 percent over these same fifty years, it did so while experiencing significant declines in the periods 1817–1827 and 1841–1846. During the independence wars in continental Spanish America between

Table 3.1. Population by gender and status, 1817–1867

	1817	1827	1841	1860	1867
White male	149,725	168,653	227, 144	468,107	491,512
White female	126,964	142,398	191,147	325.377	341,645
White total	276,689	311,051	418.291	793,484	833,157
White % of total	43	44	42	56	58
Free male of color	70,044	51,962	75,703	109,027	121,708
Free female of color	49,177	54,532	77,135	116,816	126,995
Free colored total	119,221	106,494	152,838	225,843	248,703
Free colored % of total	21	15	15	16	17
Enslaved male	137,115	183,290	281,250	218,722	203,412
Enslaved female	102,579	103,652	155,245	151,831	141,203
Enslaved total	239,694	286,942	436,495	370,553	344,615
Enslaved % of total	36	41	43	28	24

Sources: Knight, *Slave Society,* 86, and Instituto de Historia de Cuba, *La colonia,* 466–470.

1808 and 1824, Cuba was affected by both an influx and outflow of people of color. Civilian loyalists and their slaves arrived from throughout Spain's American empire. At the same time, many of Cuba's free black and mulatto militia men were sent into Spanish American battlefields.[9] External military service was just one factor that contributed to the 26 percent loss of Afro-Cuban men between 1817 and 1827. Other factors remain to be studied systematically but include the expulsions and executions of African-descended men who were charged with participating in the major political rebellions that swept Cuba between 1809 and 1844.[10] Spanish colonial administrator Mariano Torrente explained that in order to limit their revolutionary potential, in 1817 "formerly enslaved people were offered the means to return to their native [African] lands, but less than fifty accepted this offer."[11] Additionally, a royal order in 1837 prohibited the disembarkation of free African-descended people into Cuba.[12] One official reaction to the unproven 1844 Afro-Cuban anti-government conspiracy known as *La Escalera* (the Ladder) was to plan the expulsion of all free African-descended men.[13] At least 1,300 free people of color were ousted from the island between 1844 and 1845.[14]

In the reproductive domain, evidence suggests that the free population of color had higher birthrates than whites. According to the 1827 census, there was one birth for every six free women of color between the ages of twelve and forty. Whites had a lower rate of one birth for every seven women in this age range. Significantly, between 1817 and 1827 births to free African-descended women, especially pardas, increased 69 percent.[15] Owner manumission and self-purchased freedom by enslaved people also added to the number of Afro-Cubans classified as free. Although an extensive study of the rates at which Cuba's enslaved population obtained their freedom remains to be done, one analysis of nearly 30,000 slave sales indicates that the Cuban system of *coartación*, which allowed enslaved people to make incremental payments toward a fixed personal emancipation cost, operated in one out of every four slave sales transactions. And prior to 1850, African ethnics represented the majority of people who purchased their freedom in this manner.[16] However, historian Rebecca Scott notes that in 1871 (after initial governmental steps toward final abolition had begun) legally designated *coartados* were less than 1 percent of Cuba's slave population.[17] The contrast between these last two statistics makes it unclear whether enslaved people either moved quickly through the coartado category or proportionally had very limited access to self-manumission.

Many of the contributing factors in the island's sexual economy of race and the reproduction of Cuban social categories were influenced by the illegal continuation of the trans-Atlantic slave trade into Cuba. Most obviously, the illegal slave trade allowed for the maintenance of a high proportion of Africans within that population. The high numbers of African ethnics compared to black and mulatto creoles likely contributed to the low fertility rates of sugar plantations. Cuban sugar plantations retained large concentrations of Africans until the late 1860s and the true curtailment of the illegal slave trade. As noted in chapter 2, Manuel Moreno Fraginals demonstrated for the period between 1791 and 1822 some sugar plantation populations to be as much as 96 percent African. This proportion decreased to an average of 53 percent between 1827 and 1867 before the proportion of creole slaves surpassed Africans.[18] Crude natality levels on sugar plantations seemed to improve simultaneously, standing at 19 percent and 28 percent for the periods 1835 to 1841 and 1856 to 1860, respectively.[19] Although these statistics reveal significant improvement over time, they are exceedingly low in comparison to the high fertility rates that some researchers argue

Table 3.2. Gender proportions by year for free and enslaved people of color

Year	Male % of enslaved pop.	Male % of free mulatto and black pop.
1827	63.9	48.8
1841	64.4	49.5
1846	62.1	48.7
1850	62.0	49.0
1855	61.8	51.9
1862	59.0	49.2

Source: Marrero, *Cuba*, 9:178 and 181.

characterized the pre-colonial West African populations from which these enslaved people were removed.[20]

Again, general sugar plantation living conditions and continued severe imbalance in the gender ratio in favor of men curtailed slave reproduction. A comparison of slave gender ratios against those of free Afro-Cubans gives some indication of the continuing planter preference for male laborers that the slave trade appeased (see table 3.2). The gender ratio within the population of African ethnics still being illegally imported into Cuba after 1820 is documented for the smaller, but directly related, subset of people "rescued" from slaving ships. In the wake of the 1817 treaty, Cuban colonial administrators implemented new methods of managing the presence of such Africans who were not legally enslaveable. By 1825 the island's chief colonial administrator, Captain General Antonio Vives, had begun to shape the policy under which these *emancipados* (or rescued Africans) were to find a place in Cuban society. Under an elaborate administrative structure, they were to eventually gain their freedom following seven years of labor-based tutelage and receive their accumulated wages.[21] Corruption plagued this system from its inception, and emancipados were often sold into slavery with almost complete disregard for the law. Many became the objects of backdoor arrangements between colonial officials and unscrupulous buyers.[22] Nevertheless, until the removal of this classification in 1864, the presence of some 26,026 emancipados became an important new feature on the social landscape.[23]

In general demographic terms, however, the gender-ratio imbalance among the emancipados was even more pronounced that that seen in the legal slave trade of the previous era. In 1831, 65.27 percent of them were male; over the next decade this statistic increased to 77.25 percent.[24] Their presence did not improve Afro-Cuban reproductive possibilities in this regard. Yet, they joined with Cubans in other social categories to contribute to the reproduction of the Afro-Cuban population and to further modify the links between Africanness and enslavement. Such was the case in 1864 when, for example, the emancipada Florentina petitioned the Cuban Church to reclassify her baptism and that of her Cuban-born daughter Yrene to indicate they were both free. Her *patrona* (sponsor) claimed it must have been an error that both were baptized as enslaved. Fortunately Florentina had found the means to assert her rights and her freedom.[25]

Again, the largest discrepancies in the gender ratio were found on sugar plantations and in the sugar-producing regions. Moreno Fraginals estimated male gender proportions among African ethnics on sugar and coffee plantations at 69.7 percent and 59.8 percent for the periods 1823–1844 and 1845–1868, respectively.[26] In 1846, in the sugar provinces of Matanzas, Cárdenas, and Mariel, men represented 63.4 percent, 66.8 percent, and 61.2 percent respectively of the people of color of reproductive age (between sixteen and forty).[27] A traveler's anecdotal observation amplifies these statistics. An Englishman visiting three sugar estates in provincial Havana in 1849 noted, "The total number of females on the three estates we visited amounted to 108; the total number of men, 243." Thus, the male proportion was 69.8 percent.[28] Yet, the gender-ratio imbalance becomes more complex based on additional data. If one examines contemporary baptismal data from the rural town of Placetas, a more balanced gender ratio among newly baptized Africans is revealed. These generally were young people who probably escaped official oversight and categorization as emancipados. Forty-five percent of the 493 Africans baptized there in the period between 1817 and 1886 were women.[29] Similar patterns were found in an urban setting. Returning to the baptismal records of the Havana parish of Espíritu Santo, ten-year interval samples taken between 1847 and 1867 reveal great fluctuation in the gender ratio of newly baptized arrivals. African ethnic women made up 44 percent, 55 percent, and 40 percent of adult slave baptisms for the years 1847, 1857, and 1867 respectively.[30] What is interesting here is that the difference between the rural and urban proportions is not even larger, as might be suggested by greater employment of enslaved women in urban domestic labor. One is left to speculate if African men were kept in urban Havana in larger than expected numbers or perhaps they were baptized before being sold into more rural agricultural settings.

Despite the continued contraband trade in African ethnics, the ongoing gender-ratio imbalance, and the consequent negative effects on fertility, there is some indication that during the nineteenth century both the creole-slave and free-colored populations of Cuba experienced natural increases. First we return to the estimates offered by historical demographer Jack Eblen. After isolating the effects of the slave trade and manumission, Eblen extrapolated from model life tables for contemporary European and other African American population to estimate Afro-Cuban reproductive rates. He found these were very similar to those of African Americans in the same period.[31] While Elben's insights are suggestive, they should be used with caution. They only apply to the creole population and continue to accept the low natality and high mortality rates for Africans. Second, Kenneth Kiple, another scholar of Afro-Caribbean slave demographics, also concluded that those Cuban slaves not living on sugar plantations and free blacks and mulattoes probably achieved levels of natural increase at least for the two periods 1855–1868 and 1878–1886. Interestingly, Kiple further theorized that much of this increase was hidden by "a certain amount of 'whitening' of the population."[32] Finally, although unknowingly departing from the emancipado data above, Moreno Fraginals accepted that with the increased proportion of women within the contraband slave trade "a radical change took place on the plantations, causing a certain amount of upheaval in the modes of sexual behavior . . . There was a notable increase in the birth rate, which was reflected in the great increase in the Cuban-born black population."[33] He also noted that after 1860 the birthrate among the enslaved finally surpassed the mortality rate, a situation that was almost coincident with the effective termination of Cuba's slave trade.[34]

Such observations may suggest that the analysis of Afro-Cuban racialized reproduction during the slave holding period should not overemphasize the role of the sugar plantation. Its prominence in Cuba's nineteenth-century economy has led to a historiographic stress on its role in structuring other elements of Cuban social relations. The sugar plantation is often placed at the center of nineteenth-century society, with all social and economic activity radiating from it.[35] However, other agricultural and non-agricultural interests also heavily utilized slave labor. According to one calculation, in 1855, 81 percent of Cuba's slaves were employed in rural areas.[36] The direct proportion used in each labor sector is not known. It is estimated that in 1862, slightly less than half (47 percent) of the enslaved population lived and worked on sugar plantations.[37] Tobacco farms, coffee plantations, and livestock pens also employed a significant proportion of the rural labor force, and in 1862 these industries utilized 30 percent of the island's enslaved people.[38] Along with sugar, these types of production had boomed in the late eighteenth century. However, by the middle of the nineteenth century, coffee farming had begun a dramatic decline, while tobacco and livestock production continued to expand.

The labor regimes and living conditions of all three were described as much less stringent than sugar production. Cuban historians Maria de los Ángeles Meriño Fuentes and Aisnara Perera Díaz found that southern Havana province coffee plantations generally achieved better gender ratios than sugar plantations. On the five coffee plantations in Quivacan they analyzed, 48 percent of enslaved people were women in 1844. Among African ethnics on these sites, the number of women between the ages of twenty and forty exceeded the number of African ethnic men in the same age range. This outstripped the figure of 36 percent women for the general slave population of the wider Bejucal region.[39] Female labor seems to have been widely used for the harvesting and processing of coffee beans. By contrast, as we have seen in the sugar plantation gender ratio imbalances, Cuban planters generally did not seem inclined toward the labor model found on early nineteenth-century British estates, where black women predominated in sugarcane cutting.[40] Even within Caribbean slavery there were regional differences with regard to the association between black femininity and manual labor.

Table 3.3. Crude marriage rate by social status and region, 1827

	White	Free colored	Slave	Total	White pop.	Pop. of color
Western dept.	143	319	161	240	165,058	243,479
Central dept.	215	315	66	209	98,223	66,274
Eastern dept.	182	214	949	581	47,770	83,683

Sources: de la Sagra, *Historia economica-politica,* 25, and Cuba. Comisión de estadistica, *Cuadro estadístico,* 58i, 79i, and 90i.

Cuban planters were selective in their use of African-descended women in agricultural labor. However, further research is needed to determine the extent of that selectivity.

Social contrasts between slaves' experiences in sugar production and in other agricultural forms may have been present in Cuban regional differences in marriage rates. (See table 3.3.) The 1827 census demonstrates that while slave marriages were generally less frequent than those of whites, there was one region in which the reverse was true. The central region reported greater slave marriages. There, one out of every sixty-six enslaved persons was married, compared to just one out of 215 whites. Nineteenth-century observer Ramón de la Sagra attributed this difference to the declining morality of the region's white population and its contrasting maintenance among the enslaved.[41] But this explanation leads to the question of why no similar phenomenon appeared in the other Cuban regions. Other structural differences deserve consideration. At that time, a major difference in economic production between the central department and the other two was the relative lack of importance of sugar production in the former. Instead, cattle raising and tobacco remained important economic activities.[42] The control of the enslaved population associated with these was much less intense than that of those associated with sugar production, possibly allowing for greater freedom to select a partner. The central department was also the only area in which the white population exceeded that of color during this period.[43] While neither of these observations can be confirmed as the cause of such high marriage rates for the enslaved of the central department, they should be considered in conjunction with other reasons. Unfortunately, with regard to the theme of reproduction, investigation of non-sugar activities remains in its infancy, hindered by an historiographic over-emphasis on sugar and the scarcity of primary sources.

Life was somewhat less harsh for enslaved families living in urban areas even though they still faced many of the difficulties associated with bondage. The greatest contrast between rural and urban slave populations was their respective labor regimes. Those in urban areas were employed in a variety of occupations as domestics, day laborers, craftspeople, and light industrial workers. Many worked directly for their owners, while others were rented out. In terms of family formation, urban slaves enjoyed a much more balanced gender ratio and access to mates from a variety of social categories. No matter the setting in which Cuba's enslaved people were found, their lives and reproductive possibilities were not just defined by economic motives or other owner demands. Other structures within Cuban society impinged on their lives. These included the continued intervention of the Spanish colonial state into the private property rights of slave owners and the Catholic Church's socializing role associated with its religious instruction.

SHIFTING REPRODUCTIVE POLICIES AND PRACTICES

To some extent, additional colonial oversight and increased owner regard for the health of the enslaved may have contributed to gradual improvements in Cuban slave reproduction. By the early nineteenth century, the Spanish Crown had recognized the potential end of the slave trade to Cuba and realized the expedience of natural replacement. With an 1804 royal edict, it encouraged the placement of a greater number of African women on sugar plantations until they were married, and it suggested to slave owners that "aside from thus accomplishing a duty of justice and conscience, there would result for them the benefit of increasing the number of their slaves and improving their species, without the constant disbursement of their capital in buying *bozal* [newly arrived Africans] Negroes to replace those who die."[44] Here the Crown indicates a desire to maintain the institution of slavery. However, in its view, the better economic and political future lay more in the improved treatment of the existing slave population than in the continued importation of costly and potentially rebellious Africans. According to Moreno

Fraginals, many Cuban planters concurred and during the 1820s began a new policy of encouraging slave reproduction through what they called "buen tratamiento" (good treatment).[45] And with the Cuban *Reglamento de esclavos* (Slave Regulations) of 1842, the new liberal Spanish government, which had replaced the absolutist monarchy, collaborated with plantation owners to promote greater state oversight of the slave regime.[46] The *reglamento* implemented many of the protective procedures that the Crown had originally intended to establish in the late eighteenth century. It regulated the feeding, clothing, and labor regimen of the enslaved population, paying special attention to infants and other children. Article 9 mandated a type of daycare for these children, with older women minding them while their mothers worked. Article 10 required the mothers of sick children to be relieved of their labor so that they could nurse their young.[47] Oversight of these policies rested with the public office of the *síndico procurador general* (general public advocate), a holdover from medieval Spanish governance. Charged with mediating between enslaved people and owners, this office became more effective in Cuba with new regulations in 1837. Its duties were unevenly executed, however. Some síndicos favored slave owners but others worked with less bias. Enslaved people utilized this resource whenever possible, but a certain amount of autonomy from their owners was needed to access it.[48]

Even before the 1842 regulations, some Cuban administrators and planters had turned to more pro-natal policies and improved health care in attempting to maintain the enslaved population. Women were encouraged to bear more children with promises of freedom after the healthy birth of a specified number of children. Abiel Abbot, an American touring the island in 1829, noted a shift in planters' concern for the reproduction of their enslaved populations.

> As difficulties are thrown more and more in the way of importation of slaves from Africa, a greater attention is paid to pregnant females, to preserve the stock of the plantation. I trust there is with many, I know there is with some, a commiseration of female slaves in that delicate condition. They are exempt from labor for a month before and after the birth, to nurse themselves and the child, and have hours of the day for months after for the same purpose, during which others are at work.[49]

During his visit to a large sugar plantation, Abbot found thirty creole children born to the labor force of 170 enslaved workers. Continuing on to a coffee estate, he was told that "as a premium for rearing children, the mother of six living children is freed from labor for life, and has her maintenance on the estate."[50] If this practice did indeed occur, it would have represented a significant reduction from the twelve infant births required of Havana's royal slaves in the middle of the eighteenth century in order to obtain freedom.[51]

In this period, other observations of plantation life make explicit mention of "hospitals" that nursed ill slaves back to health. In his 1821 diary, Joseph Goodwin, the American manager of George De Wolf's Cuban sugar plantation, expressed genuine concern for the health of his enslaved workers. On several occasions, he noted the medical attention they received. Additionally, both Goodwin and the plantation owner were especially concerned that enslaved women bear healthy children.[52] As a matter of island-wide policy, Captain General Geronimo Valdés (1841–1843) encouraged the correction of gender-ratio imbalances in rural areas and improved treatment of enslaved infants and pregnant women.[53] This type of concern is also found in an 1862 plantation manual that suggested that, immediately following childbirth, enslaved mothers should receive a forty-to-fifty-day break from arduous tasks.[54] And in 1865, Cuban planter José Luis Alfonso, one of the most prominent members of his class, boasted that one of his sugar plantations had had twenty-nine marriages that year. He explained that this success was due to "Christian persuasion" and a prohibition on extramarital sex caused by forcing "young black women to sleep together, locked in the same large room."[55]

A Swedish traveler to Cuba in the middle of the nineteenth century also described instances of united slave families in the countryside. Fredrika Bremer wrote of one such couple. She spoke with a newly-wed female domestic and commented rather romantically, "Cecilia is only lately married to a young man of her own color; she is happy in her marriage and happy as the slave of good owners."[56] Bremer also saw some of the young children born on the plantation. She claimed that, while they were not as numerous as on American plantations, they were received with love and care.

The little ones are not here familiar and merry as they are on the plantation in America; they do not stretch out their little hands for a friendly salutation; they look at the white man with suspicious glances—they are shy; but the very little Bambinos, which are quite naked, fat, and plump, as shiny as black, or black-brown silk, dance upon their mothers' knees, generally with a blue or red string of beads around the loins, and another around the neck; they are the prettiest little things one ever saw.[57]

Regarding amorous relationships within the plantation, Bremer found little stability. "Men and women live together, and part again according to fancy or whim. If a couple, after having lived together for some time, grow weary of each other, then one will give the other some cause of displeasure, and they separate. In case of any noisy quarrel, the *majoral* (overseer) is at hand with his whip to establish peace."[58] If such instability was representative of the whole population, it would have interfered with reproduction. Again, data from other Caribbean slave societies suggest that fertility rates were much higher for stable, if not married, couples than they were for single women.[59]

In contrast to this image of instability, when Bremer asked about the existence of enduring and faithful couples, her host presented her with a remarkable couple who were both about fifty years old. They had met in Africa and had been together since their youth.[60] Their ability to survive the travails of initial enslavement in Africa, the horrors of the Middle Passage, and forced labor within a Cuban plantation speaks of a resilience few can imagine. Another of Bremer's encounters demonstrates the different tensions affecting the slave family. An enslaved couple had been prevented from marrying at the discretion of the woman's owner. But the couple had a child, and the man's owner took pity on him and gave him a peso a week toward the purchase of the woman and child on the condition that he abstain from his addiction to alcohol.[61] This combination of one owner's obstruction of slave marriage, another owner's encouragement, and the personal challenges faced by an enslaved man remind us that the pervasive oppression of slavery is not the only prism through which race and reproduction in colonial Cuba should be understood.

These cases demonstrate that simple biological increase was not the only reproductive goal slave owners had for their enslaved charges.

These owners impacted the colonial sexual economy of race in other ways. Some encouraged the establishment of legitimate families among the enslaved based on a pious commitment to the institution of marriage. In one case, Doña Antonia Pérez de Abreu, owner of Agua Santa the sugar plantation in the Bejucal region of southern Havana province, baptized fifteen young African ethnic women on May 8, 1819, and a week later returned to have these same women married to enslaved men working on the same plantation.[62] Another case of direct owner involvement in the formalization of slave marriages occurred in the rural town of Palacios in 1877. Upon learning that his "Kongo" slave, Pedro Belaza, had fathered children out of wedlock with an enslaved creole woman, the priest Don José Ylarreri bought the woman and allowed the couple's free children to live in the same house. He then performed the couple's marriage and assisted them in the process of legitimating their children.[63] On one occasion in 1878, missionary Jesuit priests married some thirty-two enslaved couples on two plantations in the town of San Juan y Martínez.[64] Another striking example is seen in the baptismal records of Espíritu Santo. All seven enslaved children baptized there in 1847 under the ownership of the heirs of Doña Ysabel Zuazo were born to married African couples.[65] These cases suggest that the owners discouraged out-of-wedlock births, following a model demonstrated for the slaves of Carlos III in the eighteenth century discussed in chapter 2.[66] Obviously, some owners actively encouraged marriage, but the prevalence of such owner involvement cannot be established from the existing data.[67]

Despite some encouragement of reproduction and in certain cases of marriage, for the enslaved, their nineteenth-century marriage rates experienced a considerable decline. Census data indicates that for 1827, 1841, 1846, and 1860, their marriages represented 38 percent, 34 percent, 23 percent, and 8 percent of the total respectively.[68] In these same years, enslaved people represented 41 percent, 43 percent, 36 percent, and 27 percent of the entire island's total population.[69] Similar declines also appeared among free people of color. The baptismal record from Espíritu Santo reflects an overall decline in paternal acknowledgment across all categories of people of color. For the thirty months between 1765 and 1767 studied in chapter 2, fathers did not appear in only 169 of

Table 3.4. Parental status in baptisms of children of color, Espíritu Santo Parish, 1847

Father	African slave	Black slave	Parda slave	Free black	Free parda	Free African	Total
				Mother			
No father	54	55	7	15	8	4	143
African slave	16	0	0	0	0	0	16
Black slave	1	11	0	0	0	0	12
Pardo slave	0	1	0	0	0	0	1
Free black	2	2	0	52	3	1	60
Free pardo	1	0	0	5	26	0	32
Free African	0	1	0	4	0	10	15
African (no status listed)	9	2	0	1	0	2	14
No status	3	4	0	3	2	1	13
Total	86	76	7	80	39	18	306

Sources: AES, libro 48 de bautismos de pardos y morenos, entries 793–868 (1847) and libro 49 de bautismos de pardos y morenos, entries 1–268 (1847).

643 baptisms, or 26 percent. For 1847, this statistic increased to 143 of 306, or 47 percent. In the samples from 1857 and 1867, an average of less than one-third (30 percent) of children were baptized with the names of both parents.[70] In the period from 1765 to 1768, only 29 percent of the black and mulatto children baptized at Espíritu Santo were born outside of wedlock, a situation which had greatly changed by the mid-nineteenth century.[71] In 1847, only 19 percent of such children were born to married parents (see table 3.4).[72]

This decline can also be analyzed in terms of the social category of the fathers. The proportion of African ethnic fathers in the Espíritu Santo Afro-Cuban baptismal records decreased from 26 percent in the mid-eighteenth century to 14 percent in 1847. The decline was even worse for pardo fathers: from 26 percent in 1765–1767 to 10 percent in 1847. An explanation of these decreases is not obvious. For pardos, demographic proportions may have been a factor. Census data indicate that pardo numbers were decreasing within the population of color: from 25.2 percent in 1776 to 17.3 percent in 1841.[73] While exact statistics on the proportions of African and black creole males within both the free and enslaved populations are not available, inferences based on the relative price of the different categories of enslaved men suggest that African ethnics were more numerous. Although a number of other factors were involved, prices from 1836 to 1865 were consistently lower for Africans than creoles.[74] There also are indicators that the proportion of African ethnics in Havana slave sales remained high at least until 1845.[75] No unqualified conclusions can be drawn from these observations. The only category of fathers to see a greater presence in the baptismal records was black creoles, increasing from 17 percent to 23 percent between 1767 and 1847.[76] White fathers were almost completely absent as self-acknowledged fathers of Afro-Cuban children in the 1847 baptisms. Only one was registered, the Spanish-born mate of a free parda.[77] This stands in marked contrast to the eight fathers noted as Spanish and ten who were probably white creoles in the 1765–1767 Espíritu Santo records (see table 2.3). The impact of the Pragmatic Sanction of 1778 restricting unequal unions clearly made itself felt with the loss of legal recognition of inter-racial families.

Comparing the 1765–1767 Espíritu Santo parental acknowledgement data against that of 1847, significant changes also appear in relation to the mothers' status. (Compare against table 2.3.) Among free parda mothers in the earlier sample, only 16 percent had their children baptized without the fathers named. By 1847, that figure increased slightly to 20.5 percent. For free African ethnic mothers, the change was more dramatic. Whereas in the earlier sample no woman in this category baptized children without a father named, by 1847 22.2 percent did. For enslaved parda mothers, 57.9 percent of their children in the eighteenth-century data were baptized without their fathers named. In 1847, astoundingly, no fathers were named for their children. Again, intra-racial differences of origin and status continued to matter in the nineteenth century, with varying social responses to slavery. While their marriage rates declined, the baptismal data suggest that as a general rule Afro-Cubans continued to be reproductively endogamous along racial lines. But this practice was further concentrated according to origin and servile status.

Several other factors may provide some cursory explanations for the general nature of these documentary changes. The cost of marriage was one such factor. At mid-century, baptisms were priced at only one peso.

By contrast, the marriage ceremony was a minimum of seven and one-quarter pesos, excluding the additional costs associated with certification of identity and previous marital status. When compared against the average wage of eight pesos a month received by free manual laborers of color, the difficulty in affording marriage is more easily seen.[78] The loss of religious instruction over this period may be the most direct explanation for declining Afro-Cuban marriage and legitimacy rates. While the African ethnics brought to labor in Cuba were familiar with their own cultural forms of marriage, most were initially unfamiliar with the Catholic modes of formalizing marriage.[79] Education in this facet of their social lives would have come through contract with Euro-Cubans (planters, plantation administrators, wage laborers, and priests) and already assimilated people of color. Of the first group, priests had the greatest responsibility for educating slaves about the spiritual and social significance of marriage. However, the ratio of clerics to the general population had been decreasing since the late eighteenth century, especially with the expulsion of the Jesuits in 1767. Between 1774 and 1846 the number of clerics in Cuba decreased by more than half, from 984 to 440, while the population grew fivefold.[80]

As had occurred throughout Cuba's colonial history, the majority of these priests were concentrated in urban areas and ministered largely to whites. By 1860, the number of clergy had increased to 779, but with over 400 of them living in Havana, the rural population was left with little sustained spiritual guidance. In some areas the ratio of clergy to enslaved people was extremely low. For example, in the sugar-producing region of Cardenas, there was one priest for every 7,500 slaves.[81] Additionally, many owners of large plantations no longer retained priests exclusively for their holdings and systematic religious education in such sites was all but abandoned.[82] It was not uncommon for newly arriving African adults and young people to be baptized without religious instruction. When one ethnic Carabalí Bibí man was asked in 1831, in connection with his criminal trial if he was baptized, he responded through an interpreter, "They sprinkled water on me."[83] If we return to Fredrika Bremer's observation that black infants on a sugar plantation were seen "generally with a blue or red string of beads around the loins, and another around the neck," the African-based religious significance of these items was lost to her. In today's Cuba, initiates into Afro-Cuban religions often wear *collares* (necklaces) and other beads to observe their links with specific *orishas* (gods or spirits in West African religious traditions). The whites administrators of the plantation Bremer visited were either similarly unaware of such practices or allowed them with impunity. Catholic education was either absent, minimal, or merged with African traditions.

The entire Cuban society experienced a decline in religious commitment that some contemporaries attributed to having stemmed from an increasing acceptance of more secular Enlightenment ideals. An 1867 report to metropolitan Spanish authorities lamented this situation and its presumably negative implications for social relations within slavery.

> As time passed, there came to Cuba the anti-Christian doctrines, the product of the school of Voltaire and the encyclopedists of the eighteenth century. Unfortunately the clergy and the highest stratum of the society accepted them, and propagated them among the people, fostering religious indifference. The chapels were abandoned; religious zeal disappeared; and the relations between master and slave lacked any other motivation than that of material interest, [but] somewhat modified still by the acquired habits and customs.[84]

The decline in marriage rates appears to have involved all classes in Havana. White marriage rates also experienced a decrease, but not one as large as seen among people of color. For white men living in Havana, marriages rates decreased from 38 percent in 1828 to 26 percent in 1862. A slightly smaller, but measurable decline in the marriage rates of white women (from 43.5 percent in 1828 to 35 percent in 1862) suggests that this phenomenon was not simply due to the mass immigration of single men from Spain and the Canary Islands.[85] These data make it difficult to attribute the decline in marriage rates among Cuba's slave population primarily to an intensification of the labor regime associated with sugar production. The decreasing marriage rate impacted not only the status of children; it also shaped the economic situation for women of color, especially their participation in the labor force. American historian Michele Reid-Vasquez reports there was a 34 percent decrease in the number of Cuban free women of color who listed their occupation exclusively as "housewife" between 1846 and 1861.[86]

Yet, the absence of marriage did not equate to the absence of other socially recognized family forms. Consensual unions increased in frequency for people of color, a development that was vehemently opposed by the Catholic hierarchy. Both Verena Stolke and Cuban historian Levi Marrero have highlighted the project by Antonio María Claret y Clará, the archbishop of Cuba (1851–1857), to eliminate what he perceived as the problem of consensual relationships. He was so committed to this project that over his six years as leader of the Cuban Church he married more than 12,000 previously illicit couples. Many of these were mixed-race couples who had not married earlier because of the restriction imposed by the 1778 pragmatic or because the white male partner had not wanted to confront the social taboo on inter-racial marriage. Despite nineteenth-century Catholic hostility toward them, it would be a mistake for modern scholars to continue to emphasize the illicit or marginal nature of these relationships. However condemned by the Church and the law, they were common, indeed more frequent than marriage, and presumably accepted by many Cubans. These unions were marginal only in that the dominant members of late colonial Cuban society exercised greater control over the sexual potential of elite women and hypocritically frowned upon those who did not do the same. Instead Afro-Cubans created their own sexuality and family formation patterns.

Many Cuban families of the period united under alternate legal or social forms. As discussed in chapter 2, both official and unofficial declarations of *hijo natural reconocido* (natural recognized child) remained an option. In 1827 a royal order curtailed the previously common practice of intentionally not naming unwed parents in their children's baptismal certificates.[87] The ninety-five hijo natural reconocido declarations for the children of color baptized at Espíritu Santo in 1847 were a mix of official and unofficial statements.[88] This number was almost double the fifty-nine legitimate births registered in the same year. The declaration of a hijo natural may have become a substitution for legitimacy for parents who desired recognition of the paternal bond despite there being no permanent ties between the two mates.

Both free and enslaved families engaged in this practice. Grouped according to origin and status, in the majority of cases found in the

Espíritu Santo documents, thirty-one free black creole couples made such declarations; free pardo couples made nine; and the remainder were couples mostly composed of partners of dissimilar color or status. Slave fathers, for obvious reasons had less ability to affect legal recognition. Only in five of the ninety-five declarations was the father clearly listed as enslaved, all in cases where both mother and father had the same owner.[89] Since the status of the father was relatively much less significant than that of the mother, it is not surprising that the status of the father often went unreported. Yet, these declarations demonstrate that some such families had to wait for a less restrictive legal environment in order to make their civil presence known. Many of these families were legally recognized only as Cuban slavery was coming to an end, although they had been started many years earlier.[90]

MAKING VISIBLE NINETEENTH-CENTURY
AFRO-CUBAN FAMILIES

Beyond travelers' accounts, snap-shot visions of Afro-Cuban reproductive and familial life, and the macro-level statistics in census data and parish records, histories of the social shifts experienced by individual families can also be recovered. More longitudinal perspectives are possible from family reconstruction methods utilizing ecclesiastic baptismal and marriage records.[91] The less common paternity recognition petitions provide additional visibility to both marital and non-marital families. In their bias toward male social reproductive choices, these paternity petitions counterbalance the general emphasis on the mother-child bond and the diminished attention to Afro-Cuban fathers found in the baptismal records of enslaved infants. Six hundred and seventy paternity petitions involving free and enslaved Afro-Cuban submitted to the Bishop of Havana between 1858 and 1893 were reviewed for this study.[92] From such data, we can consider rural families, urban families, and the interplay between them. Similar interplay among the free and the enslaved members of nineteenth-century families also becomes visible, as does their inter-racial reproductive interactions.

Meriño and Perera's in-depth study of Afro-Cuban family life on the El Recuerdo plantation demonstrates some of the general factors in

Afro-Cuban reproductive success. Among these factors were significant owner utilization of female labor, larger plantation size, owner respect for marriage or consensual families, and attention to the general
health of enslaved people. El Recuerdo was established as a coffee plantation by the Gonzalez-Larrinaga family in the late eighteenth century
in southern Havana province, but was converted to sugar production in
the late 1850s. It held 153 slaves in 1836, but that population had grown
to 226 by 1869. Some of this growth resulted from the birth of creole
children. Between 1824 and 1867, at least 142 children were born there.
A majority (55.2 percent) of these were born of legitimate marriages.[93]

El Recuerdo was the same plantation on which the couple Amalia
and Narciso, whom we met at the start of this chapter, eventually raised
seven children. The Meriño and Perera study found that the property
was worked exclusively by men until the mid-1820s, when the Gonzalez-
Larrinagas introduced enslaved women there, perhaps as a response to
the recent criminalization of the slave trade. The absence of women at
first would explain why Narciso remained single until 1824. However,
some of Narciso's male counterparts may have married enslaved women
from other properties, since weddings were recorded for them as early
as 1811. Between that year and 1865, 198 of El Recuerdo's slave couples
married. This figure, along with a number of creole births, indicates
that the plantation's female population was significant. It is unclear to
what extent enslaved people themselves or the Gonzalez-Larrinagas
prompted these marriages. The timing of these marriages was oddly
sporadic; there are several gaps and clusters of weddings. For example,
in 1837 all eight slave weddings for that year were celebrated on Epiph-
any, January 6, and in 1865, sixteen couples wed on January 22, which
suggests some level of owner involvement. But the existence of a significant proportion of children born either to consensual unions or single
mothers indicates that the Gonzalez-Larrinagas did not insist on slave
marriage.[94] Enslaved people exercised a degree of control over their
sexual and reproductive experiences.

The nineteenth-century Afro-Cuban paternity petitions reviewed here
demonstrate that a number of enslaved men and women somehow left
rural labor, settled in more urban environments, and eventually raised
families there. For example, Cristobal Baró began his life enslaved in

Matanzas. However, when he had a child with María de Jesus Molina, a creole slave from Callajabos in 1867, they immediately purchased their son's freedom. Yet his baptism record listed the father as "unknown." Even as enslaved people, they both eventually were allowed to settle in Havana together. In 1871 the couple married and eventually became enslaved to the same owner. It was only after these events that they were finally able to legally establish their son's true paternity.[95] In a more dramatic example somewhat reminiscent of Narciso and Amalia's family experiences at El Recuerdo plantation, Ambrosio Pedroso was brought from Africa at some unknown date and enslaved on one of the sugar plantations of the Conde de Casa Pedroso in Bacuranao. He had several children with an enslaved African woman, María de Jesus Mina. But both eventually gained their freedom. They married in 1867 and began the process of legitimating those children previously baptized without Ambrosio's name.[96] These cases might be exceptions to the general experiences of Cuban slaves, but they demonstrate that enslavement on a Cuban sugar plantation did not necessarily relegate men to celibate existence or the inability to create families. These cases suggest that Afro-Cuban families were formed and maintained even in the most difficult of circumstances.

Ambrosio's case also highlights the fact that often it is only with the grouping of multiple family records that it becomes possible to document the paternity of children born to unwed slave mothers. Take for example the similar situation of the children of María de la Luz Carabali and Ramón Mina. The first child was born in Guines in 1826 when María was enslaved to Don Francisco de las Cacigas. As was common, unmarried African and African-descended fathers such as Ramón were not listed on their children's baptismal certificates.[97] In 1838, María bore another child whose father was also unlisted, but she was then living in Havana and enslaved to a different owner. Typically such dispersal of family records and limited common identity markers for Maria would have made it impossible to identify any family connection between the children simply based on the baptismal certificates. Their relationship becomes apparent with Ramón's 1872 non-marital recognition of both children. María was then free and Ramón was enslaved to her former owner.[98] These documents suggest that even as an unmarried slave couple, María and Ramón moved from a rural setting to an urban one together. Although it is unclear if Ramon and María sustained their own union over those years, as she gained freedom, they began the process of legalizing their familial ties or publicly recognizing kinship. Such stories remind us that colonial Afro-Cuban baptismal documents frequently did not note paternity, despite the existence of enduring relationships. Because a child's legal status as free or slave derived directly from the mother's, it became customary to ignore paternal involvement among Cuba's African-descended population. However, an exceptional few utilized the available legal processes to create alternatives and highlight Afro-Cuban paternity.

Another extraordinary case shows that while the documentation of kinship was generally limited for rural slave families, some managed to gain freedom and financial independence, and then correct their family records. Celestino Nodal and María Joaquina Machado had both arrived as African slaves in rural Cifuentes sometime before 1840. He was Mina and she was Carabalí. By the time the married in 1840, they were both free and had previously had at least four children who were all baptized as free. However, none of these children had been baptized with their father's name. They were not legitimated until after his death in 1867 when his death certificate and final testament clarified their paternity. Celestino had owned several small properties that he left to his family.[99] Some forty-three other enslaved and formerly enslaved couples submitted similar legitimating petitions to the bishop of Havana between 1868 and 1893.[100] Most made their petitions after the termination of slavery. While this number is not large, again it does suggest that African and African-descended people not only survived slavery in Cuba, they utilized the available legal and economic means to best position their families within this hostile environment.

FREE PARTNERS FOR ENSLAVED WOMEN

Despite the fact that reproductive segregation by color, origin, and status remained the rule, a significant gender difference was seen among the enslaved in accessing sexual and reproductive partners from other social categories. Enslaved women had greater possibilities, and enslaved men faced high levels of reproductive competition from free men of all colors. The late colonial Cuban petitions to clarify paternity reveal it was not unusual for enslaved women to have children with free men. The bishop of Havana received at least eighty-seven such petitions between 1858 and 1893.[101] As the 1870 paternity petition submitted by pardo *ingenuo* (freeborn) José de las Nieves Chamizo narrates the details of the family he formed with his enslaved African wife María del Carmen Avila, it presents an exception to the general pattern of marriage within similar class and color categories. José de las Nieves had been born free, as the son of a white man and an enslaved creole woman in the rural town of Ceiba Mocha. There he met María del Carmen and in 1843 they had a child, who inherited her mother's slave status. By 1848, the couple was living together in the provincial capital of Matanzas, and José de la Nieves was earning a living as a meat vendor. They married in the same year, although María del Carmen remained enslaved.[102] According to the Espíritu Santo baptismal data, such relationships between free pardo men and enslaved black women were infrequent. Their rarity suggests Afro-Cuban intra-racial reproduction divided along lines of color, status, and origin. Additionally, Jose and María's relationship also speaks to a certain social independence from their owners that was permissible for some enslaved women within late colonial society. María del Carmen's connection to a free partner was likely outside of her owner's control.

Racialized reproduction in late colonial Cuba also involved the significant presence of indentured Asian men. Marriages between enslaved women and Asian men were extremely restricted, with Cuban marital law from this period classifying Asians as whites. Instead consensual unions occurred. Take for example the case of Joaquin Abreu. He came to Cuba as one of the 142,000 Chinese indentured laborers arriving between 1847 and 1875.[103] In 1862 he petitioned colonial authorities for permission to marry an enslaved parda. Although the government's response is not recorded, Joaquin's petition boldly challenged the formal limits on his reproductive possibilities that stemmed from his official racial classification.[104] Other couples of this type bypassed marriage altogether and created legal families based only on the bonds with their children. In 1870, Casimiro Rivero asked the Church to recognize his paternity of his son Abraham. Abraham had been born a few months earlier to the enslaved morena Cristina on the Conchita sugar plantation. Twenty similar petitions made by Asian men were identified within the records of the Archdiocese of Havana.[105] Although the fact that these men came to Cuba with few female compatriots fostered an environment for establishing relationships with Cuban women (mulattas, blacks, and whites), their acknowledgment of their mixed-race offspring was derived from their personal choice beyond the demographic factors through which such reproduction is often interpreted.[106] These inter-racial relationships also offer a different perspective on enslaved women's sexual agency than may exist when considering only black men as their prospective partners. The racial power dynamics involved were certainly different with Asian men. They labored in situations similar to enslaved people but they had a distinct social position. Yet their juridical whiteness did not grant them social power equivalent to white men. Afro-Cuban women would have had to negotiate this reality in these unions.

Given their numbers and dominant social status, white men were obviously another important factor in colonial Cuba's racialized reproduction. They intervened both to limit the reproductive possibilities of Cuba's mulatto and black men and to create another dimension in the reproductive potential of women of color. As in all slave societies in the Americas, white men in Cuba also engaged in sexual relations with enslaved women. Many such relations derived from violence and unequal power relations, but others were consensual. Social taboo, elite denigration, and governmental restriction limited the possibility of converting these long-term unions into legitimate marriages. However, some of the men participating in these relationships often differed from their counterparts in English-speaking areas of the Americas in that they not infrequently publicly recognized and accepted parental responsibility for children born of enslaved and free women of color. For example, Don Pedro Tribarreu y Goicochea owned the morena slave Caridad and had a child with her in 1874. Due to the 1870 Moret Law that ended the legal inheritance of servile identity from slave mothers to their offspring, the child was born free. A few years later in 1877, Don Pedro formal recognized the child in a notarial document. Later still, in 1880,

Caridad herself petitioned the Church for the annotation of this recognition on the child's baptismal certificate.[107] In other cases, the relationships between white men and the women they held in slavery appeared more enduring. In 1885, Don Agustin Barroso y Hector asked the Church to recognize his paternity of ten children that he had fathered with his former slave, the morena Dominga. The first two of these children had been born in 1843 and 1847 while the mother was still enslaved. However, each was baptized as free. Dominga was granted her freedom with the birth of her third child in 1849.[108] A similar situation occurred with Don Tomás de Rocha y Martel and his parda slave Dominga. Between 1862 and 1876 the couple had eight children. The six born before the 1870 Moret Law were baptized as free by a grant from Don Tomás. However, in 1878 when Don Tomás asked the Church to recognize his paternity of these children and thereby acknowledged his sexual link to Dominga, he still had not granted her freedom.[109]

Again, although sexual violence profoundly shaped enslaved women's lives, cases like those above may prompt us ask to what extent the potential reward of freedom made an owner's advances more palatable for some enslaved Afro-Cuban women. Outside the threat of violence, enslaved women may have expressed their own social agency in submitting to sexual relations with white men, and for some this choice may have been linked their expectation of gaining their freedom in exchange for bearing children with their owners. Take for example an 1859 case from Puerto Rico, Spain's other Caribbean colony. An enslaved black woman, María Balbina, complained to a local magistrate of her owner's deception and failure to free her, despite their long-term sexual relation: "On the promise of freeing me, when I was barely a teenager, my master made me the mother of his three children, born one after another. But now, unmindful of his given word and the lamentations of his conscience, he intends to sell me."[110] Her words are a reminder of the violence and oppression to which women of color were often subjected in their sexual relations with socially dominant white men. María Balbina clearly did not want to enter into this relationship but was coerced into doing so. She patiently waited year after year for her freedom. It was the threat of sale away from her children that prompted her to seek government intervention and hope it would serve her family. Her appeal could not have been based on the sexual violence to which she had been subjected. Instead, she appealed to the colonial court based on the injustice of her master's broken promise to her as the mother of his children.[111] In Havana in 1862, Juana Sánchez y Sanchez made a similar claim against her owner. Even though he denied her accusations, her owner agreed to free the child Juana presented as his daughter and set Juana's freedom price at 700 pesos. These types of cases expose spaces within Cuba's late colonial slave regime for the reproductive negotiation of freedom. For enslaved women, coerced inter-racial sex did not gain them standing before Cuban colonial courts, but becoming the mother of her owner's child did.

Besides relations with their owners, enslaved women also found mates more broadly within the white population. Both rural and urban settings provided such opportunities. Juana Fundora was a young parda slave on the Callajabos sugar plantation owned by one of the leaders of Cuban society, Don Ricardo O'Farrill, when she entered into a relationship with Don José Luciano Ramos, a white farm worker. In 1856, he was thirty-two and she was just seventeen when they had the first of their six children. After ensuring that this child was born free, Juana gained her own freedom, as demonstrated by her *libre* (free) inscription in the 1859 baptismal certificate of the next child. In his 1884 deathbed paternity recognition, José Luciano explained that the couple had lived together *"maritalmente"* (maritally) for most of their relationship.[112] A similar situation occurred in Havana for Don Rosendo Martínez and María de las Mercedes de Castro. When they began their relationship, she was a domestic slave. They had a child in 1870, whose freedom they purchased (unaware of the 1870 Moret Law mandating freedom for children born to slave mothers after September 17, 1868). By the time their next child was born in 1872, María de las Mercedes had also gained her liberty.[113] So for some enslaved women relationships with white men did prove to be a successful strategy for the acquisition of their freedom. Yet, the question remains as to what emotional price was paid by these women or what proportion failed at such attempts. The available sources do not provide any insights into this point.

With the decline in marriage rates, most Afro-Cuban families of this period have been documented through the mother-child bonds found in baptismal records. But even among these relationships, slavery's violence, the varied avenues to freedom taken by a small proportion of enslaved people, and the precarious economics of freedom complicated the possibilities of any individual's experience of family life and its emotional bonds. The traces of Petrona Medina's relationship with her daughter María Rufina found in the documentary record remind us of these limitations and the varied social experiences possible beyond legally recognized filial links. Several elements of María Rufina's life came together in the spring of 1854 as Cuba's captain general was asked to determine who should have custody of her. At that time, María Rufina was only ten years old. Her birth certificate indicates she was born in October 1843 in the small community of Guatao in provincial Havana, where her mother was enslaved to Doña Josefa de León. No father was listed. Within a year, upon Doña Josefa's death, her will granted María Rufina freedom. For reasons that are not explained in the documents, María Rufina was separated from her mother and sent to be raised by a free black woman in another town, Corralillo.

It was there in 1852, living in abject poverty, that her future guardian and employer, the lieutenant governor of the town of Santiago de las Vegas found her. He gave her work in his home as a nursemaid. Approximately a year later, Petrona Medina appeared at his door, claiming to be María Rufina's mother and demanding her return. María Rufina had no recollection of her and feared being taken from the governor's home. Petrona was turned away. A few months later, in May 1854, a free black man claiming to be María Rufina's father filed a petition for her custody with Cuba's captain general. Antonio Abad Palomino's petition offered no explanation for his or Petrona's extended absences from their daughter's life and fell just short of accusing the lieutenant governor of holding María Rufina in slavery.

The lieutenant governor's response was swift and biting. He argued that Petrona and the undocumented father were disreputable people with no standing and that they only became interested in María Rufina upon learning that she was gainfully employed in a comfortable setting. Otherwise they had abandoned her without concern. He intimated that Petrona lived through prostituting herself and only wanted to benefit from María Rufina's potential in this area. The lieutenant governor went as far as to argue that in living with an enslaved man and not María Rufina's supposed father, Antonio Abad, Petrona was demonstrating her low character. He ended pointedly with, "Someone who has so neglected the child for ten years cannot claim that her freedom is illusory." These accusations were effective. Within a week, the secretariat of the captain general ruled in his favor.[114]

The surviving record does not allow us to know who was acting in María Rufina's best interest, either economically, emotionally, or socially. All the petitioners had several possible motives, of which parental love could have been one. It is possible that like many Afro-Cuban women Petrona initially had no secure means of supporting herself and acted to protect her daughter by placing her in the care of a free black woman. Perhaps the lieutenant governor had accepted María Rufina as more than an employee and hoped to protect her from people with truly sinister motives. However, with the court's decision in favor of María Rufina's employer, white authority once again compromised black family bonds, even for free people of color living in a slave society.

CONCLUSION

The criminalization of the slave trade into Cuba impacted the island's general parameters of racialized reproduction. With the continuation of the contraband trade, some of its impact was only nominal, as with the designation of the *emancipado* category of "rescued" African laborers. Yet even as the vast majority of newly arriving African ethnics were thrust into slavery's repressive conditions, changes were occurring. Some emancipado mothers utilized judicial means to ensure their children's free births were legally recognized. This was one step in diminishing the strong symbolic link between Africanness and slavery in late colonial Cuban society. As other enslaved African and creole parents purchased their children's freedom before birth, the presumed inheritance of slave status was similarly compromised.

The proportion of women forced into Cuba by the contraband trade increased as plantation owners realized that natural slave population replacement served their long-term economic interests. Some slave owners moved to *bueno tratamiento* (good treatment) and pro-natalist practices. With the increased chances of survival for Afro-Cuban individuals and families, the racial meaning of blackness would continue to affect the bodies onto which it was written, even as that very meaning was slowly shifting. Slave owner practices were not the only factors at play. Free and enslaved Afro-Cubans also made intentional reproductive choices. Gender accorded different options, with mulatta and black women selecting partners across social categories. Despite the frequency of inter-racial sexual relations and families, racial endogamy predominated. However, intra-racial divisions along lines of color, origin, and servile status were also apparent. With other reproductive behaviors, such as the decline in marriage rates of the general population and the recognition of hijos naturales, the sexual economy of race in nineteenth-century Cuba was certainly not static. It experienced small but repeated disruptions that had lasting impacts on Cuban social identities.

4

Nineteenth-Century Racial Myths
and the Familial Corruption
of Cuban Whiteness

Although he's married and has children,
he maintains other women,
preferably those of color.
He has corrupted more young women
than he has hairs on his head.

—Cirilo Villaverde, *Cecilia Valdés*, 1881

INTRODUCTION

The nineteenth-century novel *Cecilia Valdés* by Cirilo Villaverde (1802–1894) is a classic of Cuban literature that paints a picture of a society shaped by slavery and deformed by the meanings of race created within it. Its eponymous heroine, a very fair yet racially mixed woman, is subjugated by her own ill-fated attempt to "whiten" her way out of a repressive racial hierarchy. She becomes the lover of the white creole son of a wealthy Spanish slave trader and bears his daughter. Unbeknownst to her, her lover is also her half-brother and the heir to their father's fortune. She, on the other hand, is an unacknowledged bastard relegated to life on the social margins, with her only family being her mulatta maternal grandmother who raised her. Cecilia rebuffs the attentions of her estranged father who does not reveal his true relation to her. In the above quote, Cecilia describes him as a notorious womanizer, known for his inappropriate and destructive interactions with black and mulatta women.[1]

This novel is frequently cited as indispensable primary evidence of the nature of colonial race relations.[2] Its pages describe a social world dominated by white males who ostensibly provide economic, political, and cultural order. However, much of this order was predicated on the brutalization of the island's other inhabitants. Villaverde demonstrated that in addition to the obvious brutality experienced by enslaved people, the sexual exploitation of women was another negative component of white male authority. White women were both victims of, and indirect participants in, this oppression. As its victims, they were not appreciated in their own right; instead they were valued mostly for their roles as female progenitors of the next generation of the creole elite. On the other hand, as beneficiaries and participants in Cuba's social brutality they also often collaborated in the victimization of others. They performed this role either by ignoring the pleas of their servants or punishing their blameless black and mulatto victims for the reprehensible actions of their own spouses.

Villaverde gives a true portrayal of enslaved and free people of color as those who sustained the country by laboring under heinous conditions. In addition to the economic motive for the physical violence inflicted upon enslaved people generally, enslaved women were also subject to sexual abuse at the hands of men in all social categories. Nevertheless, in many cases, free and enslaved women of African descent made their own selections of sexual partners and mates. When they had the choice of entering relationships with white men, they did so for individual emotional and material reasons. However, in his fictional vision of such choices, Villaverde portrays the women making these decisions as ultimately sowing the seeds of their own victimization. He implies that although such sexual relations brought temporary gains and whitened children, these women ultimately found themselves in worse social and economic straits. They were left with two greater burdens: additional mouths to feed and the social stigma of dishonor. Cecilia, her mother, and her grandmother are all written as typically tragic mulatta heroines who each became trapped in the vicious cycle of whitening-based desire and disappointment. In Villaverde's novel only men of color are more victimized. As the most marginalized sector within the novel, black and mulatto men are left frustrated and helpless because they possess no real means of social advancement. They are even denied the reproductive whitening option through which women of color are shown to pursue mobility.

This chapter will demonstrate that, beyond *Cecilia Valdés*, factual sources can provide some useful insights into the social significance of inter-racial relationships in colonial Cuba. *Cecilia Valdés* paints an incomplete, if not stereotypical, picture. It addresses only a very limited range of the actions involved in the politics of racialized reproduction.[3] Villaverde's emphasis on the negative motivations behind inter-racial reproduction in late colonial Cuba shields from view other sociological implications of these acts. Cuban racial identities were reproduced in a variety of familial arrangements that were ignored by Villaverde and have been largely unexplored by historians. The re-creation of racial identities was not as closely bound as Villaverde suggested.

Late colonial Cuban social agents were not left to choose solely between acceptable racially endogamous marriage or disreputable consensual unions when determining the status of their offspring.[4] While marriage has been considered the ultimate social strategy of this type, Cubans also utilized several other familial means of reproducing racial meaning and social categories. This chapter outlines such race-making familial strategies that included 1) the legal recognition of paternity for children born out of wedlock; 2) the surreptitious labeling of mixed-race children as white; 3) the official designation of whiteness in orphaned children of questionable background; and 4) the self-assertion of black and mulatto identities by individuals who had achieved white status. Shifts in racial classifications for individuals, families, and ultimately the whole society were the outcomes of these practices. These methods constructed alternate family forms through which Cubans mediated social distinctions. At times, these familial processes minimized racial distinction and at others they amplified them.

Neither the significant number of inter-racial relationships found in late colonial Cuba nor the numbers of first-generation bi-racial individuals can, in and of themselves, indicate the society's rejection of racism, just as heterosexual marriage does not indicate a lack of sexism. However, the extent to which white individuals publicly recognized and respected inter-racial families marked a departure from the rigid racial hierarchies undergirding slave and post-emancipation societies. White men possessed several options when choosing how to father and socially position the next generation. Their offspring could be almost naturally marked as white when born through the bodies of pedigreed white women. Alternately, less natural designations of whiteness could be acquired through the bodies of women of color or women of questionable racial backgrounds with either direct or secretive challenges to standard race-making practices. Or finally, white men could publicly acknowledge racially mixed, or pardo children born from their amorous unions with African-descended women. These practices were often institutionalized; those that were not sprang from an individualized redefinition of family. Recognition of these practices allows for a re-framing of the conversation surrounding inter-racial relationships, away from images of calculating and futile whitening efforts by black and mulatta women towards a consideration of the ways in which individuals and institutions shaped race through familial behaviors. Ultimately, in late nineteenth-century Cuba the tendencies to diminish the value of class and race were in constant struggle with those forces that strengthened their meanings. Only via a detailed examination of the evolving nature of this struggle can we begin to understand the various terms by which modern Cubans define themselves.

RESTRICTIONS ON INTER-RACIAL MARRIAGE AND
ALTERNATE METHODS OF FAMILY FORMATION

While the Spanish monarchy was often ambivalent toward issues of racial status in the Americas, white colonial officials were more rigorous in their approach. Cuba's colonial administrators often perceived the maintenance of a racial hierarchy as central to their political interests. The restriction, and at times outright prohibition, of inter-racial marriages was one means by which they attempted to ensure that racial differences continued to possess value. Beginning with the Military Ordinances of 1728, which required military officers to have permission from their superiors to marry, and continuing with strident local inter-pretations of the Pragmatic Sanction of 1778, the social compatibility of intended spouses was one important factor in Cuba's legal race-making practices.[5] Specifically, an 1805 Cuban clarification of the pragmatic was often interpreted by contemporaries as a broad prohibition on all inter-racial marriage with persons of African descent. Such policies ef-fectively curtailed inter-racial marriages until 1881 when the new liberal Spanish government decreased its surveillance of social practices. The most intensive application of marital restrictions coincided with the height of Cuban slavery, in the period between 1820 and 1860. Thus, in an institutionalized manner inter-racial reproduction was relegated to illegitimate forms and the racial hierarchy was reinforced.[6]

Verena Stolke (formerly Martínez-Alier) in her now classic study of these marital restrictions which has shaped much of the scholarly dis-cussion of the social dimensions of race in colonial Latin America re-views 199 petitions for and against inter-racial marriage that were brought before colonial officials in nineteenth-century Cuba. She uses these cases to demonstrate the joint actions of the colonial state and the local elite in sustaining racial hierarchy. However, her conclusions re-quire some caution. Buried in her footnotes, Stolke reveals that only twenty-five of the petitions indicate final resolutions. She found that fourteen of these were rejected while eleven were accepted. And of those that were accepted, the whites were of undistinguished common status. Only slightly less than half (44 percent) of the resolved cases were accepted. Additionally, a review of the cases in conjunction with this present study found another ten cases in which the marriages were accepted, bringing the proportion accepted to 66 percent.[7] Crucially, marriage records speak only to that segment of the population that ac-cepted the institution's social value. Many Cubans in this period, of either African or European descent, did not. This was especially true for blacks and mulattoes, both free and enslaved, for whom marriage rates consistently declined over the course of the nineteenth century. We will see below that beyond those legitimated by marriage, Cubans ac-cepted inter-racial families defined in other legal and extra-legal forms. And for those who did marry, their racial identities could be dynamic, mutable categories, adjusted to bypass legal restrictions on inter-racial relationships.

In 1786, the Marqués de Sonora José de Gálvez, the most important official in Spain's colonial administration as viceroy of Mexico and uncle to the governor of Cuba, petitioned the Spanish monarch to mediate an end to the social embarrassment experienced by a loyal Havana family by declaring the wife white. The unfortunate family had been the brunt of vicious public gossip suggesting that the wife, Doña Mariana, was actually the daughter of a previously enslaved parda woman who now worked in the Havana streets selling flowers. Her husband claimed that nothing could have been further from the truth and that the home of Doña Mariana's honorable, yet unwed, white grandmother had been frequently visited by a young parda slave with the same name and of approximately the same age as Doña Mariana's mother. People had maliciously assumed that the two were one and the same. The family presented thirty witnesses, including clerics and the former owner of the parda woman, who testified in support of their claims of whiteness. The family, it was claimed, was an honorable one that did not deserve such a perpetual stain on its reputation.[8]

When the petition reached the Spanish court, the king's advisors urged him to dismiss the request. They found it most irregular. Generally, people of quality and significant wealth first requested that a child whose parentage was questioned receive a royal legitimation through one aspect of the *gracias al sacar* procedure, through which Spanish imperial subjects beseeched and paid for royal mercy in the betterment of their formal social identity.[9] The relatives of the petitioner would testify to the claimant's familial ties and his or her white racial purity extending back at least four generations. Failing the ability of family members to testify, an extensive genealogy based on ecclesiastic records would have been used to support the family's claims. Doña Mariana had neither the public testimony of relatives nor documents from the Church proving her claim. Where were her parents or the documentary proof of their existence? Without either being presented, court advisors felt the king should deny the petition. Moreover, they asked why the royal declaration of Doña Mariana's whiteness was more important than the restoration of honor through her legitimation. Despite these objections and questions, Charles III granted the request. He did so on the explicit grounds that it was his desire to bring happiness to one of his subjects by removing this dark stain on the family and allowing it to continue to receive social distinction.[10]

Doña Mariana's story could be interpreted as revealing one individual's success at "passing"; that is, hiding any negative aspects of her ancestry. But we could also interpret the story more broadly by shifting the focus from the individual to the community. In this case, a number of good citizens and even the Spanish monarch were willing to bend the rules of racial classification for the benefit of one family. They valued the institution of family more than they valued the upholding of racially restrictive law. They were willing to confer whiteness on Doña Mariana despite her lack of merit based on the traditional measures. They engaged in what could be called a conspiracy in racial misidentification. But did not the social benefit achieved by this one family threaten society's entire racial hierarchy? If one woman of questionable background could enter the ranks of the honorable, could not others have done so? Significant fissures existed in the racial hierarchy promoted by the colonial state and the dominant class.[11] As will be demonstrated below, it was possible for children born of illegitimate unions between white men and women of color to simply become baptized as white and enjoy that designation on a legal basis. Within the files of the central archives of the Catholic Church in Havana there are several cases in which white men had their racially mixed children baptized as white.

In one such case, the free pardo Federico Mainolo petitioned the Cuban Church in 1865 for the correction of his fiancée's baptismal record so as to permit them to marry. According to Federico, his fiancée, María del Pilar Genoveva de Rosa y Acosta, had been erroneously baptized as white when in fact she was a free parda. She had lived her twenty-three years under this mistaken classification, but she would have to be reclassified to the correct parda status if the couple were to legally marry. María del Pilar's parda status was readily confirmed after she appeared before the local priest. But the Church inquired further. Her mother, the negra María del Carmen Acosta, came to testify on her daughter's behalf and explained the cause of the initial confusion. María del Carmen readily acknowledged that the items relating to maternal identity on her daughter's baptismal certificate had been falsified. Although María del Pilar's father had been correctly listed as the white Havana native Don Manuel de la Rosa, the document incorrectly registered the mother as Doña María del Carmen Acosta, and the maternal grandparents were also given the honorific title of Don and Doña to indicate their fictitious white status. María del Carmen's own baptismal certificate revealed her to be the legitimate daughter of two enslaved African ethnics. Don Manuel had also falsified the racial identities of the couple's two other children, similarly baptizing them as whites. María del Carmen claimed these distortions had been created by the now-deceased Don Manuel against her wishes. Faced with such evidence, the Church allowed María Pilar to marry her pardo fiancé by agreeing to her reclassification as parda. However, it left the white racial status of her siblings unchanged.[12]

The changing of María del Pilar's racial classification is just one example of the multiple levels of intrigue surrounding social positioning in late colonial Cuba. Her experience reveals some of the various methods Cubans used to cross the boundaries of racial identity. Here, not just one individual but family members, the Church, and the state were all involved. First, the state's role began well before Maria del Pilar's birth and continued to the time of her engagement. As we have seen, with the Spanish-American Pragmatic Sanction of 1778 and additional early nineteenth-century controls on marriage, the colonial state imposed racial limits on the selection of marital partners. Next, almost three-quarters of a century later, Maria del Pilar's white father circumvented these limitations through a questionable act, baptizing his racially mixed children as white. This allowed him to both openly acknowledge his children and legally obscure their socially disadvantageous black ancestry. Finally, however, the Maria del Pilar chose to adhere to the restrictions of the pragmatic and displayed a certain level of respect for both the state and the Church. She did this as she chose to enter a same-race marriage with another pardo rather than enjoy the legal whiteness she had been given at birth.

The archival record reveals the existence of other, similar shifts in racial classification. Two of the mixed-race children of the French émigré

Don Juan Bautista Susan were baptized as white with the mother unknown, while three others were listed as orphans of color. To ensure
each "orphan" received a portion of his estate, the father had to clarify
their paternity. The names of both parents were accordingly added to
their baptismal certificates. However, the entries for the children who
had been listed as white were not moved to the baptismal registries for
people of color and there is no clear indication that the mother's name
was added.[13] Meanwhile, in 1875 a white father, Don Francisco Franco,
returned to the Church to clarify his children's paternity and admitted
that he had aided the falsification of their baptismal certificates, listing
them as white and naming a fictitious white couple as their parents. In
reality, they were children he had had by a woman he owned as a slave
and with whom he had lived *maritalmente* (maritally) for many years.
He had wanted to give his children legitimacy, but the 1778 legislation
prevented the couple from marrying. Despite this obvious deception,
the Church allowed the children to remain listed as white after this
admission.[14]

A comparable scheme was attempted by another inter-racial couple.
Doña Teresa asked the Church to recertify the missing baptismal certificate of her illegitimate daughter. In written testimony, she and the
child's father, Don Emilio, presented themselves as white and had
the confirmation of several witnesses. The Church quickly agreed to the
petition. A local priest was about to present the restored certificate to
the father when he casually asked why the couple had not married. Don
Emilio answered that the couple could not marry because of the obvious racial difference between them. Indignant at this remark, the priest
quickly contacted higher Church officials, requesting the denial of the
new birth certificate that listed the child as white. However, the Church
let the child's white classification stand. Even when local priests complained of the falsification of white identities for a child of color, higher-
level officials often did not engage in the argument. In another case a
priest called upon the Church to change a child's classification since her
color clearly indicated that she was not white. The Church responded
that without documentation of her mixed-race ancestry no such change
was warranted.[15] In these cases, the Church's disinterest in the precise

maintenance of racial categories aided the corruption of the very meaning of whiteness. The white label had lost some of its value.[16]

In spite of the 1778 marital restriction and the historical value of race in maintaining political and social hierarchy, some Cubans changed their legal classifications from white to racially mixed in order to marry someone of previously unequal social standing. In 1817, thirty-year-old José Bonifacio Garcia had lived his entire life as legally white, but he now claimed to be a fair-skinned pardo to Church officials. He had been baptized as a white orphan who had not known his parents or grandfather. However, he had been raised by his white mother's brother. He now wanted to reject his white status in order to marry his fiancée who was clearly parda. His uncle strongly objected and pleaded with colonial authority to prevent the marriage.[17]

An 1847 case demonstrates the flexibility surrounding the assignment of legal whiteness in colonial Cuba. The white Don Ramón Moya attempted to prevent his wife's sister, Doña Encarnación, from marrying her pardo fiancé by claiming that marriage would create an unacceptable and permanent stain on his family's reputation. The young woman responded that in reality her family was not white but racially mixed. Her grandmother was of African descent and also related to her fiancé. In fact, her fiancé was also her uncle; his mother and Doña Encarnacion's grandmother were the same person. The fiancé had been conceived in her relationship with a man of color, while his older sister—Doña Encarnacion's mother—was conceived in a previous relationship with a white man. After the deaths of her parents, Doña Encarnación had been raised in the Afro-Cuban household of her fiancé's father. This was a situation that would have been truly exceptional for a young white woman of good social standing. To drive home her point, Doña Encarnación challenged even her brother-in-law Don Ramón's claims to whiteness. She suggested that he was really the illegitimate son of a priest and a mulatta slave woman. In the end, colonial officials allowed Doña Encarnacion to marry without further comment.[18]

Another challenge to the traditional forms of race-labeling came from the 1813 case of a young woman, Doña Angela Ferrer, who petitioned the Cuban colonial authorities for permission to marry her mulatto boyfriend. Her angry father insisted that the intended marriage was legally prohibited and would only bring dishonor to his family. He claimed his family was of pure Indian descent and enjoyed the right to live in the eastern Cuban town of Jiguani, an Indian *reducción* (reservation). Under Spanish colonial law, members of such communities were permitted to marry only whites or other Indians. Yet, similar to the actions undertaken by Doña Encarnación above, Doña Angela countered her father's claim by stating that her family was in fact pardo.[19] This case raises many questions about the complexity of nineteenth-century and subsequent Cuban Indian identity. Jiguani was indeed one of the last towns in Cuba designated by colonial officials as reserved for purely indigenous people or mestizos, but not mulattoes.[20] Perhaps Doña Angela's father adopted his position in order to ensure the family's continued access to Indian land. The official file does not provide a resolution to these questions.

Havana's Real Casa de Maternidad (Royal Maternity Home), commonly known as the *casa cuna* (cradle house), was an institution that also played a role in the transformation of Cuban racial categories. It was established early in the eighteenth century under the auspices of both the Spanish Crown and the Catholic Church to protect abandoned white children, offering them a chance for adoption to a good family or the right to be raised in the name of the Spanish Crown, with legal acknowledgment of a fictive legitimacy. In recognition of the casa cuna's founder, Archbishop Jerónimo Valdés, the family name of Valdés was granted to all such children and they were publicly designated an exceptional social status, with royally designated legitimacy without true genealogical knowledge of their ancestry.[21]

Despite the casa cuna's official focus solely on white orphans, nonwhite children were often clandestinely accepted. Children of all races would be left abandoned at various private doorsteps throughout the country to be later received by the Church and baptized with the annotation *al parecer blanco* (appears to be white). In this way, any infant could receive a white classification. Often the parents would then return to "adopt" or act as patrons to their own abandoned but newly whitened and legitimated children. One mid-nineteenth-century priest noted it was not unusual for adults who were obviously mulattoes to

Elegant Afro-Cuban women captioned by an American photographer as "A group of the Natives, St. Jago de Cuba," 1863. Source: The New York Public Library Schomburg Center for Research in Black Culture.

receive copies of their casa cuna baptismal certificates that listed them as white orphans. The most famous case involving the casa cuna is the fictional one in *Cecilia Valdés*. Villaverde dramatized the reality of many late colonial Cuban mixed-race families in having the infant Cecilia's receive the Valdés surname as the result of her father depositing her in the casa cuna. But for Cecilia this effort was ultimately useless. Her removal from the institution to the home of her mulatta grandmother ended any possibility of hiding her true African ancestry. Even Cecilia's fair complexion did not allow her to achieve whiteness. Villaverde portrays her racial background as an ever-present obstacle.[22]

The available sources do not indicate how successful this strategy was for real orphans. What they do suggest is that some continued to live as legal whites and others did not. One black mother petitioned the Church to change her son's baptismal certificate from the casa cuna to reflect his true parentage. She argued that the certificate listing him as white when he so obviously was not made him "the object of ridicule." Other casa cuna orphans requested deletion of their white identities as a result of an unfavorable application of the 1778 impediment against interracial marriage that restricted the possibility of sanctifying unions with African-descended partners. Take for example the case of Juana Valdés and her desire to marry her pardo boyfriend. Initially, colonial officials had denied the couple permission to marry based on racial inequality. As a royally recognized orphan, Juana was presumed to be white. After the first official rejection of her case, Juana resubmitted the petition and went to greater lengths to prove that she was in fact mulatta and that she had always associated with other people of color. She presented the required number of witnesses to affirm that point. Only then were both the changes to her racial designation and the marriage license approved.[23]

Some of the orphans who received their legal whiteness from the casa cuna realized the dubiousness of the designation. Late in the nineteenth century, a small number of these orphans insisted on additional medical confirmation of their whiteness. They submitted themselves to physical examination to verify that their anthropometric qualities belonged to the white race. One physician certified one such claim to whiteness with the statement that the young woman "pertains to the white race because [she] presents all the features that characterize and distinguish it."[24] The first request of this type found in the archbishop of Havana's archive is dated 1879.[25] It is unclear what specifically motivated these petitions, whether it was a declining social prestige for the casa cuna; other local changes in the meaning of race associated with the official end of Cuban slavery; or possibly the spread of science-based racism in the Euro-American world. Of the twenty-four such petitions extant for the period between 1879 and 1893, five were requested in 1880 when slavery was replaced by the *patronato* system that was designed as a guided transition to freedom. An additional ten were found for 1886 and 1887, when slavery was completely terminated.[26]

The process of acknowledging paternity for children born outside of wedlock was another institution by which the colonial boundaries of race and class were transformed within the context of the Cuban family. This ecclesiastical procedure allowed unwed or widowed men and women to recognize previously unacknowledged children. The Havana Catholic Church's records in this area cover the period from 1803 to the present. This study identified 670 such petitions made for Afro-Cubans with fathers of various racial backgrounds between 1858 and 1893. Even when their parents were not married, the children recognized in this way occupied a special legal space between bastardy and legitimacy. These children had the right to support from the declaring parent until they reached the age of maturity and also the right to inherit a designated minimum of their parents' estates. Of the cases reviewed for this study, 178 were declarations by white or Asian men claiming paternity of their mixed-race children. These actions created legitimate families—of a father and child—that did not conform to the limits placed on racial reproduction. Despite legal impediments and social taboos surrounding inter-racial marriages, these Cuban kinship bonds transcended attempts to define family in racially exclusive terms, where legitimacy and social recognition were reserved for whites and illegitimacy and marginalization defined the reproductive space of people of African descent.

The first inter-racial recognition encountered in the archbishop's records dates to 1860. It contains the angry testimony of a white father about the difficulties he had faced in attempting to legally recognize his *parda* daughter. Don Enrique Urbina noted that by a royal order of December 1, 1837, illegitimate children were no longer to be baptized with their parents labeled as unknown, as long as both parents acknowledged paternity to the officiating priest. The previously commonplace ecclesiastic practice of imposing illegitimacy by withholding the parents' names was supposed to cease. Therefore Don Enrique could not understand why a local priest had refused to annotate proper paternity for his namesake daughter, Enriqueta. The Church's initial response was to state that since an official impediment to the marriage of the parents existed, neither parent could be recognized on the baptismal document. This impediment sprang from their obvious racial difference and the royal cedula of October 15, 1805, which stated, "in a practice that has been constantly observed, marriages between persons of recognized nobility and purity of blood and those of the black, mulatto, or other impure classes cannot be celebrated without the permission of the president of the regional court." Despite this initial negative reaction, the child's paternity was later added to her baptismal certificate without further explanation.[27]

From that time forward, a small trickle of white and Asian men chose to claim their mixed-race children in this way. In fact, in a subsequent 1861 petition, a Church official indicated that because "there is no impediment to marriage" between an Asturian man and an enslaved woman, acknowledgment of their child's paternity should be accepted without further comment.[28] These types of recognition crossed many social boundaries and occurred among Spaniards and Cubans, and property holders and the penniless. Only members of the Cuban nobility were generally excluded from this set; as we will see shortly, the Marqués de Esteban's 1899 paternity declaration for his pardo son is the only one of its type encountered. This legal method of family formation therefore promoted a limited degree of inter-racial class coalescence.

THE RACIAL MATERIALISM OF CUBAN CLASS FORMATION

Without a reproductive component, "class" would exist only as ideological abstract, and real lived experiences would be irrelevant. Class reproduction is normally understood in isogamous terms, with working-class men and women giving birth to working-class offspring or elite men and women producing elite offspring.[29] For Cuba, as with all racially heterogeneous societies, the context of reproductive continuity or change in social status (i.e., intra- and cross-class mating) must also include the intersection of complex social identities such as race, class, and gender. White Cuban men of various classes reproduced their families through African-descended female bodies; a practice that was strictly forbidden by law. When these fathers' class (and/or occupational) markers are present in the records, there emerge stories that are not just about inter-racial families, but also about the economic base for these kin relationships. For example, an 1880 case reveals a white working-class carpenter recognizing the child he fathered with a morena woman whom he had owned at the time of the child's birth six year earlier. While the documents do not indicate the extent of the relationship between the parents, the father accepted a legal responsibility toward his son and claimed him as a family member.[30] In 1881, when a Spanish immigrant coach driver claimed the daughter he had had with a previously enslaved woman, he also contributed to a familial expansion of the Cuban working class that extended beyond racial differences.[31]

The Chinese and indigenous Mexican men brought to labor in Cuba also participated in this process of generating the Cuban working class. Witness the petition of Antonio Méndez Romero from Tabasco, Mexico. In 1882, he was a single, sixty-three-year-old day laborer when he recognized the two children he had with the morena Felipa Pérez. Their daughters had been born in 1871 and 1872, while Felipa was enslaved in Batabano.[32] Chinese men also recognized their children by white women. In 1882 the farm worker Manuel Rodríguez from Canton claimed the children he had had with Doña Gertrudis del Torro y Rodríguez. However, use of this type of family formation to reduce racial differences did have its limitations. Only in one exceptional case did a man of color claim a child with white woman. In 1884, the pardo sailor Lorenzo Cortes acknowledged his six-year-old son by Doña Serafina Pérez. The child originally had been baptized as white with father unknown. However, there is no indication that the Church ordered pardo racial designation after the recognition.[33]

While the use of this distinct family form to shape racial meaning and foster class unity was most prevalent in the working class, white men from higher social sectors also recognized their racially mixed children. In 1877, on his death bed, the co-owner of the Delicias sugar plantation claimed the three adult children he had conceived with the parda Paula Chappotin and left them a substantial part of his property.[34] In 1880, just before he returned to Spain, Captain Don Ramón Monesma y Casanova of the Spanish infantry acknowledged his son by a parda woman. In this way, the child would enjoy his father's name if not his presence. Men who described themselves as property owners and merchants also claimed their pardo children. In 1882, Spanish businessman

Don Andrés Collazo y Reyes accepted responsibility for his children by his former *parda* slave Ysabel Caro. That same year, medical surgeon Dr. Pedro Sánchez de las Cuevas recognized the children he had had with the *morena* Ysabel Duque Azrozarena. The couple appeared together before a notary and stated "que han tenido desde hace algunos años relaciones amorosas" (that they had loving relations that had lasted for several years). The first of their five children had been born fourteen years earlier.[35]

The number of such cases increased very gradually throughout the latter half of the century. The year 1860 saw the one case of Don Enrique Urbina mentioned above, while in 1862 there were eight inter-racial recognitions. These admittedly low numbers peaked in 1882 and 1887, which saw thirteen and fourteen petitions respectively. Interestingly, both of these years came after major changes in race relations in the economic domain. In 1880, the Spanish government declared that those persons then held in slavery would transition to their freedom through the *patronato* system, and in 1886 slavery was finally eliminated. The small increase in inter-racial recognitions in these years suggests a link between the creation of the meaning of class and race in the productive and reproductive domains.

These cases should not, however, give the impression that the Cuban inter-racial families formed through these combined legal and biological reproductive acts easily overcame other social divisions in which race mattered. Although the restriction on inter-racial marriages was officially lifted by the Spanish government in 1881, existing sources indicate only a modest increase in these types of marriages. A review of baptismal records for children of color in Havana's Espíritu Santo parish between 1881 and 1900 reveals only twelve children legitimately born to inter-racial couples. In the majority of these cases, a white man married a woman of color. In only four cases did a man of color marry a white woman, and two of these women were non-Hispanic.[36] With the termination of racial classification within this parish's registries at the turn of the twentieth century, no further changes in racialized reproduction were documented. However, the discontinuation of racial identifiers in itself may reflect a major change in the value placed upon racial distinctions in the reproductive domain.

"PASSING" AND GENDERED DIMENSIONS
OF INTER-RACIAL SEX

The rigidity with which colonial Cubans marked race varied not only with class. As we have already seen, gender was another ever-present factor in the social meaning of race and its legal documentation. Additional examples of this intersection are also found in the handful of cases in which single white women petitioned the Church for the correction of their erroneous parda identities listed in their children's baptismal records. In all cases, both mother and child had been initially registered in the baptismal books of people of color. However, after documentation of the mother's white ancestry, the children's records were readily transferred to the registries of whites.[37] One might think that the initial parda listings may have been simple errors. However, the original listings and subsequent corrections open themselves to different explanations. Given the colonial association of whiteness and legitimacy, these petitions may imply a clerical tendency to attribute out-of-wedlock births to African-descended people instead of to whites. Without documentation to the contrary, priests may simply have assumed that unwed fair-skinned mothers were indeed pardas. Nevertheless, such "accidental" classification of white mothers as parda would have confused even further the meaning of whiteness in Cuba's late colonial period by associating lower-status whites with the legal pardo category. Another interpretation of the reassertion of whiteness in these cases is that it represents successful "passing" by women of color. Such a view would further support the theory that, when requested, Church officials preferred to list someone as white, which ultimately aided the construction of ambiguous Cuban racial identities. The Church's ambivalence in these matters was instrumental in fostering this flexibility.

One 1840 racial reclassification request further demonstrates the impact of this institutional ambivalence. In it Antonio Soto declared himself to be a free pardo and acknowledged that his ability to marry a parda woman was compromised by the fact that his 1805 birth certificate falsely listed him as white. Because his mother was white and his father remained unnamed, Antonio had lived with white status for thirty-five years. But the restrictions on inter-racial marriage led him to seek clerical redefinition of his status. The local parish began to investigate the matter. The report on the background and conduct of the mother and son based on witness testimony stated that "yes, she does belong to the class of poor whites, and her son, who opened this investigation, is the result of her union with a man of color as indicated by his phenotype. And, for this reason, has been and is reputed to be mulatto."[38] If his mother's status was true, then this is one of the few cases from the colonial period in which a white woman was officially acknowledged as the mother of a pardo child. The existence of others may have been similarly disguised by baptizing the children as white or by ecclesiastic reclassification of such mothers as parda.

The oral family histories collected in Havana as part of this current study support the existence of this possibility. Of the twenty-three Afro-Cuban informants over the age of seventy-five consulted, three acknowledged white grandmothers. One recounted the story of the grandmother's painful banishment from her white family when she chose a black spouse at some point in the late nineteenth century. She was never again allowed to interact with her birth family and effectively became parda through her intimate contact with Afro-Cubans.[39] In contrast, in the approximately 5,800 baptisms of color recorded in Espíritu Santo between 1876 and 1904, only two white mothers are listed.[40] While there is no direct correlation between these two data sets, the discrepancy is suggestive. Together they may speak to a documentary denial of inter-racial reproduction between men of color and white women, despite limited examples to the contrary. No members of either group could reproduce themselves publicly in the bodies of the racial other, a fact that stands in great contrast to the reproductive possibilities of white men and women of color. The background of the well-remembered Cuban poet, Gabriel de la Concepción Valdés (Plácido) also speaks to the existence of this practice. He was the son of a free mulatto barber, Diego Ferrer Matoso, and a female Spanish dancer. Although he was raised in his father's home, like Villaverde's fictional Cecilia, he was initially placed in the Real Casa de Maternidad and baptized with the surname Valdés.[41] What motivated this action? Did his parents wish to protect his mother's honor, hide his father's race, or both?

An exceptional late nineteenth-century case demonstrates the possibilities open to white Cuban women in executing their reproductive options. In defending her pardo lover José de Leon against charges of kid-napping and rape, the presumably white Doña María Navarro testified that they had intended to marry and that she had threatened him "that if he didn't do it [carry her to his home], he wasn't a man." She was will-ing to break a racial taboo and risk profound social alienation for herself and legal punishment for José de Leon in order to consummate their union. And even more surprisingly, a local official supported the couple's plans. In a letter to the president of the Real Audiencia (colonial royal court), the bureaucrat cited the example of a similar case against the pardo Juan Escalona for the alleged rape and kidnapping of Doña Eusevia Yzquierdo, in which a license to marry eventually had been granted. The official suggested that based on this precedent José de Leon and Doña María should be allowed to marry, as the dishonor to the white race was already done.[42] In addition to recognizing the racial and patriarchal op-pression experienced by white women in similar circumstances, it is im-portant to acknowledge the social impact on men of color. Their pool of potential mates was greatly narrowed. Legally, inter-racial relationships between men of color and white women were permitted, but in practice social taboo restricted their fulfillment. Pleas against these injustices entered the public arena early in the twentieth century from members of the infamous Afro-Cuban Partido Independiente de Color. They urged their fellow Cubans to accept the marriages of white women and men of color as naturally as any other union were accepted.[43] In this way, race continued to have differential significance for men and women of color, just as it did for white women and men. The various ways in which they chose to shape their families at times had the power to overcome these differences while at others they only reinforced them.

LATE COLONIAL TRANSFORMATIONS
IN INTER-RACIAL REPRODUCTION

In 1882 much of elite Cuban society was shocked by the final verdict in a case that had languished in the courts for ten years. The Spanish Supreme Court overturned a series of decisions by Cuban judges to de-clare in favor of the inheritance rights of a set of "illegitimate" mixed-race children of a deceased Cuban planter, and his white nephews and nieces were left with lesser claims. The wealthy Don Esteban Santa Cruz de Oviedo had been notorious for his extensive and brutal intimacies with black and mulatta women, many of whom were slaves on his various plantations in western Cuba.[44] Before marrying into a well-respected American family late in life he was suspected to have fathered as many as twenty-six children with these women and was reputed to have been one of the few Cubans who was successful at "breeding" slaves for sale.[45] Despite his violent and scandalous reputation, he was also known to have loved and cared for many of his mulatto children. He did so to such an extent that eight of them were able to show the courts his thoughtful letters and records of his financial support. All of these had been baptized with the father listed as "unknown," but five had immediately received freedom. He had even paid for some of them to be educated in Havana, New York, or Paris.[46]

For the courts, Don Esteban's paternity of the eight petitioners was not in question, although he had never filed the required legal documents and had died in 1870 without a legal will. The fact that his marriage to a white American woman bore no children slightly complicated matters but was not decisive. Cuban judges had based their rejection of the children's inheritance rights on a strict reading of the restrictions on inter-racial marriage in the 1805 clarification of the Pragmatic Sanction of 1778. If the parents could not marry, then their offspring were fully illegitimate, without any basis for inheritance claims. All judicial actions pursued in Cuba reached the same conclusion before the Spanish Supreme Court overturned their rulings. The metropolitan judges, who were less imbued with the colonial logics of race and slave ownership, demonized the deceased Don Esteban for being an example of all-too-common slave-owner abusiveness. They read the application of the pragmatic in this suit as unjust and labeled it a "moth-eaten" document "born in rancid preoccupations that today have no bearing."[47] The judges were persuaded by the arguments of the claimants' attorney that the pragmatic would have left his clients without a known legal kinship category under Spanish law and that it was more appropriate to apply the medieval Ley de Toro, with its broader considerations of paternity. Thus these children were not illegitimate because their father's identity was known. Instead, they had rights as hijos naturales. They were just like many other such children who had successfully petitioned for inheritance rights despite lacking legal proof of paternity. The social recognition of paternity had been sufficient in many such claims, and Don Esteban left ample evidence of that social recognition. The Supreme Court's decision highlighted the late nineteenth-century differences between Spanish colonial and metropolitan evaluations of race and family. While many within the Cuban elite utilized the courts to restrict familial associations between whites and blacks, they were increasingly challenged both at home and in the metropole. Several ideologies battled on a case-by-case basis, with individuals and families deploying the strategies that best served their highly personal goals.

One final case of paternal recognition reveals just how far the association between familial legitimacy and race had shifted in the last days of Spanish colonialism. Just after the end of Spanish rule in Cuba, in January 1899, an elite Havana resident and future mayor, the Marqués de Esteban Dr. Don Pedro de Esteban y González de Larrinaga, petitioned the Church to change his son's baptismal certificate to indicate the child's previously unacknowledged paternity.[48] The baptism of the child, Ricardo, had been originally recorded fourteen years earlier in the segregated registries of blacks and mulattoes, with only the name of his parda mother documented.[49] With his father's declaration, he entered the category of *hijo natural reconocido* (natural recognized child), with the newly conferred rights to use his father's family name and to inherit some of his estate. What made this situation exceptional was that for the first time a member of the Cuban nobility was claiming his racially mixed child. The marqués was publicly joining white and black under the same elite name and demonstrating that for him the legal recognition of this family member stood above some of the social distinctions based on race. For the marqués, the secrecy previously associated with such actions was no longer justified. He did not hide the child's race or paternity, but instead acknowledged him as a legal heir. Yet it is the timing of the declaration that should hold our attention. The end of Spanish rule also ended the legal significance of titular nobility, and the consolidating liberalism of the time elevated the political rhetoric of citizenship over the previous era's royal vassalage. The official rewards once granted to elite *limpieza de sangre* (purity of blood) were to be reconceived in other racial forms, and racism would not be blithely eliminated. But perhaps Don Pedro's act reflected the hopes of many other Cubans for a multi-racial national family on the eve of independence.

CONCLUSIONS AND IMPLICATIONS

The interpretation of the value of race in the formation of Cuban families of the late colonial period found in Cirilo Villaverde's *Cecilia Váldes* is too static to offer a true picture of the reality. Actual families were created with much greater flexibility with respect to racialized reproduction than we find in the novel. Real-life Cecilias could find escape from the racial structures to which the legendary heroine succumbed. Although race, class, and gender relations are not fixed social structures, they are often perceived as such. People often act on these perceptions in ways that perpetuate them. However, within any society there exist those who place greater value on other social experiences than they do on common notions of race, class, or gender.

This chapter has argued that in choosing alternate family forms a number of late nineteenth-century Cubans initiated unintended changes to the ways in which race, class, and gender were lived and perceived at the time. At various points, the meaning of family crossed the traditional boundaries between classes and between races. The above examples are proof of the existence of these dissident acts. Between the recognition of white men gave to their racially mixed children and the norms of reproductive isolation determined by class and race, several possibilities existed. Those of African ancestry could enter the ranks of the white and the white person could choose to reclassify herself or himself as a person of color. In terms of class, the white man of wealth could choose to bear his heirs with an enslaved woman of color. Also, the white laborer could choose to create family alliances with people of color in an act that also fostered an intra-class unity that transcended racial categories.

The examples presented above also challenge earlier visions of Latin American race relations at several points. First, they demonstrate that any essentialized notion of race is questionable. For although writers in this tradition such as Carl Degler and Thomas Skidmore acknowledge that, beyond ancestry, other socio-economic conditions determine racial classification, and that "money whitens," they fail to recognize that the very definitions of racial categories were not fixed at the time. All of them were subject to internal transformations and expanded or contracted to fit a variety of socio-political situations. Even the "whiteness" that the dominant elements of Euro-American societies have held as paramount has undergone shifts in meaning.[50] By the late nineteenth century, the purity by which it had once been defined was questionable. This uncertainty was not driven only by the actions of people of color. The person of color did not simply "whiten" or "pass" into whiteness by repeated reproductive lessening of non-white physical characteristics accompanied by unproblematic socio-economic advancement.[51] Instead, the very definition of whiteness was conscientiously expanded to fit certain people of recognized mixed descent, and economic considerations were only one factor in that process. Additionally, "whitening" was a process that required active white participation beyond the biological contribution. Because the established historiography has tended to focus on the intellectual discourse surrounding race mixture, it has missed some of the nuances of the active process at work.

Second, the older scholarship assumes that all social actors were striving for advancement vis-à-vis the colonial state. All actions, including reproduction, are interpreted through this lens, and the procreative choices of the majority of subalterns are understood as "whitening." One can be critical of this perspective because of its emphasis on a unidirectional orientation and its dismissal of other possibilities in racialized reproduction. Descriptions of whitening make either the individual or the nation as the unit of analysis. The nation whitens as the demographic presence of non-white individuals decreases. The dark individual whitens with the choice of lighter individuals as reproductive partners. As shown here, there appears to have been a great deal more at play. What of the choice made by the lighter partner? Since race mixture in colonial Latin America occurred most often in consensual unions between white men and non-white women, it has been assumed that these men did not have a social investment in the offspring and did not seek to reproduce themselves in the non-white bodies of either mother or child. The literature does not consider these relations as families and instead defines this practice as concubinage or promiscuity with diluted social value. The offspring are positioned as marginal and judged according to a white-phenotype threshold. According to the literature, the partner of color whitens while the white partner remains unaffected by his or her reproductive choice.

While it is likely true that some dark individuals often did hope to whiten their offspring, viewing the process of whitening through the lens of the family or the community instead of the individual makes its legal and social limitations more apparent. As we have seen, a few people chose to be pardo rather than white. Such a perspective would also suggest that an intermediate "browning" is just as likely an interpretation. In colonial Cuba's inter-racial context, the social reproduction of race did not follow a unitary paradigm. The Latin American rejection of the U.S.-type black hypodescent or "one-drop rule" did not create only an alternate mulatto hypodescent, or an inevitable whitening. Inter-racial procreation did not have fixed results. The offspring of the same couple could have been labeled white or mulatto depending not only on skin color and economic status but also on the various strategies employed by individuals to group themselves collectively into families.

Third, one can be critical of the manner in which older studies tend to equate marriage with the height of social reproduction and expression of racial ideology. The number of inter-racial marriages is then read as the measure of the disappearance of racial preferences. With social reproduction occurring in a much more complex web of relationships than just marriage, counting the number of inter-racial marriages only is an inadequate indicator of the significance of race. Fourth, in the same vein, the older scholarship also neglects the situation that beyond the birth of children to legitimate marriages, other options existed for the social recognition of children and families in colonial Spanish America. The cases presented above of "orphans" and the intermediate status of "recognized" children demonstrate the existence of such previously unconsidered options. Ultimately, between reproduction and marriage colonial Cuban families were formed in a variety of recognized social practices and legal actions. And each form in turn reproduced racial meaning as they also had been initially shaped by race.

5

Afro-Cuban Family
Emancipation, 1868–1886

EL HOMBRE Y EL CANARIO

Plácido

... Que le adulo en la apariencia,
Piensa mi dueño, y se hechiza;
Mas, mirándolo en conciencia,
Yo engaño al que me esclaviza,
Por conservar mi existencia.

Morir por preocupación
Y sin defensa, es locura,
Suicidarse sin razón:
Vivir y hallar la ocasión
De libertarse, es cordura.

Cuanto á ser esclavo ... espera.
Te comprendo, y no te asombre,
Yo disculparme pudiera,
Y al mismo tiempo le hiciera
La misma pregunta, hombre.

Haz cuenta que yo caí
En tus redes, y ánsias vivas
No me salvaron de allí,

THE MAN AND THE CANARY

... How I flatter him with my appearance,
So thinks my owner, and he is charmed,
But looking at it thoughtfully,
I deceive he who enslaves me,
I do so for my own existence.

Dying from preoccupations
and without defenses is craziness,
Suicide without cause:
But living and finding the occasion
to liberate oneself, that is reason

How to be a slave ... wait.
I understand you and hide nothing,
I excuse myself, if I may,
to ask the same question,
of you, my friend.

You must realize that I fell
into your trap, and [my] living hopes
have not saved me from here,

| Porque tú que me cautivas | Because, you, my capturer, |
| Eres superior á mí. | are superior to me. |

¡Mas tú, que solo acatar	Especially you, who only complies
Debes al Sumo Hacedor,	as you should to the Supreme Creator,
Y de un hombre, á tu pesar,	And, to man, to your regret
Que no es á tí superior,	Who is not your superior,
Te dejas esclavizar! . . .	You allow yourself to enslave! . . .

INTRODUCTION: NINETEENTH-CENTURY
FAMILIAL LIBERATION

Although he was born free and not enslaved, the Cuban poet Gabriel de la Concepción Valdés (Plácido) sympathized with and wrote beautifully of the desire for freedom found among his fellow nineteenth-century Afro-Cubans. In his "El hombre y el canario" the caged canary decisively articulates this longing, as he mocks his enslaver's indifference. Plácido's political convictions were so strong that the Spanish colonial state executed him in 1844 for allegedly inciting an Afro-Cuban armed struggle for greater rights. Everyone living in a slave society made similar choices in accepting or contesting the system. For enslaved people, such contestations could be small or grand, personal or collective. The complete cessation of Cuban slavery in 1886 would not have occurred without their efforts. Cuban emancipatory struggles not only united free and enslaved individuals in public politics and armed revolts; they were also stories of the strategic utilization of pre-existing social networks to forge other pathways to freedom.

Familial bonds were one integral dimension of those networks and the foundations which many successful emancipatory efforts were built upon, especially those preceding the 1886 general emancipation. On this basis, one may argue that what is often termed "self-emancipation" deceptively foregrounds the individual and minimizes what might be more precisely viewed as "social emancipation." Enslaved people rarely operated as isolated actors when seeking freedom and survival; instead collective endeavors were often required. Mothers and fathers worked to free children; children sought the liberation of their parents; and husbands and wives fought to remain together. These emancipatory efforts also extended beyond physical liberation to define the survival of their social values and visions, and were also key elements in transforming the social reproduction of their communities. This chapter first discusses these freedom stories and then describes post-emancipation familial adjustments before analyzing each in terms of the sexual economy of race.

Cuban ecclesiastical archives contain a wealth of information demonstrating the results of these familial liberation processes. When several children of the same parents are identified in these sources, a family's or a parent's changing status can be observed. And as the documentation involved in the official parental recognition of children born out of wedlock often includes the baptismal certificates of several siblings, concise histories of individual Cuban families can result. For Afro-Cuban families of the nineteenth century, these records reveal their transition to freedom, especially those prior to the Moret Law of 1870 (which freed African-descended men who served in the Spanish army, royal slaves, people older than fifty-nine, and children born to enslaved mothers after September 17, 1868).

Take, for example, the case of Juan Bautista Pérez. He was not a major historical figure, and while the majority of his experiences remain unknown, his family's transition to freedom can be traced from archival sources. He was born a slave in 1793 in the small village of Sancti Espíritu. His birth family was comprised of at least two previous generations of creole slaves, as his mother and grandparents were also enslaved Cuban-born blacks. Juan Bautista also married among Afro-Cuban creoles. His first marriage ended with the death of his wife, the free parda Ana Antonia Quintero in December 1831. Her death certificate lists her as a thirty-two-year-old parda without any surviving children and the wife of the free pardo Juan Bautista Pérez. By 1839, Juan Bautista had entered a relationship with the woman who would eventually become his second wife, the free negra Ana Benigna Penton. Children were born to the couple in 1840 and 1841, before they were married. The couple wed in 1846, but pursued the legitimization of the children only much later, in 1868. The baptismal certificates of each child listed both parents as *pardos libres* (free pardos).[1] The categorization of Juan Bautista as libre in several documents would suggest that he had gained his freedom earlier in the century, before his first wife's death in 1831. At that point he would have been a relatively young man, of less than forty. Unfortunately, the ecclesiastic sources do not address the methods he used to achieve this end.

Of the several legal liberation options available to enslaved Afro-Cubans, ecclesiastic records only concerned themselves with a few, especially the purchase of a child's or mother's freedom. This documentary concern followed the property logic dictated by *partus sequitur ventrem*, where a child's servile status equaled that of the mother. For other liberation practices, alternate governmental sources allow for more specific identification of methods utilized by Afro-Cubans and their families to acquire freedom. The files from the offices of the island's many *síndicos procuradores generales* (general public advocates) retain evidence of such strategies, as enslaved people or their supporters sought the síndicos' assistance in their own individual, legal challenges to enslavement. A few of those that reached Cuba's captain generals are analyzed here.

THE CASE OF THE FREE BLACK, ROMUALDO GARCÍA, REQUESTING THE
LIBERTY OF HIS FEMALE PARTNER, OCTOBER 1837.

Romualdo García, a free black, formerly enslaved at the Santa Lutgarda
(previously "La Iberia") plantation to Don Joaquín and Don Manuel González
Arango, appears before Your Honor and says: that because he has lost his sight
and is now unable to work, his former owners granted him liberty at the price of
200 pesos. Also because he has lost his sight, he now lives in a terrible condition,
having to beg for the kindness of caring people. But he finds himself without
someone to look after him. This situation has prompted a few friends to lend him
the money necessary to obtain the freedom of his partner, Damiana, who lives
on his former plantation. Romualdo has deposited the money to free her in the
power of the responsible síndico procurador.[2]

Romualdo had given his former owners 350 pesos but they believed Damiana was worth 450 and so the case was brought before the governor. Damiana was granted her liberty a few months later, for an unspecified sum.[3] Here we see several very cynical motivating factors at play. His slave owners still required Romualdo to purchase his freedom, despite the fact that his blindness made him of little use to them. More interestingly, Romualdo had been able to pay for his freedom, despite his condition. By the same token, Romualdo's desire to liberate his female companion is described largely in terms of his own needs. His abject situation prompted friends to assist him in the purchase of Damiana's freedom. It would be interesting to know how Damiana responded to this situation. Was gratitude for liberation sufficient to bind her to Romualdo, as "partner" and helpmate? Unfortunately, additional information on the couple is unavailable, but it is clear in this case that black female labor was valued for economic production in one context and for individual (or perhaps familial) survival in the other.

Other cases present more altruistic visions of family liberation efforts. For example, Miguel Moreno's appeal to the síndico demonstrates the difficulty this enslaved father faced as he tried to purchase his daughter's freedom from another owner.

PETITION OF MIGUEL MORENO, BONDSMAN OF DOÑA MERCED POLO, TO
LIBERATE HIS DAUGHTER TOMASA, HAVANA, AUGUST 1853

... authorized by his owner and mistress, as stated in the enclosed license, [Miguel] presented himself before Coronel Miguel de Cárdenas y Chávez to try to liberate his daughter Tomasa, a black child of eleven years of age. This gentleman acceded to this emancipation at the sum of 600 pesos. This price is excessive when it is to provide benefit; this stands in opposition to her liberty. In light of this situation, Miguel has come before the síndico to request mediation. So far this prudent step has been in vain. Señor de Cárdenas y Chávez, despite having been called before the court, has ignored that citation. It appears that this situation cannot be resolved without Your Honor's authority.

[The petition also included the license for freedom dated July 23, 1853.] License to the slave Miguel to free his daughter Tomasa, of eleven and a half years of age, slave of Senor Coronel Miguel de Cárdenas y Chávez. It obligates me [Doña Merced Polo] to maintain and educate her as long as Miguel remains my slave.

Shortly after this additional petition, the síndico "settled the matter to the satisfaction of all interested parties."[4] It is curious that no mother was mentioned and that Miguel was purchasing his daughter's freedom before obtaining his own. This choice raises several questions. Perhaps the child was less costly and in freedom she could readily work toward buying her father's liberty. Additionally, Miguel's owner, Doña Merced, promised to raise the child as long as Miguel remained in her service. This is unusual. It is possible that Doña Merced had provided the money to free Tomasa and that the child would work in her home alongside her father. Doña Merced's presence in the records also speaks to the limited legal options available to enslaved fathers. In contrast to the nature of

Miguel's petition, enslaved women's petitions rarely sought an owner's permission to keep their children at their sides. That enslaved men needed to do so speaks to the greater limitations on Afro-Cuban fatherhood.

During the nineteenth-century the number of familial liberation appeals filed by Afro-Cuban men like Romualdo and Miguel decreased. In Havana during the first half of the century, men comprised the vast majority of petitioners (90 percent). Between 1850 and 1866, the proportion of female complainants increased to 27 percent. But after passage of the 1870 Moret Law, 64 percent of the liberation appeals filed before Havana's síndicos procuradores were undertaken by mulatta and black women.[5] One explanation for this shift is possibly found in contemporary decreases in Afro-Cuban legitimacy rates. As described in chapter 3, at Havana's Espíritu Santo parish, the frequency at which Afro-Cuban infants were baptized without the name of a father stood at 47 percent in 1847 and 70 percent in 1867. The ability for Afro-Cuban fathers to petition for their children's freedom was compromised as documentary evidence of paternity became less frequent. Additionally, petitions to liberate women often drew on socially accepted maternal images, for which no paternal counterpart existed for Afro-Cuban men.

Another gender difference existed in that female petitioners also referenced the sexual violence often inflicted upon slave women. The petition by Juana Sánchez y Sánchez demonstrates one way in which sexual abuse and the acquisition of freedom were intertwined.

JUANA SÁNCHEZ Y SÁNCHEZ, PETITIONS FOR HER FREEDOM AND THAT OF HER CHILD, HAVANA, AUGUST 1862.

Juana Sánchez y Sánchez, born in the city of Santiago and slave of Don Gregorio Marsá, lieutenant of the militia and resident of the same city, with the most respect and submission states that her daughter Ángela is also that of this Señor Marsá. This is sufficient reason that they [mother and daughter] should acquire liberty . . . The síndico procurador Nicolás Azcárate indicates that this mulatta maintains that she was seduced by her owner and that he is the father of her newborn child. However, even after she has presented the little girl, she still lacks the evidence to prove her assertion. Don Marsá, for his part, roundly denies this charge. But he has agreed that to avoid scandal he will declare the child free and set the price of freedom for Juana at 700 pesos, even though she cost him more than a thousand pesos.[6]

One is left to wonder if the accusation of the owner's sexual abuse was sufficient to win the child's freedom, and had other enslaved Afro-Cuban women successfully pursued such claims, either officially or more privately? The síndico's advocacy of such a claim demonstrates the limited extent to which the mid-nineteenth-century Spanish state accepted that sexual violence toward enslaved women required legal redress.

Just as parents petitioned for the freedom of their children, and lovers for the freedom of their partners, another case indicates that children did the same for their enslaved parents.

THE DRAMATIC STRUGGLE OF DIMAS CHÁVEZ TO FREE HER MOTHER, HAVANA, DECEMBER 1866

Dimas Chávez, native of Havana and resident of 53 Prado [Avenue] states: From last October, I have deposited 306 pesos with the síndico Ramón Betancourt with the intention of purchasing freedom for my mother Lorenza Chávez, who is owned by Pedro Acosta. He transferred my mother to the Los Atrevidos plantation, near the town of Colón. The síndico, in honoring his responsibility, published an edict calling Don Pedro to return my mother, but he has not appeared. Now, I am asking you [the governor-general] to demand the presentation of my mother before the courts.

Lorenza's drama did not end there. Don Pedro refused to relinquish her. On one occasion he stated she was too ill for him to release her and force her to travel to Havana. The síndico then sent armed guards to recover her, but she had been hidden at another site. Lorenza's mother and Dimas's grandmother, Mercedes, who Don Pedro also owned, testified that Lorenza had been taken to an unknown location. The case was finally settled when Don Pedro's neighbors revealed where she could be found. In March of 1867 her freedom was purchased for 300 pesos.[7] The state's intervention on this Afro-Cuban family's behalf was impressive. It not only curtailed the owner's private property rights, but it also used armed force to ensure the freedom of one Afro-Cuban individual.

This case is also instructive for demonstrating links between the rural and urban populations of color. The adult daughter lived in Havana, while the enslaved mother and grandmother worked in a rural setting; of three generations of women of color, only the youngest was free. She then worked to free her mother, while the grandmother remained in slavery. We can only speculate that the strategy was to earn freedom for the most economically viable member of the family first, then move to other family members down the economic scale.

Beyond the individual family histories revealed in petitions to the síndico procurador, collective practices can also be identified in the ecclesiastical sources. In the 1847 records of Havana's Espíritu Santo parish, twenty children were granted their freedom before baptism. Of these, the majority were identified as either legitimate or recognized hijos naturales of enslaved couples. By contrast, only one-third (seven) were baptized without an identified father of color. And of these, two were uniquely distinguished as pardos born to morena mothers. The implication of these designations is that the fathers were either white or themselves pardo. Thus, for this particular year, the often noted phenomenon of women of color earning freedom for their children with white men was of much less significance than the economic efforts of Afro-Cuban families. In both these ways, the acquisition of freedom was often a family endeavor among people of color.

TOWARD COMPLETE ABOLITION

The period between 1868 and 1886 marked the final era of Cuban slavery. With the end of slavery in the United States, Cuba and Brazil remained the only regions of the Americas with large, legal slave populations. With the loss of this last vestige of meaningful North American support for the institution, many in Cuba began to accept slavery's almost inevitable demise. Cuba's separatist Ten Years' War (1868–1878) against Spain accelerated things, as leaders on both sides used the abolition issue to garner popular support and enlist formerly enslaved fighters.[8] With the war, a gradual process of general abolition began. It occurred in several stages: the freeing of enslaved combatants; the true closure of the contraband slave trade; the 1870 Moret Law, which freed several categories of enslaved people; and finally, the 1880 *patronato* system that was designed to ease enslaved people into freedom and free-wage labor.[9] The slave population decreased by almost one half (45 percent) within a decade, going from 363,288 in 1867 to 199,094 in

Table 5.1. Cuban population 1862–1887

Year	White men	White women	Free men of color	Free women of color	Slave men	Slave women
1862	468107	325377	113746	118687	218722	151831
1867	491512	341645	121708	126995	203412	141203
1877	576272	386903	128853	143625	112192	86902
1887	607187	495702	275413	253385	—	—

Source: Ortiz, *Los esclavos negros,* 16–17.

1877 (see table 5.1).[10] All of the paths to freedom combined to make this period one of great social transformation. These transformations went beyond the economic and labor changes upon which the earlier historiography focused. For the enslaved, these changes affected not only their mode of employment. They also influenced their style of family formation.

Studies in other slaveholding societies in the Americas suggest that both during and immediately after abolition a number of alterations occurred in family structure and modes of family formation for African-descended people. For example, in many English-speaking areas, marriage rates among formerly enslaved populations increased. The limitations on marriage formerly imposed by slavery had been removed and people of color expressed their newly gained freedom by adopting marriage as a sign of personal maturity. Both for the freedpeople themselves and the historians and sociologists who later studied them, their modes of family formation became measures of conformity with the norms of the dominant society.

The speed of final emancipation in the U.S. South did not allow most enslaved people to rearrange their lives and families in anticipation.[11] Most of their adjustments were delayed until final abolition and only at that point did they begin to stabilize family life. For most of those enslaved in the United States, monogamous nuclear families were not new. They had been the predominant family form through the nineteenth century.[12] What was unprecedented were the ability to legalize the relationships and the removal of the master's potential intervention in black family life. The removal of this disruptive presence also allowed the newly freed greater social options, such as co-habitation, legal marriage, and the creation of extended multi-generational households and long-distance kinship networks.[13] "Upon their emancipation most . . . ex-slave families had two parents, and most older couples lived together in long-lasting unions."[14] Final emancipation also contributed to the lessening of the color and status distinctions among people of color. Free blacks in American slave communities were, in fact, often people of racially mixed descent who distanced themselves from their darker enslaved counterparts. The post-Reconstruction intensification of white racial animosity toward all other racial categories reinforced the once tenuous bonds between the more privileged mulattoes and the darker freedpeople.[15]

In other areas of the Americas, gradual changes to the families of freedpeople occurred both before and after final emancipation. This distinction was due to the fact that the final emancipation processes outside of the U.S. South were gradual, with stages similar to those mentioned above for Cuba. In Brazil after emancipation, the Afro-Brazilian family formation patterns closely mirrored those of whites. Urban São Paulo saw increased expression of "the value placed by 'black society' on the rules followed by the society at large, including virginity and marriage, if possible with all the formal trappings."[16] Similarly, post-abolition marriages occurred more frequently among blacks on provincial Rio de Janeiro's rural coffee plantations.[17] Marriage rates of people of color initially approximated those of whites before slowly diverging by the middle of the twentieth century. The marriage rate for Afro-Brazilians in São Paulo was 96.6 percent that of their white counterparts between 1881 and 1890. By 1930, that proportion had fallen to 91.5 percent.[18] Yet one has to bear in mind that marriages for the general population remained low. Only 23 percent of Rio's adult population were married in 1872, but by 1890 that percentage had increased to 31 percent and to 40 percent by 1906.[19] Marriage rates also increased post-abolition in the British Caribbean. Under the influence of Christian missionaries, freedpeople pursued the models of the English middle class. Marriage and female withdrawal from public labor were key aspects of that model.[20]

How did the familial context of the Cuban process compare to transformations elsewhere in the Americas? Before attempting to answer this question, one must realize how differences in social framework and in the availability of investigational sources have shaped the study of post-emancipation family transitions. Briefly, for the United States, the newly emancipated were faced with the disruptions caused by the Civil War. The federal government actively supervised the reconstruction of Southern society in its wake. As a result, the records of the Freedmen's Bureau provide access to the thoughts and actions of former slaves.[21] Much later, in the late 1930s, the interviews of formerly enslaved people undertaken by the Works Progress Administration augmented the supply of first-hand accounts of the transition to freedom in the United States.[22] For the British Caribbean and Brazil, abolition was a gradual and comparatively peaceful process, with little government oversight. However, in the former, Christian missionary societies obligated themselves to the moral socialization of the freed people. Their archives hold a wealth of material on the family matters of freedpeople.[23] Studies of Afro-Brazilians modes of post-abolition family formation are possible to the extent that race remained a marker of identity within Church registries and civil vital records.[24]

Family formation during the Cuban abolition process was not documented by records similar to those in the United States and British Caribbean, although it did have some similarities with other emancipation processes. Again, like the United States, Cuban abolition was shaped by war. For people of color, the Ten Years' War brought both destruction and mobility. Yet, Cuban abolition was also a gradual process, comparable to that in Brazil and the British Caribbean. However, neither the Spanish government nor the Catholic Church concerned themselves with the social adjustments to freedom. As a result, no surviving historical sources are fully dedicated to the experiences of Cuba's former slaves. Fortunately, however, ecclesiastic records can again provide a glimpse into their familial experiences in the transition from slavery to freedom. Additionally, these records were supplemented by Afro-Cuban ecclesiastic petitions for clarification of status, as people of color returned to the Church to clarify legal identities for themselves and their families.

Even as Cuban slavery was on the decline, families with enslaved members were challenged to maintain bonds that were not disrupted by slave masters. With the colonial state's gradual abolition process, the confrontation of those challenges also underwent transformation. Again, the 1870 Moret Law both liberated enslaved people older than fifty-nine and ended the legal application of *partus sequitur ventrem*. Thereafter, the children of enslaved women would enjoy legal freedom, but they were to remain with their mother's master until they reached maturity at age twenty-two.[25] The new policy led to families in which several members continued in enslavement but the youngest and the oldest were nominally free.

This was not an unproblematic experience. Because the law was retroactively applied to children born after September 17, 1868, a few cases appeared before Church officials in which owners and parents disputed the dates of birth and baptism for children born to enslaved mothers. For example, in 1875, in a review of the baptisms of the members of the rural community of Guamutas, the local priest noticed that two black children under the control of Don Ramón Sánchez had not been baptized. The subsequent investigation brought to light the fact that the children had been born in March 1868 and September 1869 respectively, but the mother claimed both were free. The officiating priest baptized the children but requested of the presiding bishop instructions for whether an annotation of freedom should be added to the certificates. While it is clear in retrospect that only one of the children was free, the priest may not have been confident of that fact. The dossier related to the case is incomplete and no response from the bishop was included. Another clause in the Moret Law should have protected this family's unity. It stipulated that children younger than fourteen were not to be sold away from their mother's owners. This does not seem to have won the family any greater protection, however, as the mother had already been sold to another owner by the time of the investigation.[26] Historian Rebecca Scott presented a related case in which judges in Cuba's colonial court denied the protective application of the Moret Law to the enslaved minor child of a newly freed woman. The child could be sold because the judges read the law as only applying to free-born children of enslaved mothers.[27] The existence of the law was insufficient to maintain the family bonds; its full application also required enslaved people to pursue their rights and officials who respected these interests. With major slave owners holding key positions in the body charged with enforcing the law, such advocates for enslaved families were few in number.

Another case also demonstrates the initial confusion over the Moret Law. After the law went into effect, the baptismal certificate of a black infant, Rosa, was annotated to indicate that she was free. This was an error as she was unfortunately born on August 30, 1868, sixteen days before the date indicated for the retroactive application of the law. Interestingly, Rosa's owner did not request the correction until 1878.[28] The Moret Law allowed the owners of slave mothers to keep freeborn children under their "care" until age eighteen. The owner only had to resolve the matter before Rosa reached that age in order to maintain possession of her. Cuban historians Aisnara Perera Díaz and Maria de los Angeles Meriño Fuentes have uncovered the records of one slave family's attempt to bypass the limitations of the law and create a more beneficial situation for themselves. In 1872, in the provincial Havana town of Bejucal, the unofficial arrangement that had allowed José López and Isabel Baldomera Coll, who were enslaved to different owners, to establish a family of seven children came to an end. The mother's owner, Don José Coll, wanted to leave farming and sell his holdings of both land and people. He sold Isabel and four of her children to buyers from another town. The three-year-old youngest child, Cecilia, was free according to the Moret Law and could not be sold. The law mandated that she remain under the supervision of the owner her mother had at the time of her birth. This occurrence would not have been to anyone's liking. A solution was found that allowed Don José to pass legal supervision of the child to a free woman of color, Serapia González, who lived in the same town where Jose López, Cecilia's father, remained. While the documents do not indicate how the family was to maintain contact with the child, Perera and Meriño's further research found that Serapia González was represented in this transaction by José López's owner.[29] These connections suggest that the family had utilized a network of relationships to serve the best interests of their daughter.

Over the period between 1868 and 1886, these types of conflicts obviously decreased as the percentage of enslaved mothers declined. As of 1877 only 25 percent of the children of color baptized at the Havana parish of Espíritu Santo were registered to enslaved mothers. This is less than half that found in 1847 (53 percent), and in 1857 the proportion was 43 percent.[30] Perera and Meriño have also found evidence that immediately after the law came into effect, priests involved in slaveholding were less inclined to baptize the children of slave mothers. They give the example of a priest in the provincial Havana town of Quivicán who lowered his baptism rate, going from seventy-seven during 1869 and 1870 to only twenty-eight for 1871.[31] If Afro-Cuban children were not baptized as a result, then their servile status would have been left undesignated. Again, the law was only effective if those in power permitted its operation.

The Moret Law was not the only judicial practice that impacted families of the enslaved in this period. With respect to the canonical acknowledgment of paternity, the baptisms after 1876 reflect a change from the previous requirement for notarial recognition of paternity prior to its registration in the baptismal certificate. Unmarried parents now had the possibility to declare *hijos naturales reconocido* (children with legally recognized paternity) outside the presence of a notary if they declared this status at baptism. However, declarations made after baptism still required the certification of a notary.

Despite this less rigorous approach to the acknowledgment of paternity, fathers still did not appear in the majority of Afro-Cuban infant baptisms. In 1877, slightly more than a third (38 percent) of the children of color baptized in that year at the parish of Espíritu Santo were either legitimate or hijos naturales (54 of 138 baptisms).[32] By 1887, the percentage of fathers found in these baptismal certificates had risen to 43 percent (65 of 150 baptisms).[33] These figures were significantly higher than the 30 percent reported for the same parish in both 1857 and 1867 and this suggests that legal recognition of paternity within the Afro-Cuban population increased to a degree with the approach of abolition. Unfortunately, official census data are not clear on this subject. Censuses were undertaken in 1861 and 1877 by Spanish authorities and in 1899 by the U.S. government, which was then occupying the island, and none makes any mention of extra-matrimonial declarations of paternity. Instead they focus on marriage rates, while the 1899 census also discusses consensual living arrangements. Among Afro-Cubans of all ages, only 6.2 percent were married in 1841. This statistic increased slightly in 1861 to 8.1 percent. No such data were reported in 1877. The 1899 census indicated a return to the 1841 rate. This census also made explicit mention of racial differences in marriage and cohabitation. "Unions by mutual consent were more than three times as prevalent among colored as among whites . . . Of the total unions among whites 81 per cent were lawful marriages. Of the total unions among colored 28 per cent were lawful marriages."[34] Any changes associated with the process of abolition are undocumented, with the thirty-eight-year interval between the 1861 and 1899 censuses. Moreover, none of the census data included information on parental status at birth.

The incidences of ecclesiastic recognition of paternity *after* the initial baptism also experienced a slight increase as final emancipation approached. Records from the headquarters of the bishops and archbishops of Havana held the first of this type of recognition for people of color as of 1859.[35] For whites, post-baptismal paternal recognitions appear in the ecclesiastical records as early as 1804.[36] In the first year of such documents for a child of color, one legitimization was reported. In this case, a freed African couple recognized and legitimized the two children they had had prior to their marriage of the same year.[37] By 1871, the number of these later Afro-Cuban paternity recognitions had risen to twenty-one, and there were four legitimizations reported. The peak number was reached in 1887, a year after final emancipation (see table 5.2). The families found in the ecclesiastic recognition or legitimation records are those who accepted a degree of conformity with the norms of Hispanic society. They realized the social benefits their children received by something as simple as having two surnames, which was standard for freeborn legitimate children.

Researcher Michael Zeuske has analyzed how the absence of one or both surnames remained an indelible stain of past bondage and illegitimacy in late nineteenth- and early twentieth-century Cuba. As former slaves gained their freedom and encountered the bureaucratic and legal apparatus of the state, they were often simply classified on the basis of their surnames. To be recorded as someone *sin otro apellido* (without another surname) continued the marginalization begun in slavery into the post-emancipation period.[38] Some corrected this omission by reclaiming

Table 5.2. Afro-Cuban post-baptismal paternal recognitions

Year	Recognitions	Recognition with legitimations	Year	Recognitions	Recognitions with legitimations
1858		1	1876	17	9
1859	1	1	1877	24	3
1860	4	0	1878	28	6
1861	4	0	1879	20	1
1862	6	1	1880	15	6
1863	15	0	1881	16	12
1864	6	3	1882	29	9
1865	3	1	1883	28	6
1866	5	2	1884	29	6
1867	10	7	1885	16	10
1868	14	5	1886	14	2
1869	15	4	1887	30	5
1870	14	3	1888	16	5
1871	21	4	1889	12	3
1872	6	10	1890	11	9
1873	12	7	1891	16	16
1874	22	9	1892	12	18
1875	7	2	1893	3	10

Source: Reconocimientos, leg. 3, exp. 8 (1858) to leg. 116, exp. 61 (1893).

the names of undocumented fathers. The people approaching the Church to complete this task quietly utilized the available legal tools to ensure that at least their textual marginalization was minimized.

Some of the recognitions occurred in the same year as the child's birth, but most occurred much later, by an average of nine years.[39] In one of the more tardy of these cases, a free moreno father acknowledged paternity thirty-four years after the birth of the first of his two children born to a free morena woman. This 1879 petition does not include an explanation of the delay. Although the petition lists both parents as free, one cannot assume that slavery had not complicated their family life. Either one of the parents may have been enslaved at some earlier point.[40] Take for example free moreno Cipriano Valdés's 1877 paternity declaration. It was only through the annotation of his Lucumi ethnicity that his previous bondage was known. His daughter Cornelia Cipriana was born much earlier, in 1841, with only her enslaved morena creole mother, Justa, listed. When the couple married in 1864 both were free. However, they waited another thirteen years to request clerical legitimation for their daughter.[41]

Marital legitimizations of children were generally delayed much longer than the recognition of paternity. The former was a much more complicated procedure. For example, in 1871 legitimation occurred on average eleven years after the birth of the couple's first child. In the most protracted case of 1871, two *morenos ingenuos* (blacks born into freedom) married and legitimated their four children some twenty-seven years after the birth of the first child. The couple, José del Carmen Luna and Loreto Manzano, had married as early as 1863 but had not asked the Church to change the status of their children until nine years after their marriage. Unfortunately again, this record does not contain any explanation of these delays. The couple only indicated that they were poor, and they married to fulfill their commitment to their Church, themselves, and their children.[42] This record has another unique feature. Although Loreto had been initially baptized in 1824 with her parents unknown, in her children's baptism both maternal grandparents were listed. The similar omission of parents also occurred in the baptismal record of one of Loreto's children. Her third child had been baptized in 1849 with *padres no conocidos* (father unknown) listed.[43] This alludes to a practice described in chapter 3: earlier in the nineteenth century, some priests would not register the name of either parent for children born out of wedlock.[44] It is only when Afro-Cuban families actively sought correction of their legal status, as controlled by Church-recording practices, that the nature of private family bonds became apparent.

As the Church imposed official checks on the baptismal indications of parentage, people of color found other ways to use these documents to suggest heritage. In a few cases, relatives of the omitted fathers presented themselves as godparents. This practice is revealed in subsequent documents of parental recognition. In several of these cases, fathers explicitly stated that their relatives had been the godparents of their children and in others similarities between last names are suggestive. For example, in 1881, when pardo ingenuo José Ochoa y Flores legally recognized his daughter, twenty-five-year-old Justa Germana, the supporting documents reveal that both his mother and brother earlier had acted as godparents to the child at her baptism. But José was completely absent from the baptismal certificate, which followed the standard practice of reporting a *padre no conocido* for mulatto and black children.[45] Such unreported but socially known family connections are apparent in another case from 1885. The *moreno* Pablo García sought official annotation of legitimacy for himself and his siblings after their parents' deaths. He testified to Church officials that his parents had legitimated their children by marrying well before their deaths. Pablo also noted that he had in fact acted as godfather to two of his siblings, even though his father was never mentioned in any of the original baptisms.[46] Such acts remind us that the official documents only tell part of the story. They obscure many social bonds that Afro-Cubans enjoyed but were not expressed outside their intimate circles.

Church records also reveal the increase in internal migration of individuals and families of color as slavery gradually declined. In Espíritu Santo's 1867 registries, only thirteen parents in 178 infant baptisms were registered with non-African, non-Havana origins. By 1877, that figure had increased to 30 of 138 baptisms and in 1887 to 45 of 150 baptisms. The 1867 migrants arrived from areas largely within the province of Havana. By 1887, however, their origins were much further afield. Migration from Cuba's coastal town of Trinidad was prominent within this group, followed by Puerto Príncipe and Bayamo. These three towns had experienced some of the greatest difficulties associated with the Ten Years' War. That the last two had been especially hard hit likely contributed to the increased migration to Havana.[47]

SLAVERY, FREEDOM, AND AFRO-CUBAN FAMILY STRUCTURES

As slavery waned, Afro-Cuban families were constructed in various forms based on the status of the parents and their legal relationship to each other. Continuing a trend first observed after 1820, children of single mothers represented the majority of infant baptisms in this period. Beyond single mothers, parent couples appeared in various arrangements. One example of these forms comes from the documentary record of the family of the morena libre Marcelina Cárdenas. She initially appeared in the 1877 baptismal records of Espíritu Santo as a single mother and with the above description of her color and free status.[48] Yet, the description of this family as a single-parent one was erroneous. Six years after this first documentation of Marcelina, her mate, a man of unknown status and race, petitioned for the recognition of his paternity of this child and another born in 1881. The associated documents also indicated that the couple shared a Havana residence.[49] Therefore, based on the collected documents we have a co-residential couple and their offspring who can now be easily reclassified as a consensual nuclear family. Such classification would not have been possible without compilation of the family's various appearances in documents created over several years. Marcelina later baptized another child for whom the father remained unnamed.[50] At this point it becomes unclear if that child was born to the initial pair, or if Marcelina had found another unnamed partner.

On occasion, men of color appear in the recognition documents in association with children of different mothers. Such is the case of the pardo ingenuo Clemente Bergara of Matanzas. On June 15, 1871, he recognized three children. The first child, José Clotilde, had been born in 1857 and initially baptized as the child of unknown parents. However, Clemente's recognition petition reveals that the child's mother was actually the parda ingenua Yrene Rodríguez.[51] The next two children were born in 1860 and 1864 to another parda woman, Dominga Ferrer. In neither case did Clemente marry the women.[52]

In a similar case, the link between the free moreno José del Pie y Faura and his female partners is not so obvious. His separate recognitions of paternity were several years apart, although two of the children were born within a two-month period. In November 1867, the enslaved morena Dorotea Domínguez gave birth to his daughter Eugenia. This child was baptized at the inter-mural Havana parish of Santa Angel.[53] In January 1868, the enslaved parda Jacinta Campos gave birth to another of José's daughters, Luciana. The two families lived in different parts of Havana. Luciana was baptized just outside the city wall in the extramural parish of Monserrate.[54] Their close dates of birth were not the only characteristics that Jose's daughters shared. Even though both

"Native Colored Family." Source: United States, War Department, Cuban Census Office, *Report on the Census of Cuba, 1899.*

mothers were enslaved, both children were baptized as free. Despite these similarities, the legal relationships the two girls had with their father differed. José provided legal recognition to Eugenia a little more than a year after her birth, in December 1868. His recognition of Luciana was delayed by more than six years, however, and occurred in September 1874. At the same time, Luciana was also legitimated. José maintained his relationship with her mother Jacinta on a long-term basis, and the two married. The couple had other children in 1872 and 1881.[55] It is not apparent what happened to José's relationship with Dorotea.

The documents also reveal how the moreno ingenuo Francisco Sesabier from the town of Regla also killed two birds with one stone with respect to paternity. In February 1884, he declared his paternity of three children. The first and third were born to the free morena Ciriaca Medina in December 1873 and April 1875, respectively. The second was born to another woman of color in November 1874. These dates suggest that Francisco's relationships with these women overlapped each other. Interestingly, the documents reveal that while Francisco did not live with either of the women, they lived at numbers 66 and 88 of the same street in the village of Regla, across the harbor from Havana.[56]

Another family type was one in which the couple first recognized children born out of wedlock, later married, and then had additional legitimate children. The family of Simón Carsi and Anastasia Sánchez followed this pattern. Five of their children were baptized at Espíritu Santo between 1876 and 1883. The first of their children encountered in the records was registered shortly after her birth as the couple's hija natural. There Simón is listed as a free black creole and Anastasia is described as a free African from the Congo.[57] Anastasia subsequently had twins, who were registered solely in her name. Simón is absent from both baptismal certificates.[58] But in 1881 and 1883, the couple had two other children that were by now legitimate at the time of their baptisms.[59] Other families also demonstrated this pattern. The family of the pardos libres Joaquín Díaz and Susana Osma was another in which the first born child was not legitimate but was recognized as a hijo natural by both parents. This daughter was born in 1873.[60] The couple later married by 1876 and their next five children were baptized as legitimate.[61]

In other cases, either the mother or father of a recognized child would later marry someone else and have other legitimate children. While it is impossible to determine to what extent the relationship between the first child and the parent continued, a legal obligation still existed. This occurred with the pardo Manuel Mantilla. He first appears in the Espíritu Santo baptismal records as the father of a hija natural born to an unclassified woman in 1876.[62] He reappears six years later in 1882 as the legitimate father of another child, born to a woman of parda classification like him. That couple would have two more children before disappearing from the records of Espíritu Santo.[63] A similar situation also occurred for the family of the morena Beatríz Acosta. She first appears in the baptismal records of Espíritu Santo as the enslaved mother of her daughter baptized in July 1878. No father was recorded at that time.[64] Two months later, the same child was baptized for a second time under a different name. This time, Beatríz's parents were listed, and she herself was described as free. Additionally, a father was named and the child recognized as an hija natural.[65] Their relationship is confirmed by documents from the bishop of Havana's archives, which indicate that in that same month the free black craftsman Jorge Gómez had petitioned the Church for the acknowledgment of this child and another daughter he had fathered with Beatríz in 1875. It is also clear from the documents that the couple lived separately.[66] The existing legal system permitted them to either create one non-residential family or to live so that each parent constructed separate relationships with their children without being married to each other.

Beatríz Acosta next appears in 1879 in the baptismal records, again as a single mother. Interestingly, the maternal grandmother listed is not the same as that given for previous children. The 1879 name is the same as that previously listed as the mother of Jorge Gómez, although he was not mentioned directly.[67] This hints, without proof, at his continued involvement with the family. Beatríz makes a final appearance in the 1882 baptismal record of another daughter. By then her civil status had changed. This child was born of the legitimate marriage of Beatríz and a new man, Remigio Díaz.[68] Again, the legal system bonded Jorge Gómez to his daughter by Beatríz but did not restrict parents taking other partners for themselves. This pattern may be read as a precursor to the blended families we accept as unproblematic today.

The baptismal records became more complete with the passing of time. For example, when the first child of the parda Rosario Cárdenas appears in the records in 1876, only her name and that of her mother were entered.[69] With the next two children born in 1878 and 1881 respectively, both maternal grandparents were listed, along with their origins.[70] In the registration of the last of her children found in the records, the father had provided recognition of his paternity. The black creole father, Esteban Azpeitia, was listed along with the names and regional origin of his parents. A final important piece of information found in the baptismal registration is that both parents lived together, along with the maternal grandmother.[71] When the family of Polonia Mendíola first appeared in the baptismal records of Espíritu Santo in 1857, only a few facts were noted. She was an enslaved parda owned by Señora Doña Lorenza Mendíola de Croza who had managed to have her daughter baptized as free.[72] Twenty years later, a 1878 request to recertify her baptism indicated that Polonia had been born to an enslaved black woman in 1831. By the time of the request Polonia had gained her freedom, again following the pattern of the majority of Cuba's formerly enslaved people.[73]

Polonia next appears in the documents in 1888, when her son, Ricardo Mendíola, baptized the first of his legitimate children included in the records of Espíritu Santo. Since this occurred after final emancipation, it is not certain that Ricardo shared the good fortune of his sister in being baptized as free. But he did list himself as a coachman, one of the more respected professions then open to people of color. Polonia at this time lived with Ricardo and his wife.[74] At the baptism of another of her son's children in 1895, Polonia was listed as deceased and the name of Ricardo's father was listed for the first time; Ricardo reclaimed his surname, Croza.[75] The family had therefore gone from an enslaved one in which only matrilineal links were recorded to a free one in which paternity was consciously reasserted.

Such reassertion of family links took various forms. Of the approximately 6,300 baptismal and recognition records reviewed for this study, one unusual case of non-marital paternal recognition from this period deserves special mention. In the 1876 baptism of his daughter, the freedman Luís Santochi Dovi-Yalena presented himself as a prince of the Araraes Sabalu African nation and listed his parents as Acovejachi Dovi Yalenn and Fume Glono.[76] This is the only case of this type to both affirm both the specific names of the African grandparents and assert royal heritage. A similar declaration of pride in African ethnic heritage appears in the notarial archives of Cienfuegos, in the form of an 1885 paternity declaration:

> The moreno Antonio Pérez, without second surname, native of the town of Yisá, of the Lucumí nation in Africa, single, fifty-one years of age, field

worker and from this place . . . the neighborhood Pueblo Nuevo . . . says: in consequence of the relationship which he had with one of his class, morena libre Regina Pared, native and citizen of this city, single, adult, and already deceased, the latter gave birth the twentieth of December in 1878 to a child that her son and that of an unknown father and was baptized . . . with the name Julio Domingo the thirtieth of January [1879] . . . Concerning this child, moreno Antonio Pérez . . . declares and acknowledges as his natural son the named Julio Domingo . . . who therefore gains the right to alimony and education and to follow him as his heir before the law . . . empowering him to use his surname; wishing to record for the proposed opportunity that the grandparents of the acknowledged child were Yícocun Hova and Fá Chipe, both native of the aforementioned town of Yísa and already deceased, and the person appearing [Antonio Pérez] was baptized about the year 1850 [at age sixteen] in the parish church of the hamlet of Guaracabuya, as belonging to the dotación of the cattle yard called "El Plantanal."[77]

This father carefully provided his son with not only the promise of material support, but also with a clearly articulated lineage that is meant to instill genealogical pride. Antonio Pérez was ensuring that his African family heritage was not ignored in the documentary record, nor lost to his son.

The story of the family of Luciana Peñalver also demonstrates how legal recognition of family bonds became more complete in later documents. Luciana experienced several transformations as slavery ended. She was first recorded in the baptisms of Espíritu Santo in 1874 simply as an enslaved single mother. The only other identity marker was the name of her owner, Don Isidro Domínguez. No information about her family was offered. Her next child was born in 1876 and Luciana was found in the same situation.[78] The 1877 and 1878 baptisms of other children found Luciana with a new owner, Doña Antonia Silva, and with the 1878 child, the maternal grandparents were listed for the first time.[79] But with the baptism of a child born in 1879, she was free, following the pattern of many of Cuba's formerly enslaved people who gained their freedom well before final emancipation in 1886.[80] The other major transformation in Luciana's life was the acknowledgment of the paternity of these children by the free black cook Melchor Peñalver. He had first erroneously appeared as the legitimate father of one of their daughters in 1880, although the couple were not actually married at that point.[81] In 1882 Melchor officially declared paternity of this child, a son born in

1881, and the three born in 1874, 1876, and 1877 respectively. The child born to Luciana in 1879 was not mentioned, suggesting either that the couple avoided the expense of recognizing a deceased child or Melchor was not the father. The couple married at some point before 1884, when the first of four other, now legitimate, children was baptized.[82] The collection of documents demonstrates the complexity of the family's relations as it left slavery and took steps for the legal acknowledgment of the bonds between its members.

In recognizing his children born out of wedlock, Melchor Peñalver may have followed a tradition established by his brother. Eight years earlier, in 1874, Luis Peñalver, a freeborn black craftsman, also recognized his paternity of several children. The sibling relationship emerges from their separate appearances in the baptismal records of Espíritu Santo and recognition documents of the bishop of Havana. Both had the same parents listed, Gregorio and Ygnacia Peñalver. In fact, both men named the first of their reported children after their father. Luis's daughter Luisa Gregoria was born in 1867 and Melchor's son, Gregorio Vicente, was born in 1874. Both of these children were baptized only in their mothers' names, without the initial acknowledgment of the fathers.[83] However, while Melchor and Luciana eventually married, the documents do not indicate that Luis and the mother of his children, Teresa Rubio, did. Luis only petitioned for the legal recognition of these children. In this case, like that of Luciana, Teresa had once been enslaved. However, the date she gained her freedom is not clear. In the baptismal record of Luisa Gregoria her status was not listed. The next child born in 1868 was registered with *padres reservados* (parents' identity withheld). For two subsequent children, Teresa appeared in the documents as a *parda libre*. Knowledge of her enslavement comes from a copy of her baptism included in her children's recognition file, which indicated she was born to an enslaved mother in 1848.[84] An additional unique feature of this recognition process is that Teresa used the moment to reassert her family's surname. Teresa had been known at various times by the surnames Zayas or Lavin, which may have been associated with her previous owners. At her birth, her mother had been enslaved to a Don Manuel Zayas. With the recognitions, Teresa claimed that her family name was really Rubio, the surname of her mother.

The family of the two African ethnics Francisco Sevillano and Victoriana Sánchez experienced similar dramatic changes in the final two decades of Cuban slavery. The couple first appear in the documents with an 1876 petition to recognize and legitimate their children born out of wedlock. Francisco described himself as an enslaved African from the Macua nation. His wife was also African, from the Ganga people. Unlike Francisco, Victoriana was initially registered as an emancipada. Their first child was born in 1869 and baptized at the Havana parish of Pilar, outside the old city wall. Only the mother's name appears on the certificate. The same was true for the next two children. However, in those cases, the family was registered at different Havana parishes, first at Espíritu Santo and then at Santo Angel; and Victoriana's condition differed each time. For the second child born in 1871, she had gone from being an emancipada to a morena libre consigned to a white patron, an infantry captain. With the third child in 1875, she was simply a morena libre, without further qualification. The couple returned to the parish of Espíritu Santo and married in December of that year.[85] Yet Francisco remained enslaved. And his condition had not changed by the time of his final appearance in the documents, the 1877 baptism of the next, now legitimate, child.[86]

These cases are exceptional in that they allow the tracing of changes in parents' partners. In cases where the mother is listed solely and her parents are not named, it is difficult to establish the relationship between persons of similar names. In this way, it becomes easier to trace families for which both parents and both sets of grandparents appear. With single mothers predominating in the registries, the task becomes more difficult. One family stands out as the only case among Espíritu Santo's Afro-Cubans in which only the father was named. The documentary record for the family of the freeborn pardo Rafael Suárez is a very unusual one. In both 1878 and 1879 he baptized a child with solely his name. In both instances, the mother remained unlisted, with the annotation *madre reservada* (mother's identity withheld).[87] Historian Ann Twinam has demonstrated that such ascriptions were not infrequent within white populations of colonial Spanish America. She attributes their occurrence to a general desire on the part of fathers to protect the honor of mothers by guarding their anonymity from potentially judgmental public scrutiny. The honor of a white woman would have been threatened in cases of out-of-wedlock birth, of racial difference between parents, and other forms of parental dissent.[88] Such considerations for the honor of women of color were less common but not unknown. The mother of Rafael Suárez's children could have been from any social category, but it was her honor that merited protection. If she were African-descended, then Rafael's action attributed to her a sense of honor that most did not receive. While his action may also have shielded the children from the social stigma associated with slavery, the late date of the children's births ensured that they would have been born free regardless of whether the mother herself was enslaved. If she were a white woman, Rafael was attempting to preserve any honor that a relationship with a man of color would have compromised, but doing so would have cost the children the social prestige of at least second-generation whitening.

For Espíritu Santo and in the records of the Cuban bishops of this period, only a few baptisms clearly linked a father of color to a mother possessing the Doña title generally reserved for whites. In an 1885 baptism, the pardo Manuel Cabada y Gómez declared a hijo natural with Doña Fermina Valdés. However, no parents were listed for Fermina and by virtue of the infamous Valdés surname, she was likely an orphan of questionable racial background.[89] In another case, the mother's white identity is much less ambiguous. In 1884, the freeborn pardo Lorenzo Cortes in the rural town of Batabano recognized his paternity of a son born to Doña Serafina Pérez. The mother's parents were listed as Don and Doña, respectively. This declaration came thirteen years after the child's birth and after the death of Serafina and the marriage of Lorenzo to a parda wife.[90] Perhaps with her death, Serafina's honor was no longer at stake.[91]

It is unusual for the honorific titles of Don and Doña to appear in the baptismal records for parents of color in Espíritu Santo. Spanish colonial law during Cuba's slaveholding period prohibited the application of such an honor to people of African descent, but this policy may have lost some of its rigor as final abolition approached. Five consecutive such baptisms were registered in January 1877. In most of these cases the family does not appear in subsequent baptisms, which implies that they did not have extended contact with the parish. Nor was there any marginal annotation of a possible error in racial categorization, as frequently is the case when such errors occurred.[92] One can only speculate on these families' social status. Perhaps they were families of color who informally gained the titles as recognition of some advanced social position. Yet, that their children's baptisms remained confined to the book of color suggests that their legal advancement was limited. One specific family of this type is insightful on this point. Late in 1877, the registration of a child with Don and Doña parents and grandparents occurred for the Solano and Álvarez family. Yet, when this same family later baptized another child in 1879, the person previously listed as Don Pedro Solano became the pardo libre Pedro Solano. The same occurred for his wife, who was listed earlier as Doña Juana Álvarez.[93] Even though the family's racial identity was now known to the parish officials, no revisions were made to the earlier baptism. By the 1880s more Afro-Cubans were claiming the Don and Doña titles in the baptism of their children. Initially this shift was made by men who were militia leaders or in public service. This is seen in the case of José Bernabeu and the baptisms of his three children. For the first two, in 1856 and 1867, José was listed as a pardo ingenuo. However, with the 1880 baptism of the last child, the listing of José as a "Captain of the Havana Firefighters" seems to have qualified him for the honorific "Don."[94] Although some parda women had on occasion appeared with this designation earlier, José Bernabeu was one of the first Afro-Cuban fathers to be given it in what appears as an intentional act. In 1880, the moreno Don Bonifacio Perez Arcano, the freeborn son of an enslaved morena mother, similarly claimed this honorific title, based on his service as a sergeant in a colored militia battalion.[95] Others followed, and by the 1890s these titles were more consistently applied to the now entirely free population of Afro-Cubans as they strove for racial equality.

CONCLUSION

The available sources allow for only a few direct comparisons of the effects of abolition on family formation in Cuba with those in other slave-holding societies in the Americas. The Cuban census data indicate a decline in marriage rates among people of color during the emancipation process and in its wake. This was the exception to the general rule of increased marriage rates found elsewhere in the Americas among freedpeople. However, marriage within Cuban slavery seems to have been initially more prevalent than the British-American experience. Cuba's declining rate therefore needs to be seen in context: marriage was a comparatively new form of legitimacy in other areas. By contrast, both free and enslaved Afro-Cubans had a long history of accessing it. Additionally, Cuban family formation was not simply limited to the choice between illegitimacy and marriage. The category of recognized children allowed for the establishment of legal bonds between parents and children without the need of marriage. Therefore, even in light of the lower marriage rate, one should not infer that Cubans of color were less committed to family. Many such families had a unique status not found elsewhere.

Finally, abolition in Cuba was not solely a process by which slave families became free families. The modes of family formation among Cuba's enslaved people varied over the course of the nineteenth century. As seen above, many families slowly gained their freedom before final abolition occurred in 1886. When this fact is added to the frequent occurrence of inter-racial family formation it becomes difficult to speak of Cuban "slave families" in the final decades of slavery. Instead, some families were composed of members who never experienced slavery while other members had endured it for the majority of their lives. However, all were deeply affected by it. So as children born free to slave mothers, African emancipados, and white men were found in respective unions with enslaved people, their families were neither completely enslaved nor completely free. These situations demonstrate the classificatory flexibility that continued to characterize Cuban families as they frequently crossed the standard social boundaries. Although Afro-Cuban families did not conform to the model of their white counterparts, they did demonstrate many of the same elements and even shared family members across racial boundaries. Cuban social reproduction continued to follow racial rules, but these were never rigid ones.

6

"Regenerating" the Afro-Cuban Family, 1886–1940

SINFONÍA EN NEGRO MAYOR
Enrique Andreu (1915)

SYMPHONY IN BLACK MAJOR

Te canto por ser negra; pues, en la vida
todo cuanto sea negro es de mi amor
que, con luto, su espíritu prestigia

en voluptuosidades raras de color . . .
Nada me importa el histórico pasado
vivido por tu raza, ni su fausta leyenda;
cual pintor unicromo, sólo el matiz
  recabo
del paisaje previsto a través de la senda.
Mis ritos pasionales perecen [pues] muy
  negra;
mi esperanza, por prieta, parece de
  carbón; y
siendo el porvenir mi más densa tiniebla,
  ¿por
qué no ha de ser bruna mi querida
  ilusión? . . .
Por eso yo te canto, mujer negra, mi
  amada . . .

I sing to you, woman, for being black,
for in Life all that is black has my love
And that, with mourning, your spirit
  valorizes
In rare pleasures of color . . .
It does not matter to me, the historic past
Lived by your race, nor its Faustian legend,
Which the monochromatic painter only
  outlines
As a landscape seen only from the road.
My passionate rites perish [then] very
  black,
My hope, so dark, seems like coal, and
  Being my
Future such dense darkness, why should it
  not be
Brown, my dear
  illusion? . . .
For this I sing to you, black woman, my
  love . . .

Y haciéndote mi Diosa preferida y macabra,	And I shall make you my favorite and macabre
en la noche del Tiempo y el Espacio infinito,	Goddess; on the endless night and in the infinite
salmodiaré tu Gloria rimando con mis alas	Space, I will sing your glory, rhyming with my
el acompañamiento de un erótico mito . . .	Wings the accompaniment of an erotic myth . . .
Y entonces: todo negro, pero negro de magia,	And then: all is black, but black like magic,
negro alucinatorio, negro de apoteosis, será (por	Hallucinatory black, black apotheosis; it will be
los Oficios) fecundación que haya lanzado para	(By the gods) the fertility that has launched to
el mundo lo negro de su Gnosis . . .	The world, blackness of your Gnosis . . .
Y los milagros negros dirán al Universo	And black miracles will tell the Universe of
las negruras fatales de los negros enigmas	The fatal blackness of black enigmas
contenidos, ocultos, por quienes, como negros	Contented, hidden by those, who like black
dardos, disparan los más blancos estigmas.	darts, shoot the most white stigmas.
Estigmas que no dañan mis espíritu de vida;	Stigmas that do not harm my joy for life, for,
pues, mujer, tu negrura, sugiriendo del Amor, me	woman, your blackness, suggesting Love, hid me
oculta con su sombra; cuyo luto prestigia mis	with its shadow and whose mourning validates my
voluptuosidades raras de color . . .	rare pleasures of color . . .

THE RACIAL PRIDE ASSERTED BY AFRO-CUBAN WRITERS SINCE the early nineteenth century found new form and urgency after the abolition of Cuban slavery in 1886 and in the context of Cuban anti-colonial struggles against Spain. Nation-building required acceptable definitions of citizenship, with new political rights and responsibilities. For Afro-Cubans, inclusion in the nationalist project had to be earned and structured against negative white presumptions. The poet Enrique Andreu was one of many to advance such efforts in the ideological terrain. In focusing on love and reproductive "fertility" to elevate Afro-Cuban experience above its "Faustian legend" and other limitations of the "monochromatic painter," he joined other Afro-Cubans in reshaping the sexual economy of race into a nationalist frame and giving Cuban blackness new post-colonial value. They did not do so in isolation. They were participants in a wider discourse on Cuban identity that contained voices from multiple political and social backgrounds.

JOINING RACE AND FAMILY IN THE TURN-OF-THE-CENTURY NATIONALIST PROJECTS

By the end of the nineteenth century, the dominant Euro-Cuban nationalist vision represented Cuba's cultural identity as essentially Spanish in origin, but distinguished by geographic uniqueness and the unfortunate, although now transcended, experience of slavery.[1] This emphasis on a European cultural heritage provided white Cuban nationalists with a means to justify Cuba's membership in the family of modern civilized nations, as opposed to that of the presumably barbarous, uncivilized countries of the world who did not have the right to political sovereignty.[2] This outlook ignored possible inclusion of the African-based components of Cuba's ethnic identity, despite their continuation within the Afro-Cuban population. Leading Euro-Cuban nationalists believed that any residual African practices eventually would disappear in light of their incompatibility with the nation's modernizing destiny.[3]

While such rejection of African-based components fostered within much of turn-of-the-twentieth-century Cuban nationalism a monocultural outlook, this nationalism was decidedly multi-racial. Instead of holding a racially homogeneous view of Cuban ethnicity, based on pure European biologically descent (comparable to what occurred in the United States), Cuban intellectuals acknowledged that their nation could contain several races, with sufficiently acculturated blacks, whites, mulattoes, and Asians peacefully co-existing. Race mixture was also part of this vision. A segment of the white leadership accepted that the ongoing miscegenation common in Cuban society through relationships of women of color with white men was largely unproblematic since it would eventually whiten the darker components beyond recognition.

This mono-cultural, multi-racial, and reproductively permissive approach to *cubanidad* (Cubanness) can also be found in the political writings of the Cuban national hero José Martí (1853–1893). He famously provided the most concise formulation of the multi-racial nation in his phrase "Lo cubano es más que blanco, más que mulato, más que negro" (Cuba is more that white, more than mulatto, and more than black).[4] Yet Martí, despite his consistent articulation of a belief in racial equality, placed that equality within a limited cultural context. He did not consider that cubanidad might embrace an Afro-Cuban mentalité or symbolism. This limitation is seen when Martí asks himself the rhetorical question, "Would you marry your daughter to a black man?" His answer was exceptional for a white father of his era, when few amorous unions between white women and Afro-Cuban men received white public approval. He responded in a positive, but qualified, manner that any father would want the best for his daughter and he would approve of a black groom "if he demonstrates not only the conditions of raw and simple generosity . . . but also the conditions of exceptional character and culture necessary to have my daughter love him."[5] With this approval of only the *exceptional* black man, Martí implies that ordinary men of color are culturally undeveloped, but could eventually educate themselves in ways appropriate to contemporary Cuban society.

Several white authors took a more eugenic approach to Cuba's racial future and suggested that those who were perceived as incapable of the appropriate level of cultural assimilation were doomed for racial extinction. These writers designated the Afro-Cuban masses as the likely victims of that process.[6] From the middle of the nineteenth century through the first two decades of the twentieth, demographic statistics appeared to support the Social Darwinist claims of the most pernicious racists. The Afro-Cuban proportion of the Cuban population had been steadily decreasing since the complete cessation of the slave trade in the late 1860s. In 1827, free and enslaved people of color represented 58 percent of the island's total population.[7] Almost a century later, in 1919 that proportion had dramatically fallen to 28 percent.[8] While it was obvious that large waves of Spanish immigration, deaths from the independence wars, and high mortality rates associated with poverty were contributing factors to this decline, some wondered if Afro-Cuban

Table 6.1. Percentage of Cuban population by race, 1899–1953

	1899	1907	1919	1931	1943	1953
White	66.9	69.7	72.2	72.1	74.4	72.8
Black	14.9	13.4	11.2	11.0	9.7	12.4
Mulatto	17.3	16.3	16.0	16.2	15.5	14.5
Asian	0.9	0.6	0.6	0.6	0.4	0.3

Sources: de la Fuente, "Race and Inequality," 135, and Castellanos and Castellanos, *Cultura afrocubana*, 2:355.

behaviors or culture were not also implicated.[9] Whatever the perceptions of a decreasing Afro-Cuban presence, through the remainder of the first half of the twentieth century the racial proportions of the Cuban population held fairly constant, with only a slight increase in the proportion of whites within the population (see table 6.1).[10]

In attending to the demographic and cultural elements of race, nationalist intellectuals also considered family organization and gender norms in their social and political visions of the nation's future. They attempted to define the normative gender roles and sexual practices by which the legitimate members of the nation were to be characterized.[11] Their aim was to reform the local sexual economy of race in a manner that they regarded to be more nationally appropriate, more in line with what they considered beneficial, civilized characteristics. So while Cuban political liberalism was radical in prioritizing national values and the concept of sovereignty, it remained conservative with respect to gender and family-formation practices. Instead, its adherents remained committed to patriarchal social models. Among middle-class and elite Cubans, before the 1930s the Spanish adage "El hombre está hecho para la calk y la mujer para la casa" (Men are made for life in the streets, women for life within the home) succinctly captured the separate nature of male and female spheres of activity.[12] White men were publicly to lead both their families and their communities by demonstrating a masculinity which embodied intellectual ability, physical prowess, and civic responsibility. In contrast, women were to have important domestic responsibilities, solely under men's authority as daughters, wives, and mothers. They were to be selfless and sentimental, nurturing and pious, "the perfect counterpoints to materialistic and competitive man, whose strength and

Table 6.2. Proportion of illegitimacy by age and race, 1919

	Percentage of illegitimacy		
Age	All races	Native whites	Colored
Under 5 years	23.2	13.6	49.9
5 to 9 years	23.5	13.5	52.0
10 to 14 years	24.1	13.5	53.9
15 to 19 years	25.3	14.0	55.2
20 to 14 years	25.0	12.8	54.8
25 and over	23.9	11.0	56.8

Source: Cuba, Dirección del Censo, *Census of the Republic of Cuba* (Havana: Maza, Arroyo, 1921), 366, cited in Stoner, *From the House to the Streets*, 64.

rationality suited him for the rough and violent public world."[13] If Cuban women were to possess any social power, it was to be found solely in the moral superiority that they demonstrated through religious piety and that offered no potential challenge to men's authority.[14]

At the turn of the twentieth century, marriage remained the institution through which the family existed as the base that "preserved class and familial authority."[15] Although legal restrictions on the marriage of social unequals were rescinded in 1881, the beliefs that had sustained them continued to inform social patterns into the republic. Cuban marriages continued to be largely endogamous with respect to race, even beyond the elite and into the white working class. In Havana's ecclesiastic marriage records for the period between 1900 and 1940, only 0.5 percent of white men married women of color, and a miniscule 0.2 percent of white women married men of color. Yet, a limited possibility of greater numbers of inter-racial marriages existed in that 13.5 percent of all men wed partners without racial classification, as did 14 percent of all women.[16] Legitimate marriage marked social status and appeared to confirm racial differences in sexual behaviors. The 1919 Cuban national census indicated that approximately an eighth of whites and half of all people of color had been born out of wedlock. Interestingly, the statistics suggest that these rates were increasing for whites while declining for people of color (see table 6.2). And for all races between the 1899 and 1953 census years, the percentage of persons admittedly involved in consensual unions increased from 12.6 to 18.2 among men and from 13.9 to 21.3 among women.[17]

FAMILY, RACE, AND POST-EMANCIPATION
AFRO-CUBAN INTELLECTUALS

Nationalist concerns about the Cuban family were not exclusive to white leaders. Afro-Cubans were actively involved with these issues. They fully participated in late nineteenth- and early twentieth-century attempts to delineate the ideological characteristics of the emergent nation, and employed the concepts of masculinity, femininity, race, and styles of family formation in these projects. Afro-Cuban nationalism, unlike its Euro-Cuban counterpart, however, was informed by the obvious need to minimize the negative perceptions of Afro-Cuban racial identity. As Afro-Cubans presented themselves as individuals and communities with positive social valuation, they attempted to separate the trope of "civilization" from its close association with European racial identity. From the perspective of racialized reproduction, this effort placed Afro-Cuban nationalist intellectuals in a difficult position. They engaged in the seemingly contradictory process of trying to minimize the nationalist discourse on race while simultaneously contributing to the internal reform and strengthening of Afro-Cuban communities. Their racial *regeneración* or "racial uplift" goals contained both a black existential quality and racist assumptions of European cultural superiority. This philosophy argued that through education and moral reform under middle-class guidance, the Afro-Cuban masses would renounce their "primitive" lifestyles and embrace the "civilized" norms of the Euro-Cuban elite.[18]

Imitation of European patriarchal notions of heteronormative sexuality and family formation was a central feature in Afro-Cuban social reform models. They promoted similar visions of patriarchal leadership and female domesticity. In this way, turn-of-the-twentieth-century Afro-Cuban nationalism often failed to address many of the social-reproductive elements of Cuba's racial reality. Afro-Cuban intellectuals tended to minimize discussion of the racist social restrictions experienced by Afro-Cuban men and women and the relative economic and socio-sexual "freedom" of Afro-Cuban women. They also faced an existential question in regard to inter-racial unions. How were Afro-Cuban leaders to provide a new moral compass for racial and national advancement when faced with a stark contradiction between what many perceived as the immoral nature of the consensual unions so prevalent within their communities and a belief popular among some blacks and whites that inter-racial unions were essential to both the cultural assimilation and economic progress for people of color? Ultimately, instead of questioning the nature of the Euro-Cuban patriarchy and realizing its inappropriate fit for their community, late nineteenth- and early twentieth-century Afro-Cuban writers explained the Afro-Cuban masses' supposed non-conformity to these models in terms of their lack of education and morality which continued as legacies of slavery. Through this strategy, these writers could avoid direct confrontations with racist claims that Afro-Cuban cultural inferiority was a permanent, inescapable state. Instead, they would portray themselves as models for Afro-Cuban racial *regeneración* that the masses could emulate.[19]

Elements of this discourse were developed in a variety of sites, especially in social clubs and periodicals. Within the pages of Afro-Cuban newspapers and columns, gender and class conflicts within their community are easily revealed, as middle-class Afro-Cuban intellectuals attempted to fit elite Euro-Cuban models of gender roles and family relations to the Afro-Cuban community. Afro-Cuban publications such as the magazine *Minerva: Revista Quincenal Dedicada a la Mujer de Color* (Minerva: The Biweekly Magazine for the Woman of Color) and the column "Palpitaciones de la Raza de Color" (Heartbeats of the Colored Race) in the Havana daily newspaper *La Prensa* provide especially useful insights into the place of the family in Afro-Cuban nationalist ideology. Continuing a long-established tradition of Afro-Cuban public polemics, *Minerva* and "Palpitaciones" strove toward a positive image of Afro-Cuban identity and for social and political inclusion.

Minerva was founded by middle-class Afro-Cubans in 1888, shortly after the final abolition of slavery in 1886. From its pages, female authors projected the appropriate intellectual and social orientation of their compatriots.[20] A similar project was pursued by contributors to "Palpitaciones" between August 1915 and September 1916. While *Minerva* was directed almost exclusively toward Cuban women of color, as a column in a mainstream periodical "Palpitaciones" reached a wider audience. The column's editor, Ramón Vasconcelos, intended to present Afro-Cuban issues and concerns before Cubans of all races. In its subtitle, Vasconcelos described the column as "Crónica escrita para negros sin taparrabos, mestizos no arrepentidos y blancos de sentido común" (A chronicle written for blacks without loincloths, unrepentant mulattoes, and whites with common sense). This language expressed both racist stereotypes and community-integrating hopes. Only the blacks worthy of engagement with Vasconcelos were the supposedly cultured ones without any association to the primitiveness symbolized by the loincloth. The "sentido común" attached to whites is intentionally ambiguous, either asking them to practice common sense or prompting them to find common cause with Cuba's other social categories. Following patterns seen since the colonial period in reproductive endogamy and other social relations, Vasconcelos also simultaneously differentiated blacks from *mestizos* (very far skinned, African-descended people) and joined them collectively under *una raza* (a race).

The surviving biographical data on people involved in *Minerva* and "Palpitaciones" are minimal, but suggest that their contributors were typically from families that had lived for a significant period as free people of color under slavery and many were racially mixed to some degree. They represented a numerically small but organized and educated Afro-Cuban class that constructed and presented their visions of the proper relation between Afro-Cuban people and the rest of the nation.[21] For example, one of *Minerva*'s agents in Havana was Angela Rodríguez de Edreira. Baptismal records from Havana's Espíritu Santo parish reveal that she was the illegitimate daughter of a black mother and white father. Although her father never officially established legal paternity, before her marriage Angela had publicly carried his last name. Her husband, Nicolás Edreira, was a tailor and also bi-racial. Unlike his wife, he had been publicly claimed as a hijo natural reconocido by his white father.[22] When the couple married in 1880, both husband and wife were listed as free pardos and there was no indication that either had ever been enslaved.[23] Another of *Minerva*'s Havana agents, Modesta Álvarez de O'Farrill, was also a mulatta with a mulatto husband. Both were themselves the children of mulatto parents. When one of their children was born in 1879, the records revealed no hint of an experience of enslavement for either.[24]

HABANA, 30 DE DICIEMBRE DE 1888

Minerva

REVISTA QUINCENAL DEDICADA A LA MUJER DE COLOR

Año I	Dirección y Administración, Compostela 6	Núm. 6

PUNTOS DE SUSCRIPCION

La suscripción á MINERVA en la Habana está abierta en los puntos siguientes:
Muralla 64, Librería de Alarcia (interior)—Aguacate 88, Sr. Enrique Cos.—Villegas 61, Sr Agustín Izquierdo.—Rayo esquina á S. Rafael, Sra. Dª Julia Milián de Gálvez.—Paula 27 Srita Carolina Fuentes.— S. Nicolás 108. Barbería. y en la Redacción y Administración, Compostela 6.

SUMARIO

¡RAZA DE COLOR ELEVATE!

LA FAMILIA.

SI la raza de color desea cordialmente dignificarse, y ocupar en las funciones públicas el lugar á que están llamados todos los elementos componentes de la sociedad, empiece por formar la familia dentro de los preceptos dictados por la moral, y exigidos por las leyes.

Tenga presente que sin familia no hay organización sociológica posible.

Medite que es irrealizable la familia sin el matrimonio.

Reflexione que sin respeto propio, sin amor ni estimación á los demás individuos de la propia raza, no hay matrimonio; que sin este vínculo sagrado no existe el amor á la gloria, ni hay interés en conservar un nombre limpio que trasmitir á los hijos, ni razón para acumular riquezas que representen privaciones sin cuento, sacrificios supremos, esfuerzos increíbles, pues que no hay á quien dejarlas con amor, ni quien las pida con dolor y con justicia. No hay en fin esa consoladora prolongación de la vida que conocemos con el nombre de sucesión legítima.

Piense que cuando la madre tiene perfecto derecho para titular esposo al padre de sus hijos, se enorgullece con tan augusto título, y ese noble orgullo la eleva de tal modo, que á su altura no llegan por lo regular los dardos de la perversión. Y entonces tiene más autoridad sobre sus hijos porque se les muestra como ejemplo vivo de la dignidad, y del exacto cumplimiento del deber, y casi siempre es imitada, tributándosela desde luego más respeto y más cariño.

Cuando la mujer es esposa del

Minerva, December 30, 1888. Frontispiece.

Ramón Vasconcelos came from a similar background. Born in 1890, he was a very fair-skinned, self-described "mestizo," the illegitimate son of a wealthy white father and a mulatta mother. His parents' relationship was short-lived. His father followed custom by marrying and starting a legitimate family with a white woman. But he maintained a close bond with his racially mixed first son. In fact, in a situation that paralleled the denial of the mulatto family seen in the novel *Cecilia Valdés*, Ramon's father had hoped to raise his son within the new household and encouraged him to live as white. His mother, however, would not tolerate her son's separation from her family. As a compromise, Vasconcelos enjoyed his father's wealth and connections while maintaining strong links to the Afro-Cuban community. Despite the disruptions occasioned by Cuba's second independence war (1895–1898), Vasconcelos completed secondary education and began his professional life as a teacher. After his travels to Mexico and much of southern Europe in 1910, he turned to a career in journalism in Cuba.[25] Upon his return, he founded the newspapers *El Liberal, El Cuarto Poder,* and *Universal.* He also contributed to several others, including *La Prensa.* He held the coveted office of the Historian of Havana from 1920 to 1924. And between 1927 and 1933, he represented Cuban businesses in Europe. He was president of the nationally influential Liberal Party between 1933 and 1940, and he served as a senator from Havana for two separate terms, one beginning in 1936 and the other in 1944. He was also a cabinet minister to President Fulgencio Batista on two separate occasions: minister of public education in 1942 and minister of communications in 1954.[26] This biography is valuable for understanding his public standing and the diverse audience for his writings on race.

Many contributors to *Minerva* and "Palpitaciones" supported the belief that the Afro-Cuban masses would gain respectability and minimize racial discrimination most effectively by first taking responsibility for their and their children's education. One editorial letter to "Palpitaciones" clearly outlines the project of Afro-Cuban social acceptance as one of gaining honor through imitation of Euro-Cuban, or European, behaviors. It states, "We should work with the necessary morals in all our actions and we should try to imitate what is honored and extolled."[27] *Minerva's* authors frequently highlighted the themes of morality, virtue, and civilized action, but they never explicitly delineated which qualities structured this morality, except in the discussion of stable, legitimate families. They advocated for a vigorous, collective struggle against the backwardness presumably persisting in the wake of slavery. One woman writing in *Minerva* explained this project in gendered terms that outlined specific responsibilities for Afro-Cuban women. She noted that for 400 years Cuban women of color "have been the objects of caprice and amusement, the toys of cruel men, but today following the signs of the time . . . we lift ourselves up and make the heroic effort to reconquer the dignity that I ask the heavens to concede to our sisters."[28] In their emphasis on European family forms, many accepted that slavery had taught people of color to live immorally and not provide their children with appropriate family models. In the words of one woman, "the truth is that the period of slavery never produced marital partners, only concubines. But now that it has ended, the degradation also ends." She continues:

> If the colored race sincerely wishes to dignify itself and occupy in public functions a place to which are called all the component elements of the society, [it must] begin to form the family within the rules dictated by morality, and demanded by the laws. It must remember that without the family, sociological organization is not possible. It must recognize that the family without the marriage is unrealizable and reflect that without self-respect, without love, nor esteem for other individuals of the same race, there is no marriage. That without this sacred bond, there is no love for greatness, nor is there interest in conserving a clean name that to can be transmitted to children. There is no reason to accumulate wealth that represents supreme, untold sacrifice and incredible efforts, since there is no one with whom to leave such wealth lovingly nor who request them with pain and justice. In the end, there is not that consolatory prolongation of the life that we know with the name of legitimate succession.[29]

For her, group respectability could only be achieved if legitimate families provided the base for all other social development. It is also important to note the emphasis she places on "without self-respect, without love or esteem for other individuals of the same race, there is no marriage." Here, she implies that marriage should be restricted to partners of the same race. Was she advocating that belief or simply acquiescing to endogamous local custom? In either case, she denied inter-racial consensual unions any positive social value and instead promoted the internal survival of the Afro-Cuban community.

With such belief in the social necessity of marriage, these Afro-Cuban intellectuals generally displayed a tacit patriarchal vision. Although the discussion of gender roles contained in "Palpitaciones" was still linked to a communal emergence from slavery, it also occurred within the context of an emergent Cuban debate over the social value of marriage and divorce mentioned above. Contributors to "Palpitaciones" suggested that Afro-Cuban men "gallantly" take their "rightful" place at the heads of their households while they also become involved in the leadership of their communities. For example, Vasconcelos called upon them to "renovate or die, . . . and accept their responsibilities. For now was the time to enter true manhood."[30] A male reader added, "With hard-working black men, virtuous and unassuming families, happy homes, and decent customs, this completely shows progress, civic aptitudes, and competence for a life of liberty, and above all, . . . we can and should establish the racial pride, naturally favorable for the enjoyment of democracy and knowledge."[31] We see here the suggestion that Afro-Cuban men assume the role of the patriarch within the family. Also, he should become its chief breadwinner, freeing his wife from the necessity of work outside the home. A female reader concurred with these masculinist opinions, suggesting that in society and marriage "el hombre es el más fuerte, el que impone leyes y costumbres" (the man is the strongest, he who makes laws and customs).[32] The Afro-Cuban man's role as father was to be confirmed if he conceived children solely with a wife in official wedlock. Children born to illegitimate relationships only demonstrated that he had not recognized his responsibility for civilized behavior and that he continued in a barbarous state.

Additionally, the discussion of the need for Afro-Cuban self-development, education, and cultural uplift also emphasized the important role of Afro-Cuban women within the proposed patriarchal system. Like the expectations ascribed to the elite Euro-Cuban woman, the Afro-Cuban woman was to assume responsibility for domestic life. As a wife, she was to be affectionate, faithful, discrete, thrifty, and modest: "the angel of the home, the queen of society, and the glory of the nation."[33] Although she may lack "una vasta cultura" (extensive education or culture), her responsibility was to utilize her knowledge in the creation of a suitable home and in the moral education of her children.[34] One female contributor to "Palpitaciones" offered, "The woman's duty is to educate and guide the family from the home."[35] As a decent woman, she was to instill virtue, morality, and proper culture in the next generation by living an exemplary life.[36] Vasconcelos both honored the Afro-Cuban woman and limited her to the community reproduction needs when he described her as "the critical element of regeneration, she is the true touchstone."[37] In this way, he placed much of the responsibility for overall Afro-Cuban social progress with her. Several letters from *Minerva* and "Palpitaciones" readers praising such expressions indicate the acceptance of these gendered views of Afro-Cuban social relations.

This tendency toward a strong patriarchal model was not without some qualification, however. National debates regarding changes in marriage law and the implementation of divorce were occurring between 1914 and 1918 and Afro-Cubans addressed these issues as they related to their community. In an article reprinted in "Palpitaciones" from the journal *Albores* from Camagüey in central Cuba, an Afro-Cuban woman and man, Inocencia Silveira and Mariano Castillo del Pozo responded to a set of questions related to marriage, divorce, and sexual definitions of responsibility and honor. Silveira commented that female fidelity to marriage depends on the contributions of her mate, as well the marital respect she receives. Thereby she rejects the unequivocal position expressed by Vasconcelos. For her, husband and wife shared the responsibility of protecting the honor of the family and neither was more powerful than the other. "In marriage, the guardian of honor should be the husband, but the woman should also be the guardian of honor."[38] On the indissolubility of marriage, Silveira demonstrates some ambiguity, but suggests that rigidity of the law is overridden by the level of spousal commitment.

> It is my opinion that the bonds of mutual affection between husband and wife are what form unbreakable marital bonds, not in the structure of the law: because the first is the true foundation of morality and the marital happiness and the second is simply a social codification of natural law. We view with pain cases in which [marriage] without voluntary and mutual bonds are formed only with respect to the law, causing disturbances and immorality.[39]

Castillo del Pozo responded to the question of male marital obligation by also noting it depends on the circumstances, "el ambiente social" (the social environment), and "la idiosincracia del hombre" (the
man's idiosyncrasies). Therefore, a man was to choose a wife who would
be content with his attitudes. As to the permanence of marriage, he suggested that it depends on the compatibility and love of the partners.
Castillo made no direct reference to legal divorce but, comparable to
Silveira, indicates that martial stability rests within a specific couple.[40]

Despite the small qualifications to their social outlook, most of the
writers for both *Minerva* and "Palpitaciones" committed themselves to
the correction of what they perceived as social deviance among Cubans
of color. The obvious standard to follow was that espoused by the Euro-
Cuban or European elite. When Vasconcelos argued that "What consti-
tutes modern nations is the solidarity of the peoples' moral and material interest," he was not proposing the blending of Euro-Cuban and
Afro-Cuban standards, but the demise of the latter. Given the hege-
mony of Euro-centric values, he was denying the possibility of socio-
cultural variation within the boundaries of the Cuban state and also
denying any potential validity to Afro-Cuban culture. Indeed, what
Afro-Cuban intellectuals hoped to demonstrate was that their racial
difference in no way prohibited their acquisition of the appropriate cultural standards of the nation. Generally, they felt the majority of Afro-
Cuban people were living in a dishonorable manner. These sentiments
were not only implied but, at times, stated as fact. Moreover, those who
maintained African-based practices were frequently described as "barbaric," "filthy," and "ignorant." Again, Vasconcelos called only to "blacks
without loincloths."

DISJUNCTIONS BETWEEN AFRO-CUBAN HISTORY
AND CONTEMPORARY REALITY

Afro-Cuban intellectual goals of providing a model that fostered the
social acceptance of the masses ultimately failed in its projection of a
patriarchal vision that did not address specific Afro-Cuban possibilities
in labor relations, public politics, and the sexual economy. Intellectuals
within this community were well aware that the majority of its mem-

bers did not conform to the proposed model, but they continued to believe that such conformity was just a matter of will. Their polemic assessments of the lack of responsible behavior, especially in accusations
directed against black and mulatta women, did not match with the official observations on family-formation patterns. The 1919 Cuban census
suggests that such harsh criticism may have been undeserved since
marriage rates for Afro-Cuban women were slightly higher than those
of Afro-Cuban men. The Afro-Cuban nationalists also failed to incor-
porate into their gender philosophy an acknowledgment of the racial
divisions of labor that continued to be a salient feature of Cuban society
and of which they were all too well aware. Except for a few successful
middle-class individuals, the majority of Afro-Cubans held only the most
menial and under-paid jobs. Afro-Cubans were greatly over-represented
in the lowest levels of agriculture, manufacturing, and domestic service
and greatly under-represented in the professions.[41] The few in the professions did not receive salaries comparable to their white counterparts.
This situation only worsened early in the republic, with ever-increasing
Spanish immigration and continuing employer preference for white workers in every occupation beyond manual labor.[42] Therefore, most Afro-
Cuban men found it difficult to support themselves and their families,
and they could not provide Afro-Cuban women an escape from outside
employment.

Likewise, Afro-Cuban men found it difficult to achieve the community-
leadership component of patriarchy. Beyond perpetuating a supposi-
tion of Afro-Cuban intellectual and cultural inferiority, racist ideology
hindered Afro-Cuban male leadership in two additional ways. First,
most did not achieve the educational prerequisites or the sponsorship
of a strong (and preferably white) patron that success in the Cuban political arena necessitated. With respect to the importance of patronage,
reviewing the republican-era difficulties experienced by the black independence war hero Quintin Bandera demonstrates patronage functioned alongside race to control social mobility. Although his military
capability had earned him the rank of general in the Liberation Army
and he was the highest-ranking Afro-Cuban military leader to survive
into the republic, Bandera did not receive the economic and social
rewards obtained by many white veterans. The only position he was

offered by the newly formed national government was janitor to the congress. His supposed illiteracy may have been a factor in this indignity. But his African phenotype, very dark skin, and unproven accusations of strong adherence to African-derived religious practices also were at play in white disregard for him.[43] Bandera's situation may have been the most egregious of its kind, but many other mulatto and black men suffered similarly. They constantly agitated in political and military ways for equality, but in the early years of the republic many of their efforts were stifled.

Second, just as Afro-Cuban male leadership of non-race-specific constituencies was hindered, so too was their general political effectiveness within those Afro-Cuban organizations with overt political objectives.[44] These objectives were intentionally obstructed both by whites and by more cautious Afro-Cubans. Such was the case with the early twentieth-century formation of Cuba's first and only exclusively African-descended political party, the Partido Independiente de Color, and its 1912 revolt against a racially repressive national law that criminalized all race-based political entities (but which in operational terms only applied to Afro-Cubans). The protestors were perversely charged with anti-white racism and brutally crushed by the Cuban government.[45] Without the possibility of Afro-Cuban political self-determination, in at least public form, Afro-Cuban men were limited in their ability to develop the authority over subordinate men that was another necessary element of patriarchy. Overall, Afro-Cuban patriarchy did not have the necessary foundations for the practice of male authority with which to sustain itself comparable to those that were available to its Euro-Cuban counterpart.

Comparable limitations affected Afro-Cuban female adherence to the patriarchal model. Again, the economic reality of Afro-Cuban life necessitated that the majority of women had to work outside the home. During the early republican era, labor-force participation for Afro-Cuban women was three to five times that of Euro-Cuban women.[46] However, they worked most frequently in low-wage occupations such as laundresses, servants, seamstresses, peasant farmers, tobacco workers, dressmakers, midwives, and healers. Only a few secured reliable occupations as nurses, merchants, teachers, and clerical workers. Until the

1930s and changes in national immigration policy, Afro-Cuban women were continually displaced from meaningful occupations by newly arriving Spanish women, similar to what had occurred in the male case.[47] Therefore, Afro-Cuban women in the first post-abolition generations did not have the time needed to cultivate the domesticity recommended by the intellectuals. Labor outside the home was incompatible with the image of the virtuous, generous, and humble female homemaker.

Just as the Afro-Cuban gendered division of labor was distinct from that of their Euro-Cuban peers, so too was Afro-Cubans' operation within the local sexual economy of race. The predominance of consensual unions among them socially differentiated the group from its white compatriots. Similarly, inter-racial unions, but not marriages, between white men and Afro-Cuban women were encouraged by what U.S. literary critic Vera Kutzinski described as mulatta women's depiction as the height of sensual beauty within Cuba as of the late nineteenth century.[48] By contrast, social taboo and white patriarchal control limited the ability of Afro-Cuban men to form open sexual relationships with white women. Such relationships would see the woman lose her standing in the white community. Moreover, the reproductive potential of such unions was thought not to serve the nation-building project. Republican-era Euro-Cuban women could not socially whiten children conceived with African-descended partners in the way that Euro-Cuban fathers could advance their mixed-race children. Thus, Afro-Cuban women had greater access than did Afro-Cuban men to the presumed social benefits of producing lighter children.

An implication of this observation is that even in the post-emancipation context, *blanqueamiento* (whitening) for Afro-Cuban families continued through women of color. These raced and gendered limitations of Cuba's sexual economy also suggest that blanqueamiento on a national level would have occurred at a much slower rate had such restrictions not existed.[49] But even with these factors, the occurrence and rate of blanqueamiento also depends on further material and ideological practices related to racial meaning. The higher proportion of whites than blacks in Cuba's republican-era population also resulted from the comparably larger loss of Afro-Cubans in the wars of independence, the mortal impact of racially concentrated poverty, continuing Spanish immigration, and restrictions on black immigration. Therefore, members of the smaller African-descended population would have had a smaller pool of potential partners if their choice was racially self-segregated. Such reproductive racial exclusivity was actually what the Afro-Cuban intellectuals' emphasis on legitimate marriage proposed. It pitted Afro-Cuban existential survival against the inter-racial sexual freedom of black and mulatta women.

This form of Afro-Cuban female sexuality was especially troublesome to many writers in the turn-of-the-twentieth-century Afro-Cuban press. They feared that a large proportion of illegitimate unions would contribute to the extinction of people of color, and consistently spoke of the supposed prostitution, ignorance, and lack of mortality of the Afro-Cuban women who involved themselves in these types of relationships. His own family history notwithstanding, Vasconcelos was very critical of these relationships and saw Afro-Cuban women as more immoral than Afro-Cuban men. He argued, "the major obstacle to the achievement of the uplift of the black is the woman." And "the woman of color is the greater co-efficient in consensual unions and in prostitution."[50] Vasconcelos also claimed these inter-racial consensual unions were encouraged by Afro-Cuban mothers, who he imagined telling their daughters, "Listen, I don't want you to be a fool, look for a man who gives you money even though you don't like him and before you marry a black man, I prefer that you become a sweetheart [lover] of a white."[51] He continued, "The mulatta and even the black woman, has just reached puberty when she begins to dream of a white lover . . . what controls this disdain toward men of color? Are there aesthetic reasons? Are there spiritual reasons or economic ones, or is it in the social order? Perhaps all of these combine, but more than the others it is the social."[52] This statement stands as an open challenge to the process of race mixture and whitening. Again, despite his own status as the product of such a relationship, Vasconcelos questions their general utility for the Afro-Cuban community. He had not yet arrived at the appreciation of race mixture expressed by male Cuban intellectuals of the *vanguardista* period of the late 1920s and 1930s. As we will see in chapter 7, both black and white intellectuals of that era came to praise race mixture (in contrast to whitening) for the former's ability to distinguish a "true" Cuban identity in the face of cultural intrusions from the United States.[53]

The desire of intellectuals like Vasconcelos to limit the formation of relationships between white men and women of color extended beyond the discursive arena. Afro-Cuban social clubs and mutual aid societies also attempted to minimize encounters between their female members and white men. When asked for this study about inter-racial relations in the early republican period, two female informants indicated that their clubs had warned them against association with white men. One related the story of an incident from the 1940s that illustrates such pressure on women of color. As a young woman she had been walking home when she encountered her white employer. They innocently stopped to talk. The next day one of the leaders of Unión Fraternal, an Afro-Cuban mutual aid society, threatened her with expulsion if she were to continue such inappropriate behavior.[54] This story makes visible the rarely acknowledged censure of inter-racial amorous unions by African-descended people. Some did not assess the possibilities of whitening and the associated consensual unions favorably.

Turn-of-the-twentieth-century critiques of Afro-Cuban female sexual behavior did not stand without challenge. Other writers rose to their defense. Both men and women claimed that Afro-Cuban women were in fact better educated and more pious than Afro-Cuban men. They offered examples of many Afro-Cuban female teachers and Catholic worshipers. One male reader from the eastern part of the island observed, "In Oriente and Camagüey, the mulatta is almost always superior in culture to the man, she is dignified, moral, and virtuous. The black woman is on the same plane . . . These women know how to be ladies and young ladies in the same proportion as those of the white class."[55] This gender difference in education is supported by 1919 census data that indicate slightly higher literacy rates for Afro-Cuban women than for men (54.4 percent to 51.9 percent).[56] A young woman in Havana, "Indiana," explained both martial separation and the high incidence of consensual unions as the result of both the educational and moral superiority of Afro-Cuban women in comparison to Afro-Cuban men. She added that women made these alternative sexual choices because Afro-Cuban men were often abusive. Even Vasconcelos conceded the existence of domestic abuse in too many Afro-Cuban relationships: "As a general rule, the black man does not marry for the love of his woman, he marries to submit her to brutality . . . This has as its result that the fragile woman associates with whomever treats her with less despotism."[57] He also accepted that if in fact black, mulatto, and white men all had treated the Afro-Cuban woman solely as an object of pleasure and acted abusively toward her, this would indeed have obstructed her ability to create a "proper" home. Thus, he implicated all men who preferred consensual unions to marriage in the decline of the community of color. One woman harshly castigated such a man as "unworthy of being a man, he is a slave to the basic instinct who does not know that the spiritual satisfactions are much sweeter than physical pleasures."[58]

While these accusations focused on contemporary gender conflicts, others re-examined the historical basis for these tensions. As was noted above, several *Minerva* and "Palpitaciones" contributors suggested that the Afro-Cuban inability to establish stable homes was, at least in part, a legacy of slavery. They asserted that under its destructive force Afro-Cuban women had learned to behave sexually *only* as instruments for the reproduction of human capital for their owners. Previous chapters of this study examined the historical evidence for this point and found that broader reproductive and family forms existed. Some eighteenth-century slave owners seemed to have encouraged marriage and familial stability among the charges. It was only in the period of open legal trade (1790–1820) that slave owners were certain in their estimates that the replacement costs of slave purchase were less than the costs associated with raising children.[59] After the end of the legal slave trade in 1820, pro-natal, economic strategies reappeared among some owners.[60] Additionally, the better-situated Afro-Cuban families of the colonial period had availed themselves of Spanish imperial legal resources to maintain family bonds. While they were frequently unsuccessful, they countered slavery's social destructiveness as best they could. Similar caution applies to the emphasis that contributors to *Minerva* and "Palpitaciones" placed on Afro-Cuban women's experience of the unwanted sexual advances of their owners. While such violent behavior undoubtedly occurred, its reproductive value and weight in propagating distinct

Cuban social categories is uncertain. For example, evidence presented earlier in this study revealed that most births of children designated as pardo occurred outside the institution of slavery and the term did not signify "biracial." Instead, it indicated any degree of combined European and African descent. Thus many pardos had pardo fathers. It also would be unwarranted to accept that all inter-racial relationships in the slaveholding period were the result of sexual coercion from white men or some calculus of social and economic benefit on the part of Afro-Cuban women. Other emotional and social considerations were often at play.

The Afro-Cuban writers discussed here did not limit their indictment of slavery solely to its corruption of Afro-Cuban women. They also suggested that under the degenerate moral values of slavery, Afro-Cuban men also had learned to disregard the social value of marriage and to enjoy sexual relations outside wedlock.[61] While this opinion reveals an obvious gender bias that assumes men controlled sexual expression and women were passive actors, its critique of male disregard for marriage could have applied equally to Afro-Cuban women. These women also could have questioned the value of marriage and seen no need to limit their sexual experiences to its confines. In either case, to address this perceived problematic legacy, "Palpitaciones" contributors promoted the communal obligation to reverse these tendencies through conformity with the dominant patriarchal model, despite its improper fit with the unique aspects of Afro-Cuban life and history.

TRANSFORMING THE LEGAL STATUS OF CUBAN FAMILIES

The Afro-Cuban intellectual concern for the legitimacy of Afro-Cuban families was set within the context of a changing legal status of marriage within Cuban society. The legal definition of family did not continue unchanged in the Cuban transition from colony to republic. As a succession of less traditional political ideologies such as liberalism, socialism, and feminism gained currency, each influenced reforms of the legal definitions of family. The ascendance of a liberal political culture occurred in Cuba well after it had in continental Latin America. In the latter, this process evolved from the late eighteenth century on and contributed to ultimately successful anti-colonial efforts. By contrast, it was only toward the end of the nineteenth century that the ascendance of Spanish metropolitan liberalism affected the separation of Church and state in Cuban civil law.[62] Peninsular liberal politicians rejected the continuing strictures of the ancien régime, which they perceived as still operating principally through the Catholic Church, and created more open forms of political participation.[63]

One of the points of their attack was the Church's then exclusive right to verify civil status through control the registries of baptism, marriage, and death. Although these registries were mainly used by the Church to mark the fulfillment of the related sacraments, they also generated small Church incomes and influenced family-formation practices. In limiting these possibilities, the liberal Spanish government created civil registries in the peninsula for the first time in 1870 and extended them to Cuba in 1883.[64] The establishment of the civil registries also marked one of the more radical transformations of the legal definition of family seen since the requirement for the clerical sanction of marriage created by the Council of Trent in the middle of the sixteenth century. Thus, with the co-existence of both secular and ecclesiastic forms of family recognition, the previously obligatory religious dimension of family formation was eliminated for those Cubans who chose to accept it solely as a social contract with economic implications. The establishment of the civil registry also brought the termination of official racial designators. Partially as a result of the pressure brought by the centralized Afro-Cuban *Directorio Central de las Sociedades de la Raza de Color* (Central Directorate of Societies of the Colored Race) in 1893, markers of race and color no longer had legal standing.[65] With the removal of racial designators from the state's vital registries, race was no longer officially imposed. For the first time, Cubans did not have to carry official racial labels marking their social status. Even before independence, the island's inhabitants were not entered into the civil birth registries as white, black, or mulatto, but solely as Cubans (albeit still as Spanish subjects).

This is not to suggest, of course, that the value of race disappeared from Cuban society. Race continued to shape many of the interactions among Cubans. The 1893 civil regulation did not apply to the Catholic Church. Cuban ecclesiastic registries had been separated according to race since the middle of the seventeenth century. Through the nineteenth century, the racial restrictions on marriage created by Pragmatic Sanction of 1778 and the royal cedula on marriage of 1803 only fostered further distinction. The diocese of Havana ended the racial separation of its vital registries in 1904.[66] But as the U.S. sociologist Enid Logan has demonstrated, Church officials did not mandate the elimination of racial classifications at baptism. The inclusion of racial labels within many ecclesiastic registries persisted until 1940, when a new Cuban Constitution prohibited the practice.[67]

The suppression of racial designation in civil documents allowed Cubans more flexibility with socially constructed non-governmental and self-selected forms of racial identification, instead of limiting them to categories derived from a long-standing legal template. One can imagine that the primary beneficiaries of this greater flexibility would have been those ambitious men and women of color whose phenotype and ambiguous ancestry would allow them to "pass" as white once state documentation to the contrary no longer existed. By the same token, lower-class whites lost one of the legal distinctions between themselves and people of color. But as legal definitions of race were removed, the space for the social discussion of their characteristics was expanded. It was this opening that nationalist intellectuals availed themselves of.

Transformation in the official designation of race in Cuba also occurred as the indirect result of other changes to the Cuban legal system. Prior to independence, Spanish liberals consolidated centuries of royal dictates into more comprehensive statutes with the Civil Code of 1889. This legislation altered many of the Spanish government's earlier social policies. On the one hand it placed new economic restrictions on the illegitimate family by discontinuing a previous requirement for the parental support of those "recognized" children born and raised outside of wedlock. It also removed the inheritance rights of surviving partners of consensual unions. Both practices had existed as part of Spanish imperial law since the medieval period, in the Siete Partidas and the Leyes de Toro. However, some of the inheritance rights lost to women in consensual unions were regained by their offspring. The Siete Partidas had established that recognized children born outside of wedlock could inherit a maximum of one-fifth of their father's estate. The newer civil law adjusted this to one half of the amount guaranteed to legitimate children, or a maximum of one-quarter of their father's estate.[68]

The reforms to family law implemented by late nineteenth-century Spanish legislators remained largely stable in the transition into the republic. The Civil Code of 1889 continued through the initial period of U.S. intervention with few changes. The occupying American military government, present in Cuba from 1899 to 1902, also attempted to limit the social importance of the Church by ending the parallel existence of both ecclesiastical and secular vital registries and by denying the legitimacy of Catholic marriage in favor of civil marriage; only the latter effort held legal validity.[69] Cubans, however, did not rapidly conform to this policy. In 1901, the military government made modifications and accepted the validity of both civil and religious marriages as long as clergy filed their certificates with civil authorities.[70] And the filing cost of secular marriage was set to a nominal level, one U.S. dollar, in an era when the annual average worker's wage was $175.[71] All births were also to be registered civilly.[72] Judicial changes to the nature of the Cuban family also occurred in post-independence politics. Especially in the period between 1914 and 1918, the separate debates over divorce and the property rights of married women reignited earlier questions about the distribution of social authority between the Cuban state and the Church, between the state and the family, and ultimately between men and women. Previously, married women had no legal personality apart from their husbands, full divorce had not been permitted, and spouses only had the option of legal separation in a limited set of circumstances.[73] Again, the motivation to change these practices came from contemporary liberal political currents which suggest that the nation progressed as its individual members were liberated from long-standing, corporate obligations and privileges, such as those of the Church, and that the demise of colonial controls would leave the state with the responsibility for balancing social order against individual rights.

Racialized reproduction within Cuba was also impacted when feminist views joined the liberal mission and extended the vision of the responsible citizen beyond its male archetype to women. Early in the republic, Cuban women's political involvement steadily increased. Initially, early feminists organized themselves into women's groups that

supported a number of social welfare causes and promoted female empowerment in limited arenas. They often sought a form of women's liberation consistent with some of the more conservative Catholic beliefs
and accepted that politically active women would make better mothers
for a progressive nation. Women's nation-building potential could be
more fully realized if women were freed from the unrestricted domination of husbands, some of whom were deemed unfit for such authority.
By 1918, classic liberalism and a feminism that centered on a progressive
but nationalistic form of motherhood combined to legalize divorce and
allow for greater female access to marital assets.[74] The next major
changes to the legal status of Cuban family had to await the revolutionary upheaval of the 1930s.[75] By 1930, frustration with both Gerardo
Machado's dictatorship and long-entrenched political corruption brought
a younger generation into the political arena. And with them came a
shift away from both liberalism's emphasis on the individual and from
the traditional hierarchies of Cuban society. These ideologies were to be
replaced with a more egalitarian and democratic ethos that responded to
the popular classes and their needs.[76] Many Afro-Cubans were attracted
to socialist or communist ideals and organized effective multi-racial political bodies (clubs, unions, and parties) around them.[77]

Although family was directly addressed in little of the new reformist
legislation emerging after 1933, a few related items were very significant.
Cuban women won the right to vote in 1933 (although it was not fully
realized until the 1940 constitution), and multi-racial feminist activism
allied with leftist political movements to address women's conditions in
a number of spheres including labor rights and social welfare. In 1934,
new legislation forced employers to contribute to a national maternity
insurance for working women. This progressive policy provided six
weeks of leave on a subsistence income for new mothers, regardless of
marital status.[78] It was a small acknowledgment of the economic difficulties faced by working families, where women's incomes were essential for survival. It also recognized that men were often absent from these
families or that their economic contributions were often insufficient.
Unfortunately, many women of all races remained unprotected by the
legislation, as domestics, who represented 42 percent of female employ-
ees, were excluded. Afro-Cuban women were the majority in this field.[79]

Reformist fervor also prompted reconsideration of the relationship between the state and the family through constitutional changes. The constitutional convention of 1939 provided the platform for generating and achieving reforms. Representatives ran the gamut of Cuban political positions from conservative to left-liberal. However, the liberal and left-leaning forces dominated. Under their auspices, the new constitution would become known for its transformative elements. It answered several political and social questions with a progressive outlook reminiscent of the Mexican Constitution of 1917.[80]

With respect to the legal status of the Cuban family, the reformist 1940 constitution fostered such change in important two articles. Article 43 stated:

> The family, motherhood, and marriage are under the protection of the State.
>
> Only marriages authorized by officials having legal capacity to affect them are valid. Civil marriage is gratuitous and shall be recognized by the law ...
>
> The tribunals shall determine the cases in which, for reasons of justice, the union between persons with legal capacity to contract marriage shall be deemed comparable, in stability and special status, to civil marriage.
>
> Allowances for support in favor of the woman and the children shall enjoy preference with respect to all other obligations, and this preference may not be derogated by any condition of unattachability of property, salary, pension, or economic investment of any kind whatever ...[81]

These clauses demonstrate a compromise between progressive views of marriage and those from the nineteenth-century liberal tradition. The state remained the central agent in the process and common-law marriage remained unrecognized. And yet the words "the union between persons with the legal capacity to contract marriage shall be deemed comparable ... to civil marriage" opened possibilities for positive legal comparison between formal marriage and enduring, stable consensual unions. Without establishing firm guarantees, the new law was an effort to give consensual unions some level of legal standing and acknowledge that the many non-marital Cuban families would benefit economically from such change. Toward this end, the last paragraph of the article refers not to the wife and legitimate children, but to "the woman and the children," leaving the issue of legitimacy open.

The constitution's next article broached the issue of the legal comparison between the legitimate and illegitimate family more directly. It is quoted here in its entirety.

> ART. 44. Parents are obliged to support, tend, educate, and instruct their children, and the latter to respect and assist their parents. The law shall assure the fulfillment of these duties with guarantees and adequate penalties.
>
> Children born out of wedlock to a person who at the time of conception may have been able to contract marriage, have the same rights and duties as are stipulated in the preceding paragraph, except for what the law prescribes in regard to inheritance. For this purpose, children born out of wedlock, of married persons, when the latter acknowledge the children, or when the filiation is established by declaration, shall also have equal rights. The law shall regulate the investigation of paternity.
>
> All qualifications on the nature of filiation are abolished. No statement may be made differentiating between births, either upon the civil status of the parents in the written records of the latter, or in any registry of baptism or certificate referring to the filiation.[82]

Legislation requiring the parents of illegitimate children to provide the latter with equal economic consideration as those born in wedlock also impacted the legal nature of the Cuban family.

With these changes, the 1940 constitution reformulated the contours of Cuban family law that were to remain in use until the changes brought by the 1959 revolution. While it did not remove the social distinction between legitimate and illegitimate families, it did permit the latter to sue for economic support. Earlier in the republic, economic support for the illegitimate had been left to the father's discretion. With the establishment of the right to investigate paternity, men potentially lost some of this liberty. As Afro-Cuban families demonstrated higher rates of illegitimacy, they also potentially stood to gain more from the new legislation. Afro-Cuban families formed in consensual unions were made legally comparable to those formed by marriage, as predominated among white Cubans. Such legal changes had implications for many

Cuban families. If one compares the legal status of families created after 1940 to the frequent inter-racial families from the late nineteenth century, the former had greater standing. No law prevented racially dissimilar partners from marrying. The stigma of racial labeling no longer carried official, legal value, and therefore children of these unions were no longer baptized or registered as mulatto or white. Instead, they were legally recognized solely as Cuban. Regardless of their parent's marital status, the children received their father's surname and guarantees of his economic responsibility toward them. In these ways, illegitimacy had lost much of its former meaning.

One has to be careful, however, to distinguish between these legal changes and the complete elimination of racial discrimination within the context of the Cuban family. The most obvious example of such discrimination is illustrated by the experience of President Fulgencio Batista (1940–1944, 1952–1958). He came from an impoverished, racially mixed background and rose through the military to become the most dominant person in Cuban politics in the three decades prior to 1959. He first appeared on the Cuban political scene with the 1933 revolution, organizing the army's lower ranks against the officials linked to the unpopular President Machado. After betraying the 1933 revolutionaries and repressing their more radical objectives, he undertook his own political rehabilitation by projecting a reformist political image. He sided with the progressive political elements of the 1930s and 1940s to support a new interest in the popular classes. In fact, he called the 1939 constitutional convention and ensured the representation of all political sectors.[83] He was also noted for including mulattoes and blacks, such as Ramón Vasconcelos, in higher political circles.[84] Yet, Batista's family life did not reflect the progressive image of his post-1934 politics. He attempted to hide his mulatto identity and "pass for white." Despite these efforts, Batista could not erase his popular nickname, "el mulatto lindo" (the handsome mulatto). He was still not permitted to enter Cuba's most exclusive social settings that remained reserved for whites.[85] This is evidence that, even in this progressive era of Cuban politics and even for the most important politician of the era, Afro-Cuban advances had their limits. And race mixture, in and of itself, did not result in social mobility.

Similarly Afro-Cuban nationalists were faced with the choice of assimilating into white Cuban culture or projecting Afro-Cuban experiences into the national design. An acceptance of Cuban cultural unity required both the discussion of the supposed cultural deficiencies of the Afro-Cuban masses and the development of corrective strategies. Family organization and gender roles became two of the important areas upon which Afro-Cuban nationalists concentrated their social-reproductive and reformist discourses. In this regard, they asked themselves what role inter-racial relationships would have for their mode of inclusion. More specifically, they questioned whether the sexual unions between white men and women of color would lead to the rise of a valued, culturally mediating population or to the eventual disappearance of the Afro-Cuban population. Their negative responses centered on Afro-Cuban physical survival, but one mediated by cultural assimilation. As we shall see in chapter 7, the next generation of Cuban intellectuals (including many whites) reconsidered this question, resolved it in favor of the former alternative, and embraced the ideal of a mulatto Cuba.

7

Mestizaje Literary Visions and Afro-Cuban Genealogical Memory, 1920–1958

Our elements have been mixed spontaneously and naturally.
And from Spanish and creole whites, African blacks, or Indians,
there has been created an intermediate race that is not white, nor black.
It has come to be the Cuban race, an ideal and uniform race.
Fortunately, all differences, all the small antagonisms that bother us
today will disappear with it. Within a century, with the constantly
blending [*mestizaje*] of races, these problems will not have a reason to exist.

—"La Raza Cubana,"
Diario de la Marina (June 26, 1928), 8

INTRODUCTION

In June, 1928 an anonymous reader of "Ideales de una Raza" (Ideals of a Race), the Afro-Cuban column of the leading Havana paper *Diario de la Marina,* offered a pointed definition of "the Cuban race," one with biological and cultural race mixture (mestizaje) among its essential components. The perspective on race mixture expressed above stood in contrast to many previous renderings of the role of race in Cuban nationalist projects. It did not present whitening as its ultimate goal, it therefore differed from common mid-nineteenth century visions, such as that presented in Cirilo Villaverde's novel *Cecilia Valdés,* or in José

Antonio Saco's earlier insistence that "No nos queda más que un reme-dio: blanquear, blanquear, y entonces hacernos respetar (We have no other solution than this: whiten, whiten, and in this way make ourselves respected)."[1] It also differs from general images of the Cuban body poli-tic associated with the independence movement, where whites, blacks, and mulattoes politically and militarily co-existed in forging the emer-gent nation. Instead, the anonymous author's alternative articulation of mestizaje defined a new Cuban type produced through biological and cultural fusion.

This transformed perspective on *la raza cubana* had not developed in isolation. It was one of many similar redefinitions of Cuban iden-tity that began to appear in the late 1920s, within a broader context of shifting Western visions of blackness. Like similar African-diasporic Negritude movements of the period, Afrocubanismo, or the Afro-Cuban Movement, brought new public acknowledgment of the African-derived elements of Cuban life. The vogue was to insert Afro-Cuban voices, art, and religion into mainstream popular culture. This was done not with the contemptuous buffoonery of previous generations of Euro-Cuban cultural agents. Instead, new articulations deemed Afro-Cuban culture as a positive, if not essential, component of *cubanidad* (Cubanness). But Afrocubanismo was also more complex. One later observer distinguished it from other Cuban intellectual efforts based on its emphasis on universalism, allusions to the social conflicts gener-ated by past slavery and continuing racial discrimination, positive as-sessment of race mixture, attention to black and mulatta sensuality, and engagement with Afro-Cuban rhythms and religious ritual.[2] With res-pect to a new reproductive vision of race, family, and nation, this new movement contained many variations, some of which continued to hold problematic notions of blackness. Simultaneously, beyond artistic representation of race, everyday Afro-Cubans of this period continued to make sexual and reproductive choices that ran the racial spectrum from intentional self-segregation to deliberate race mixture. In doing so, they increased the complexity of the twentieth-century Cuban sex-ual economy of race.

VISIONS OF MESTIZAJE WITHIN
AFROCUBANISMO LITERATURE

Although critics have charged many of the contributors to Afrocubanismo with ambivalence toward true racial equality and with ultimately
trivializing Afro-Cuban life through an over-glorification of its exotic
and sensual elements, its significance to Cuban cultural nationalism
should not be underestimated.[3] It represented one of the seminal moments in the evolution of Cuban identity, as several major intellectuals
and artists from all colors and classes created new images of Afro-
Cuban forms. Authors and artists such as Nicolás Guillén (1902–1989),
Ramón Guirao (1908–1948), José Zacarías Tallet (1893–1989), and Alejo
Carpentier (1904–1980) projected their more inclusive perspectives on
Afro-Cuban life and aesthetics to a white public who previously had
either ignored them or amused themselves with portrayals of the black
buffoon or the misguided tragic hero. These writers brought a new sensibility to Cuban literature. Their mission may have sprung from the
commonality of being born into a generation that had never experienced Spanish colonialism or slavery. They saw Cuba with fresh eyes
and novel possibilities. According to literary critic Vera Kutzinski, the
movement differed from earlier allusions to Afro-Cuban forms because
it "contained and defused potential ethnic threats to national unifica-
tion by turning them into original (and ordinary) contributions to Cuban culture." This was a new form of nationalist expression that utilized
Afro-Cuban references to oppose the penetration of U.S. culture in Cuban life and created what Kutzinski has labeled an "anti-imperialism in
blackface."[4] This symbolic blackface combined problematic racial imagery with insightful social critique.

   Afrocubanismo played a valuable role in consolidating the theme of
mestizaje in Cuban public consciousness.[5] It expressed in literary terms
the links between real family-formation practices and a positive vision
of a national race. The sexual politics and imagery associated with
Cuban nationalism of this period celebrated race mixture as a counter-
hegemonic trope or an "antidote to Wall Street," to quote Alejo Carpentier. It offered the basis for a new positive evaluation of Cuban identity
in the confrontation with the U.S. economic and cultural imperialism

implemented formally with the 1899 military intervention and continued explicitly with the U.S. oversight of Cuban national politics that resulted from the Platt Amendment to the 1902 Cuban Constitution. This position was comparable with the advancement of the ideal of the *raza cósmica* (cosmic race) by other contemporary Latin American nationalists, especially in Mexico.[6] According to Kutzinski, Cuban intellectuals of this period also employed the concept of mestizaje to "celebrate racial diversity while disavowing troubling social realities . . . and nourishing Cuban nationalism."[7]

Although Kutzinski presents important insights, a more subtle reading of the emerging appreciation of race mixture associated with the movement is warranted and can be performed by outlining an intellectual history of the differing perspectives on race within Afrocubanismo. The newer articulations of mestizaje were not the same for all proponents of Afrocubanismo. Instead, it appeared in at least two forms. One accepted the combination of European, African, and, at times, Asian elements in Cuba's cultural terrain and in the realm of social behavior. The other emphasized the biological interaction of previous races as the foundation of a new Cuban race, one in which biological and cultural blackness was sanitized with white blood. Often the race of the author influenced which of these projects was emphasized. The different styles of addressing racial issues often distinguished the white writers within the movement from their black and mulatto counterparts.[8]

White writers largely treated cultural themes and tended to limit the range of behaviors and values permitted to their fictional Afro-Cuban personages. Afro-Cuban musicians, dancers, and expressive, religious ceremonies became their favored subjects. In these works, people of color could sing, dance, and shake with religious fervor, but few other activities were expressed. The works of white Afrocubanismo writers also differed from those of their black and mulatto peers in that the former's limited engagement with the ongoing difficulties of Afro-Cuban life equated with an absence of any political considerations for that group. As people of color were presented as existing in a perpetual state of musical or sensual contentment, these writers avoided the thornier challenge of addressing the real inequalities experienced by Cuba's mulattoes and blacks. They did not have to consider ways to sustain an Afro-Cuban future and could instead rely on its history and continuing aesthetic contributions as sources for their own artistic innovation. These elements could then be defined as essential characteristics of national culture that could be used to confront a perceived invasion of external materialism.

These essentialist perspectives also explain the manner in which white writers minimized the sociological aspects of the Afro-Cuban presence and the process of race mixture. The characters of color found in their works are constructed with little social context. They do not have social rights, responsibilities, or families. They exist in the moment. In addition to the denial of their future, they appear without human ancestry, except for an inescapable connection to an almost mythical Africa. People of color remained distinctive, if not problematic, Cubans. White writers largely continued to envision them as permanent links to Africa's dark skin and dark cultures, on the margins of true Cuban identity. These writers positioned themselves at the center of a world still perceived in largely Hispanic terms and became literary anthropologists or voyeurs within their own country. They gave themselves the responsibility for reporting for their readers those lifestyles that, although they occupied the same geographic terrain, had previously gone unacknowledged. Many of these white writers could offer seductive snapshots of an imagined Afro-Cuba from the outside. Yet, they did not display a true understanding of the depths of co-existence among whites and people of color. In other words, the majority of white writers within Afrocubanismo imagined the legacy of African descent in Cuba as existing parallel to a separate white space, without real integration. Race mixture was understood only at the most superficial level.

The white poet Ramón Guirao's *Orbita de la poesía afrocubana, 1928–1937* (1938) provides a summation of the movement that both affirms this new acceptance of Afro-Cuban culture and critiqued its lack of attention to political reform. For him,

> *afronegrista* poetry, that is poetry about black themes, is the most genuine manifestation of our insular sensibility . . . This vigilant passion for blackness made us believe . . . in the possibility that the Negro could achieve equality of opportunities, the right to co-exist [with whites] on a harmonious plane of

mutual comprehension and understanding. We have seen that these incursions into the rich veins of the black quarry have not changed the social destiny of black people. The reality is different. A careful distance from that [European] spell of negrophilia makes it necessary to confess that its objective was very cruel. It was a matter of adding another string to the bow of the Western artist to give his art a little luster . . . If one invited the blacks to share the bread, if one seated them at the table for just a few moments, it was with the expectation that they would leave something original on the starched white tablecloth.[9]

He recognized that Cuban *afronegrismo* did not realize its potential to be something genuinely profound. Even his own poetry emphasizes the more limited, exotic notion of Afro-Cuban culture. "Bailadora de Rumba" (Rumba Dancer) (1928) is typical. It begins,

Baildora de guaguancó	Guaguancó dancer
piel negra	Black skin
tersura de bongó.	smoothed by the bongo.
Agita la maraca	Shake the maracas
de su risa	of your smile
con los dedos de leche	with the milky fingers
de sus dientes . . .[10]	of your white teeth . . .

Here, the black female dancer is described in sensual terms, lost in the musical rhythms. But she is little more than a caricature of presumed primitive freedoms. The harsh realities of contemporary Cuba do not enter her world. She has no existence or concerns beyond the moment. While Guirao alludes to her African past, he denies her any other social agency, including the ability to shape her own future.

Despite its limitations, Guirao's representation of black female sensuality highlights another shift in racial thought. Previously, late nineteenth-century allusions to sensuality among women of color almost exclusively involved mulattas. They often were described as sensual temptresses who were born to beguile all men, especially whites. By contrast, pure black women remained trapped in images of laborers and haggard broodmares. They were not publicly read as objects of desire; instead they were depicted solely as objects of both labor-related and sexual brutality. In literary and iconographic imagery, both types of women were imprisoned by a male oppression centered on the use of their bodies. What differentiated them was the suggestion of several authors and artists that the mulattas participated in the fulfillment of their own oppression. These mixed-race women were often represented as confident in their desirability and willing to use it for social gain, even if ultimately their sexual intrigues brought tragic results in a manner reminiscent of *Cecilia Váldes*.[11]

These late nineteenth-century tropes continued largely unchanged in Cuban literature and art into the early twentieth century. But with the Afrocubanismo of late 1920s, the black Cuban woman was cast in a new light. For the first time she entered the iconographic stage as an exotic, yet strangely nationalist, symbol, a place previously held solely by her mulatta sister. She embodied an extreme sense of distance and purity in the face of the corrupting, imperialist presence of the United States that Cuban nationalists struggled to reject. For many white authors, the mulatta, with her racially mixed ancestry, became less useful for their anti-imperialist purposes. Some, like Guirao, turned with new interest to a sensual, black female form. "¡Negra, de tu carne se venga del alma de los demás (Black woman, from your flesh comes the soul of the rest)," penned the writer Alfonso Hernández Cata. The poet Emilio Ballagas collapsed *mulata* and *negra* into the same category and pleaded, "Morena, ¡ven a mis brazos!" (Brown woman, come into my arms!). And José Antonio Portuondo's "la negra Pancha" is nothing but sexual energy:

¡Negra Pancha,	That Black Francesca,
qué pimiento! . . .	How hot! . . .
¡Negra Pancha,	That Black Francesca
qué lujuria! . . .[12]	How luxurious! . . .

This almost exclusive attention to the black woman marked another distinction between white Afrocubanismo artists and their counterparts of color, who, as well as paying new attention to the black woman, continued to uphold the mulatta icon in their own self-interested fashion, as we shall see below.

The limitations found in Guirao's Afrocubanismo poetry were found elsewhere in the movement. The well-known poetry collection

Jose Garcia Benitez's 1939 depiction of the black woman, beyond the standard visions of the mulatta. Source: *Carteles*, August 30, 1939.

by Agustín Acosta, *La Zafra* (The Sugar Harvest) (1926), has often been cited as one of the finest examples of the nationalist literature produced in this period. It too includes a new awareness of a parallel Afro-Cuban cultural presence and history, painting a sympathetic picture of enslaved people from Cuba's not-too-distant past. Instead of perpetuating the negative images of the cultural barrenness typically thought to derive from the brutality of slavery, Acosta permits the slaves in his poem to survive their oppression while retaining both traditions and memories from their homelands:

Bajo el cubano sol—canícula perpetua—	Under the Cuban sun—the continual dog days—
inmunes a la fiebre de las insolaciones	Immune to the fever of its hot waves
bajo el cubano sol que aduerme y emborracha	Under the Cuban sun, that soothes and intoxicates
iban las negras dotaciones	Go the black slave women
Llevaban en los ojos un lejano misterio:	Their eyes carry a far-off mystery:
el fetichismo ilógico de su país natal;	The illogical fetishism of their native lands;
el sol inexorable de Congo y Mozambique	The perpetual sun of the Congo and Mozambique
y las noches del Senegal . . .[13]	And the nights of Senegal . . .

Despite a desire to create a more positive image of African heritage, the Africa remembered here remains a harsh, mysterious, and illogical place. But the slaves drawn by Acosta have managed to bring it forward into their Cuban existence. It is not something that was to become lost in the experience of slavery. And by writing them in this way, Acosta was asking all Cubans to recognize African manifestations in their own land.

Likewise, Alejo Carpentier's early Afrocubanismo excursions produced similar images. His *¡Ecue-Yamba-O!* (God Be Praised!) (1933) was once labeled the "only novel Afro-Cubanism produced."[14] It explores the experiences of the rural black population as it traces the life of its protagonist, Menegildo Cué. His life provides literary testimony of Afro-Cuban distinctiveness. Although the novel's temporal setting remains vague, it suggests that Menegildo's family had barely escaped the practices of the slave plantation. They continued to live and labor according to the rhythms of sugar production. Their days were spent either in the fields or in the mills, but their nights were left to the worship of their African gods and the love and otherworldly pleasures that they believed this worship might bring. But for Carpentier, Cuba's salvation lay in these acts.

> Only the blacks ... fervently preserved an Antillean character and tradition.
> The bongo drum, antidote to Wall Street! The Holy Spirit venerated by the Cué
> family did not allow Yankee sausages between pieces of his votive bread! ...
> No hotdogs for the saints of Mayeya![15]

When Menegildo is forced into an urban environment his links to Afro-Cuban ritual become even more profound. People of color continue in their lives, physically closer to whites, but still separated on a parallel plane of mystery and magic. Looking into this world from the other side creates the magic realism that Carpentier made famous. Nevertheless, Carpentier would later admit just how inaccurate his descriptions of Afro-Cuban life were:

> Well then: after twenty years of investigation into the syncreticisms of Cuba,
> I have concluded that all the depth, truth, and fullness that I have pretended to
> paint in my novel was actually outside of my reach. For example, the animism of
> the rural black; the lives of the black in the forest; certain initiating practices
> that were faked for me by the practitioners with a disconcerting ability.[16]

One segment of contemporary Cuban anthropology provided social scientific parallels to the literary productions of Afrocubanismo. From its late nineteenth-century beginnings, Cuban anthropology had been rooted in a racially oriented understanding of criminology that linked African-derived physical features and cultural elements to illicit activity. This approach to the study of race continued through the 1930s in the studies of Cuban scholars Israel Castellanos and Julio Morales Coello. The well-respected Cuban ethnographer Fernando Ortiz (1881–1969) began his scholarly career informed by the same perspectives. In his earliest works, from the turn of the century, he expressed views that the "primitive" African elements, especially African-derived religions, were largely responsible for anti-social behaviors among the Cuban lower classes. A 1906 work clearly indicates this interpretation:

> The black race is the one that under many aspects has been able to mark the bad
> Cuban life, characteristically, communicating its superstitions, their organizations, their languages, their dances, etc ... and its legitimate children are the
> witchcraft and the ñañiguismo, that means so much in the Cuban underworld.[17]

Ortiz displays a remnant of this view even as he asserts in 1924 the importance of African-derived elements in the formation of Cuban culture.

> It was impossible that the customs and national languages of Africa were so
> soon forgotten, and even today we find abundant survivals of this undeniable
> *primitiveness* that rise to the surface through the superstructures of the culture.
> Among these are the very peculiar words that the Africans have managed to
> inlay in the vernacular of Cuba . . . and [it] is interesting to observe how our
> people in those *vulgarisms* unconsciously reproduce certain ideas, concepts and
> judgments that solely belonged to Africans many decades ago.[18]

In this moment, Ortiz accepted that the supposed "primitiveness" of
African culture and the "vulgarism"of its language were negative behaviors to be studied, managed, and eventually exorcised from the nation.
Importantly, however, this work and his government-requested revi-
sion to the Cuban penal code, *Proyecto de Código Criminal Cubano*
(1926), also mark his transition away from a theory of Cuba's racial ata-
vism to a nascent envisioning of his seminal transculturation theory.[19]
He began to reconsider the bounded link between race and culture, to
perceive profound cultural interconnections between the racial elements in Cuban society. In 1943 Ortiz would proclaim, "Without the
black, Cuba would not be Cuba."[20]

In the 1930s, Ortiz launched a new ethnographic approach to the study
of Cuban race relations. He, his former student Rómulo Lachatañeré
(1909–1952), and later Lydia Cabrera (1899–1991) attempted to method-
ically document the more positive aspects of the African presence
within Cuban culture.[21] These influences in the areas of music, language, religion, and folktales began to receive significant attention.[22]
However, many of these studies again tended to separate whites and
people of color into different cultural domains. So in their analysis, African influences continued to be something found only among the latter. White involvement with these practices remained largely undis-
cussed. Instead, in a style that paralleled developments in the literary
domain, the social observers influenced by Afrocubanismo assigned
themselves the task of promoting a new awareness of African elements
to culturally dominant whites who previously had been ignorant or dis-
missive of them. Although it may appear somewhat contradictory, the
novelty of the later stages of Afrocubanismo was the sense that once-
distinct cultural traditions were being combined to create a new sense

of Cuban identity. Both its literary and social-scientific components united in recognition of Cuba's cultural mestizaje. From the point of view of those involved in the movement, Cuban identity was no longer to be perceived in exclusively Hispanic terms. Afro-Cuban "contributions" were to be valued for the first time. However, the regard for these contributions was not uniform, and varied among those participating in the movement.

As his interest in race evolved, Ortiz distinguished himself more completely from the approach taken by most white proponents of Afrocubanismo. Instead of discussing African and European cultural elements as separately existing within the same national terrain, Ortiz proposed a more integrationist model. In this, the African and European cultural elements did not solely co-exist, they merged into something new and originally Cuban. In 1940, Ortiz had coined the term "*transculturación*" (transculturation) to denote the mutual exchange between Cuba's ethnic groups. He used this term to express the highly varied phenomena that have come about in Cuba as a result of the extremely complex transmutations of culture that have taken place here, without knowledge of which it is impossible to understand the evolution of the Cuban people, whether in the economic, institutional, legal, ethical, religious, artistic, linguistic, psychological, sexual, or other aspects of their life.[23] Here again was a newly articulated theory of cultural mestizaje that stood in stark contrast to earlier anthropological theories that had emphasized a unidirectional cultural flow from the presumably superior to the inferior. For Ortiz at this stage of his career, modern Cuba was born from and would continue to survive based the "integration of the races."[24]

It is important to note that these important transformations in Ortiz's outlook on race did not occur in a vacuum. Other white Cuban writers expressed a similar sense of the close intertwining of once-distinct African and European experiences. A good example of this orientation comes from Felipe Pichardo Moya. His poem "Filosofía del Bronce" (1925) transforms the mulatta "Virgincita del Bronce" from Villaverde's tragic Cecila Valdés into the heroic mother of a new Cuba, rescuing her from the image of the unfortunate soul formerly drawn in the novel.

¡Tendrás de tus antepasados
sabe Dios cuanta gente!
¡Cuántos pedrigrées ignorados
que forman tu modo presente!

You have all those ancestors
That only God knows how many!
How many ignored pedigrees
Form who you are today!

!Sangre bárbara y sangre nuestra
bajo el sol cómplice mezcladas

por bendición de la siniestra
mano, son luz en tus miradas! . . .

The barbarous blood and our blood
Have mixed with the assistance of the
sun
With the blessing of its sinister hand,
They are the light in your eyes! . . .

Quizás tuviste un ascendiente
que fue de sangre real,
y en el negrero algún marino, bajo el
puente
unió a su sangre el porte rubio de boreal.

Perhaps you had an ancestor
With royal blood,
And in the slave ship, some sailor, under the
staff,
Lent his northern blood.

¡O el abuelo noble y español,
cedió al impulso que le daba,
en una siesta ebria de sol,
la carne negra de la esclava!
Idilio monstruo entre los cortes de las
cañas,
concepción contra las leyes . . .
¡Visiones de cosas extrañas
exacerbando las nostalgias de los
bueyes! . . .[25]

Perhaps a noble Spanish grandfather,
Gave into that driving impulse,
During a afternoon escape from the sun,
To enjoy the flesh of a black slave woman!
What monstrous idyll between the cut
rows of cane,
Conception that opposed the laws . . .
Visions of strange things
Exacerbating the nostalgia of the
oxen! . . .

The mulatta becomes the sensual representation of the nation for her ability to dually *bear* historical memory and future national creation that seamlessly combined both the African and the European, as "sister of ours, and of theirs." In the last stanza one finds the suggestion that her painful past gave her the strength to rise and unite her brothers of all races.

Y así llegaste hasta nosotros,
hermana nuestra y de los otros,
suprema flor de la injusticia,
que conviertes en bravos potros
las palomas de la caricia.

And that is how you came to us,
Sister of ours and of theirs,
The supreme flower of injustice,
You convert into wild hawk
The once caring doves.

With this, Pichardo Moya put forth a new way of inserting Cuba's past into in the nation-building process. Slavery, in his reflection, is no longer solely a shameful facet of Spanish colonialism. For all its horrors, it also provided the setting for the sexual processes that forged a new Cuba, or better yet, a new Cuban race, destined for greatness based on its unique cultural and biological origins.

Literary and anthropological notions of transculturation also drew on similar currents found among Afro-Cuban intellectuals. Their treatment of race and race mixture varied greatly from that of the majority of white participants in Afrocubanismo. Obviously, the inclusion of Afro-Cuban elements in visions of the national identity was not something that they proposed from an external standpoint, as did their white counterparts. The public dismissal of those elements was part of their lived experience. They felt themselves to be equally as Cuban as their white counterparts imagined themselves to be. Afro-Cuban polemicists also realized that this conviction would only become more generalized if Cuba was no longer thought of solely in Hispanic terms. Earlier efforts for racial inclusion based primarily on black cultural assimilation had had limited success. They had left the masses behind and created the small Afro-Cuban middle class, whose members were exceptions to the perceived general incompatibility between civilization and African descent. With the greater Western interest in the cultural "other" that followed World War I and influenced white Cuban intellectuals, Cubans of color also changed their approach to the public conversation about race. Previously, Afro-Cuban intellectuals had rarely discussed Afro-Cuban cultural manifestations in a positive light. By the 1920s, this had changed. They, too, began to demonstrate a new appreciation for African-derived practices. In one of the aspects of this movement that has received a limited level of scholarly attention, these Afro-Cuban intellectuals, in conjunction with this new cultural direction, also began to openly discuss what they perceived to be the positive sociological effects of mestizaje.

Social and physical mestizaje in their works was no longer the tragic event it had represented for earlier Cuban writers. Instead, Afro-Cuban writers now reclaimed it as their own proud history. This was especially true for writers who were themselves of racially mixed backgrounds. No one embraced the theme of Cuban race mixture better, or more famously, than Nicolás Guillén. While many other commentators have reviewed this element of his work, it is useful here to place it in the context of other writers and examine the role of the family within it. It is also important to realize that although he did not initiate a transformed projection of mestizaje, he did bring it to new heights.[26] He was a proud member of that Afro-Cuban middle class, which had advanced through education and acquired some social prominence by the end of the nineteenth century. His father had been a journalist and publisher of a small newspaper, and eventually became a national senator during the second decade of the Cuban republic. Much later, Guillén explained his background in the following way: "If someone were to ask me to what class my family belonged, I would say with confidence the small black bourgeoisie."[27] By the time Afrocubanismo was emerging, the younger Guillén had only just begun to establish himself as a journalist and minor poet. In 1929, he began to provide social commentary for the Afro-Cuban column "Ideales de una Raza," edited by his friend Gustavo Urrutia. Guillén was an outspoken opponent of racial discrimination who challenged his white compatriots to re-evaluate their assumptions of black cultural deficiency and to make a greater effort to reform their racist behavior.[28]

His early poetry followed the modernist forms then popular in Spanish American literature and an African-descended element is not apparent in these works.[29] However, his 1930 *Motivos de son* (Motives of *Son*) collection marked a major transformation for him and for Cuban poetry more generally. These "poemas mulatos," as he labeled them, brought Afrocubanismo away from voyeuristic stereotypes to offer a more intimate entry into the issues and rhythms of Afro-Cuban urban life. The music of the *solar*, or tenement house, provides a background, but music was only one aspect of the lives lived there. Guillén also raised concerns about racial discrimination, as well the stress on color distinctions among Afro-Cubans themselves. He glorified the continuing struggle to overcome the difficulties of poverty, as he challenged the penetration of U.S. culture into Cuban life. The poems were "mulattoes," not only because they drew attention to mulattoes and blacks, but because they demonstrated how integrated these lives were to larger Cuban social and cultural patterns.[30]

For Guillén, whites and people of color shared more than earlier authors had been willing to indicate. This attitude is most evident in his "La Canción del Bongo."

> But my profound voice convokes the black and the white, that dance to the same *son,* bodies brown, souls black, more blood that sun . . . In that land, blending African and Spanish, Saint Barbara on one side and Chango on the other, there is always a grandfather missing.[31]

Guillén saw the absence or genealogical dismissal of one grandfather as the explanation for Cuba's racial divisiveness. Whites were relegated to one side and blacks to the other, as each group had forgotten its common ancestry. Guillén assigned himself the task of lessening this divide:

> I think that our creole poetry will not be thorough if it forgets the black. The black—from my point of view—supports the very essence of our cocktail . . . As of now, the spirit of Cuba is racially mixed. And from the spirit to the skin, the definitive color will come to us. Someday it will be called "Cuban color." These poems attempt to advance that day.[32]

While the proposal of "Cuban color" might initially appear to parallel the nineteenth-century suggestion of *blanqueamiento* (whitening), the two were very distinct. The ideal of "Cuban color" was not the belief that a future based solely on biological race mixture would solve Cuba's racial problems. Instead, it placed greater emphasis on the creation of a new history, a history that noted the points at which Cuba's races and families were already integrated. Guillén re-iterated the familial aspect of this objective in his famous "Balada de Los Dos Abuelos" (Ballad of the Two Grandfathers). The recollection of the two grandfathers heralded the proud heritage created as two once separate paths became intertwined in their descendants. "Sombras que sólo yo veo, me escoltan mis dos abuelos ([In] shadows that only I see, my two grandfathers follow me)."[33]

Interestingly, Guillén's highlighting of both forefathers is a notable contrast to the more typical, older image of Cuban race mixture in which the haggard black woman bore the mulatta as a result of either sexual brutality or the sexual intrigues linked with a black desire for racial "advancement." Previously, the entire notion of race mixture had been a highly feminized one. Males were not imagined as actively involved progenitors or as offspring. Guillén attempted to correct these untenable omissions and to demonstrate the inclusion of men in the project of race mixture, both as initiators and in the outcome. Guillén's own family history exemplified the recall of such memories and the acknowledgment of such heritage. Both of his parents were mulattoes. His paternal grandmother came from a white family whose members did not distance themselves from her after her marriage to a mulatto. As an adult, Guillén recalled fondly that during his childhood one of her brothers would frequently visit his family, even after her death.[34] From this foundation it is easy to understand how Guillén could develop a sense of Cuban identity associated with a more positive history of the multi-racial family.

The multi-racial vision of Cuban identity and history was supported by other Afro-Cuban intellectuals of Guillen's generation. For example, when the black former congressional representative Primitivo Ros Ramírez publicly stated that most Afro-Cubans were "the descendants of those Africans who came to Cuba to enrich her with the sweat of their brows and whose descendants hardly possess Spanish blood," he was vehemently challenged. The black intellectual Benjamin Muñoz Ginarte submitted the correction that the majority of Afro-Cubans were mulatto, having at least half Spanish blood.[35] In this way he minimized the often-mentioned biological and cultural distance between Afro-Cubans and Euro-Cubans. Muñoz wanted both elements included in a new Cuban consciousness. Yet, he also called on all the descendants of Cuba's mythical "Mama Inés" to never forget the contributions of this symbolic black grandmother, regardless of how light their skin color or how culturally assimilated they were to Hispanic norms.[36]

Returning to the quotation that opened this chapter ("Our elements have been mixed spontaneously and naturally . . . It has come to be the Cuban race, an ideal and uniform race"), this sense of a new Cuban race was also found in the larger Afro-Cuban population as a unique entity worthy of preservation. In providing this definition, the unidentified Afro-Cuban reader of "Ideales de Una Raza" also called for limits on immigration from Afro-Caribbean nations in order to protect the characteristics of the "Cuban race."[37] Interestingly, the author makes no mention of possible limits on white immigration, which at that point continued to be much larger than Afro-Caribbean immigration. Therefore, although the author did not promote whitening, she did not appear as disturbed by its potential as she was with the prospect of further national darkening or the infusion of the presumably more primitive aspects of other Afro-Caribbean people.

The column's editor, the black architect Gustavo Urrutia, addressed this contradiction. He advanced what he believed to be a more appropriate program for creating the new "Cuban race."

> We do not now aspire nor desire to stop being blacks, because color does not prevent us from being Cuban. However, we are enchanted by and committed to the noble idea of creating the Cuban Race, as a special ethnic identity, with all its intermediate character, with all its interactions.[38]

Urrutia's "Cuban Race" was unified but not homogenous. It could still have "all its intermediate character." Urrutia lived this philosophy to such a degree that when his granddaughter was to be registered by school officials as white, he objected. He had no desire for members of his family to view lightness of skin color as an opportunity to "escape" from the race, nor as confirmation of white racial superiority. He preferred to emphasize for all Cubans the "salutary goal of uniting humanity with dignity and justice."[39]

Among Cuban authors existed different notions about the constituents of this newly uniform "Cuban race." For some, it resulted from a process of the biological mixture of races, which would continue until the original white and black inputs were eliminated and only mulattoes remained. For others, it was mainly the cultural fusion of the constituent backgrounds, where biological race mixture was insignificant. Both Ortiz and Urrutia proposed this model. Yet, the two differed in that Urrutia was suspicious that the persistence of the biological process of race mixture would be dangerous to the survival of blacks. And for others, following Guillén's example, both the biological and cultural processes of race mixture were ongoing. However, these processes could help eliminate racial problems only if they were restated as a new, familial Cuban history. This new history would eliminate the recriminations that normally associated mestizaje with reproductive illegitimacy. There were to be none of the venomous attacks seen in the turn-of-the-century writings of Ramón Vasconcelos, which questioned the morality of those women of color sexually involved in a strictly biological vision of race mixture. The past was reconfigured with pride and the future with great possibility.

FAMILY HISTORIES OF RACE MIXTURE

Polemical literary discussions of mestizaje were paralleled by the experiences of many Cuban families, and just as the discursive presentation of these choices was not unproblematic, the personal options related to racialized reproduction were also highly complex. The previous chapters of this study have demonstrated that familial mestizaje co-existed alongside more endogamous, racially isolationist practices of both Cuba's whites and blacks during the colonial era. The difficulty in positioning oneself and family with respect to these options was just as true later in the republican era. But the context was changing. In the post-emancipation, post-colonial setting, all Cubans had greater social flexibility. However, in academic research, analysis of the personal possibilities in racialized reproduction has largely been subsumed under a focus on the more generalized polemical conversations. In order to move beyond the limits of intellectual discourse, this study now turns to oral family histories from Cuba's republican period to reveal the complex and emotional living memories of the types of intimate interactions that transformed Cuban racial meaning. These histories reveal the continuing personal tensions associated with race that existed outside the harmonious picture often painted by nationalist authors; a few of them are discussed here.[40]

Proud Passing?

Alfredo Barrera Bondi was born in a provincial town outside Havana in 1932. He was the son of a mulatto day laborer and the daughter of Italian immigrants. This racial background challenges the general wisdom that relationships between African-descended men and white women were not permissible within pre-revolutionary society. Despite his father's color, Alfredo described himself as white and felt comfortable in his prejudice against Afro-Cubans. Even though as an adult Alfredo often found himself in relationships with African-descended women, he viewed these unions with a degree of contempt. He explained the sexual escapades of his youth in racial terms:

> A lot of blacks lived in Las Yaguas and racial prejudice was strong. For example, we white fellows laid black girls oftener than white girls because the poor things weren't so well looked after by their parents. The daughters of black families were always getting knocked up. If people saw a black girl with a white boy, right away they'd begin to criticize her. They'd say, "You're a slut and a fool. That white boy is going to break your pussy and then leave you with a big belly." And they were right, that's what happened . . . What did I care? If a girl's father tried to call me to account, I'd say to him, "What do you expect? I'm a man. It's up to you to keep your daughter home."[41]

A surprising element of the story is the community consensus within this poor, racially diverse neighborhood that relationships between white young men and black young women brought no benefit to the women involved. These women were publicly chastised. Any presumed whitening goal was not one that met with community approval.

Alfredo's very sexist and racist sentiments were still at play when he later married a mulatta woman. "I wanted to start a home of my own, to have someone to wash my clothes, cook my meals, and look after me." He clearly envisioned his spouse solely as a tool of domestic labor. After his first wife died, he had two subsequent marriages to black women. Despite these marriages, Alfredo was critical of the choices of all of his sisters to marry black men. He was unembarrassed in stating, "I didn't want all that blackness in my family." He did not see the inconsistency between his own family-formation choices and his racist beliefs. He continued to instill these notions in his children and was proud that some were lighter than he, although they had dark mothers. He felt pity for his darker daughters, but it seems skin color was more significant than ancestry or social contact in Alfredo's conceptualization of race. His white self-identity was not compromised by his bi-racial genealogy, marriages, or children.

Los mestizos

JUAN

The interview with Juan was of one of the first formally conducted for this study. My Cuban assistant, Julían, describes Juan as a *mestizo claro*. Juan described himself simply as a mestizo, the son of a white Cuban man and a woman he described as *una mulata linda* (a beautiful mulatta). He was born in Havana in 1915. Juan indicated that his parents had been married, not in a church, but through the civil registry. He expressed some concern that he had no documentation for this civic marriage. His maternal grandparents had a similar relationship, a nineteenth-century one formed between a white man and a black woman. When asked if this was a secret relationship, Juan responded, "no, no, not hidden, but neither did they marry. They lived together. And that's where they began. He kept her and he also had his 'thing' over there. But he kept her and had three daughters with her."

> KYM: So, he had another family?
> JUAN: Yes, of course. He had one in Guira de Melena, a provincial town over there. He had his wife.
> KYM: Did you know this family, this white family?
> JUAN: Yes, I knew them, from a distance.

His grandparents' relationship was not secret, but neither was it legitimate. This white grandfather maintained two families, the white one in the rural setting and the one of color in Havana. Juan accepted this practice as normal and felt no reservation about discussing what he knew of it. He described his grandfather as a white politician who eventually became an important government administrator of provincial Havana. This was not a lower-class white without the means to support a respectable white family. Nor was this grandfather someone for whom a demographic shortage of white women supposedly had sent him into the arms of a woman of color, as some lay explanations have posited of Cuban interracial relations. This was a man who had made an intentional choice to create dual families. This history of dual families and race mixture has obvious parallels with the fictional one in *Cecilia Valdés*. Both were nineteenth-century stories of race mixture. In both cases, the white man took financial responsibility for his mixed-race offspring. But Juan's grandfather had one important difference from the fictional Candido Gamboa. He did not attempt to hide his paternity from his mixed-race offspring. However, he probably was not as forthright with his white wife.

Juan's family was the product of a long line of women of color, many of whom had relationships with white men. He described his great-grandmother as "una negra de nación," indicating that she was African. She had arrived in Cuba at some point in the mid-nineteenth century. That he described his grandmother also as black suggests that she was not born of an inter-racial relationship, unlike his mother and her siblings. Once the family's history of inter-racial relations began, it continued into the next generation. Juan's mother and one of his aunts married white men. Juan had gained a certain degree of social advancement because of these relationships. Since that aunt had no children of her own, he was raised more in her home than in his parents'. She was "married" to an Asturian shoemaker. Because Juan's father was a tobacco worker, he and Juan's mother lived in Tampa for at least four years, sometime during Juan's childhood. On such occasions he stayed in his aunt's home and often visited his father's family. He eventually received his primary education at a school at which one of his father's sisters was teaching. Juan's career choice was another area influenced by his white family members. After primary school, Juan learned the printing trade. One of his father's brothers was associated with a shop that printed the famous journal *Bohemia*. After a time in printing, Juan returned to his studies and completed secondary school. Eventually, with his uncle's help, he was able to enter university at some point immediately after the fall of President Gerardo Machado in 1933. Juan explained that he was able to achieve entrance only because his uncle "estaba muy relacionado" (was well connected). He acknowledged that racism had prevented many good students of color from obtaining similar success. He was among the lucky few that had bypassed prejudice and lack of opportunity.

Juan's university career began like so many others at the time. He wanted to study law. However, he was not successful and he eventually left university without completing a degree. By the late 1930s, Juan had married and started a family with a young black woman. At that point he also turned to a career in acting. He achieved much more success in this area. This allowed him to travel throughout Latin America and live for a time in Mexico after his first marriage fell apart in the early 1950s. He returned to Cuba in the late 1950s and was a recurring actor on the Cuban soap operas of the 1960s and 1970s. At separate times he established relationships with women of different racial backgrounds. His second wife was white and together they had two children, both of whom eventually settled in Miami. Juan also had children in a third long-term relationship, this time with a mulatta. So Juan's children covered a broad spectrum, from dark to white. However, the extent of their involvement in their father's life is uncertain. At the time of his interview, Juan was living in one squalid, flea-infested room in a *solar* (tenement house) in Old Havana. He did not appear to be benefitting from any remittances sent by his children in Miami.

Before ending this description of the role of race in Juan's family and his life, one final moment during the interview deserves mention. My assistant was prompted by Juan's near-white features to ask if he had ever "passed" or pretended to be white. He responded,

> Well, I don't suppose that I passed much, because I never liked that. I am not, never was a racist, never, never, never. Here it was a delirium before [the 1959 revolution]. The mulatto would put on a lot of powder and such, to be whiter. I never had no this defect of those no, no, no . . . but I never liked this problem that you are white, you are black, and you are . . . I never was into that. This [sentiment] began with my father, who was white [but], did not allow that my case [for anyone] to speak of race nor any of that.

Here was a family that was trying to erase the racial differences in which they were deeply embedded. But this attempted erasure should not be interpreted as the equivalent of whitening or passing. To this family, this erasure of racial differences appeared to be the common Cuban condition.

CARMEN AND JULIA

We were fortunate to conduct separate interviews with two sisters, Carmen and Julia, which result in a detailed picture of one family. They were originally from the eastern city of Manzanillo. Carmen was born in 1912 and Julia in 1916, two of the youngest in a family of twelve children. Like Juan above, they were fair-skinned people who described themselves as mestizas. However, their family's history of race mixture was a bit more complex. Both of their parents were also mestizos. Both were the children of mulattos and white women, a situation that has often been considered highly unusual for the late nineteenth century. However, the repetition of such stories may connect to the possibility that white women in such relationships were socially reclassified as African-descended, except among their descendants who held onto the valuable genealogical memory of their whiteness.

Julia and Carmen could not recall much about their father's family except that they were impoverished *colonos* (sharecroppers). They never knew their paternal grandparents, but they did know that their grandmother had died at a relatively young age. They recalled their maternal history much better. Their maternal grandfather, Fernando, was a rich mulatto of French and African ancestry. He owned a great deal of property in Manzanillo. He was also a transporter of rural produce and ran his own mule train. In an era before mechanized transportation, this was an important source of wealth. He had married twice. His first wife, a mulatta, had died after the couple had a large number of children. Julia and Carmen could not remember how many.

Fernando's second wife, Rafaela, was Julia and Carmen's grandmother. She was from a poor white family. She also was a widow. Her first husband, a white man, had died when she was only seventeen. At that time, Rafaela already had one daughter and had no opportunity to support herself. When Julia was asked if she had been told how the couple met, she responded with the cliché, "Esta fue una verdadera, triste historia de amor y dolor (This was a sad, true story of love and pain)." She told us how her grandmother had a good friend, a poor black woman, whom she used to visit frequently. Their grandparents met when the grandfather also visited this woman. Once their relationship developed, Rafaela's family objected. However, the couple married anyway. At that point, Rafaela's mother disowned her, declared her dead, and never again acknowledged her daughter's existence. Rafaela's familial connections to whiteness were severed. The couple eventually moved from their hometown and settled in Manzanillo. However, their relationship was short-lived. Rafaela died when their only child, Paula—Julia and Carmen's mother—was only two years old.

Carmen and Julia indicated that much of this history occurred during the Ten Years' War (1868–1878). However, other information they gave suggests that it was probably toward the end of that war, if not during the Guerra Chiquita (1879–1880), or in the last independence effort (1895–1898). They explained that at some point during the war their grandfather moved to Costa Rica. His oldest son stayed and fought. Paula remained in Cuba and was raised by an older sister. Her father left money to provide for her maintenance and her education at the hands of private tutors. Her family's position and wealth were confirmed by the fact that, unlike most Afro-Cuban women of the period, she never worked before she married.

Carmen and Julia were less clear about the circumstances under which their parents met. Carmen only said vaguely that "era una cosa de raza, en ese tiempo la gente fue bien vanidosa (it was a race thing, at that time the people were very vain)." It is unfortunate that we do not have a clear picture of what drew these two people from different class backgrounds together. Here was a peasant boy marrying a young woman of some means. The pair married sometime around Cuba's second war of independence, which began 1895. The first of their twelve children was born in approximately 1897. Carmen stated that her oldest brother, Rafael, was about fifteen years older than she.

The sisters did not emphasize the value of national independence for their family's history, but the independence struggle did engender one strong sentiment. Carmen was firm in stating, "tengo orgullo de ser de la raza de Maceo (I am proud to be of Maceo's race)." Their father, Joaquín, had been a veteran of the war. He received no personal benefit for his effort. He returned to the life of a simple farmer. Carmen and Julia did not comment on the American presence on the island after the war, except to say that the Americans often believed that their mother was white. They did not clarify in what capacity Paula would have had encounters with Americans. After her marriage, she had begun to work as a seamstress and concentrated the rest of her time to raising her children. Julia recalled that although her mother was fair enough to pass for white, the family was socially embedded in a black and mulatto context. The family participated in the local "Maceo" social club for people of color and was excluded from the white clubs. Julia said that not even "una mestiza blanconaza como yo pudiera entrar (a very fair woman, like me, could enter)."

The next generation continued to live relatively undistinguished lives. The boys farmed with their father and the girls became seamstresses, like their mother. One by one, they married and began their own families. Their spouses covered the spectrum of Cuban color categories. Four married persons described as mulattoes. Two of the sisters married white men and one married a black architect. Paula and her four youngest girls moved to Old Havana in 1928, initially settling with her second daughter Clementina and her Spanish husband. In 1940, Carmen married a white Cuban, Tomás, a warehouse worker. After her wedding, she never worked on a regular basis again, although she took the occasional sewing job at home. Carmen and Tomás seemed to define themselves not so much in racial terms but according to class. The social clubs defined by Spanish ethnicity were not for them, nor were the Afro-Cuban social organizations. Their greatest participation was in "la logia y el síndicato" (the lodge and the union). Carmen noted with pride Tomás's political allegiance to the activities of the black labor leader Lázaro Peña.

Julia was just sixteen when she married Ernesto, a mulatto plantation supervisor. He had been a longtime friend of the family. Together the couple had two children before he died. Shortly after his death, Julia relocated her family to Havana, where they briefly lived with Carmen and her husband. She was a widow for five years before she remarried. This marriage was to a white friend of Carmen and Tomás's. They remained together until his death in 1986. They never had children. As the interview ended and the recorder stopped, Julia was asked why she did not have children with her second husband. She responded, "no quería crear confusión racial para mis hijos (I did not want to create racial confusion for my children)." This response could lead one to wonder about the limits of whitening and racial integration. Julia knew racism was a fact of Cuban life that did not respect the privacy and intimacy of the home.

GILBERTA

Gilberta was the oldest of the female subjects interviewed. She was
ninety-two, a woman labeled by my Cuban assistant as mestiza. Although she was as fair as the two sisters described above, Gilberta described herself as "una morra," a term that is currently used by Cubans
to describe a dark person with straight hair. She was born in Havana,
the daughter of a "negro prieto" (dark-skinned black) and a woman she
variously described as mestiza or blanca. She also indicated that her
maternal grandfather was a mulatto claro while her grandmother was
white. She explained that for this reason her mother "salío blanca,
blanca, blanca (turned out white, white, white)." Both her parents were
from the small town of Manacas in the province of Villa Clara. Her
mother, Josefa, had run away with her father, Pedro, in order to escape
her abusive drunken father. According to Gilberta, her grandfather
then asked the police to pursue the matter and the young couple were
forced to marry after knowing each other only very briefly. Together
they settled in Havana before separating after a short time. Their relationship lasted only three or four years, just enough time to bear two
daughters.

Josefa and Pedro were from two different worlds. Gilberta recalled
that Josefa was from an economically stable family. Her father was a
public works inspector. Oddly, Josefa's mother also worked. She ran a
small fruit stand. This description is inconsistent with the general image of turn-of-the-twentieth-century white Cuban women. According
to that image, they would not enter relationships with men of color or
work in such a presumably undignified occupation as fruit vendor. Gilberta's description of her father's background is more consistent with
the general image of Afro-Cuban men. She does not remember her
father having any stable employment. He often had no money, "ni para
café (not even for coffee)." Socially, it was difficult for Josefa to have a
black husband and mestiza children. She was often called *cochina* (dirty
slut) when she walked in the streets with them. She had failed to uphold
the racial exclusivity expected of white women.

Gilberta remembers that although her parents separated, they were
not able to divorce for a long time. This was prior to legalized divorce
in Cuba, and in any case Pedro did not want to lose Josefa. Gilberta

recalled that on one occasion the couple was caught in a massive fight. It actually involved three people: Pedro, Josefa, and Josefa's Spanish lover. All were arrested. Nearly a century later, Gilberta still recalled the situation with pain.

> As my father did not have money, he was kept in prison. The Spaniard was released because he could pay the bond. And there it went on for a few years. And my mother was under house arrest at the home of one of my aunts. At that time, the laws were severe in this respect. And if a woman was found with a man other than her husband or in an inn [brothel?] she received four years in prison. It was [President] Batista who ended this and allowed divorce.

The couple was only able to divorce many years after their separation. Afterward, Josefa lived with the Spaniard, first in Manacas and later in Havana. He bought her homes in each case. Despite this financial assistance, Josefa worked outside the home to a limited extent. At some point after Gilberta was grown, Josefa trained and practiced as a midwife. She attempted to regain a level of social respectability. But race had always mattered within the home. Gilberta declared that her mother treated her and her sister Martina as maids and did not tell people they were her children. The Spaniard was a person of some means, a plantation owner who sold sugar to Americans. He never married Josefa, since he already had another legitimate family. Gilberta believed that there had not been much love between the Spaniard and his wife. When Gilberta was older, her mother told her that the two had married despite the objections of the wife's rich family, after she had become pregnant. The Spaniard frequently told Josefa, "Si yo pubiera encontrar a quien me diera el certificado yo la mato (If I could find a doctor to write the [death] certificate I would kill her)." That never occurred.

As an adult, Gilberta's own life contained some of the turbulence of her parents'. She received only a limited education and became pregnant at a young age by a white friend of one her cousins. At the time, she had not known that he was already married with two children. Her mother and "stepfather" were somewhat supportive when they learned this news. They would have allowed Gilberta to stay in their home, but her pride would not permit it, especially since her mother continued to treat her as a maid. Gilberta went to live with various friends. For a short time she stayed with a girlfriend. She then found another man to take care of her. He even provided her with a furnished apartment. She stayed with him until just after her son was born. She explained her next move: "When my son was born, this man was already old. I didn't like that and I went to live with someone else. I stayed with him for a time, until my son was older. That is how I spent my life." At that time Gilberta moved on to her third partner. This time it was a black man that she recalled as "era jubilado de los cigarros y todavía cogío buena pensión (already retired from the tobacco industry and receiving a good pension)."

Gilberta and her family reveal the darker side of amorous relationships in general. For Josefa, men seemed to have been the means of escaping her economic limitations. And Gilberta followed the same pattern. Their survival depended on their ability to attract and maintain relationships with economically viable men. Therefore, in and of itself, color did not appear to be foremost in their selection of partners. It existed in the background and obviously shaped economic possibilities. However, race/color played a direct role in generating the shame projected onto Josefa for having first a black husband and then mestiza daughters.

Los mulatos

ELBA

Elba was eighty-seven when she sat down for our interviews. Her family was from the central provincial capital Cienfuegos. She was described by my assistant as mulatta. She, on the other hand, would not place herself in any color category, except to say *"clarita"* (a little fair-skinned). She spoke of very little race mixture in her family. She seemed a bit perplexed and irritated at us even asking. Again, Elba would only describe her family as "eran de color, así como de mi color, claritos" (they were of color, just like my color, a little clear). She recalls growing up in a big house with her parents, both sets of grandparents, and her five brothers and sisters. The family lived a simple, stable, and economically adequate life.

The gender roles within the family seemed relatively straightforward. The men worked at agricultural labor and the women managed the home. Since the family lived in the city, the men would leave every morning for the countryside. Elba's mother took in sewing and her father, Ernesto, supplemented their income by playing clarinet in a municipal band. Her father exercised a great deal of freedom with respect to his marriage. Elba labels him "un diablito . . . era un poco mujeriego (a little devil . . . he was a bit of a womanizer)." Her father even had three children from other relationships, who were accepted by all.

Socially, the family was well integrated into the Afro-Cuban social organizations. Ernesto was a founding member of the La Minerva de Cienfuegos club. It is not possible to determine if that club was directly connected to the magazine *Minerva* discussed in chapter 6. That magazine first appeared in 1888 and reappeared in 1910 under new management and with a broader focus.[42] Elba described Ernesto's club as reserved for "lo mejorcito (the best families)." It had dances and excursions exclusively for its members of color. Elba suggested that the members were especially protective of the young female members. They were constantly chaperoned and not allowed to leave the house alone.

> ELBA: We were a group of young girls whose parents were always with us. They brought us to the dances and we did not go alone. [That is how it was] with respectable families, not like it is today with young women coming home at four in the morning.
>
> KYM: And when a young girl had a boyfriend, how was that arranged?
>
> ELBA: She had to go out with everyone, or if not, with a respected person, not solely with the boyfriend. That was not done.
>
> KYM: And for the young men, what was the process of obtaining a girlfriend?
>
> ELBA: They had to speak with the oldest person in the house, I agree with this. A [young girl] could not go out solely with the boyfriend. Her mother had to accompany them.
>
> KYM: And what of a young girl who went out with a young white man, what if she had a boyfriend like that?
>
> ELBA: They rejected her.
>
> KYM: Even if he was a good person?
>
> ELBA: Even if he was a good person, yes.
>
> KYM: Therefore, if a young girl had a white boyfriend, what did the people think of her?
>
> ELBA: It simply was not done that a respectable girl went out with a young white man. Not in that era, no.

These actions reveal the community's vigilance against both inter-racial relations and the sexual freedom of women of color. This community acted in a manner that suggests it perceived the social costs of inter-racial relations as very high.

Elba's own marriage had been to a young teacher whose family was from the same social group. They met at a dance and began a two-year courtship under the supervision of her mother. They married and eventually moved to Havana. There their lives continued in much the same way they had in Cienfuegos. Her husband belonged to a masonic lodge and the couple attended events at the well-known Afro-Cuban club Unión Fraternal. Elba's image of the lives of her family members is very different from the ones drawn for the mestizo families above. For the former, respect within the bounds of their racially defined group was valued more than material benefits of race mixture. They reflected the beliefs of the generations of prominent Afro-Cuban intellectuals who emerged immediately after slavery and independence. They did not confront racism directly but maintained selected moral standards of their community while simultaneously supporting its survival in positive racial terms.

Ana

Ana's background was very similar to that of Elba. She was seventy-nine at the time of our interview. She was born in the small town of Cartagena, in the province of Santa Clara. She labeled herself mulatta, born into a family of mulattoes. She described her father as a "mulatto claro" born of a "mulatto jabao" (fair-skinned man with black features, especially coarse hair) and a Spanish woman. Ana's knowledge of her paternal grandfather was pieced together from family stories. He had died before her birth, but her paternal grandmother was a central figure in her life. Ana's family visited her grandmother's home on a regular basis. In fact, Ana had been named for her. Ana described her mother's family as again one of mulattoes. One of the great-grandparents was from the Spanish province of Viscaya. Ana believed that it was her great-grandmother, but could not say with certainty. She was more sure of her maternal grandmother was the descendant of local indigenous people. This grandmother was an "india alta" (tall Indian).

Everyone in the family was an agricultural worker, mostly cane cutters. The family lived mostly from the income of her brothers. Ana was the youngest and her father died when she was four. Although the family was economically very humble, they belonged to one of the Afro-Cuban societies that guarded the integrity of the group. One year, Ana even became the "queen" of the Sociedad Maceo de Santa Clara. She was quick to point out that the queens in the black and mulatto societies were distinct from those in the white societies. The former chose their queen according to personality, while the others chose beauty queens. However, this statement has to be taken with a grain of salt since, even near eighty, it was obvious that Ana was once a stunning woman. As the club's queen, she was expected to comport herself with dignity. This was tested once as she happened upon her mother's employer. He was a white businessman and a politician. He was sitting in the park with a few friends and, upon seeing Ana, called her over. In a warm greeting, he kissed her on the cheek and embraced her. This was well outside the norms of decency for respectable Afro-Cuban women. Normally, Ana would not have spoken to a man on the street, but since he was her mother's employer, she felt it necessary. The town gossips ran back to her family with this news. Some even wanted to remove her as the society's queen. Fortunately, one of her brothers defended her honor, explaining the choice she had had to make. Here we have the extension of familial and institutional honor to an Afro-Cuban woman, a practice that has not received sufficient scholarly attention.

Like Elba above, Ana also met her husband through the society. She was eighteen when they met at a dance. He was a cane cutter like her brothers. Their relationship lasted for ten years before ending in divorce. Ana could not bear his continuous infidelity. During their marriage, she also worked at home as a seamstress, and after her divorce she supported herself in the same manner. She remarried to a mulatto after her son was grown. She faced many economic difficulties and barely managed at times. For this reason, she admitted to having had eight abortions. "Precisamente por no pasar necesidad y porque mis hijos no pasaran necesidades; eso es un delito, pero hasta cierto punto a mi entender fue necesario (This was precisely so as to not live in poverty and that my children would not suffer. It is a crime, but I understood it to be necessary)." One has to wonder how many other Cuban women, especially those of African descent, faced similar choices.

When she was asked about the issue of whitening, Ana spoke about the choices she had made in that realm. She indicated that the practice had been very prevalent and still existed.

> That idea abounds here, it still abounds here, even with the revolution. Even today there are those who have their little sin with this behavior. Although I have not lived it, I know that this legacy existed. This was something very difficult here, very difficult. Do you know what it is like to deal with a person, and just because they are white, they believe themselves to be superior? [But] as our history says, "He who does not have something from the Congo, has something from the Carabalí." Here we are all blacks and forgive me this expression, but Fidel speaks very clearly on this point . . . and we have the proof. Our race came most to Cuba: blacks such as ourselves.

Ana spoke passionately on this point and chastised those who have considered blanqueamiento as a possibility. Nonetheless, she also rejected the idea that all race mixture is whitening. She points to her own sister's marriage to a white man and how it was formed by love on both sides. However, there was a slight contradiction with the picture she painted earlier of restrictions placed on the interaction of respectable women of color with white men. She qualified that point by saying that her brother-in-law was not really white but "trigueño, ultimamente se decian blancos (wheat-colored, which is now called white). The attempts by their Afro-Cuban social organization to restrict the sexual choices of women of color may have worked in Ana's case, but it did not work with her sister.

Pilar

Pilar was one of the women extensively interviewed from 1969 to 1970 by the team of researchers led by the American ethnographers Oscar Lewis, Ruth Lewis, and Susan Rigdon.[43] She was twenty-seven at the time of those interviews and had lived in various Havana neighborhoods all her life. She defined herself as mulatta, and was the descendant of two generations of consensual unions between black women and white men, beginning with her maternal grandparents. Her maternal great-grandmother was African, but Pilar did not have many details to share about her. She had more firsthand observations of her maternal grandparents' union. She described her grandfather as a white former soldier who was very abusive toward his inter-racial family. Her grandmother was a black housewife who was very submissive and accepting of her husband's domestic tyranny. They had three daughters, including Pilar's mother. Pilar commented very little on her maternal grandparents' economic situation and only hinted at their poverty. Despite their economic difficulties, neither Pilar's grandmother nor mother worked outside the home. Both also had limited education.

When Pilar's parents married, her father's white family was disapproving. They believed he was "lowering himself by marrying a mulatta."[44] But he ignored this censure to commit to the woman he loved. Her father's family was better off economically than her mother's. Both paternal grandparents were private teachers who taught classes in their home. Her father, however, was constantly facing economic difficulties, although he appeared to have been very hardworking and educated. He would hold multiple jobs at a time. His work and his wife's mental-health challenges left the children largely unsupervised. Pilar spent a great deal of time with her black maternal grandmother. Her paternal grandmother was not as receptive and favored Pilar's light-skinned younger sister. Pilar was pained that

> My grandmother came right out and said that she took Francisca with her because my sister could pass for white and colored people weren't allowed in the places she went. My brother Aurelio was also on the light side, but Susana Xiomara and I were dark-skinned and she was embarrassed to be seen in public with us. Little Susana was even darker than I, and Grandmother used to call her "the monkey of the family."[45]

Pilar had completed only the sixth grade before educational costs forced her parents to remove her from school and at age thirteen she became a live-in maid. Shortly afterward, Pilar decided marriage was the solution to her problems. She was still thirteen when she turned a friendship with a twenty-seven-year-old white day laborer into something more serious. She married at fifteen. She had a daughter a year later and was separated a year after that. She then turned to prostitution and earned a living that way until the revolution.

For the next generation of women in Pilar's family, racial concerns continued to be important. By the time Pilar's oldest daughter was a young teenager working in revolutionary labor camps her father was monitoring what he read as her inappropriate attraction to black boys. He disapproved of possible inter-racial relations for his white daughter, even though she had been born from his marriage with a mulatta. Similarly, Pilar's light-skinned sister feared that people would notice even the slightest African features in her daughter, even though her African origins were four generations removed. By contrast, as the daughter Pilar had with a "dark-skinned man" after the revolution grew older, Pilar had taught her to have pride in being *mulatica*. The racialized reproductive choices made by members of Pilar's family attest to the multiple possibilities to define race anew in each generation. Some conceded to hegemonic patterns and accepted notions of white superiority; others lived their own personal resistance.

Los negros

Reyíta

In the mid-1990s, when Daisy Rubiera Castillo sat down to record the biography of her more than ninety-year-old mother, they both created a rare and valuable source that highlights the multi-generational dynamics of racialized reproduction in Cuba. Afro-Cuban ancestry and race mixture were among the important themes captured in María de los Reyes Castillo Bueno's, or Reyíta's, testimonial. Reyíta begins her family's history by demonstrating the deep historical links to Africa that were evident even during Cuban slavery. The memory of her maternal grandmother's specific African homeland of Cabinda survives. That grandmother, Tatica, was captured along with two sisters, and remarkably all three were shipped together and purchased by the same slave owner. Although the majority of their extended family bonds had been severed, these siblings managed to cling to one another through the difficulties of slavery and into their post-emancipation lives.[46] And this was a point of pride that Reyíta transmitted to her children.

As an enslaved woman, Tatica struggled to maintain the integrity of her Cuban family. She kept her relationship with a fellow slave, Basilio, a secret from their owner, despite the fact that the two had a son together. Her subsequent rape by that owner produced a daughter,

Reyíta's mother, Isabel. Tatica and Basilio continued as a couple despite this violation. They gained their freedom together and had another child. Reyíta's retelling of her grandmother's trauma accentuates for her readers the links between Cuba's slave past and its racial present. The importance of such transhistorical links is further emphasized by the realization that Reyíta's own twentieth-century decisions about marriage and children were fundamentally shaped by the legacy of the racism and sexism freely practiced in the nineteenth century, even within her own family.[47]

Isabel's birth after the September 1868 implementation of the Moret Law, the so-called free womb law, did little to differentiate her condition from the enslaved members of her family. She was forced to labor for her white father's household. After general emancipation, her father even used his paternal rights to retain her under his control as a worker. Isabel eventually fled, but found herself in abject poverty. Her gender was no reprieve from intense labor, and she survived by becoming a cane cutter. Her intimate relationships also defined her existence. Reyíta knew that although her mother had one long-term relationship with a black man, her father, Isabel continually found herself attempting to resolve her persistent material deprivations through ultimately disappointing relationships with white men. Despite the fact that she was born of a white male's sexual abuse of an African woman, Isabel accepted that black and mulatta women had few other options for sustaining themselves or for advancing socially. Reyíta implicitly read Isabel's choices as internalization of racism. This was also manifested in Isabel's deep-seated sense of racial shame toward her three dark-skinned children, including Reyíta, as opposed to the affection she demonstrated toward her mestizo children bore of white fathers. Isabel subjected the darker, "negro" three to abusive behaviors, such as insisting that they eat in a separate area from their lighter siblings, constant correction, and assignment of harsher chores. Reyíta became increasingly desperate to escape these abuses as she grew older.[48]

Reyíta was a young adult when she came to participate in Garveyite movements within Cuba.[49] This African-conscious politics may have partially equipped Reyíta against some of the psychological elements of racism, but it did not intervene against her profound desire for a white husband. She even prayed for this to the patron saint of Cuba, la Vírgen de la Caridad del Cobre. Many years later, as she explained to her daughter the material motives behind this desire, the reproductive politics of whitening were still present, although subdued.

> It goes without saying, now, that I love my race, that I'm proud to be black, but in those days marrying white was vital . . . I didn't want a black husband, not out of contempt for my race, but because black men had almost no possibilities of getting ahead and the certainty of facing a lot of discrimination. Their best chance was in sports: being a boxer . . . But anyway, apart from that, if a black man dreamed of getting away from poverty, back then, he had to set himself up as a huckster or a thug, and in the end, what? The penitentiary or death, and the reformatory for the younger ones . . . That's why I asked my Virgencita for a white husband. I wouldn't have been able to put up with seeing my children humiliated, harassed, mistreated, and much less living a life of vice. That's why I married a white man.[50]

Here, the pursuit of better material conditions for herself was coupled with a desire for children who would not be socially read as fully black. In Reyíta's mind, having a white father would ensure they would not be as mistreated as blacks. Within a year of her prayer, Reyíta met and "married" Antonio Amador Rubiera Gómez, a white Cuban of working-class origin. As the couple shared a life together and their family grew, she believed her hopes had been fulfilled. Only many years later did Reyíta learn of the false nature of her marriage. Although her union with Antonio would last until his death in 1975, he never formally registered the marriage, as she had initially believed. His parents and siblings did not accept the relationship and never acknowledged it. Reyíta and her children felt that rejection.[51] Although they lived in various racially diverse settings, they encountered racial discrimination both inside and outside their home.

FERNANDO, ESTELLA, MARCOS, AND GLORIA

Fernando, Estella, Marcos, and Gloria were interviewed separately, but shared very similar family histories. Each was initially described by my Cuban assistant as negro. As they shared their respective stories, it became clear that Marcos and Gloria also possessed some Chinese ancestry. Neither was very specific on the point, and both spoke only vaguely of Chinese grandfathers. Like Reyíta above, any potential claim to a racially mixed background was obscured by predominantly black physical features and the lack of social ties to white or Asian relatives. Marcos was seventy-eight and born in Güines. Gloria was eighty-two, and a Havana native. Estella was seventy-six, and also from Havana. Fernando was the oldest, at ninety-two. He had been born and raised in Matanzas. Their testimonies are grouped together here, not because their life experiences were less valuable than those told above, but because the most common factor in their lives was labor. Their personal histories and those of their ancestors were remembered largely in terms of work. Each had little or nothing to say about Afro-Cuban racial pride or the processes of racial mixture in their families. Marcos spoke about his experiences as a dock worker on the Havana wharf. Fernando had originally been a cane cutter, but he eventually settled in Havana and became an elevator operator in the Capitol building. Estella and Gloria had been maids. Each of them had begun their work lives at very young ages. Each of them remembered working outside their homes by age eight.

Of their families, they said very little. The separation of their respective parents was common; Gloria was the only one whose parents had not separated or divorced. The others spoke of being raised by their mothers, with occasional visits from their fathers. Each explained this as one of the reasons they had to enter the labor force at such young ages. Their own experiences with their partners had been similar. Marcos spoke about the two mothers of his three children, but he had never married. Fernando had married late in life, in his late forties. He then divorced after a few years. Estella had married at a young age and then divorced a short time later. Although she and her ex-husband had a daughter together, she had been solely responsible for her economic support. For this reason, she did not bother with most men afterward. To her, they did not seem worth the trouble.

This group represented those for whom mestizaje had minimal significance in their lives. However, none of them attributed this experience to any specific cause. As with all of the cases presented, one cannot distinguish between the possibilities and limitations created by personal choices and those imposed by structural constraints. However, in these four cases, extremely demanding working conditions and difficult family situations may have been factors that limited their interaction with partners of other races. It also important to understand from these personal histories that the study of shifting racial meaning within Cuba cannot be solely presented in terms of race mixture. Many families and individual continue to define themselves solely as black.

SPIRITUAL MESTIZAJE

Both discourse and practice related to mestizaje appear within a third Cuban social site, beyond intellectual renderings and standard family formation. Afro-Cuban religions allowed for new consideration of race through the interactions of their African-descended and European-descended participants. Outside of the standard Euro-American kinship forms, the spiritual kinship patterns established through Cuba's African-derived religions have generated alternative social identities and constructed independent notions of race. People initiated into African-derived religions were not just attesting to a belief in another set of gods and spirits; they were also committing themselves to spiritual families of profoundly extended genealogies and social value. At least since the end of the nineteenth century, these spiritual families or *ramas* have been inter-racial networks that often trace their genealogy to a specific ethnic community of continental Africa.[52] Like all initiates, the whites connected to these networks often profess an African spiritual ancestry with the same force that they profess their biological lineages. The very term "Afro-Cuban religion," while accurately indicating origin, obscures centuries of white involvement in these practices. Oral histories and other sources attest to white initiation at least since the middle of the nineteenth century, and in 1882, a group of white practitioners of Abakuá formally incorporated themselves according to government regulations.[53] Yet, due to a long history of perceptions of barbarism and state repression, public disclosure of participation by Cuban whites may be reserved for moments when the initiated person believes herself to be in contact with someone who shares a similar background. As a dark-skinned foreign traveler in Cuba, this author often encountered people of white phenotype who were quick to note their Yoruba or Kongo ancestors of either spiritual or biological affiliation.

While this study did not thoroughly interview persons affirming such identities, one of the interviews conducted by the Oscar Lewis team provides some insights in this area. Argentina Bondi spoke to the Lewis team to provide additional information associated with the team's more in-depth ethnography of her son's life. Elements of Alfredo Barrera Bondi's life history were presented above and reveal a social outlook filled with racism. His mother was the daughter of Italian immigrants who came to Cuba at the turn of the twentieth century. Her father was a skilled construction worker whose income fluctuated greatly. After a time in Havana, the family was able to purchase a small farm, but its income was unstable. Argentina Bondi married very young to a white local farmhand, but that marriage was very brief. She was still in her teens when she entered her second, more longer-lasting relationship with a mulatto day laborer. As she matured she came more involved with Santería (an Afro-Cuban religion primarily of West African, Yoruba ethnic origin) and invested a great deal of time, money, and energy into its rites. She described herself as a devotee of the Yoruba goddess Yemaya and explained that many other whites secretly were strong Santería adherents. In her commitment to her religion, her *madrina* (the woman who initiated her) was an important focus of her social life. Argentina surrounded herself with other believers from the same rama, many of whom were presumably black. Their *casa templo* (house temple) was likely similar to what several commentators have described as the smaller sites of Afro-Cuban religious veneration that began to replace the government-regulated *cabildos de nación* at some point in the middle of the nineteenth century.[54] Her testimonies reveal a woman for whom race had little of its typical negative meaning. It is not clear if this is a result of her marriage, her religious beliefs, or simply her personal convictions. She was not as troubled as her son Alfredo that many of her children had married Afro-Cubans, or that her grandchildren had mixed racial ancestry. She welcomed all.

Similar accounts of white adherence to Yoruba ethnicity are also documented elsewhere. For many, what begins as a momentary and reluctantly-pursued reliance on the orishas to intervene in a crisis often becomes a more permanent spiritual and social re-orientation. Such was the case of Evelio Iglesias Quintana. He was born in Cuba in 1909, into a middle-class white family. While he was a young child, his unbelieving family had been told that he eventually would be initiated into Santería. In his early adulthood he also had disparaged this possibility.

> I felt myself to be refined; I was a teacher, an instructor of stenography and typing. I also taught algebra. I surrounded myself with fine and decent people. I saw some people speaking and said to them, "Why the hell would I mess with that nonsense, with those blacks and whites, and those dirty and insignificant people."

However, prompted by an intense illness, he sought the assistance of a local santero and was initiated in 1944. He went on to become one of the most respected priests in Cuba before going into exile in Miami. He openly asserted his devotion to the Yoruba gods and highlighted his spiritual genealogy to a prominent nineteenth-century black priestess from Matanzas, Fermina Gómez. "This lady brought *Olukun* [an orisha associated with the sea] to my godfather, and the first Olokun that he initiated, was mine. Ferminita Gómez, is my grandmother in Olokun, and the great-grandmother of my godchildren in Olokun, because they also have my Olokun spirit."[55] In this way, Evelio traced the type of African-based spiritual genealogy that is accepted by many Cubans, regardless of the biological ancestry or phenotypical identification that are often (mis)interpreted as race.

Cuba's African-derived religions have created a collective spiritual identity among initiates. This is the case regardless of race. So when one is initiated into Santeria, for example, one becomes *un negro Lucumí* (a black of Lucumí or Yoruba ethnicity). These religions then become sites for uncoupling biological race from social race. The anthropologist Stephan Palmie writes, "*Africanity and blackness* are not coterminous in the world of Afro-Cuban religion. Nor have they, for what must surely be a long time, more than partially overlapped in complex and ill-understood ways."[56] As Cubans negotiate these overlaps, they redefine the biological and cultural meaning of race to allow for less restrictive alternatives. Cuban opinions on inter-racial interactions and amorous relationships have varied. Some, like Alfredo, celebrated the passage to whiteness. Others celebrated "Cuban color" and notions of common genealogy as ways of minimizing the causes of social discrimination. Some fostered collective black and mulatto unity and survival. And still others traced the origins of their spiritual genealogies to Africa, and made a racially inclusive Africanity, instead of biology, the source of modern *cubanidad*. The epilogue will discuss how Afro-Cubans utilized race and gender policies after the 1959 revolution to redefine these familial experiences of mestizaje to pursue a more unified image of the Cuban nation.

EPILOGUE

Revolutionary Social Morality and the
Multi-Racial National Family, 1959–2000

INTRODUCTION

What are the present ramifications of Cuba's long history of racialized reproduction? Many commentators begin by pointing to the island's specific and often debated demographic proportions of mulattoes, blacks, and whites. The most recent Cuban census, from 2012, reports these proportions by "skin color" as 64.1 percent white, 26.6 percent mulatto, and 9.3 percent black.[1] By contrast, a 2007 U.S. Central Intelligence Agency assessment listed those proportions at 51 percent mulatto, 11 percent black, and 37 percent white.[2] Important questions arise from these statistics: Which group in fact numerically predominates, and why should it matter? Some scholars focus less on demographics and more on the political value of race, often noting the continuing presence of anti-black discrimination within the context of proclaimed revolutionary egalitarianism. For them, the presence of a racial democracy is called into question. Yet, beyond politics and demography, a more complete inquiry into racial meaning in Cuba would also acknowledge the additional complexity found in more intimate and reproductive domains. Such an analysis would account for the everyday notions Cubans hold about self, otherness, and familial concepts of belonging.

Like so many other narratives that tie together the multiple strands of family life and history that make up Cuban racial identities, one family's story highlights the links between the pre- and post-revolutionary intimate behaviors associated with race-making. In 1970, three Cubans sat down with a Jamaican interviewer to speak of the personal transformations brought by the 1959 Cuban Revolution and inadvertently highlighted the sexual and reproductive elements of race. Sylvia, a black physician, began the conversation. She spoke of the revolutionary transformations largely in positive terms. The revolution had defined her professional success. Prior to it, she believed the goal of becoming a physician would have been unobtainable for someone like herself. As a teenager, she had been barely literate, and had lived and worked in her family's small bar. However, by the time of her interview, she was a respected doctor, with a decent Havana apartment.[3]

Yet Sylvia was ambivalent about one aspect of the revolution. Her relationship with her racially mixed teenage son, Miguel, remained unsettled.[4] He was a young man with whom she had little contact. He had been born of her brief relationship with a white neighbor, George, six years before the triumph of the revolution. Sylvia described their short-lived union with some anguish.

> He [George] was a soft white man and I would do anything for him—work for him, lie down for him, have a baby for him, but I didn't dare hold him. I loved him. He wasn't the kind of young white Cuban who would pass and put his hand on your front. That kind of brute I could [not] deal with. But George would hang around feeling very romantic—till the sperm was out of his sack of course, and then he was off. Days he would pass the shop and forget I was there. Then he'd way-lay me at night, push me up against a tree, then down on the ground, and curl up on my body like a baby. I am a woman who feels her rights, from very young; for example I knew where black men stood with me. I was reserved for white. Then I was pregnant and never saw George.[5]

Racialized notions of sexuality and love abound in Sylvia's vision of her interaction with George. She was adamant about her disinterest in black men and claimed this dismissiveness as a right. Only white men would do. Yet she would not tolerate outright sexual abuse from them and had to be courted to some extent. George did that for a time, until he had won her over sexually. He then ended any public acknowledgment of their relationship and limited their interactions to fleeting sexual encounters. Despite longing for something more permanent, Sylvia resigned herself to their second-class liaison. Her pregnancy bought all these issues to the fore. George disappeared from Sylvia's life. However, he later returned to claim their child.

After their son Miguel was born, George kidnapped the baby from her home. Sylvia was distraught and desperate for Miguel's return. But her pleas to the government were ignored. She believed racism had shaped the Batista government's inaction, since, at that time, the responsible parties assumed a white father would have been better for the child than a presumed ignorant, black mother. Sylvia only saw her child from a distance, as George had restricted all access. However, a change occurred at some point after 1959, when the new revolutionary authorities stepped in. Under their auspices, Miguel was taken from George and raised in state facilities. From that time forward he had little contact with either parent.[6]

The continuation of Sylvia's story revealed her new, post-revolutionary outlook on racialized sexual relations. Prior to the revolution, she had been exclusively interested in white men. Afterward, she reconsidered the basis of that preference.

> When I entered medical school I went out with a white boy who kept telling me how to behave, and whose father, a revolutionary, approved of me because the coupling would "improve the race." Our children would be whiter than me. He mentioned that old shit in my hearing, in a sadistic sort of way, and the fellow revolutionary he said it to winked at him. Right in my face. It was on that business I broke with the son. He saw what happened, same as me, and would not admit it. Would not admit, because really at bottom he wasn't all that upset about it. He didn't hate it.[7]

If whitening had been an option for Sylvia earlier, it certainly was not now. While one cannot definitely claim that the revolution caused Sylvia to rethink her racial attitudes, it provided the context for a shift. Both racial and economic equality were its much vaunted goals, and Sylvia had benefitted from access to better education. She also gained a new sense of self-worth and was comfortable in later marrying a black man. However, the revolution did not fix her broken relationship with her son, and she continued to regret their minimal contact.[8]

George, the father of Sylvia's son, told the story of their interaction somewhat differently. She had been nothing more than a cheap sexual diversion for him. When she bore his only child, George believed it necessary and honorable to save Miguel from the miserable life Sylvia presumably would have offered him. George absconded with his infant son one day when Sylvia was away from her home. While he wanted no further contact with Sylvia, George had nothing but love and concern for his son. He remembered his family life and Sylvia just before Miguel was taken from him by revolutionary authorities:

> The boy was mine, had no dealings with his mother, none whatsoever, a little black girl in a bar—he didn't even know that. There were many times I thought of moving because I believed people around her would shame him with that, but they respect us too much. They say nothing about the mother. There have been one or two damn careless remarks, and the boy is alert, but nothing much. He never knew her. That class of person could never be in his life, till this government exposed him.[9]

George acknowledged that his son was in his term "colored." Yet he had firmly believed he could raise the child without knowledge of his black ancestry. And he expected his community to participate in the subterfuge and allow the child to live without connection to his mother's black past. George believed that the white portion of his son's background was sufficient to give Miguel a sense of identity.

Miguel's interview revealed his complete disinterest in both parents and a more revolutionary identity. Despite the fact that his white grandmother had initially taught him to reject the revolution's ideals and programs, the seventeen-year-old Miguel made vehement claims to a revolutionary mulatto and black identity:

> I am a worker, a soldier . . . am a mulatto, a negro, a black working man. My friends are black working men. I'm happy with them . . . And white Cubans I dislike. Any whitey who tells me he feels equal with a black Cuban is a liar. My revenge is to have minimum dealings with them. Polite. No more. One of my hobbies is to watch black men climb up in the revolution.[10]

Years in socialist boarding school and other life experiences had changed him. He came to define himself through his close association with blacks and other mulattoes.

In these histories, three distinct visions of the connections between the concepts of race, family, and revolution appear. Before the revolution, Sylvia could not imagine herself with a black partner and had allowed herself to be sexually exploited by the white George. After the revolution, she no longer permitted white racial superiority to define her relationships. Before the revolution, George saw no problem in having a casual sexual relationship with the black Sylvia. He did not contemplate anything more between them. However, he received their mixed-race child into his family and home and fully loved his son. He would have continued to shield his son from the black side of his heritage if the revolution had not occurred. In his words,

> I was very well assured that I could look after my son and my mother. The boy is colored but his grandmother had no doubts about how her friends up there [perhaps in the United States] would react. I had doubts. You never can tell—strangers, you understand—the boy is colored, would that put gum in the works, ha, ha, now I wasn't sure, but the grandmother had no doubts, and she of course knew substantial people.[11]

There are obvious racial tensions in this statement. George was not sure what his mother's friends "up there" would have thought of his mulatto son. After 1959, George had attempted to get the child out of the country, but that plan failed when the authorities had Miguel sent away to boarding school. For Miguel, that experience taught him that the ideals of the revolution were more valuable than his relationship to his biological family. He also had learned to reject the white dimension of his ancestry. He was mulatto and linked in struggle with blacks. Nothing else mattered.

The above testimonies also reveal just how much post-1959 Cuban notions of race had changed from those of the nineteenth century; we see publicly asserted black pride alongside ambivalence toward inter-racial reproduction. Yet, one has to be careful in considering the new perspectives revealed by these stories. What was the agent of change? It is too easy to assume that the revolution was exclusively responsible for these notions of race and family. Such a view of transformation would fail to acknowledge the various interlinked constructions of race and family that existed prior to the revolution. These were not simply created anew after 1959.

Despite its intended complete social transformation, the revolution was built on the foundation of older social practices and beliefs. Prior to 1959, many had been subaltern practices, existing unexamined below the standard discourse. But with the revolution they became more apparent and more fully incorporated into the official image of the nation. This study ends with a discussion of that process. However, we will first revisit and summarize the conclusions from earlier chapters related to Cuba's pre-revolutionary history of race in the domain of the family.

REPRODUCING RACE: VALUES AND PRACTICES PRIOR TO 1959 SUMMARIZED

The central aim of this study is to explore the links between race and family formation in Cuba. This objective has been developed around the premise that race is not solely an abstract concept. Races, like nations, need the presumed characteristics that define them and the material bodies to populate them. Selective reproductive acts provide the mechanisms through which both these elements of race are achieved. To demonstrate the specific details of these processes, this study began by questioning the ideological and demographic factors in Afro-Cuban reproduction under colonial slaveholding. The reproductive practices of free and enslaved African-descended people were inextricably bound to the ways race was imagined and lived.

While the existing Cuban race relations historiography has frequently explored the political and intellectual dimensions of racial formation, the familial space in race relations studies remains underdeveloped. As a fundamental building block for social relations in Cuba (and elsewhere), "the family" represents the collective identity and continuity given to selected reproductive acts and their outcomes—offspring. Ethnicity and race emerge from the family in terms of biologically defined concepts of reproduction, and people use notions of family to negotiate social belonging and exclusion.[12] Through this negotiation family becomes an active agent of historical change. The family, in both concept and structure, is not solely a lens through which to view change, as much of the existing historiography suggests. Ideas about family, and their social relations and practices, also have the power to reconfigure other social categories, such as race. The ideologies behind mating and family formation define how one comes to occupy a racial category. To comprehend these ideologies and their associated acts, it is first necessary to accept that a child is not born into some a priori black, mulatto, or white body. Instead he or she comes to occupy one of these categories based on a number of familial and societal choices.

These reproductive acts are normalized, and also continually transformed, by what I posit as a *sexual economy of race,* which operates within racial heterogeneous societies to classify sexual behaviors and the resulting offspring. Within any particular setting, the sexual economy of race begins with the designation of social-sexual agents by race, class, gender, and so on. Mate selection follows, with an awareness of the permissible limits of racial choice. These limits then are used to classify the nature of the sexual relationship—as marriage, consensual union, concubinage, or rape. With procreation, the offspring are categorized based on all of the preceding inputs. Memory of the previous steps and the practices of preceding generations contribute to each classificatory moment. One accepts (or contests) a racial classification based on knowledge and valuation of ancestry. The status of each social-sexual agent is, at least in part, based on public knowledge of one's progenitors. The white person rejects the presence of non-European progenitors, while the black person might make the opposite claim. The final element in this racialized reproductive calculus is the family's normative or disruptive relationship to the existing social order.

Taking the family as a critical agent of Cuban history, slavery initially defined the characteristics of early Cuban sexual economy of race. It stipulated one's initial legal identity based on the doctrine of *partus sequitur ventrem,* whereby maternal identity defined the child's and paternity was made less relevant. Slavery also prompted a racial endogamy that maintained the boundaries between groups according to labor status. Through the concept of *limpieza de sangre* (purity of blood), honorable images of the white family were central to the regulation of social behavior in the colonial period. White men were discouraged from marrying women of color, and honorable white women were secluded from the public in order to protect them from social engagement with, and more importantly, from intercourse with, men of lesser status, especially mulattoes and blacks. However, while these behaviors initially appear to be unquestionably standard, they in fact existed within a much more complex constellation of sexualized race-making behaviors. Cubans of African descent also exercised family agency to survive as a racially defined group. One might also speak of Afro-Cuban racial groups, depending on the extent to which reproductive self-isolation has been maintained between blacks and mulattoes.

While most of Cuba's reproductive practices generated the expected classificatory results, where either whiteness or blackness was unquestioned, some outcomes were less obvious. These non-normative responses played a decisive role in changing racial definitions. Examples include the extension of social honor to the families of African-descended men who led Spanish colonial militias; the conspiratorial community efforts to establish white legal identities for mixed-race children; and "whites" who refused the benefits of the accepted racial hierarchy and reclassified themselves as people of color. It is not race mixture alone that transforms racial meaning in these cases. The respective modes of survival of white and black families, and the repetition of both subversive and normative practices, also contributed to this transformation.

This study began by considering Afro-Cuban reproduction and family formation in relation to other transformations in Cuban slavery. Afro-Cuban reproduction (for both the free and enslaved) was examined according to the major temporal divisions with that system: the period prior to 1762; 1763 to 1789; 1790 to 1820; 1821 to 1867; and 1868 to 1886. Each period was defined by the distinct legal or economic patterns that characterized the institution of slavery. Within early Spanish colonial reproductive policies the goal of re-creating a Catholic, Hispanic society has to be understood alongside the enforcement of racial distinctions. Even the treatment of the enslaved reflected this goal and influenced a unique sexual economy of race that would distinguish itself from those of later periods. Through the seventeenth century and prior to the British invasion of Havana in 1762, enslaved people were engaged largely in urban non-agricultural settings. Cuba's transition from a society with slaves to a slave society paralleled the growth of capitalist authority and social perspectives. Pre-existing feudal thought and practices were weakened. Afro-Cubans lost their earlier social value as potential Catholic defenders of the Spanish empire to become seen almost exclusively as laborers of the island's booming economy. The large-scale importation of African ethnics not only changes economic relations; it also transformed the intimate, personal landscape of those mulattoes and blacks with a multi-generational family presence in Cuba.

Pre-nineteenth-century documentary sources relevant to Afro-Cuban reproductive lives remain limited. Baptismal records for Havana's Espíritu Santo parish from 1765 to 1767 reveal several patterns. The population was mostly locally born, and births expanded it more than did the forced arrival of African ethnics. More of the parish's Afro-Cuban infants were baptized as free than enslaved. A significant number were free despite birth to enslaved mothers. Evidence from this period suggests caution when interpreting Afro-Cuban access to freedom largely as the result of inter-racial unions and reproduction. That access is more likely due to the work of Afro-Cuban family efforts, whether it occurred before birth, at baptism, or later.

Most infants, whether free or enslaved, were born to married couples. However, free children were more than twice as likely to be legitimate. Despite their low numbers in this study's mid-eighteenth-century sample, free African mothers did not baptize illegitimate children. These findings support the conclusions of other scholars that African cultural elements did not proscribe Christian marriage, even during enslavement. By contrast, the majority of children born to enslaved parda women were baptized without fathers named. This information suggests some concurrence with the observations from the British Caribbean that decreased regard for marriage seems to have increased along with the proportion of American-born slaves. However, in this sample, the majority of children born to enslaved black creole women were legitimate. That Afro-Cuban reproductive patterns more closely approximated those of whites suggests that at this stage of Cuban history, few associated blackness with an innate moral or social difference from whites. That notion emerged at some later point. Additionally in this period, inter-racial marriages were socially acceptable. Their numbers were low yet they marked a degree of familial interaction between whites and people of color and suggest that at that time mixed-race people were not assumed to be illegitimate. The 1778 Spanish pragmatic on unequal marriage curtailed legitimacy for bi-racial children and exposed them to assertions of questionable moral heritage.

The Espírtu Santo baptismal records also reveal the presence of alternative forms of family construction, including both legal and illegal variants that existed beyond marriage. For example, families created by the paternal recognition of *hijos naturales reconocidos* (recognized natural children) appeared for the first time. In the legal process associated with these recognitions, parents (usually fathers) accepted responsibility for the welfare and education of children born out of wedlock. These bonds between parent and child created family regardless of the relationship between the parents or their living arrangements. The parents who made such recognitions established a legal commitment to their children that existed in a social space distinct from the normally understood categories of legitimate and bastard. This alternative family form maintained an important social presence for the remainder of Cuba's colonial period and provides valuable analytical insights into both the survival of previously unconsidered Afro-Cuban families and inter-racial families.

For the period between 1790 and 1820, again, most Afro-Cuban children were born into legitimate marriages. This phenomenon was followed by an abrupt increase in illegitimacy that paralleled the intensification of plantation slavery. Simultaneously, the distinctions between rural and urban slavery also increased, despite the continued interaction between the two. The gender-ratio imbalance found within rural slavery became more pronounced. African men vastly outnumbered their female counterparts. The anecdotal evidence indicates few marriages and low reproduction rates in rural areas. By contrast, in urban areas women and free people of color predominated. Mulatto and black reproduction in these areas remained strong. Yet, in these regions marriage rates also declined. Moreover, with even greater restrictions on inter-racial marriage few inter-racial families were legitimated. It was at this point that many in the dominant social sectors began to associate race mixture with a morally questionable ancestry and that the social distance between whites and people of color increased even further. The legal avenues of family formation had become more defined by race.

On the other hand, inter-racial mating continued in illegal relationships, and many white fathers continued to socially acknowledge their inter-racial children. They and their recognized children constructed more positive images of *mestizaje* (racial mixing). Their public recognition of inter-racial families limited the possibility of viewing race mixture as a shameful occurrence. These families belied the image of these practices as ones in which white fathers wanted little connection with their mixed-race offspring and women of color solely sought them as a whitening strategy. Those families that formalized their relationships were able to distinguish themselves from their counterparts in other areas of the Americas where such paternal bonds were often not reinforced in the law.

The documentary evidence also reveals more subversive family practices that corrupted Cuban standards of racial classifications. In a number of cases, Cuban family members illegally manipulated the legal identities of white fathers, the mulatto or black mothers, or the offspring so that their children could receive white standing. And the agents of these manipulations often went beyond just the immediate families. At times, larger institutions such as the Church and Church-controlled orphanages participated in racial reclassification. In this way, the assignment of black, mulatto, and white identities operated beyond some semi-official calculus based on the status of the parents. For example, whereas in most of Latin America the social formula of white plus black equaling mulatto was the norm, late colonial Cubans could exercise family strategies that allowed white plus black to equal white. Thus, nineteenth-century Cuban racial classifications demonstrated even more flexibility than the simple social whitening according to wealth seen elsewhere in Latin America.

After 1820, reproduction and family formation within Cuban slavery were shaped by several additional factors. First among these was the criminalizing of the slave trade. Although the illegal trade continued to be sizable, the Spanish government's promotion of more protective, and even pro-natal, policies was seen in some quarters. However, because of the limitations in existing documentary and demographic data, it is difficult to assess the extent to which such policies had any impact. Additionally, the fact that slave reproduction did not occur within a closed system (i.e., slaves reproducing only slaves) only increases the analytical challenge of evaluating the demographic growth rates. While in the strictest sense Cuban slaves demonstrated little natural increase, other factors in slave reproduction must also be considered. A measurable percentage of enslaved people were able to eventually gain freedom. The significant population of free people, new groups of *emancipados* (those Africans rescued from illegal enslavement after 1820) and indentured Asians transformed the social borders of slavery, as well as its reproductive dimensions. The likelihood of an Afro-Cuban child being born to two enslaved parents decreased. Also, marriage rates among both free and enslaved people of color continued to decline significantly from what they had been in the eighteenth century.

The next period discussed in this study, 1868–1886, was bounded by the beginning of the wars of independence and its concomitant abolition efforts at one end and the granting of final emancipation at the other. An important reform was the 1870 Moret Law that freed several categories of enslaved people, including children born after September 17, 1868. This study considered how the gradual abolition of Cuban slavery affected the modes of family formation for people of color. This issue was framed in relation to similar situations in other slaveholding regions of the Americas. Whereas initial increases in marriage rates with emancipation were seen in other African American populations, the Cuban case was the exception. Cuban mulattoes and blacks therefore were less likely to marry as freedom approached. On the other hand, as slavery waned, some re-established family bonds through the continued practice of recognizing children born out of wedlock. Again, Cubans had open to them this intermediate family form, distinct from the standard legitimate and illegitimate category.

When considering the decreasing marriage rates, it is important to note that when compared to other slaveholding societies, marriage was a less novel experience for Cuban blacks and mulattoes. The records indicate that, despite the difficulties of slavery, many still had access to marriage. Structural limitations to slave marriage developed more out of the lack of priests, the persistent gender-ratio imbalance, and restrictions on inter-racial marriage than any generalized desire of the master class to restriction such unions. And Afro-Cubans also had options beyond marriage for the legal recognition of non-marital families.

After 1886, in the years toward the end of the colonial era and beginning of the republic, the rise of an Afro-Cuban political and intellectual leadership was critical to transformations in race relations. This engagement first had been seen within the slave society. And then the quest for national sovereignty and stability brought this group even more into prominence. In the slave-holding period, the acquisition of freedom was obviously a key element of the creation and advancement of Afro-Cuban leaders. In considering some of the methods by which freedom was obtained, the intervention of family appears to have been very valuable. While masters often contributed toward freedom, it was largely Afro-Cubans who pursued freedom for themselves and their family members. Once emancipated, free people of color occupied a variety of socio-economic positions within Cuban society. While many barely managed to sustain themselves through their physical labor, others managed to acquire wealth and prestige. Education and the command of a marketable skill distinguished the men in the latter group from the former. Possibilities existed for both blacks and mulattoes. Thus, for people of color, economic and other social distinctions that approximated class existed alongside the color distinctions that were so prominent within Cuban society.

Family structure and the modes of its formation were two of the more important concerns described in the post-emancipation Afro-Cuban self-improvement ethos. By the beginning of the twentieth century, private questions of illegitimacy and race mixture had become part of the larger public debates on the nature of Cuban society. The concept of "civilization" became the major trope against which a nation's right to sovereignty was measured and many Afro-Cuban intellectuals joined their white counterparts in using the imagined ideal of the European patriarchal family as the standard to which Cubans should conform. Their perceptions of Afro-Cuban failures in this area generated angry critiques of the sexual freedom of the lower classes and the ability of women of color to engage in inter-racial consensual relationships.

Despite the strength of these negative perceptions of non-marital families, more liberal views of the family also entered the political arena. By 1940, Cuban feminists had established an important political space for themselves. Together with other progressive forces, they won major reforms to marriage laws, including the right of divorce and the legal acceptance of illegitimate families. This in turn minimized the legal distance between legitimate and illegitimate families and changed perceptions of the distance between Afro-Cuban and white styles of family formation. In a parallel process, the removal of legal markers of race within Cuban vital registries also revealed a major shift in racial distinctions in family formation. Children no longer received official racial labels at birth. Yet, in other social and economic practices, important racial distinctions persisted.

Mestizaje also remained important in early twentieth-century articulations of Cuban identity. While it had been hidden under much of the public discourse related to the quest for national sovereignty and respectability, mestizaje underlay many Cuban social and cultural experiences. By the mid-1920s, fresh ideas about race and race mixture were advanced by a new generation of Cuban intellectuals, those who had never known either slavery or Spanish domination. For many participants in the Afrocubanismo movement, Cuba's racial diversity and uniqueness became a new point of pride and national identity. The African-derived elements were brought to the fore in literature and the arts.

It is important to note that Afrocubanismo was not a monolithic movement. Noticeable differences concerning the meaning of race were found among its members. Some emphasized mestizaje as a cultural process and others concerned themselves with its familial or biological aspects. Only rarely were there any efforts to unite these two perspectives. Additionally, while whites tended to emphasize the Afro-Cuban exotic, writers of color highlighted racial integration. They drew upon a sense of family genealogy in which once divergent racial identities merged. In doing so, they walked a fine line between a vision of mestizaje that promoted a homogeneous Cuban identity that removed the black and white extremes and one that allowed for continued racial diversity.

The family practices of ordinary people should not be left out of this picture of the familial dimensions of race in the early republic. Beyond the intellectual discussions, race obviously continued to be significant in everyday familial experiences. Race was an ever-present factor in both economic survival and social choices. Very personal family histories collected from several older Cubans of color expressed some of those choices. Some selected partners according to race. Others did so in spite of it. While the range of racial variation in sexual and marital practices would have been striking to a North American observer, social pressures for endogamous selection remained strong. The older Cubans interviewed for this study also revealed one previously unacknowledged factor in race relations: the protectiveness practiced by Afro-Cuban families and social organizations toward young women of color. This stemmed from a belief in their vulnerability to the sexual predations of white men. A few of this study's informants spoke of the means by which these societies attempted to prevent relationships between white men and women of color. In doing so, these societies not only attempted to control female sexuality, they were also demonstrating a concern for the racial survival of Afro-Cuban people. While they could appreciate the history of race mixture in the heritage of many of their families, they were concerned that the mulatto and black presence in Cuba might disappear with the continued practices of mestizaje. In this way, the testimonies to these more typical Afro-Cuban informants indicate that the realities of race and race mixture remained even more complex than their portrayal in the writings of Cuban intellectuals.

REVOLUTIONARY PROMISES AND PROGRAMS

It is easy to see in the family stories that began this chapter that many of the old tensions surrounding the value of race in family formation continued into Cuba's post-1959 revolutionary era. Again, race was central in the white George's decision to disavow any connection to the black Sylvia despite the fact that she was the mother of his child. On the other hand, the love and profound sense of responsibility George felt for his son mulatto Miguel appeared much less affected by the social distinction of race. In this way, George acted in a manner similar to those white fathers of the nineteenth century who established a legal connection to their mixed-race children. New meanings of race were subsequently displayed by Sylvia, the mother, and Miguel, the son. Sylvia rejected her previous exclusive preference for white men, and Miguel defined himself as a revolutionary and man of color. He also distanced himself from any association with his white ancestry. Although the revolution gave these sentiments a new public space, it built on older notions of family and race to provide an opening for the ongoing rearticulation of Cuba's racial identity. As early as 1959, Fidel Castro proclaimed the revolution's new official position on race: "We all have lighter or darker skin color . . . lighter skin implies descent from Spaniards who themselves were colonized by Moors that came from Africa. Those who are more or less dark-skinned came directly from Africa. Moreover, nobody can consider himself as being of pure, much less superior race."[13] Such a statement would have been unimaginable under President Batista, despite his own racially mixed heritage. Castro's words offered a new governmental re-iteration of the public esteem given to Cuban racial diversity that originated in the late nineteenth-century independence efforts and was aggressively advocated by the Afrocubanismo movement of the 1920s and 1930s. In both the post-revolutionary and Afrocubanismo instantiations of this theme, all Cubans shared a similar African heritage. The racial differences were minimized as relatively unimportant questions of social distance. Later, in association with Cuba's military intervention in Angola in 1975, Castro furthered this notion of bi-racial national identity by declaring Cubans to be a "Latin-African people."[14]

It is important to note the distinction between such statements and late nineteenth-century calls for racial harmony. Both were nationalistic, but in slightly different ways. When the independence hero José Martí spoke of Cuba "as more than white, more than black, more than mulatto," he was not referring to a common history and a common genealogy. He spoke not of a familial past or future, but of a social and political future. In contrast, Castro squarely called upon a common history to create a unified Cuban future. This strategy was based— consciously or not—on the commonality generated by many Cuban families' earlier transcendence of racial boundaries. In addition to the projection of Afro-Latin identity, the 1959 campaign for racial equality that drew upon an image of a young black boy pleading for respect and expressing the hope that one day his son would not hear "there goes a negrito" and instead hear "there goes a child," reinforced the revolution's egalitarian mission. It was paralleled by the 1968 call to "Produce as Much as Your Slave Grandfather" associated with that year's ten-ton harvest proposal.[15] This was a new public acknowledgment of a slave grandfather who could often be found in Cuban family trees, despite the skin color of his descendants and lack of previous recognition.

As the revolution focused on the elimination of class-based inequality, the social value of Cuban racial difference also decreased. Educational reforms were among the more important mechanisms utilized. The exclusive private schools of the republican era were eliminated in favor of more inclusive public schools. At least through the junior-high school level, Cubans of various backgrounds received similar instruction. Based on this success, African-descended people increasingly entered those professional occupations that earlier had been more racially selective. Black and mulatto families were also relocated into neighborhoods where they previously had not been welcome. Social organizations that had been segregated by race were completely eliminated. This last change affected not only white clubs, but the Afro-Cuban ones as well. All of these sites had formerly been important areas through which race had been reinforced. Despite the revolution's achievements in decreasing several measures of racial inequality, many commentators have described its inability to eliminate racial discrimination or achieve racial parity in political representation. Moreover, before racially conscious initiatives in the first decade of the twentieth first century, Cuban blacks and mulattoes had been under-represented in every prominent sphere of public life and the revolution permitted little discussion of Afro-Cuban social difference outside the folkloric domain (which I will review below).[16]

Leaving these observations aside for a moment, the revolutionary government's attention to issues of class and racial inequality had unintended consequences. First, the most racially conservative social elements—the vast majority of whom were white—were demographically reduced with the post-1959 emigration of the nation's upper classes.[17]

The social shifts associated with this exodus had more than demographic value. This exodus also removed much of the local ideological opposition to the new rhetoric of racial unity. Second, the revolution's reconsideration of gender and family as important sites of social reform also impacted the racialized visions of Cuban identity and modes of reproducing social difference. First with the Fundamental Law of 1959 and later with the 1975 Family Code, the Cuban government was committed to women's equality in both public and private spheres. Women were encouraged to work and their labor force participation rates increased from 13 percent in 1955 to 34 percent in 1990.[18] Women also gained greater acceptance in occupations once dominated by men. At the same time, their domestic duties gained greater official regard and the government encouraged fathers to accept a greater share of responsibility in the home. State-supplied day care for the children of working women, while insufficient to meet demand, eased some of the domestic responsibilities traditional faced by such mothers. Additionally, the legal definitions of marriage and divorce were formally liberalized to allow for greater flexibility by both partners.[19] These reforms tempered the need for Cuban women to conform to older systems of patriarchal control. Educational opportunities and youth work brigades away from home also lessened the force of parental authority.

Newly available employment opportunities especially impacted white women, making many less economically dependent on both their families of origin and their marital families. The public idea of white female honor was shifted away from sexual purity to the projection of revolutionary nationalism and egalitarianism. Just as the revolution envisioned the "new man," it also fostered the creation of the new liberated woman.[20] This new Cuban woman could choose to form her family in a variety of styles with partners from a variety of social backgrounds. Her reproductive capacity was to be less dedicated to the maintenance of class and racial boundaries. The nineteenth-century standards of the sexual economy of race that had been retained with only slight modification during the republican era now faced a new set of challenges as the concept of white femininity was reshaped. There was less patriarchal insistence that white femininity serve as the womb with which to reproduce the older patterns of social hierarchy; the sexual and reproductive unions between African-descended men and white women, once considered taboo by Cuban elites, received greater acceptance after 1959.

Cuban sociological research conducted in two Havana neighborhoods during 1993 and 1995 offered one of the first empirical explorations of the racial familial composition for the post-1959 period. Among the participants 32.5 percent described themselves as members of multiracial families.[21] This statistic contrasts with the low percentages of inter-racial marriages found for three Havana parishes between 1901 and 1940. In these formal Church records, only 0.5 percent of white men and 0.3 percent of white women married partners of an identifiable racial distinction.[22] The more recent data reveal a greater openness to inter-racial unions that implicitly confirms the social liberation of white women and the increased permissibility of their entry into inter-racial unions.

Such shifts in racialized reproductive practices did not, however, eradicate older types of disavowal. Cuban studies from the late 1990s and the first decade of the twenty-first century acknowledge the persistence of social barriers to inter-racial unions. Respondents in these studies who opposed such relationships were frequently vague about their motives, other than they "simply did not function." When pressed for more specific explanations, some said "that if a relationship was one of a black man and a white woman, 'his jealousy would not allow her to live in peace.' For a black woman with a white man, 'the white man believes himself superior . . . and laughs at her.' For these reasons, it is better to avoid such unions, 'so as not to feel discrimination, with anxiety.' "[23]

American anthropologist Nadine Fernández's qualitative research on inter-racial relationships in Havana during the early 1990s found intimate unions across racial lines to be very common, but not unproblematic. Her interviews of eight such couples detailed the tensions between the older traditions of self-segregating racial hierarchy and the revolutionary ideals of equality.[24] One of the stories captured by Fernández was that of Yanet and Victor. At that time (1993), Yanet was a twenty-two-year-old white female psychology student at the University of Havana. Victor was a twenty-three-year-old black recent university graduate. The couple met while they were doing compulsory agricultural work one summer. They married in December 1993, despite the intense objection of Yanet's father and maternal grandparents. In fact, Yanet felt forced to choose between her grandparents and her fiancé. Her mother was much more accepting of the relationship, due in part to the fact that she had herself remarried to an Afro-Cuban man.

The objections of Yanet's grandparents, and even those of her young friends, were clearly based on racial difference. With the exception of color, Victor's family possessed many of the markers of higher-class status. Fernández noted that, "there is a notable class difference between the families with Victor's family more educated and Yanet's more firmly working class."[25] Victor owned a car, lived in a nice neighborhood, and possessed a university degree. His mother was a physician and his late father had been an air force combat pilot. All of this was insignificant in assuaging the objections of Yanet's family and friends to the relationship. It is worth quoting at length Yanet's comments on the negative reactions to her relationship.

> With my grandparents, I can understand [their rejection], but I have a sister with whom I was very close, but she has not been able to deal with [my relationship] She's young, 26 years old. She . . . and her husband won't even speak to me . . . My case is a reflection of many cases. [A reflection] of a latent prejudice [that shows itself] in the extreme reactions like in my case, in other cases maybe [the prejudice] is underlying, but it seems to me that it is a problem among many people. I've been with people who haven't said anything to me [about my relationship] but they didn't like the idea and that's a form of prejudice too. Or when people meet Victor they say, "Ah, this boy is almost white!" and they start to joke with me. I myself had never really thought about it . . . And sometimes people look at us in the street or on the bus and I hear them say, "Oh, that poor white girl look at who she's ended up with." At first I used to feel ashamed, but now it doesn't bother me.[26]

When asked of her decision to marry, Yanet remarked further:

> Everything I've always needed I have now. I am going to graduate. He [Victor] is already working and we want to start a family. We're going to be independent because his mother is giving us half of her house so we can live alone. I am going to marry because I have left everyone else behind. I had to break with many things for this [relationship]. But time will tell . . . I tell you, if we break-up, we'll break-up because of me or him, not because of any other person or some prejudice. The only thing that I've gotten out of this experience is that I know I won't forget this when I have a child. I will never make him go through what I did. And this child and his generation will have less pressure, and I imagine that

[this will happen] in each successive [generation]. I don't know, I think that time this will be overcome, because this is dragged from the past . . . Because I'm not the only one who breaks with all of this. Each time there will be more people that are able to, and age has a lot to do with it. I wasn't able to do it at seventeen, but I'm almost an independent woman. I've had other relationships, and I know what I want.[27]

On the one hand, one sees in Yanet's comments just how strongly the force of racial prejudice has continued in Cuban society. Negative public reaction to inter-racial couples is not infrequent. On the other hand, one also sees how central the liberation of white women was to the transformation of racialized reproduction. Yanet could exercise personal choices even when they received disapproval from her intimates because she was an "independent woman." Without that liberated consciousness, even the rhetoric of racial equality would not have removed the sexual boundaries of race and allowed white women to more openly participate in inter-racial relationships if they wanted to. Revolutionary ideals allowed young white women like Yanet to believe that their choices were at least compatible with contemporary Cuban politics.[28] And she looked forward to the less discriminatory environment her mixed-race children would face.

In turn, the sexual element of white women's liberation fostered greater sexual possibilities for African-descended men. Under the revolution, both groups were allowed a new social maturity that they once had been denied. They could more openly choose partners who had been previously restricted to them. They could participate in reproducing the nation in the inter-racial manner that had been previously restricted to white men and women of color. Similarly, for women of color, the material motives for preferring white partners were lessened. The rationale described by Reyíta in chapter 6 became less likely in the revolutionary environment. The increased economic opportunities for mulatto and black men also made them more viable partners for all categories of Cuban women.

While these examples identify increased possibilities for inter-racial coupling, one should note that they may also continue reproductive racism. This issue also arises in a published 1999 interview with another young black physician, Dr. Nuria Pérez Sesma, who responded to the question, "How is it for blacks in terms of relationships among the young?"

> That's a hard one right now, especially [with] mulattos. When mulattos get somewhere, they discriminate against blacks. They look for another mulatto or white, to whiten the race. That exists especially among my generation, both in men and women, but more so in the men. That's to say, it's more frequent to see a mulatto man discriminating against black women than it is to see a mulatto woman discriminating against black men. Of course, this is not the finding of any scientific study, it's only a view based on my observations.[29]

Nuria interpreted the access of mulatto men to inter-racial relation-ships as a preference and suggested that whitening is still the goal. She continued, noting her reaction to this situation:

> I imagine this very situation in which we are discriminated against, and which values the white race over the black, is the cause of this kind of whitening. . . . Maybe the mulatto man thinks that if he marries a white woman his children will benefit more, will stand a better chance. As a black woman, this touches me close up, it hurts. I'm affected by this kind of situation, I feel it a lot, it's hurtful and damaging to me. I have felt rejection from people of my own race and that makes me depressed. I'm twenty-six years old and at this age a woman needs a stable relationship with a man, a stable home.[30]

This comment makes clear that in contemporary Cuba not everyone perceives race mixture as benign or beneficial. In Nuria's view, there was still the potential for whitening to minimize the value of the mu-latto and black segments of the population. Since the late nineteenth century, that possibility has co-existed with the potential for race mix-ture to become the basis of a unifying national discourse. When one is aware of the contest between these views, it becomes more appar-ent that the force of race mixture and all other acts of racialized re-production cannot simply be measured in terms of the demographic results these practices generate. Their importance is also determined by the ideological framework that they are given; only when practices that counter a racial hierarchy of white over black are upheld as natural and historical elements of the Cuban national identity is their transforma-tive value appreciated. One sees in the above testimonies that some Cubans do not acknowledge the historical moments at which Cuban families were racially integrated. They prefer to highlight distinction, or to view race mixture as beneficial whitening. Others, however, take an alternative position and embrace the histories of mestizaje, noting commonalities.

REVOLUTIONARY ACKNOWLEDGMENT
OF AFRICAN RELIGIOUS "ANCESTORS"

While the revolution created a new sexual politics that redefined the familial future of race in Cuba, its often contradictory policies toward African-based religions simultaneously opened an unexpected space for new racial visions of the nation's familial past. Under the auspices of new revolutionary cultural projects, the continuing power and relevance of "the ancestors" within Afro-Cuban cosmology emerged from a previously marginalized existence to appear subtly in the government-approved public discourse about Cuban national identity and the historical components from which it flowed. As such, Cuban social reproduction was influenced by alternate genealogical memories that rhetorically displaced the previous primacy of whiteness in favor of fostering the image of a third world-oriented, resistive Cuba, which could be visualized as either multi-racial, non-racial, or black.

On this point the preamble to the 1976 Cuban Constitution is instructive. In a style quite distinct from other Western constitutions, it is uniquely structured in a fashion reminiscent of the *moyuba* opening prayers found in West African ritual traditions, especially those of the Yoruba who gave rise to the Cuban Regla de Ocha or Santería religion. Moyuba means "to pay homage to" or "I bow to you," as a gesture of submission and request for guidance. Moyuba sequences are often the first rituals in longer Afro-Cuban religious ceremonies. Although each spiritual lineage of believers (*rama*) follows its own well-established and regulated pattern, typically the veneration of *eggun* (ancestors) often proceeds from the oldest, most esteemed (often the god Olofí, the supreme creator) to the most recent (normally one's decreased biological and spiritual parents).[31] In secular form, this ethos informs the Cuban constitution. It follows a similar pattern, beginning with "WE, CUBAN CITIZENS, heirs and continuers of the creative work and the traditions of combativeness, firmness, heroism and sacrifice fostered by

our ancestors . . ." In chronological order, it pays homage to both biological and ideological ancestors ("Indians," "slaves," "patriots," "Marx,"
and "Lenin").

In many West African traditions, direct communication with a desired spiritual power is preceded by the essential practice of first opening the path. In Santería, this act becomes *abriendo camino*—a call
upon a facilitator spirit (typically the god Eleggua Eshun) to initiate
less obstructed connections with more remote gods.[32] With caution,
one might even suggest that the preamble invokes a non-religious version of Eleggua, with a symbolic personification of the revolution that is
then combined with a political mythologizing of Fidel Castro and José
Martí. The preamble declares, "the triumphant Revolution [as] headed
by Fidel Castro . . . initiated the development of socialism and it continues with the goal of building the communist society." Before moving to
the constitution's statutory elements, the preamble offers Martí's words
as its aim: "I want the highest law of our republic to be the ultimate gift
of Cubans to the full dignity of humanity." With this, the paths to a lib-
erating national, and then international, communism are rhetorically
opened.

Similarly subtle presentations of Afro-Cuban forms have had a long
history within Cuban politics. The most famous occurred as white
doves settles on Castro's shoulders while he delivered his first general
speech to the Cuban people after the defeat of Batista, on January 8,
1959. Many Cubans familiar with African-based religious have interpreted these doves as a sign of Castro's favor with the *orishas* (primary
gods and goddesses of the Yoruba religion) and Castro has never dis-
credited such views. Similarly the red and black colors of his July 26
Movement also represent for many another link to Eleggua, through
which Castro discretely acknowledges his reliance upon Afro-Cuban
spiritual potential. The comments of one santera (Santiera priestess)
elucidate the ways in which Castro's subtle displays of African-base religion can be read:

> As a santera I reaffirm that he [Fidel Castro] is a believer because every 13th
> of March he makes an act in the park in front of the University of Havana in
> commemoration of José Antonio Echeverría, a martyr of the Revolution. He
> begins the act by mentioning all the martyrs and the public responds, "Present!"

as he mentions each name. In our religion, we santeros use a ceremonial stick to pound the floor in ritual. Before performing a rite we call upon our ancestors and the participants respond with "*Ibaé*" [I salute you]; we call the dead so they know about and can authorize what we are going to do. The Comandante makes the same rite when he calls the name of each martyr. This is called the "*yumbon-iar* [from moyuba, "to pay homage"] the ancestors." This is the observation that the people of Cuba have had, and because of this they say he has "made Ocha."[33]

American ethnographer Ivor Miller reads such occurrences as "coded performances" that contain distinct levels of semiotic meaning for formal politics and for interaction with the masses. In the former, the standard, Western symbols of state power are utilized. In this respect, the constitution has inherent meaning, regardless of its contents, as it places the Cuban nation in the same dialogic plane as other Western nations. Despite what can be read as the covert usage of Afro-Cuban religious symbolism in the constitution's preamble, its secular character remains explicit. The communist authors' ideological commitment to atheist scientific materialism prompted them to disallow direct references to West African gods and strip the typical Yoruba ceremonial opening of its overt spiritual dimensions. But its ethos remains and is expressed at the mass level of the "coded performance," where the subtle use of Afro-Cuban symbolism demonstrates the government's access to what Miller terms the "local secrets and esoteric power" that are not defined by external and presumably imperialist forces. Layers of Afro-Cuban meaning exist as guarded secrets exclusive to a subaltern community of believers, those outside Western liberal notions of power. For centuries, to survive against state and Church repression, practitioners of Afro-Cuban religions have quietly encoded and decoded public political symbols with their own meaning.[34] The Cuban Constitution becomes a grand public object through which to project such a coded process.

Through the mobilization of secularized West African forms, this state declaration is a Cuban nationalist challenge to the liberal notions of time and citizenship that frame the constitutions of most Western nations. Whereas liberal philosophical traditions posit the universal, ahistorical citizen, the Cuban text makes specific racial genealogies relevant, acknowledging that each citizen carries a particular history forward. Ancestry matters. In a West African sense, the dead are not de-

Fidel Castro addresses a Havana crowd celebrating President Fulgencio Batista's defeat, January 8, 1959. Source: CorbisImages AP Collection.

parted, but continue to interact with the living. In liberal Western politics too, ancestry is not truly absent; it is only silent. It is often conflated in unarticulated ways with race. The Cuban Constitution accepts that conflation and articulates what is often left implicit for many Western nations: the racial dimensions of citizenship. Interestingly, while the choice of the terms "Indians" and "slaves" marks indigenous and black racial categories quite directly, "patriots" is much more racially ambiguous. Whiteness is submerged. The term invokes anyone, regardless of race, who has dedicated himself or herself to the quest for national self-determination. Collectively, these terms at once suggest an interesting ambiguity between the universal, non-racial project of the revolution and its attention to African-descended racial specificity.

Well before the 1976 constitution, these tensions between naming race and homogenizing the nation were present in the early post-1959 projects of the revolution's cultural agents. Throughout the 1960s and 1970s they highlighted secularized forms of Afro-Cuban rituals to present the deep historical roots of their newly won sovereignty. These government agents were selective in their use of Afro-Cuban aesthetics in the process of defining the anti-imperialist contours of the nation. The black cultural elements they utilized were those thought to conflict least with the atheist, scientific materialist framework accepted as most useful for the modernizing nation. State organizations, such as the Instituto de Etnología y Folkore founded in 1959, were key to the selection and dissemination of the new and newly recovered forms of revolutionary culture. They did for Cuban history and anthropology what an earlier generation of Afrocubanismo writers had done for literature and repositioned the positive value of African contributions as an essential component of the nationalist project.

For the Instituto de Etnología y Folkore, the height of this expression was the 1966 publication of Miguel Barnet's *Biografia de un Cimarron* (Biography of a Runaway Slave). In this now classic work, Barnet was one of the first to capture with some deference, instead of the usual condescension, the previously unfamiliar first-person voice of a member of the Latin American underclass as he documented the historical experiences of the former runaway slave Esteban Montejo. Although in Barnet's work Montejo holds himself aloft from the religious practices of the Yoruba and Congo slaves with whom he had been raised, it is clear that their cultural philosophies informed his behavior and those of many other African-descended Cubans. In undertaking this research, Barnet was part of a small, but increasingly influential cadre of young scholars such as Natalie Bolívar and Rogelio Martínez Furé who had been encouraged by the seminal voices of Afro-Cuban studies: Fernando Ortiz, Lydia Cabrera, and Argeliers León.[35]

One mission of this new generation of Afro-Cuba proponents was to promote its artistry for nationalist purposes but to eliminate what they saw as the residual primitive and superstitious elements. According to Barnet, in recovering Cuba's socio-cultural past "We are seeking to do more than document an era; we want to judge it" and those judgments would be "based on the principles of dialectical and historical material-ism."[36] Another senior Cuban anthropologist of the period, Isaac Barreal, was even more direct in articulating the methods for eliminat-ing the cultural features that were irrelevant for revolutionary society: "All elements that appear to have a religious function or a superstitious base, those characterized as a game of stakes or chance, those resem-bling outmoded class or racial divisions, acts of useless cruelty to ani-mals, or those that endanger the physical or moral integrity of people, etc., must unfailingly be discarded."[37] In his well-received *Dialogos Imaginarios,* Rogelio Martínez Furé outlined which Afro-Cuban ele-ments were to remain in the nationalist vision after this selective cut-ting. Those elements that featured a spirit of collective resistance and creative alternatives to European forms were most esteemed, for exam-ple ritual dance and drumming. Those that demonstrated wise adapta-tion to the particulars of Cuba's social politics were also acceptable. In this way, Esteban Montejo's personal history as a runaway slave was easily chosen by Barnet over the life stories of other black centenarians who had not demonstrated such obvious resistive qualities.

The political manipulation of Afro-Cuban culture also should be inter-preted within the context of the state's relation to all religions. After 1959, the government's shift toward scientific atheism did not occur immediately; it coincided with the state's gradual shift toward Marxism more generally. Religious organizations initially had been welcomed alongside other components of Cuban civil society in the struggle to oust Batista, and as members of the largest publicly recognized religious body, even ardent Catholics were active in this effort. In 1957, Enrique Canto, the president of the Santiago chapter of Catholic Action, became the national treasurer of Castro's July 26 Movement, and Father Guillermo Sardiñas served as chaplain to the Rebel Army. Four other priests subsequently joined him. Shortly after Batista's defeat, the archbishop of Santiago, Monseñor En-rique Pérez Serantes, warmly congratulated his personal friend Castro.

This goodwill was short-lived, as a strong alliance between the revo-lutionary leadership and the previously ineffective Communist Party emerged. In small, local settings communists had the tacit support of the Fidelista forces in effectively shutting out Catholics from decision making in trade unions and other political arenas. For their part, Cuban

Church officials were at first cautious in light of the political aspirations of Fidelistas and had even greeted the sweeping Agrarian Reform of 1959 with approval, acknowledging its social justice objectives. It was only after the increasing government restriction of traditional civil liberties that local Church officials asserted the same staunchly anti-communist position that the Vatican had developed in relation to European (and particularly Soviet) communism. Their opponents read these actions as the election of imperialism over revolutionary nationalism. As tensions mounted, revolutionary leaders and the high-level Cuban clergy missed opportunities for a united pursuit of the social reforms that they all sought. The government forced the closure of independent media outlets, including those producing widely circulated Catholic titles. In May 1961, all private schools, both parochial and non-religious, were nationalized and foreign priests expelled. Restrictions on public religious manifestations increased. But the practices themselves were not criminalized.[38]

Perhaps the most direct statement of the new government's relationship with religion was articulated by Blas Roca, a pre-eminent Afro-Cuban member of the pre-revolutionary Communist Party. Roca was also one of the few old communists to gain a significant leadership position within the newly consolidated revolutionary state, as first president of the National Assembly of People's Power (Poder Popular). In 1975 he became the lead author within the committee charged with producing the new constitution of the revolutionary state. His 1963 "La Lucha ideological contra las sectas religiosas" (The Ideological Fight against Religious Cults) is an often-cited text that addressed what he interpreted as the imperialist orientation of mainstream religions. He stated, "Yankee imperialism and all the enemies of the [working] class have utilized religion in their counterrevolutionary attempts. First they use the organization and influence of the Catholic Church ... They want to deceive the population in the name of God, to oppress a people in their effort to construct the new socialist society." Interestingly, Roca said nothing in direct relation to Afro-Cuban traditions. However, his euphemistic language suggests a politically utilitarian complacence with respect to them. He conceded, "We must respect the religious sentiments of the rural people."[39] This distinction in the treatment of

African-based and Judeo-Christian religions became a part of the political culture of the revolutionary government.

Practitioners of Afro-Cuban religions were not initially perceived by
revolutionary forces to hold the same potential counter-revolutionary
and imperialist threat implied in the international institutional character of Judeo-Christian groups. At the same time, there continued the
high levels of secrecy that had allowed African-based beliefs to survive
colonial-period persecution and republican-era derision. There were few
publicly recognized Afro-Cuban religious organizations. So whereas
individual practitioners were often identifiable as they donned ritual-
specific clothing, devotional assemblages were not widely known. In
the first few years of the revolution, Afro-Cuban religious practitioners
were hopeful that they could create more positive relations with the
new state than had been the experience with previous governments. A
few public events gave some indication of that possibility. For example, renowned drummer Felipe García Villamil tells a credible but undocumented story of early revolutionary interaction between the new
government and the Afro-Cuban faithful. Here again, one of the leading Afro-Cuban communists of the older generation, Lázaro Peña,
was key.

> Almost a year after Batista fell, a great *egbó* [offering to the orishas] was held,
> authorized by the government. Lázaro Peña was the one who authorized it. This
> big fiesta was celebrated in Guanabacoa's stadium. The stadium was one of the
> headquarters, but the main headquarters was the cemetery. The government
> gave horses to march through the streets, they gave everything. It was to
> celebrate a mass for all of those who had died in the revolution and it was called
> the Great Egbó. There were sheep, goats, and such walking through the streets in
> costume, with their *manteles* [decorated aprons], and those white horses . . . The
> drummers from my house went to play in the Great Egbó. We were there with all
> the cabildos that played. We also played in the house of Arcadio, that was called
> the house of the brujo of Guanabacoa, that was the society of Saint Anthony.[40]

Similarly the highly secretive, Afro-Cuban Abakuá societies con-
vened an unprecedented national congress in 1960.[41] Abakuá societies
had first appeared in early nineteenth-century Cuba as highly secretive
black fraternal orders, or lodges, based on male initiation groups in the
Cross River region of present-day Nigeria. White authorities from the

colonial era on had viewed them with a degree of trepidation and sought to disrupt what was perceived as their criminality and disregard for the norms of the dominant society. For their members to stage such a public gathering so early into the revolution suggests Abakuá societies had an expectation of new acceptance. Few cases of direct Afro-Cuban religious persecution were reported through the 1960s, in comparison to members of Christian groups. However, caution is needed on this point. Afro-Cuban worshipers had limited access to Cuban media, and proportionally few left the island in the 1960s and 1970s. Those who did met with more intense perceptions of primitiveness than they had encountered on the island. Therefore, in contrast to the Christians subject to state repression, they did not have the opportunity to tell their stories more freely abroad.

Despite the benign appearance of the initial revolutionary position on Afro-Cuban religions, by the late 1960s there occurred several notable instances of the same type of cultural racism that had been the pre-revolutionary norm. In the fall of 1968, *El Militante Comunista* ran several articles that demeaned Afro-Cuban religions, finding them, "*sumamente arcaicas*" (thoroughly archaic).[42] And in December 1975, the first post-revolutionary congress of the reconstituted Communist Party commented on Afro-Cuban religions (labeled "syncretic cults") primarily in terms of folkloric artistry and an inherent primitiveness that could threaten the social order. "Our political approach to these sects, in that it needs to be specific, is directed to prevent any anti-social activities and behaviors, those that are dangerous to the public health and the unity of the people, and contrary to the public good. The folkloric cultural values of music, dance, etc. that these support, the ethnicity of these groups, should be assimilated and purged of mystical elements."[43]

Beyond these limited perceptions of Afro-Cuban religion, Cuba's involvement with the Cold War politics of Africa also had significant implications for domestic race relations. Castro's visit to Guinea in 1972 opened the officially proclaimed "Africa Decade," in which ideological and biological links with a mythical African homeland received new prominence. Elements from a Castro speech on the Angolan war are telling, as he accentuated the "blood" ties between the two communities. "Many are the things that unite us to Angola: our cause, our common interests, politics, ideology. But we are also united by blood, and blood in the two senses of the word, blood of our ancestors and blood we shed together on the battlefields."[44] Ultimately, the revolutionary leadership attempted both to reform those African-based elements they saw as retrograde and to capitalize on those that offered nationalist possibilities.

Any inappropriate, lingering notions of the primitive character of Afro-Cuban religions are displaced by an awareness of the complexity of their underlying cosmology and philosophy. To concisely summarize the features most relevant to our discussion of the familial dimensions of race in Cuba, the well-researched patterns of Santería can serve as a guide. Similarities are found in the male-dominated Regla de Kongo (originating from the regions of Angola and southern Congo) and Abakuá. The ideas central to Yoruba cosmology include the existence of a remote supreme god; the influence on human experiences of lesser, but more immediately accessible gods and spirits; the continuing role of the deceased in the lives of the living; and the potential reincarnation of the dead. Both the gods and the ancestors are believed to be rooted in very localized West African sites. Their veneration by the living brings cosmological harmony, as the former are nourished with material goods and the latter are protected and guided. Biological and spiritual ancestors are those closest to a believer. They act as the first line of assistance in the quest for spiritual and material harmony.

This Afro-Cuban reliance on spiritual and familial ancestors has been a source of continuing African racial identification and pride. It has provided another type of genealogical memory and an understanding of the value of the past in the present that has not been acknowledged in Western historical thought. Western norms accept that familial antecedents contribute during their physical lifetimes to the material, intellectual, and spiritual well-being of their descendants. With death such contributions end, and the living are left to their own talents and circumstances to make their own may in the world. By contrast, West African spiritual philosophies recognize the ongoing, after-death involvement of ancestors in the lives of their descendants. Additionally, local African gods are believed to attach themselves and serve as guides to persons without direct biological heritage in West Africa. However, the helpful involvement of these spirits with the living does not arrive unsolicited. It must be encouraged and renewed. African religious practices (both on the continent and in the Americas) are thought to provide the rules for ensuring the beneficial presence of both the immediate ancestors and more distant gods. As a first step, acknowledgment of local ancestors and gods is obligatory for one's real-world grounding. One must know who are his or her specific spiritual guides. Santeros or *babalao* priests read such knowledge for each individual and indicate the best methods for maintaining beneficial relationships with the ancestors and orishas. In the process, the initiate becomes a member of a new spiritual family, entering a long African-based lineage of devotees.

Each *casa templo* (house temple) headed by a santero or babalao becomes a site for organizing connections within this spiritual family. Each priest is the godfather to the many spiritual godchildren, who have voluntarily sought his guidance. Through him, the godchildren are incorporated into spiritual lineages of great historical depth. Many ramas proudly trace their spiritual ancestry back to Yoruba origin site of Ile Ife. One highly esteemed leader in Afro-Cuban religions, who as a santero, babalao, and *palero* (a priest of the Palo Mayombe religion) explained the creation of this new, non-racial spiritual ethnicity:

> Belonging to the Yoruba people does not only mean that one is born in that country or that one is the descendant of the slaves brought to the Americas. It is sufficient that one belongs to the religion after one has been initiated in or accepts the Yoruba Orishas. It is something very beautiful and grand. Imagine whites, Indians, whoever, no matter what language they speak. If they practice the Yoruba religion they are considered brothers [and sisters], as a member of the same family, like one more Yoruba person.[45]

Instances of the non-biological acceptance of Yoruba ethnicity abound within Cuba. Again, the West African physical features of this author often encourages even the most phenotypically white Cuban to share this sense of themselves in ways that they are unlikely to share with white visitors and researchers. There was the taxi driver who proudly beamed of his *antepasados yorubas* (Yoruba ancestors). Or the white santero at the sugar plantation, Mejico or Alava, just outside the town of Colón who proudly displayed the most sacred objects of his *padrinos esclavos* (slave godparents). One of these was a statue of Eleggua that he claimed had been carried from Africa by "a slave, one of my religious ancestors." An ethnographic observation by the early twentieth-century American researcher Irene Wright highlights the continuing tensions between views of Cuban racial identity based on phenotype and those based on cultural affiliation. She was guided into an Afro-Cuban community in Cerro, Havana, by a middle-aged mulatto who was a respected santero and then introduced to an African elder who was the senior priest of the community. Along their path, a young woman, who "could pass for white," stopped to offer a ritual salute to her guide.[46] These three generations of Afro-Cuban religious practitioners (an African, a mulatto, and a nearly white woman) demonstrate the simultaneous processes of phenotypical whitening and the maintenance of an African cosmological outlook. These processes indicate that inter-racial families that have been such a significant part of Cuban social development should not be read as inevitable stepping-stones to ideological whitening. Multi-generational choices in social reproduction have drawn a much more complex picture of racial identities and have been critical in defining Cuba as a multi-racial nation with a strong African cultural orientation in informal arenas.

CONCLUSION

So where does this leave our study of the familial and reproductive dimensions of race in Cuban history? There can be no doubt that racism continues to exist in Cuba. However, Cuban notions of race have not simply equated phenotype and behavior in any permanent manner. Like the meanings of race in most societies, Cuban racial ideologies have evolved under their own particular set of historical circumstances, many of which also relate to the concept of family. The extended review of Cuban social history undertaken in this study allows one to appreciate the familial factors in Cuban race relations. Over time, these have included the following:

· legal acceptance of the medieval doctrine *partus sequitur ventrem,* where a child's initial servile status equaled that of the mother;

- pre-capitalist appreciation of Catholic families, although qualified by race;
- nineteenth-century heightened regard for racial purity by many white families;
- the frequent recognition of mixed-race children by white men;
- familial and institutional flexibility in racial classification;
- the tenacious, but frequently challenged, survival of families of color;
- a colonial form of slavery that allowed for the acquisition of freedom under a limited set of circumstances and in which familial strategies for liberation were critical;
- the elimination of restrictions on inter-racial marriage in the late nineteenth century;
- post-emancipation Afro-Cuban efforts to assert patriarchal family forms;
- the elimination of official markers of racial identity with the emergence of the republic in the early twentieth century;
- the elevation of the legal status of consensual unions during the middle of the twentieth century;
- the development of intellectual and political discourses that attributed positive value to the history of race mixture;
- the revolutionary political efforts to eliminate social segmentation according to race;
- the social liberation of white women, beginning with the feminist movements of the early republic and continuing with the 1959 Cuban Revolution; and
- a post-1959 revolutionary nationalism that incorporated a limited version of African cosmological visions of "ancestors" to redefine the boundaries of citizenship.

Many of these factors may appear to contradict each other, and collectively they have not eliminated anti-black racism. However, they reflect the specifically Cuban power struggles embodied in the inseparable concepts of "family," "race," and "nation." The selective genealogical memory used to foster nationalism is similar to those from which notions of familial and racial identity emerge, each giving rise to strongly felt visions of "us" and "them." The familial, racial, or national "we" each derives from dynamic, social reproduction processes, with individuals, families, civil institutions, and government policy makers manipulating ideological arguments to create the material conditions most advantageous to themselves. Thus, while our trinity of "family," "race," and "nation" may carry some universal significance, they are quite particular to place and time.

It is not by some coincidence of insular geography that Cubans have claimed a unique national identity. They have created themselves as such through multi-generational social reproduction in which concepts of race and family mattered. Cuban families simultaneously existed as racialized tools for achieving social mobility, maintaining status, or measuring compatibility with the norms of "the civilized." These processes shaped a domestic domain in which racial hierarchies were similar but not equal to those established in the domain of public politics. While many private choices in mating and family formation replicated the dominant racial discourse, in others Cuban individuals also selected reproductive behaviors that minimized accepted meanings of race and disrupted these hierarchies. It is in this context that, as some white men promoted the white family as the sociopolitical ideal, other white men sought public recognition of their mixed-race children. Similarly, families of color physically survived the difficulties of slavery, racial discrimination, and pervasive notions of whitening to also promote the inclusion of African ancestry in ideological visions of the nation. All of these experiences drove the question of whether Cuba would be articulated as a white, mulatto, or black nation.

An observation by the contemporary Cuban writer Eliseo Altunaga (1941–present) indicates the degree to which that question remains unresolved. Continuing in the tradition of the mid-twentieth-century Afrocubanismo movement, Altunaga suggests that the ongoing quest for Cuban national unity will reach successful conclusion only when the long-standing intimate inter-racial connections of ancestry and culture became more fully articulated and accepted. For him, history has created a truly mestizo Cuban culture, whose African ancestral significance was still unrecognized.

I think that the negation of any of the components of Cuban culture and the obstinate desire to marginalize a component that has been forged, wishing only to select four or five features—music, poetry, Santería, rhythm—as what is black in Cuban culture, weakens that culture terribly. I think they have no alternative but to look at themselves in the mirror; if they want to perpetuate themselves as a nation, the members of that nation must recognize themselves as black as much as white.

What is black in Cuba resides in the spirituality of Cubans and is expressed in their food and clothing, in their way of seeing the world, speaking Spanish, using music. I think the black is what makes Cuba different from Spain and from Europe. It's what the black put in the pot, it's what the black changed. I think that the Cuban black is not African, nor is the Cuban white European. I think the Cuban white is black and that the Cuban black is white, and the idea of a mestizo society is the only one that can save the nation. I think the Cuban has a white aesthetic and a black ethic. This is where the struggle lies. There is the idea that a man who looks in the mirror and won't recognize himself for what he is, is weakened by that. I honestly think that one of the ways Cuba can be salvaged as a nation—when all economies are the same, money is the same, commercial values and cultural cosmopolitanism are the same—is recognizing it is black.[47]

The battle over race in the symbolic representation of the Cuban national family continues. Some would whiten this picture, and others would blacken it. As Cubans have been shaped by the forces of Spanish colonialism, slavery, African ethnic cosmologies, nineteenth-century liberal nationalism, and revolutionary socialism, they have developed very fluid forms of racial identification and have often chosen the most socially expedient racial self-representation for themselves, their families, and their nation. They take these historical processes with them into the next phase of Cuban nation-building.

NOTES

INTRODUCTION

1. Personal interview of "Julia," conducted by the author, Havana, October, 1999. The pseudonym is use to protect her identity.

2. We will return to oral histories related to the role of race in Cuban family formation in chapter 7.

3. While colonial Spanish American designations of African ethnic or regional origins are known to be geographically imprecise, the term "Carabalí" had been used in Cuba from the seventeenth century to denote people from what is today eastern Nigeria and northwestern Cameroon. See Rafael L. López Valdés, *Los Africanos de Cuba* (San Juan: Centro de Estudios Avanzados de Puerto Rico y el Caribe en colaboración con el Instituto de Cultura Puertorriqueña, 2001); and Jorge Castellanos and Isabel Castellanos, *Cultura afrocubana*, vol. 1, *El negro en Cuba, 1492–1844* (Miami: Ediciones Universal, 1988).

4. In addition to Cuba, this saying is commonly found throughout Latin American regions with significant African-descended populations. See Peter Wade, "Afterword: Race and Nation in Latin America, an Anthropological View," in *Race and Nation in Modern Latin America*, ed. Nancy P. Appelbaum, Anne S. Macpherson, and Karin Alejandra Rosemblatt (Chapel Hill: University of North Carolina Press, 2003); and the poem "¿Y tu agüela, a'onde ejtá?" by Puerto Rican poet Fortunato Vizcarrondo, reprinted in *Personalidad y literatura puertorriqueñas*, ed. Hilda E Quintana, María Cristina Rodríguez, and Gladys Vila Barnés (Madrid: Editorial Plaza Mayor, 1996), 195–196.

5. The term "Afro-Cuban" is used throughout this study as a synonym for "African-descended." It is a term that has limited but growing currency among contemporary Cubans in marking a lived social identity. It may be used in association with folkloric representations of the historical presence of Africans in Cuba. In this study, "Afro-Cuban" also at times stands in for the collective of blacks and mulattoes. While the latter term may offend some North American readers, it is a distinct social category in Cuba that is both attributed and self-proclaimed.

6. See for example Melina Pappademos, *Black Political Activism and the Cuban Republic* (Chapel Hill: University of North Carolina Press, 2011); Alejandra Bronfman,

Measures of Equality: Social Science, Citizenship, and Race in Cuba, 1902–1940 (Chapel Hill: University of North Carolina Press, 2004); Alejandro de la Fuente, *A Nation for All: Race, Inequality, and Politics in Twentieth-Century Cuba* (Chapel Hill: University of North Carolina Press, 2001); Ada Ferrer, *Insurgent Cuba: Race, Nation, and Revolution, 1868–1898* (Chapel Hill: University of North Carolina Press, 1999); and Aline Helg, *Our Rightful Share, the AfroCuban Struggle for Equality, 1886–1912* (Chapel Hill: University of North Carolina Press, 1995).

7. Brackette Williams, "Classification Systems Revisited: Kinship, Caste, Race, and Nationality as the Flow of Blood and Spread of Rights," in *Naturalizing Power: Essays in Feminist Cultural Analysis,* ed. Sylvia Yanagisako and Carol Delany (New York: Routledge, 1995). Also see Patricia Hill Collins, "It's All in the Family: Intersections of Gender, Race, and Nation," *Hypatia,* 13, no. 3 (1998): 62–82; and Pierre Bourdieu, "Marriage Strategies as Strategies of Social Reproduction," in *Family and Society: Selections from Annales: Economies, Sociétés, Civilisations,* ed. R. Forster and O. Ranum (Baltimore: Johns Hopkins University Press, 1976). For a study that emphasizes the ideological construction of modern nationalism see Benedict Anderson, *Imagined Communities: Reflections on the Origins and Spread of Nationalism,* rev. ed. (London: Verso, 1991), 143–144, 149, and 154. For a study of the link between family genealogy and the public politics of race in early modern Spain and its American empire see María Elena Martínez, *Genealogial Fictions: Limpieza de Sangre, Religion, and Gender in Colonial Mexico* (Stanford: Stanford University Press, 2008).

8. This study prioritizes heterosexual ideologies and practices. Other forms of sexuality are valued, but are outside its scope of inquiry.

9. Much of the scholarship on the links between sexuality and nationalist movements is influenced by Michel Foucault, *The History of Sexuality,* vol. 1, trans. Robert Hurley (New York: Pantheon Books, 1978), and a growing body of literature has continued to address the issue. See for example earlier works such as George Mosse, *Nationalism and Sexuality: Middle-Class Morality and Sexual Norms in Modern Europe* (Madison: University of Wisconsin Press, 1985); and Andrew Parker et al., eds., *Nationalism and Sexualities* (London: Routledge, 1992). Important studies by Robert J. Young and Ann L. Stoler, respectively, associate these issues with questions of race-making in the colonial context; see Young, *Colonial Desire: Hybridity in Theory, Culture, and Race* (London: Routledge, 1995); and Stoler, *Race and the Education of Desire: Foucault's History of Sexuality and the Colonial Order of Things* (Durham, N.C.: Duke University Press, 1995) and *Carnal Knowledge and Imperial Power: Race and the Intimate in Colonial Rule* (Berkeley: University of California Press, 2002).

10. I initially explored this concept in Karen Y. Morrison, "'Whitening' Revisited: Nineteenth-Century Cuban Counterpoints," in *Africans into Spanish America: Expanding the Diaspora,* ed. Sherwin Bryant, Rachel O'Toole, and Ben Vinson (Urbana: University of Illinois Press, 2012), 163–185.

11. Within a very rich, feminist literature on the social value of reproduction see Janet Saltzman Chafetz, "Feminist Theory and Sociology: Under-Utilized Contribution for Mainstream Theory," *Annual Review of Sociology* 23 (1997): 97–121; Randall Collins, Janet Saltzman Chafetz, Rae Lesser Blumberg, Scott Coltrane, and Jonathan H. Turner, "Toward an Integrated Theory of Gender Stratification," *Sociological Perspectives* 36, no. 3

(Fall 1993): 185–217; and Mary O'Brien, *Reproducing the World: Essays in Feminist Theory* (Boulder, Colo.: Westview Press, 1989). It is also important to note the value of black feminist perspectives on racialized reproduction, seen for example in Williams, "Classification Systems Revisited"; Patricia Hill Collins, *Black Feminist Thought: Knowledge, Consciousness, and the Politics of Empowerment* (Boston: Unwin Hyman, 1990); Evelyn Brooks Higginbotham, "African-American Women's History and the Metalanguage of Race," *Signs* 17, no. 2 (Winter 1992): 251–275; and Hortense J. Spillers, "Mama's Baby, Papa's Maybe: An American Grammar Book," *diacritics* 17, no. 2 (1987): 65–81.

12. See Anne McClintock's reading of Frantz Fanon, *Black Skin, White Masks* (New York: Grove Press, 1967) in "No Longer in a Future Heaven: Nationalism, Gender, and Race," in *Becoming National, A Reader,* ed. Geoff Eley and Ronald Grigor Suny (Oxford: Oxford University Press, 1996).

13. Similar exposition of a libidinal economy predicated upon colonial and post-colonial racist violence is seen in Saidiya Hartman, *Scenes of Subjection: Terror, Slavery and Self-Making in Nineteenth-Century America* (New York: Oxford University Press, 1997); Frank B. Wilderson, *Red, White, and Black: Cinema and the Structure of U.S. Antagonisms* (Durham, N.C.: Duke University Press, 2008); and Jared Sexton, "People-of-Color-Blindness: Notes on the Afterlife of Slavery," *Social Text* 28 (Summer 2010): 31–56.

14. See Peter Wade, *Race and Sex in Latin America* (New York: Pluto Press, 2009) for a valuable exploration of the shifting relationship between race, sex, and national identity in colonial and modern Latin America. While Wade and the African Americanist authors in note 13 above emphasize the connections between libidinal economy and political economy frame, this study emphasizes social reproduction over individual, bodily desire.

15. Isabel Mendizabal et al., "Genetic Origin, Admixture, and Asymmetry in Maternal and Paternal Human Lineages in Cuba," *BMC Evolutionary Biology* 8 (2008): 213.

16. Oficina Nacional de Estadísticas, *Cuba, Censo de población y viviendas 2012.* http://www.one.cu/resumenadelantadocenso2012.htm, accessed December 16, 2013.

17. See works cited in note 6 above. On black existential thought and praxis see Lewis R. Gordon, *Existentia Africana: Understanding Africana Existential Thought* (New York: Routledge, 2000).

18. Michael Omi and Howard Winant, *Racial Formation in the United States* (Los Angeles: Psychology Press, 1994), 55.

19. Anthony Good, "Kinship," in *Encyclopedia of Social and Cultural Anthropology,* ed. A. Barnard and J. Spencer (New York: Routledge, 1996), 311–318, provides an introduction to broader considerations of family forms. Anne McClintock, *Imperial Leather: Race, Gender, and Sexuality in the Colonial Contest* (New York: Routledge, 1995), 5; and Kathleen M. Brown, *Good Wives, Nasty Wenches, and Anxious Patriarchs: Gender, Race, and Power in Colonial Virginia* (Chapel Hill: University of North Carolina Press, 1996), 4, offer novel insights into the power of sexual expression to create other social forms such as class, race, and nation.

20. Sheila McIsaac Cooper, "Historical Analysis of the Family," in *Handbook of Marriage and the Family,* 2nd ed., ed. M. Sussman, S. Steinmetz, and G. Peterson

(New York: Plenum Press, 1999), 13–37; and Tamara Hareven, "Family History at the Crossroads," *Journal of Family History* 12, nos. 1–2 (1987): xxiii.

21. The classic work on the African American family is Herbert Gutman's *The Black Family in Slavery and Freedom, 1750–1925* (New York: Pantheon Books, 1976). Also see Jacqueline Jones, *The Labor of Love, Labor of Sorrow: Black Women, Work, and Family from Slavery to the Present* (New York: Basic Books, 1985); Justin Labinjoh, "The Sexual Life of the Oppressed: An Examination of the Family Life of Ante-Bellum Slaves," *Phylon* 35 (1974): 375–397; Herman Lantz, "Family and Kin as Revealed in the Narratives of Ex-Slaves," *Social Science Quarterly* 60, no. 4 (March 1980): 667–674; and Ann Patton Malone, *Sweet Chariot: Slave Family and Household Structure in Nineteenth-Century Louisiana* (Chapel Hill: University of North Carolina Press, 1992) offer important contributions to this topic.

22. For general surveys of Latin American family historiography see Elizabeth Kuznesopf and Robert Oppenheimer, "The Family and Society in Nineteenth-Century Latin America: An Historiographical Introduction," *Journal of Family History* 10 (1985): 215–234; Robert M. McCaa, "Introduction" [to special issue on Latin American family], *Journal of Family History* 16 (1991): 211–214; Nara Milanich, "Whither Family History: A Road Map from Latin America," *American Historical Review* (April 2007): 239–259; and, most recently, for colonial Spanish America, Bianca Premo, "Familiar: Thinking beyond Lineage and across Race in the Spanish Atlantic," *William and Mary Quarterly* 70, no. 2 (April 2013): 295–316.

23. Verena Martinez-Alier, *Marriage, Class and Colour in 19th-Century Cuba: A Study of Racial Attitudes and Sexual Values in a Slave Society* (Cambridge: Cambridge University Press, 1974), which is discussed in greater detail in chapter 4, and M. Sherry Johnson, *The Social Transformation of Eighteenth Century Cuba* (Gainesville: University Press of Florida, 2001), 8–9, for Cuba. A seminal work that laid the foundations for much of the colonial Latin American race relations scholarship is Magnus Morner, *Race Mixture in the History of Latin America* (Boston: Little, Brown, 1967). While many of its interpretations have been superseded by new research, it continues to influence notions about the *social* positioning of persons of mixed-race heritage. For alternative approaches see for example Peter Wade, "Afterword, Race and Nation in Latin America"; Kathryn Burns, "Gender and the Politics of Mestizaje: The Convent of Santa Clara in Cuzco, Peru," *Hispanic American Historical Review* 78, no. 1 (February 1998): 5–44; Douglas Cope, *The Limits of Racial Domination: Plebeian Society in Colonial Mexico City, 1660–1720* (Madison: University of Wisconsin Press, 1994); and Rachel Sarah O'Toole, *Bound Lives: Africans, Indians, and the Making of Race in Colonial Peru* (Pittsburgh: University of Pittsburgh Press, 2012).

24. The "Evarista Party" was the Partido Independiente de Color (The Independent Party of Color). It will be discussed in chapter 6.

25. See for example, Martínez-Alier, *Marriage, Class and Colour;* Franklin Knight, "Cuba," in *Neither Slave nor Free: The Freedman of African Descent in the Slave Societies of the New World,* ed. David W. Cohen and Jack P. Greene (Baltimore: Johns Hopkins University Press, 1972), 278–308; Sergio Aguirre, *Nacionalidad y nación: En el siglo XIX cubano* (Havana: Editorial de Ciencias Sociales, 1990); Jorge Duany, "Ethnicity in the

Spanish Caribbean: Notes on the Consolidation of Creole identity in Cuba and Puerto Rico, 1762–1868," in *Caribbean Ethnicity Revisited,* ed. Stephen Glazier (New York: Gordon and Breach, 1985), 15–39; Armando García González, "En torno a la antropología y el racismo en Cuba en el siglo XIX," in *Cuba: La perla de las Antillas,* ed. Consuelo Naranjo Orovio and Tomas Mallo Gutierres (Madrid: Doce Calles, 1994), 45–64; and Aline Helg, "Race in Argentina and Cuba, 1880–1930: Theory, Policies, and Popular Reaction," in *The Idea of Race in Latin America, 1870–1940,* ed. Richard Graham (Austin: University of Texas, 1990), 37–69.

26. Further discussion of Stolke's *Marriage, Class, and Colour* can be found in chapter 4.

27. I also draw conceptually on Pierre Bourdieu's habitus in his *Outline of a Theory of Practice* (1977) and his *Distinction: A Social Critique of the Judgment of Taste* (1984). However, where Bourdieu emphasizes the discursive elements of social reproduction and positioning, I see the material elements of biological reproduction as mutually constituent of discourse.

28. Robert Cottrol, *The Long, Lingering Shadow: Slavery, Race, and Law in the American Hemisphere* (Athens: University of Georgia Press, 2013); Edward Telles and Tianna Pascal, "Beyond Fixed or Fluid: Degrees of Fluidity in Racial Identification in Latin America" (paper presented at the International Congress of the Latin American Studies Association, San Francisco, California, May 23–26, 2012); and Peter Wade, "Afro-Latin Studies: Reflections the Field," *Latin American and Caribbean Ethnic Studies* 1, no. 1 (April 2006): 105–124.

1. ASCENDANT CAPITALISM AND WHITE RE-ASSESSMENTS

1. Often praised as the first Cuban nationalist poet, Heredia was forced into exile in the early 1820s by Cuba's Spanish colonial authorities for his pro-independence beliefs and participation in the major 1823 nationalist conspiracy of the multi-racial group the Soles y Rayos de Bolívar (Suns and Rays of Bolívar).

2. "Descripción de la isla de Cuba con algunas consideraciones sobre su población y comercios," in *Nicolás Joseph Ribera,* ed. Olga Portuondo Zúñiga (Havana: Editorial de Ciencias Sociales, 1986 [1757]), 128. Ribera's own pro-slavery orientation is apparent when he continues, ". . . an openness to African slaves is the only way to rapidly fill the island with great towns," 143.

3. Analysis of *partus sequitur ventrem* has been central to many feminist discussions of slavery and race relations in the Americas. Within the rich associated literature, several works have been especially useful for this current study: Camilia Cowling, *Conceiving Freedom: Women of Color, Gender, the Abolition of Slavery in Havana and Rio de Janeiro* (Chapel Hill: University of North Carolina Press, 2013); Jennifer Morgan, *Laboring Women: Reproduction and Gender in New World Slavery* (Philadelphia: University of Pennsylvania Press, 2004); and Joseph C. Dorsey, "Women without History: Slavery and the International Politics of *Partus Sequitur Ventrem* in the Spanish Caribbean," *Journal of Caribbean History* 28, no. 2 (1994): 165–207.

4. *Real cédula de 21 de octubre de 1817 sobre aumentar la población blanca de la Isla de Cuba* (Imprenta del Gobierno y Capitania General, Havana, 1828).

5. See for example Gabriel B. Paquette, *Enlightenment, Governance and Reform in Spain and Its Empire 1759–1808* (Basingstoke, UK: Palgrave Macmillan, 2008); and Paquette, ed., *Enlightened Reform in Southern Europe and Its Atlantic Colonies, c. 1750–1830* (Farnham, UK: Ashgate, 2009).

6. The term "African ethnics" is used to remind the reader that consciousness of a united continental vision of Africa was a much later ideological creation that captives did not initially possess. They were, however, aware of distinctions in community identification, although the European slave trade labels for these communities often did not match the self-identity claimed by individuals.

7. See María del Carmen Barcia, *Los ilustres apellidos: Negros en La Habana colonial* (Havana: Editorial de Ciencias Sociales, 2009), 48; and Fernando Ortiz, "Los cabildos afrocubanos," in *Ensayos etnográficos* (Havana: Editorial de Ciencias Sociales, 1984).

8. See Frank Tannenbaum, *Slave and Citizen: The Negro in the Americas* (New York: A. A. Knopf, 1946); Eugene Genovese, "Materialism and Idealism in the History of Negro Slavery in the Americas," *Journal of Social History* 1, no. 4 (Summer 1968): 371–394; Gwendolyn Midlo Hall, *Social Control in Slave Plantation Societies: A Comparison of St. Domingue and Cuba* (Baltimore: Johns Hopkins University Press, 1971); and Franklin Knight, *Slave Society in Cuba during the Nineteenth Century* (Madison: University of Wisconsin Press, 1970). For a review of studies that have challenged Tannenbaum's conclusions see Alejandro de la Fuente, "From Slaves to Citizens? Tannenbaum and the Debates on Slavery, Emancipation, and Race Relations in Latin America," *International Labor and Working-Class History* 77 (Spring 2010): 154–173; and "Slave Law and Claims-Making in Cuba: The Tannenbaum Debate Revisited," *Law and History Review* 22, no. 2 (Summer 2004).

9. See for example Manuel Moreno Fraginals, *El ingenio* (Havana: Editiorial de Ciencias Sociales, 1978), vol. 1, 130.

10. Ramón Suárez Polcari, *Historia de la iglesia católica en Cuba* (Miami: Ediciones Universal, 2003).

11. Levi Marrero, *Cuba: economía y sociedad,* 15 vols. (Río Piedras, P.R.: Editorial San Juan, 1972–1992), 8:208. On colonial black social mobility through Catholic education see also Biblioteca Nacional José Martí, Havana (hereafter "BNJM"), Colleción Manuscripta, Franco 2, 2nd box; and Archivo General de Indias, Seville (hereafter "AGI"), Ultramar, leg. 2, 10, N.3; and Eduardo Torre-Cuevas, "Ensayo introductorio: Hacia una Interpretación del Obispo De Espada y Su Influencia en la Sociedad y el Pensamiento Cubanos," in *Obispado de espada, papeles* (Havana: Casa de Altos Estudios Don Fernando Ortiz), 1–163. In Cuban usage, *pardo* does not equate with the English meaning of mulatto, as born of one black and one white parent. Instead the term often designates a person with any degree of both Afrifcan and European biological ancestry.

12. Barcia, *Los ilustres apellidos,* 58; and Carmen Montejo Arrecha, *Sociedades de instrucción y recreo de pardos y morenos que existeron en Cuba colonial* (Veracruz: Instituto Veracruzano de Cultura, 1993), 16.

13. AGI, Filipinas 335, leg. 17, F. 62V–64R.

14. On the role of lineage in African social identity formation, see Lucy Mair, *African Societies* (London: Cambridge University Press, 1974), 6 and passim.

15. For basic discussion of African religious beliefs see for example Kwame Gyekye, *An Essay on African Philosophical Thought: The Akan Conceptual* Scheme (Philadelphia: Temple University Press, 1995); John S. Mbiti, *Introduction to African Religion*, 2nd ed. (London: Heineman, 1991); and E. Bolaji Idowu, *African Traditional Religion: A Definition* (Maryknoll, N.Y.: Obis Books, 1973).

16. Barcia, *Los ilustres apellidos*, 93.

17. For examples of recent scholarship on Afro-Cuban spiritual geneaology see David Brown, *Santeria Enthroned: Art, Ritual, and Innovation in an Afro-Cuban Religion* (Chicago: University of Chicago Press, 2003); and Andrés Rodríguez Reyes, "El Cabildo Lucumí de Santa Teresa en la Ciudad de Matanzas," undated manuscript, Centro Provincial de Superación para la Cultura, Matanzas. For application of this concept to Afro-Cuban structuring of affinitive kinship bonds, see Maria del Carmen Barcia, *La otra familia: Parientes, redes y descendencia de los esclavos en Cuba* (Havana: Casa de las Americas, 2003), 84–85.

18. Nicolás Duque de Estrada, *Explicación de la doctrina Christiana acomodada a la capacidad de los negros Bozales: Contiene todo lo que debe saberse asi con necesidad le medio, como con necesidad de precepti, para beneficio de los mismo negros, de los Capellanes encargados de su instrucción, y de los amos* (Havana: Arazoza y Soler, 1818).

19. Eduardo Torres-Cuevas and Edelberto Leiva Lajara, *Presencia y ausencia de la Compañía de Jesús en Cuba* (Madrid: Fundación Ignacio Larramendi, 2005), 20, citing AGI, Santo Domingo, 151, for a 1689 report of Bishop Compostela. Also see Marrero, *Cuba*, vol. 3.

20. Pedro Pruna Goodgall, *Los jesuitas en Cuba hasta 1767* (Havana: Editorial de Ciencias Sociales, 1991), 19, and Torres-Cuevas and Leiva Lajara, *Presencia y Ausencia*, 34.

21. Eduardo Torres-Cuevas and Edelberto Leiva Lajara, *Historia de la Iglesia Católica en Cuba: La Iglesia en las patrias de los criollos (1516–1789)* (Havana: Publicaciones de la Oficina del Historiador de la Ciudad, 2008), 106.

22. Mercedes García Rodríguez, "Presencia jesuita en la economía de Cuba" (PhD diss., Universidad de la Habana, 1999), 95.

23. BNJM, Colección Manuscripta. Franco 2, 2nd box; AGI, Ultramar, leg. 2, 10, N.3; and Torres-Cuevas, "Ensayo introductorio."

24. Johnson, *Social Transformation*; Matt Childs, "The 1812 Aponte Rebellion," in *Cuba and the Struggle against Atlantic Slavery* (Chapel Hill: University of North Carolina Press, 2006); Pedro Deschamps Chapeaux, *Los batallones de pardos y negros* (Havana: Editorial Arte y Literatura, Instituto Cubano del Libro, 1976); Barcia, *Los ilustres apellidos*; and Michele Reid-Vazquez, *The Year of the Lash: Free People of Color and the Nineteenth-Century Atlantic World* (Athens: University of Georgia Press, 2011).

25. Allan Kuethe, *Cuba, 1753–1815: Crown, Military, and Society* (Knoxville: University of Tennessee Press, 1986).

26. Herbert Klein, "The Colored Militia of Cuba 1568–1868," *Caribbean Studies* 6, no. 2 (July 1966): 17–27.

27. Calculated from ibid., 20.

28. For the participation rates see Johnson, *Social Transformations*, 62–63.

29. *Reglamento para las milicias de infanteria, y caballeria de la isla de Cuba aprobado por S.M* (Madrid: n.p., 1769).

30. Kuethe, *Cuba, 1753–1815,* 74.

31. Deschamps Chapeaux, *Los batallones,* 21–23.

32. Marrero, *Cuba,* 8:164.

33. Childs, *1812 Aponte Rebellion,* 80–81.

34. Jane Landers, *Black Society in Spanish Florida* (Urbana: University of Illinois Press, 1999), 62–65; and Ralph Johnson, "Freedom's Trail: The Florida Cuba Connection" (paper presented at the National Park Service, U.S. Department of Interior Conference, "Places of Cultural Memory: African Reflections on the American Landscape," Atlanta, Georgia, May 9–12, 2001).

35. Johnson, *Social Transformation,* 67–68.

36. Childs, *1812 Aponte Rebellion,* 112. "Lucumí" is an ethnic label used in colonial Cuba to describe a subset of Yoruba-speaking people.

37. Ann Twinam, *Public Lives, Private Secrets: Gender, Honor, Sexuality and Illegitimacy in Colonial Latin America* (Stanford: Stanford University Press, 1999), 96; Gary M. Miller, "Bourbon Social Engineering: Women and Conditions of Marriage in Eighteenth-Century Venezuela," *Americas/Franciscans* 46, no. 3 (January 1990): 261–290; and Leslie B. Rout, *The African Experience in Spanish America: 1502 to the Present Day* (Cambridge: Cambridge University Press, 1976), 140.

38. Martínez, *Genealogial Fictions,* 56.

39. Twinam, *Public Lives, Private Secrets,* 41–48; and Martínez, *Genealogial Fictions,* chap. 3.

40. Martínez, *Genealogical Fictions,* 62 and passim.

41. See Robert B. Ekelund Jr., Donald Street, and Audrey Davidson, "Marriage, Divorce, and Prostitution: Economic Sociology in Medieval England and Enlightenment Spain," *European Journal of the History of Economic Thought* 3, no. 2 (Summer 1996): 183–199, on the Spanish Enlightenment philosophers Pablo de Olavide, Gaspar Melchor de Jovellanos, and Francisco de Cabrrús.

42. The pragmatic is reprinted in Joaquín Amóros, *Discurso en que se manifiesta la necesidad y utilidad del consentimiento paterno para el matrimonio de los hijos y otros deudos: conforme a lo dispuesto en la Real Pragmatica de 23. de marzo de 1776* (Madrid: Blas Roman, 1777), 6–8, with my emphasis.

43. *Pragmatica Sanción,* reprinted in Amóros, *Discurso,* 15.

44. Francisco Chacón Jiménez and Josefina Méndez Vázquez, "Miradas sobre el matrimonio en la España del último tercio del siglo XVIII," *Cuadernos de Historia Moderna* 69, no. 32 (2007): 70.

45. Reprinted in Richard Konetzke, ed., *Colección de documentos para la historia de la formacíon social de Hispanoamerica* (Madrid: Consejo Superior de Investigaciones Científicas, 1953), vol. 3, 1 n. 247.

46. Joseph Hechavarrría, *Reglamento que el ilustrísimo señor Dr. Dn. Santiago Joseph de Hechavarría, obispo de Cuba, ha formado para los ministros de su curia, y párrocos de su diócesis con motivo de la Pragmática, Real cédula de S M e instrucción de la Real Audiencia del distrito sobre matrimonios* (Colegio Seminario de San Carlos, 1780), in AGI, Santa Fe, 727. I thank Steinar Saether for making this source available to me.

47. Martínez, *Genealogical Fictions*, chap. 8.

48. Carlos IV, Real decreto de 10 de Abril de 1803, reprinted in José María Laina Gallego "Libertad y Consentimiento Paterno para el Matrimonio en la Legislación Española (de la Pragmática de Carlos III al Proyecto de Código Civil de 1851)" (PhD diss., Universidad Complutense de Madrid, 1991), 569–570.

49. Quoted in Martinez-Alier, *Marriage, Class and Colour*, 13, her emphasis.

50. Andres A. Orihuela, *El sol de Jesús del Monte* (Paris, 1856), quoted in Deschamps Chapeaux, *Los batallones de pardos y morenos libres*, 53.

51. Johannes Postma, *The Dutch in the Atlantic Slave Trade, 1600–1815* (New York: Cambridge University Press, 1990), 42–44.

52. *The Assiento, or, Contract for allowing to the subjects of Great Britain the liberty of importing Negroes into the Spanish America: signed by the Catholick King at Madrid, the twenty-sixth day of March, 1713.*

53. Ibid.

54. For sixteenth-century Cuba, the only gendered statistics of captives that survive are those of the 1532 voyage of the ship Sao Antonio. Of 201 African ethnics, a third on this ship were female, which matched the regulations. However, in general practice, the gender proportions varied widely between ships. As the ship Concepcion brought its cargo to Spanish America in 1547, an incredible 68 percent were women or girls. By contrast, as another ship disembarked in the region in 1549 only 7 percent of its captives were female. Finally, in a late-seventeenth-century example of the continuing variation in the trade's sex-ratios, the James, a ship owned by the British Royal Africa Company, disembarked captives in Cuba in 1675 of whom 57 percent were male. This evidence suggests that some traders remained attentive to the royal mandate, while others did not. See the TransAtlantic slave trade database (TSTD), Voyage Database at http://www.slavevoyages.org/tast/database/search.faces (accessed August 18, 2010).

55. Although it does not engage the anti-imperial potential of slavery, for discussion of the persistent colonial contest between Spanish Americans and the Spanish monarchy, see David A. Brading, *First Americas: The Spanish Monarchy, Creole Patriots and the Liberal State 1492–1866* (New York: Cambridge University Press, 1993).

56. Quoted in Hugh Thomas, *The Slave Trade: The Story of the Atlantic Slave Trade, 1440–1870* (New York: Simon and Schuster, 1997), 215.

57. Charlotte A. Cosner, "Rich and Poor, White and Black, Free and Slave: The Social History of Cuba's Tobacco Farmers, 1763–1817" (PhD diss., Florida International University, 2008).

58. Julio Le Riverend, *Historia económica de Cuba* (Havana: Ensayo Instituto del Libro, 1967); and Mercedes García Rodríguez, "De productores empíricos a hacendados ilustrados, el mundo del azúcar que precedió a Francisco de Arango y Parreño," in *Francisco Arango y La Invención de la Cuba Azucarera,* ed. María Dolores González-Ripoll and Izaskun Álvarez Cuartero (Salamanca: Ediciones Universidad Salamanca, 2009), 85–104.

59. Le Riverend, *Historia económica de Cuba.*

60. Thomas, *Slave Trade*, estimates 3,500; Juan Pérez de la Riva, *Cuántos africanos fueron traídos a Cuba?* (Havana: Editorial de Ciencias Sociales, 1977), 4,000; Matt Childs and Manuel Barcia, "Cuba," in *The Oxford Handbook of Slavery in the Americas,*

ed. Robert L. Paquette and Mark M. Smith (Oxford: Oxford University Press, 2010), 90–110, estimate 7,000; and Fernando Ortiz, *Los negros esclavos* (Havana: Editorial de Ciencias Sociales, 1996), 10,000.

61. Gloria García, "El auge de la sociedad esclavista de Cuba," in Instituto de Historia de Cuba, *La colonia: Evolución, socioeonómica, y formación nacional* (Havana: Editora Política, 1994), 227–228.

62. Moreno Fraginals, *El ingenio.*

63. Real cédula de 6 de febrero de 1789, ANC, Reales Cédulas y Órdenes, libro IX, fol. 103.

64. Marrero, *Cuba,* 9:23.

65. With the establishment of constitutional government, Spanish peninsular liberals allied with colonial planters to create a variant of these regulations in 1842. See Jean-Pierre Tardieu, *"Morir o dominar," En torno al reglamento de esclavos de Cuba (1841–1866)* (Madrid: Iberoamericana, 2003).

66. Thomas, *Cuba, or the Pursuit of Freedom,* updated ed. (New York: Da Capo, 1998), 72–73; Instituto de Historia de Cuba, *La colonia,* 288; Alfonso Quiroz, "Free Association and Civil Society in Cuba, 1797–1895," *Journal of Latin American Studies* 43 (2011): 39.

67. Knight, *Slave Society in Cuba.*

68. María Elena Díaz, *The Virgin, the King, and the Royal Slaves of El Cobre: Negotiating Freedom in Colonial Cuba, 1670–1780* (Stanford: Stanford University Press, 2000).

69. Jane Landers, "Cimarrón and Citizen: African Ethnicity, Corporate Identity, and the Evolution of Free Black Towns in the Spanish Circum-Caribbean," in *Slaves, Subjects, and Subversives: Blacks in Colonial Latin America,* eds. Jane Landers and Barry Robinson (Albuquerque: University of New Mexico Press, 2006), 111–147.

70. On the anti-slavery politics of free Blacks in the United States, see for example, Benjamin Quarles, *Black Abolitionists* (New York: Oxford University Press, 1969); and Patrick Rael, *Black Identity and Black Protest in the Antebellum North* (Chapel Hill: University of North Carolina Press, 2002).

71. Childs, *1812 Aponte Rebellion,* 27–28.

72. Thomas, *Cuba, or the Pursuit of Freedom,* 72–73; Instituto de Historia de Cuba, *La colonia,* 288; and Quiroz, "Free Association and Civil Society in Cuba," 39.

73. See for example Franciso Arango y Parreño, *Obras,* vol. 1 (Havana: Ciencias Sociales, 2005). Proposals were offered through 1803.

74. Ibid., "Representación hecha a su majestad con motivo de la sublevación de esclavos en los dominios franceses de la isla de Santo Domingo," 140.

75. Ibid., "Discurso sobre la agricultura de la Habana y medios de fomentarla," Madrid, January 17, 1793, 144.

76. Ibid., 170.

77. Arango, *Obras II,* "Representación de la Ciudad de la Habana a las Cortes, el 20 de julio de 1811, con motivo de las proposiciones hechas por D. José Miguel Guridi Alcocer y D Agustín de Argüelles, sobre el tráfico y esclavitud de los negros; extendida por el Alférez Mayor de la Ciudad, D. Francisco de Arango, por encargo del Ayuntamiento, Consulado y Sociedad Patriótica de la Habana," 19–52.

78. Arango, *Obras I,* "Discurso," 183–185, and "Informe que se presentó en 9 de junio de 1796 a la Junta de Gobierno del Real Consulado de Agricultura y

Comercio de esta ciudad e isla por los señores Don José Manuel De Torrontegui, Síndico Procurador General del Común, Y Don Francisco de Arango Y Parreño, Oidor Honorario de la Audiencia del distrito y Síndico de dicho Real Consulado," 271–273.

79. Arango, *Obras II,* "Representación de la ciudad de La Habana," 29–30.

80. Ibid., 19–52.

81. Arango, *Obras I,* "Discurso," 177.

82. Ana Irisarri Aguirre, "El Informe del Obispo Joaquín de Osés Alzúa: Un intento ilustrado de Promocionar el Oriente Cubano," in *Grupos sociales en la historia de Navarra, relaciones y derechos: actas del V Congreso de Historia de Navarra.septiembre de 2002* (Pamplona: Ediciones Eunate, 2002), 90, citing AGI, Santo Domingo, 2.235, Royal order of December 18, 1793, which requests the bishop's assessment; Bishop Osés's response is dated November 30, 1794.

83. José Luciano Franco, *Las minas de Santiago del Prado y la rebelion de los cobreros, 1530–1800* (Havana: Editorial Ciencias Sociales, 1975), 31; María Elena Díaz, *The Virgin, the King,* 273.

84. Bernardo O'Gavan, *Observaciones sobre la suerte de los negros del Africa, considerados en su propia patria, y trasplantados á las antillas españolas: y reclamación contra el tratado celebrado con los ingleses el año de 1817* (Madrid, 1821), 9.

85. José Agustín Caballero, "En defensa del esclavo," in *Obras* (Havana: Editorial Ciencias Sociales, 1999), 200.

2. SLAVERY AND AFRO-CUBAN FAMILY FORMATION

1. R. R. Madden, ed. and trans., *Poems by a Slave in the Island of Cuba, Recently Liberated; Translated from the Spanish, by R. R. Madden, M.D. With the History of the Early Life of the Negro Poet, Written by Himself; to Which Are Prefixed Two Pieces Descriptive of Cuban Slavery and the Slave Traffic, by R. R. M* (London: Thomas Ward and Co., 1840), 55–56.

2. For the application of "re-Africanization" to Brazilian history and U.S. history, respectively, see Stuart Schwartz, "Rethinking Palmares: Slave Resistance in Colonial Brazil," in *Slaves, Peasants, and Rebels: Reconsidering Brazilian Slavery* (Urbana: University of Illinois Press, 1992), 103–136; and Ira Berlin, *Many Thousands Gone: The First Two Centuries of Slavery in North America* (Cambridge, Mass.: Belknap Press of Harvard University Press, 1998), 314–316.

3. Antonio Saco, *Historia de la esclavitud de la raza africana en el Nuevo mundo y en especial en los paises américo-hispanos* (Barcelona: J. Jepús, 1879), 325.

4. Hubert Aimes, *A History of Slavery in Cuba, 1511 to 1868* (New York: Putnam and Sons, 1907), 36–37.

5. Thomas, *Slave Trade,* 272. Levi Marrero reported a lower figure of 20,000 in 1768; see his *Cuba,* 9:11.

6. Kenneth Kiple, *Blacks in Colonial Cuba, 1774–1899* (Gainesville: University Presses of Florida, 1976), 4, 26, and 29.

7. The 1829 plantation inventory is reprinted in Moreno Fraginals, *El Ingenio,* 2:16–17. Robert Paquette, *Sugar Is Made with Blood: The Conspiracy of La Escalera and the Conflict between Empires over Slavery in Cuba* (Middletown, Conn.: Wesleyan University Press,

1988), 59, citing Arango, *Obras*, 2:238–241, incorrectly does not subtract the number of children in obtaining the size of the adult workforce.

8. Cuban baptismal records were often segregated by color until the first decade of the twentieth century.

9. The classic debate related to the concept of creolization among the African-descended population references the African retention approach proposed by Melville Herskovits, for example, in *The Myth of the Negro Past* (1941) and the New World created approach articulated by Mintz and Price in *The Birth of African American Culture: An Anthropological Perspective* (1976). For a review of recent literature on creolization and a critique of the uncritical application of the term, see Stephan Palmié, "Creolization and Its Discontents" *Annual Review of Anthropology* 35 (2006): 433–456.

10. For the British Caribbean see for example B. W. Higman, *Slave Populations of the British Caribbean, 1807–1834* (Kingston: University of the West Indies Press, 1995), 121–123.

11. Archivo de la parroquia de Espíritu Santo (hereafter "AES"), *libro 8 de bautismos de pardos y morenos, 1759–1767* (hereafter *libro 8*), entries 1364, 1622, 1805, and 1932.

12. Ibid.

13. José María de la Torre, *Lo que fuimos y lo que somos o la Habana antigua y moderna* (Havana: Spencer and Co., 1857), 92; and Manuel Cuadrado Melo, *Obispado de la Habana, su historia a traves de los siglos* (Havana, 1970), 290; both state this figure as 1,100. This is corrected to 11,000 in Johnson, *Social Transformation,* 21. The latter number is much more plausible given that Espíritu Santo was one of Havana's four parishes and according to Jacobo Pezuela, *Diccionario geográfico, estadístico y histórico de la Isla de Cuba,* 4 vols. (Madrid: Mellard, 1863–1866), 3:52, Havana's total population was 75,648 in 1773.

14. Cuadrado Melo, *Obispado de la Habana,* 292.

15. The 1774 census indicates that the combined enslaved and free African-descended population represented 43.8 percent of the total (calculated from the de la Sagra figures appearing in Kiple, *Blacks in Colonial Cuba,* 26). If we accept the parish's population to be 11,000, this equates to 4,818.

16. See David Weir, "Life under Pressure: France and England, 1670–1870," *Journal of Economic History* 44, no. 1 (1984): 37 for crude birthrates.

17. AES, *libro 8,* entries 1317–2083.

18. Rout, *African Experience,* 88; Herbert S. Klein, *African Slavery in Latin America and the Caribbean* (Oxford: Oxford University Press, 1986), 156–157 and 228; and Rosemary Brana-Shute, "Manumission," in *A Historical Guide to World Slavery,* ed. Seymour Drescher and Stanley L. Engerman (New York: Oxford University Press, 1998), 262.

19. Evidence of this experience remains anecdotal and requires further research.

20. Higman, *Slave Populations,* 357–362; Michael Craton, *Searching for the Invisible Man: Slave and Plantation Life in Jamaica* (Cambridge, Mass.: Harvard University Press, 1978), 96–97. This evidence must be adapted to Cuba with great qualification. Both these sources are based on sugar plantation labor. The case under review here is an urban one.

21. AES, *libro 8.* Sixteen baptisms of "adult" African women were registered in the period, with ages reported for eight. See entries 1352, 1401, 1410, 1412, 1414, 1424, 1684, and 1784.

22. There were four children born free to enslaved mothers.

23. Ibid., entries 1398, 1584, 1685, 1727, and 1974.

24. Ibid., entries 1317–2083.

25. Ibid., entries 1762, 1796, 1797, 1800, 1808, 1820, 1828, 1834, 1836, 1837, 1846, 1847, 1851, 1859, 1876, 1887, 1923, 1924, 1934, 1940, 1947, 1951, 1989, 2013, 2017, 2024, 2045, 2046, and 2078.

26. *Código negro carolino,* Cap. 25, quoted in Hall, *Social Control,* 94. On royal slaves see *Reglamento para el gobierno, militar, político, y ecónomico de la Compañía de Artelleria compuesta de negros de S.M. y sus familias* (Havana: D. Blas de los Olivos, 1768), reprinted in *El curioso Americano,* epoca (series) IV, año (year) 4, no. 1 (January–February 1910): 22–28. The men in this company were encouraged to marry and have large families: "el Intendente bucará negras para casarlas con estos [negros], a fin de obviar los desordenes á que estan expuestos" (The military supervisor will seek black women in order to marry them to these [black] men, with the goal of avoiding the disruption that these men are disposed) and "tendrán libertad el negro y negra casados que llegaren a tener doce hijos vivos" (Those married black men and women who have twelve live children will gain their freedom) (26).

27. See *Dictamen sobre las ventajas que pueden sacarse para el mejor fomento de la Isla de Cuba,* cited in Marrero, *Cuba,* 12:188, as an example. Marrero attributes this undated document to 1766.

28. AES, *libro 8,* entries 1375, 1445, 1465, 1472, 1493, 1507, 1530, 1608, 1620, 1622, 1626, 1644, 1647, 1743, 1819, 1932, and 2054.

29. Ibid., entry 1620. The mother in this case was a free black creole.

30. See for example Archivo del Arzobispado de La Habana, Fondo Reconocimientos y Legitimaciones (hereafter "Reconocimientos"), leg. 105, exp. 38 (1891).

31. References to the Ley de Toro 11 on this point are found in José Portuondo de Castro, *La filación* (Havana, 1947), 7, and Enrique Gacto Fernández, *La filación no legítima en el derecho histórico español* (Seville: Universidad de Sevilla, 1969), 81, 131, and 140–141. The process is distinct from legitimation by *gracias al sacar* described by Ann Twinam. The former was a procedure controlled by local ecclesiastic authorities and the latter required Crown approval; see Twinam, *Public Lives, Private Secrets,*16 and passim.

32. AES, *libro 8 de bautismos de pardos y morenos, 1759–1767,* entries 1620, 2054, 1507, 1743, 1448, and 1445.

33. No mention of the status of these children is made in Spanish law before the eighteenth century. See Federico Puig Peña, "Hijos de Padres Desconocidos," *Nueva Enciclopedia Jurídica* (Barcelona: Editorial Francisco Seix, 1962), 10:9–10. However, the *Actas del Concilio Provincial de Santo Domingo (1622–1623)* mandates that abandoned children be labeled "exposito" and their baptismal records reflect the homes in which they were placed. *Exposición del Ayuntamiento de la Habana al Escmo Senor Ministro de Ultramar acera del establecimiento municipal de las Reales Casas de Beneficiencia y Maternidad* (Havana: P. Fernández, 1890), 14–16, and Ondina González, "Abandonment in Havana: The Response of the State and the Church, 1700–1750" (paper presented at the International Congress of the Latin American Studies Association, Miami, Florida, 2000), traces eighteenth-century royal, clerical, and elite efforts to found an orphanage for the abandoned children of Havana.

34. Real Cédula, "Libertad de Comercio de Esclavos" (Royal Order "Freedom of the Slave Trade"), February 6, 1789, reprinted in Hortensia Pichardo Viñals, ed. *Documentos para la historia de Cuba*, 2nd edition (Havana: Editorial Pueblo y Educación, 2000), I:168–171.

35. Laird W. Bergad, Fe Iglesias García, and María del Carmen Barcia, *The Cuban Slave Market, 1790–1880* (Cambridge: Cambridge University Press, 1995), 21.

36. David Eltis, *Economic Growth and the Ending of the Transatlantic Slave Trade* (New York: Oxford University Press, 1987), 245.

37. The statistics stated by both Alexander von Humboldt and Ramón de la Sagra are rectified and cited in Kiple, *Blacks in Colonial Cuba*, 5 and passim. Again, Johnson (*Social Transformation*, 24) urges caution with the estimates of the white population as peninsular military men were probably excluded from the count.

38. Knight, *Slave Society in Cuba*, 124–125.

39. Saco, *Historia de la esclavitud de la raza africana*, 3:16; Ortiz, *Los negros esclavos*, 329–334; and Hall, *Social Control*, 103–105.

40. Knight, *Slave Society*, 125–126; Manuel Lucena Salmoral, "El reglamento de esclavos de Cuba," *Del Caribe* (Santiago de Cuba) 25 (1996): 89; and Garcia, *Esclavitud desde la esclavitud*.

41. Childs, *1812 Aponte Rebellion*, 65.

42. Herbert S. Klein, *The Middle Passage: Comparative Studies in the Atlantic Slave Trade* (Princeton: Princeton University Press, 1978), 214.

43. Moreno Fraginals, *El ingenio*, 2: 67, 71, 73–76; and Marrero, *Cuba*, 9: 189.

44. Bergad et al., *Cuban Slave Market*, 27.

45. Parroquia de Iglesia Mayor de la Catedral, *libro de barajas, seccion de bautismos, 1590–1600*.

46. Cited in María de los Ángeles Meriño Fuentes and Aisnara Perera Díaz, *Un Café para la Microhistoria: Estructura de Posesión de Esclavos y Ciclo de Vida en la Llanura Habanera, 1800–1886* (Havana: Editorial de Ciencias Sociales, 2008), 100.

47. Pablo Tornero Tinajero, *Crecimiento ecónomico y transformaciones sociales: esclavos, hacendados y comerciantes en la Cuba colonial (1760–1840)* (Madrid: Ministerio de Trabajo y Seguridad Social, 1996), 60–61.

48. Herbert Klein, "Women in the Atlantic Slave Trade," in *Women and Slavery in Africa*, ed. Claire Robertson and Martin Klein (Madison: University of Wisconsin Press, 1983), 32–33.

49. Moreno Fraginals, *El ingenio*, 2:39.

50. Bergad et al., *Cuban Slave Market*, 61–62.

51. David Eltis and Stanley L. Engerman, "Was the Slave Trade Dominated by Men?," *Journal of Interdisciplinary History* 23, no. 2 (Autumn 1992): 243.

52. Jack Ericson Eblen, "On the Natural Increase of Slave Populations: The Example of the Cuban Black Population, 1775–1900," in *Race and Slavery in the Western Hemisphere: Quantitative Studies*, ed. Stanley L. Engerman and Eugene Genovese (Princeton: Princeton University Press, 1975), 211–247.

53. Moreno Fraginals, *El ingenio*, 2:86.

54. Higman, *Slave Populations*, 358; and Herbert S. Klein and Stanley L. Engerman, "Fertility Differentials between Slaves in the United States and the British West Indies:

A Note on Lactation Practices and Their Possible Implications," *William and Mary Quarterly* 35 (1978) 357–374.

55. Moreno Fraginals accepted "a family unit within the sugar plantation was a foreign body, naturally rejected," *Ingenio* 2, 45. Rebecca Scott made initial revisions to Moreno Fraginals's comments by demonstrating family actions related to self-emancipation; see Scott, *Slave Emancipation in Cuba: The Transition to Free Labor, 1860–1899* (Princeton: Princeton University Press, 1985).

56. John Dumoulin, "Los matrimonios santiagueros en el siglo XIX: apuntes para un debate sobre esclavitud y ciudadanía en las Américas," in *Ciudadanos en la Nación*, ed. Olga Portuondo y Michael Zueske (Santiago de Cuba: Fritz Thyssen Stiftung/Oficina del Conservador de la Ciudad, 2002), 154–158.

57. Aisnara Perera Díaz and María de los Angeles Meriño Fuentes, *Esclavitud, familia, y parroquia en Cuba: Otra mirada desde la microhistoria* (Santiago de Cuba: Instituto Cubano del Libro, Editorial Oriente, 2006), 163.

58. Ibid., 153.

59. These average rates were calculated from a series of population reports (*padrones*) that noted the civil statuses submitted by each district. AGI, Cuba, leg. 1470. For Bahia Honda, the reporting years were 1791–1795. For Jibacoa, the years were 1791, 1792, and 1794. For Yaguaramas, the years were 1791, 1792, 1794, 1795, and 1796. I thank Sherry Johnson for making these data available to me. These averages were calculated to minimize significant variations in the original data that were presumably caused by migration and reporting inaccuracies.

60. Ramón de la Sagra, *Historia ecónomico-política y estadistica de la Isla de Cuba, o sea de sus progresos en la poblacion, la agricultura, el comercio y las rentas* (Havana: Las Viudas de Arazoza y Soler, 1831), 24.

61. Klein, *Slavery in the Americas,* 96 and 97.

62. Knight, *Slave Society in Cuba,* 106.

63. Africanist historian John Thorton suggests that decreasing the proportion of Central African ethnicities may also be at play, as many from the Kongo Kingdom would have known Catholicism prior to enslavement in Cuba (personal conversation Havana, July 2013).

64. AES, *Libro 8 de bautismos de pardos y morenos, 1759–1767,* entries 1317–2083.

65. AES, *Libro 22 de bautismos de pardos y morenos, 1800,* entries 1–447; and *Libro 33, 1820,* entries 334–943.

66. See Eblen, "On the Natural Increase of Slave Populations," for similar estimations that do not discuss gender.

67. Higman, *Slave Populations,* 368–367.

68. For an example from the region of Nueva Granada (now Colombia) see María Eugenia Chaves, *La estrategia de libertad de una esclava del siglo XVIII: las identidades de amo y esclavo en un puerto colonial* (Quito: Ediciones Abya-Yala, 1999), 51–52. This office was not fully defined until 1789 and in Cuba the 1842 slave regulations gave it greater authority.

69. AGI, Escribania, 48B.

70. See de la Fuente, "Slave Law and Claims-Making."

71. On the discrepancy in Manzano's date of birth see Ivan Schulman's introduction in Manzano, *Autobiography,* 13.

72. Ibid., 44–47.

73. Ibid., 50–53.

74. Ibid., 55.

75. Ibid., 44.

76. Herbert Klein, *Slavery in the Americas: A Comparative Study of Virginia and Cuba* (London: Oxford University Press, 1967), 196–200.

77. Manzano, *Autobiography,* 77.

3. THE ILLEGAL SLAVE TRADE AND THE SEXUAL ECONOMY OF RACE

1. María de los Angeles Meriño and Aisnara Perera Díaz, *Matrimonio y Familia en el ingenio: Una utopia posible, La Habana (1825–1886)* (Havana: Editorial Unicornio, 2008), 66, 68–69, appendix VIII.

2. José Luciano Franco, *Comercio Clandestino de Esclavos* (Havana: Editorial de Ciencias Sociales, 1980); Arthur Corwin, *Spain and Abolition of Slavery in Cuba, 1817–1886* (Austin: University of Texas Press, 1967); and Murray, *Odious Commerce.*

3. Knight, *Slave Society in Cuba,* 31.

4. Joseph Goodwin, "Diary 1820–1827," November 28, 1821, New York Historical Society Museum and Library, New York.

5. David Eltis, "The Nineteenth-Century Transatlantic Slave Trade: An Annual Time Series of Imports into the Americas Broken Down by Region," *Hispanic American Historical Review* 67, no. 1 (1987), 109–138.

6. Philip D. Curtin, *The Atlantic Slave Trade: A Census* (Madison: University of Wisconsin Press, 1969), 40.

7. Eltis, "Nineteenth-Century Transatlantic Slave Trade," 121–128.

8. Instituto de Historia de Cuba, *La colonia,* 466–467. Cuban historian Juan Pérez de la Riva offers higher estimates of the nineteenth-century slave trade, suggesting the arrival of 1,110,000 Africans in "El monto de la inmigración forzada en el siglo XIX," *Revista de la Biblioteca Nacional José Martí* 16, no. 1 (January–April 1974): 77–110.

9. Reid-Vazquez, *Year of the Lash.*

10. Ibid.

11. Quoted in Ortiz, *Los negros esclavos,* 1916, p. 330.

12. Hall, *Social Control,* 128.

13. Ibid., 130–132.

14. Reid-Vazquez, *Year of the Lash,* 82.

15. Ibid., 22.

16. Bergad et al., *Cuban Slave Market,* 128 and 141.

17. Scott, *Slave Emancipation,* 14.

18. Moreno Fraginals, *El ingenio,* 2:86.

19. Ibid., 2:88.

20. Joseph C. Miller, "Demographic History Revisited," *Journal of African History* 25 (1984): 94 and John Iliffe, "The Origins of African Population Growth," *Journal of African History* 30 (1989), 165–166.

21. Regarding conflicts in the status of the emancipados see Ines Roldan De Montaud, "Origen, Evolución y Supresión del Grupo de Negros 'Emancipados' en Cuba (1871–1870)," *Revista de Indias* 42, nos. 169–170 (July–December 1982): 560–641.

22. Ibid., and Knight, *Slave Society*, 29, 102–103.

23. Knight, *Slave Society*, 29.

24. Roldan de Montaud, "Origen, Evolución y Supresión," 584.

25. Reconocimientos leg. 7, exp. 29, 1864.

26. Manuel Moreno Fraginals, "Africa in Cuba: A Quantitative Analysis of the African Population in the Island of Cuba," *Annals of the New York Academy of Sciences* 292, no. 1 (1977): 191.

27. Marrero, *Cuba*, 14:256.

28. Richard Robert Madden, *The Island of Cuba* (London: C. Gilpin, 1849), cited in Louis Pérez, *Slaves, Sugar, and Colonial Society: Travel Accounts of Cuba, 1801–1899* (Wilmington, Del.: Scholarly Resources, 1992), 52.

29. Nery Gómez Abreu and Manuel Martínez Casanova, "Contribución al estudio de la presencia de las diferentes etnias y culturas africanas en la región central de Cuba: zona de Placetas (1817–1886)," *Isla* 85 (September–December 1986): 118.

30. AES, *libros 48, 49, 52,* and *54 de bautismos de pardos y morenos* (hereafter *libro 48, libro 49, libro 52,* and *libro 54*).

31. Eblen, "On the Natural Increase of Slave Populations."

32. Kiple, *Blacks in Colonial Cuba*, 25. Kiple described the possibility of natural increase for "urban slaves and others not on sugar estates, along with the free coloreds" over the period 1855–1899, but appropriately excluded the period of high mortality occasioned by the Ten Years War (1868–1878).

33. Moreno Fraginals, "Africa in Cuba," 192.

34. Moreno Fraginals, *El ingenio*, 2:56.

35. Among the leading proponents of this position see Ramiro Guerra y Sánchez, *Azúcar y población en las Antillas* (Havana: Cultural, S. A., 1927); and Moreno Fraginals, *El ingenio*.

36. Knight, *Slave Society in Cuba*, 63.

37. Scott, *Slave Emancipation*, 12–13.

38. Ibid., 12.

39. Meriño Fuentes and Perera Díaz, *Un café para la microhistoria*, 86–89.

40. On use of slave women on British Caribbean sugar plantations, see Richard S. Dunn, *Sugar and Slaves: The Rise of the Planter Class in the English West Indies* (Chapel Hill: University of North Carolina Press, 1972); Craton, *Searching for the Invisible Man*; and Higman, *Slave Populations of the British Caribbean*.

41. de la Sagra, *Historia economico-politica*, 25.

42. Le Riverend, *Historia económica de Cuba*, 172.

43. Ibid, 180.

44. Hall, *Social Control*, 26, citing a royal order of April 22, 1804.

45. Moreno Fraginals, "Africa in Cuba," 193.

46. Tardieu, *"Morir o dominar."*

47. Hortensia Pichardo, ed., *Documentos para la historia de Cuba* (Havana: Editorial Pueblo y Educación, 2000), 316–326.

48. Scott, *Slave Emancipation*, 75–76; and de la Fuente, "Slave Law and ClaimsMaking."

49. Abiel Abbot, *Letters Written in the Interior of Cuba* (Boston: Bowles and Dearborn, 1829), 41.

50. Ibid., 42 and 142.

51. *Reglamento para el gobierno militar, politico, y economico de la Compania de Artilleria compuesto de negros,* 26.

52. Goodwin, "Diary 1820–1827," see for example July 22, 1821.

53. Paquette, *Sugar Is Made with Blood,* 149.

54. *Cartilla prática del manejo de ingenios ó fincas destinados á producir azúcar* (Irun, 1862), 82–83, cited in Paquette, *Sugar Is Made with Blood,* 59–60.

55. Moreno Fraginals, *El ingenio,* 2:44.

56. Fredrika Bremer, *The Homes of the New World: Impressions of America,* 2 vols., trans. Mary Howitt (New York: Harper and Brothers, 1854), 301.

57. Ibid., 335.

58. Ibid.

59. Higman, *Slave Populations,* 349–351; for the Bahamas see Michael Craton, "Changing Patterns of Slave Families in the British West Indies," *Journal of Interdisciplinary History* 10, no. 1 (Summer 1979): 15.

60. Bremer, *Homes of the New World,* 336–337.

61. Ibid., 385–386.

62. Perera Díaz and Meriño Fuentes, *Esclavitud,* 152.

63. Reconocimientos, leg. 46, exp. 63 (1877).

64. Reconocimientos, leg. 52, exp. 15 (1878).

65. AES, *libro 49,* entries 109, 110, 111, 154, 173, 178, and 220 (1847).

66. See chapter 2.

67. David M. Stark has found that for eighteenth-century Puerto Rico approximately half of slave marriages involved the pairing of enslaved people to the same owners; see "Discovering the Invisible Puerto Rican Slave Family: Demographic Evidence from the Eighteenth Century," *Journal of Family History* 21, no. 4 (1996): 395–421. Similar studies of the Brazilian experience have found much higher occurrences of this practice; see Stuart B. Schwartz, *Sugar Plantations in the Formation of Brazilian Society: Bahia, 1550–1835* (Cambridge: Cambridge University Press, 1985), 383; and Alida C. Metcalf, *Family and Frontier in Colonial Brazil: Santana de Parnaiba, 1550–1822* (Berkeley: University of California Press, 1992), 169.

68. Marrero, *Cuba,* 14:43 and 47.

69. Calculated from Kiple, *Blacks in Colonial Cuba,* 5–7.

70. AES, *libros 48, 49, 52,* and *54.*

71. See chapter 2, and AES, *libro 8,* entries 1317–2083 (1765–1767).

72. AES, *libro 48,* entries 793–868 (1847), and *libro 49,* entries 1–268 (1847).

73. Based on data found in *Cuadro estadístico de . . . 1827* (Havana: Oficina de las Viudas de Arazoza y Soler, 1829), 26; *Resumen del censo . . . 1841 . . .* (Havana: Impr. del gobierno, 1842), 20; and Kiple, *Blacks in Colonial Cuba,* 3.

74. Bergad et al., *Cuban Slave Market,* 68, 162–172.

75. Ibid., 44–47, 85. These authors urge caution on this point, emphasizing that the sale of Africans was illegal after that time.

76. AES, *libro 48,* entries 793–868 (1847) and *libro 49,* entries 1–268 (1847).

77. Ibid., *libro 49,* entry 25 (1847).

78. For wages and the price of marriage in the middle of the nineteenth century see María Dolores Pérez Murillo, *Aspectos demograficos y sociales de la isla de Cuba en la primera mitad del siglo XIX* (Cadiz: Universide de Cadiz, 1988), 199 and 205–209.

79. John Thornton qualifies this point by noting that some captives from West Central Africa would have arrived from societies already familiar with Catholicism (personal conversation, Havana, July 2013).

80. Marrero, *Cuba,* 13:85.

81. Knight, *Slave Society,* 107–109.

82. Hall, *Social Control,* 43–50.

83. Archivo Nacional Cubano (ANC), Fondo Miscelánea de Expedientes, leg. 207F transcribed in Gloria Garcia, ed. *La esclavitud desde la esclavitud: La visión de los siervos* (Mexico: Centro de Investigación Científico "Ing. Jorge de Tamayo," 1996), 132.

84. *Informe presentado a la junta informativa de ultramar . . .* (Madrid: J. Peña, 1869), translated and quoted in Knight, *Slave Society,* 112–113.

85. Statistics for 1828 are found in Manuel Pastor, ed., *Año de 1828, Censo de la siempre fidelisima Ciudad de la Habana, capital de la siempre fiel isla de Cuba* (Havana: Imprenta del Gobierno y Capitanía General, 1829), 10. Statistics for 1862 are calculated from Centro de Estadistica, *Noticias Estadisticas de la isla de Cuba en 1862* (Havana: Imprenta del Gobierno, Capitanía General y Real Hacienda, 1864). Both are based on populations above age fifteen. The situation in Havana differed from that in the rest of the island, which saw marriage rates increase from 42 percent in 1827 to 48 percent in 1862. See *Cuadro estadistico de la siempre fiel isla de Cuba correspondiente al año de 1827* (Havana: Arozoza y Soler, 1828), 60; Centro de Estadistica, *Noticias Estadisticas de la isla de Cuba en 1862* (Havana: Imprenta del gobierno, 1864); and Martínez-Alier, *Marriage,* 60.

86. Michele Reid, "Negotiating a Slave Regime: Free People of Color in Cuba, 1844–1868" (PhD diss., University of Texas, 2004), 211–212.

87. Reconocimientos, leg. 4, exp. 57 (1860) references this 1837 royal order.

88. See for example AES, *libro 48,* entries 801, 805, and 812 (1847).

89. Ibid., *libro 48,* entry 842, (1847) and *libro 49,* entries 27, 64, 114, and 248 (1847).

90. See chapter 5.

91. For the use of ecclesiastic records in colonial Cuban life-cycle and family reconstruction, see Guy Bourdé, "Fuentes y métodos de la historia demográfica en Cuba, siglos XVIII y XIX," *Revista de la Biblioteca Nacional José Martí* 65, no, 1 (January–April 1974): 21–68; and for Afro-Cuban families, see a series of publications by Aisnara Perera Díaz and María de los Angles Meriño Fuentes, beginning with *Esclavitud, familia y parroquia en Cuba: otra mirada desde la microhistoria* (Santiago de Cuba: Editorial Oriente, 2006).

92. Reconocimientos, legs. 1–116 (1800–1893). The first Afro-Cuban petition dates from 1858. After 1893 racial identifiers are found less consistently in the petitions, making it difficult to distinguish Afro-Cuban family experiences.

93. Meriño Fuentes and Perera Díaz, *Matrimonio y Familia en el ingenio,* 36.

94. Ibid.

95. Reconocimientos, leg. 22, exp. 95 (1871).

96. Ibid., leg. 24, exp. 114 (1868).

97. Ibid., leg.4, exp. 57 (1860) references a 1837 royal order that lifted previous restrictions on the naming of unmarried parents in their children's baptismal certificates.

98. Ibid., leg. 29, exp. 94 (1872).

99. Ibid., leg. 42, exp. 3 (1876).

100. Ibid., leg. 18, exp. 79 (1870); leg. 21, exp. 41 (1870); leg. 21, exp. 47 (1870); leg. 21, exp. 76 (1870); leg. 22, exp. 95 (1871); leg. 24, exp. 114 (1867); leg. 29, exp. 94 (1874); leg. 31, exp. 40 (1873); leg. 35, exp. 21 (1874); leg. 35, exp. 94 (1874); leg. 36, exp. 79 (1874); leg. 36, exp. 40 (1874); leg. 38, exp. 22 (1875); leg. 41, exp. 94 (1876); leg. 42, exp. 3 (1876); leg. 42, exp. 20 (1876); leg. 46, exp. 23 (1877) ; leg. 46, exp. 82 (1876); leg. 49, exp. 62 (1878); leg. 52, exp. 58 (1878); leg. 61, exp. 70 (1880); leg. 61, exp. 88 (1881); leg. 62, exp. 25 (1880); leg. 63, exp. 58 (1881); leg. 67, exp. 61 (1879); leg. 67, exp. 78 (1882); leg. 68, exp. 93 (1882); leg. 71, exp. 38 (1882); leg. 73, exp. 51 (1883); leg. 73, exp. 61 (1883); leg. 76, exp. 25 (1883); leg. 77, exp. 39 (1883); leg. 77, exp. 55 (1884); leg. 79, exp. 99 (1885); leg. 81, exp. 76 (1885); leg. 82, exp. 53 (1885); leg. 84, exp. 33 (1885); leg. 91, exp. 13 (1887); leg. 93, exp. 17 (1888); leg. 97, exp. 55 (1889); leg. 101, exp. 77 (1890); leg. 101, exp. 78 (1890); leg. 105, exp. 39 (1891); leg. 106, exp. 69 (1891); leg. 107, exp. 58 (1890); leg. 108, exp. 72 (1891); leg. 111, exp. 67 (1892).

101. Reconocimientos, legs. 1–116 (1800–1893).

102. Ibid., leg. 21, exp. 76 (1870). María del Carmen is listed alternately as Mandinga and Carabali.

103. On the number of Chinese indentured laborers arriving in Cuba see Denise Hely, "Introduction," *The Cuba Commission Report, A Hidden History of the Chinese in Cuba*, trans. Sidney Mintz (Baltimore: Johns Hopkins University Press, 1993), 20.

104. Archivo Nacional de la República de Cuba, Havana (hereafter "ANC"), Fondo Gobierno Superior Civil (hereafter "Superior"), leg. 925, no. 32318 (1862).

105. Reconocimientos, leg. 19, exp. 81 (1870).

106. Other recognitions by Chinese men of the children they had with enslaved women are found in ibid.: leg. 21, exp. 24 (1870); leg. 24, exp. 26 (1868); leg. 31, exp. 19 (1873); leg. 39, exp. 53 (1875); leg. 41, exp. 16 (1876); leg. 41, exp. 74 (1876); leg. 44, exp. 84 (1877); leg. 45, exp. 93 (1876); leg. 49, exp. 89 (1878); leg. 50, exp. 33 (1878); leg. 51, exp. 29 (1878); leg. 55, exp. 8 (1879); leg. 77, exp. 19 (1883); leg. 78, exp. 9 (1884); leg. 80, exp. 2 (1884); leg. 82, exp. 27 (1885); leg. 84, exp. 87 (1885); leg. 89, exp. 87 (1885); leg. 105, exp. 4 (1891); and leg. 114, exp. 73 (1893).

107. Ibid., leg. 58, exp. 20 (1880).

108. Ibid., leg. 83, exp. 76, (1885).

109. Ibid., leg. 73, exp. 43 (1883).

110. Benjamín Nista Moret, ed., *Esclavos prófugos y cimarrones de Puerto Rico, 1770–1870* (Río Piedras: Editorial Universitaria, 1984), 201, trans. and quoted in Dorsey, "Women without History," 172.

111. On enslaved women and sexual violence see, for example, Angela Davis, "Reflections on the Black Woman's Role in the Community of Slaves," *Black Scholar* 3, no. 4 (1971): 2–15; Marietta Morrissey, *Slave Women in the New World: Gender Stratification in the Caribbean* (Lawrence: University of Kansas Press, 1989); and Barbara Bush, *Slave Women in Caribbean Society, 1650–1838* (London: James Currey, 1990).

112. Reconocimientos, leg. 90, exp. 38 (1887).

113. Ibid., leg. 88, exp. 12 (1886). For other recognized children of enslaved women and white men see leg. 4, exp. 83 (1861); leg. 5, exp. 49 (1862); leg. 23, exp. 27 (1871); leg. 28, exp. 14 (1872); leg. 30, exp. 67 (1873); leg. 34, exp. 54 (1874); leg. 36, exp. 56 (1875); leg. 43, exp. 26 (1876); leg. 45, exp. 20 (1876); leg. 46, exp. 56 (1877); leg. 48, exp. 12 (1877); leg. 51, exp. 17 (1878); leg. 53, exp. 17 (1878); leg. 53, exp. 87 (1878); leg. 58, exp. 20 (1880); leg. 62, exp. 94 (1881); leg. 65, exp. 90 (1881); leg. 66, exp. 90 (1881); leg. 71, exp. 28 (1882); leg. 79, exp. 18 (1884); leg. 80, exp. 11 (1884); leg. 83, exp. 76 (1878); leg. 85, exp. 61 (1886); leg. 88, exp. 25 (1886); leg. 89, exp. 77 (1887); leg. 90, exp. 13 (1887); leg. 93, exp. 1 (1888); leg. 101, exp. 7 (1890); leg. 103, exp. 62 (1890); leg. 103, exp. 63 (1890); leg. 105, exp. 22 (1891); leg. 110, exp. 59 (1892); and leg. 114, exp. 68 (1893). Further discussion of inter-racial relationships can be found in chapter 4.

114. Transcribed from ANC, Fondo Gobierno Superior Civil leg. 949, no. 33543 in García Rodríguez, *La esclavitud desde la esclavitud*, 114–115.

4. RACIAL MYTHS AND THE CORRUPTION OF WHITENESS

Elements of this chapter previously appeared in Karen Y. Morrison, "'Whitening' Revisited: Nineteenth-Century Cuban Counterpoints," in *Africans into Spanish America: Expanding the Diaspora*, eds. Sherwin Bryant, Rachel O'Toole, and Ben Vinson (Urbana: University of Illinois Press, 2012).

1. Villaverde, *Cecilia Valdés*.

2. See for example Reynaldo González, *Contradanzas y Latigazos* (Havana: Editorial Letras Cubanas, 1983), 24–26 and passim; Yolanda Aguirre, "Leonardo Gamboa y la juventud cubana en su tiempo" and Raimundo Lazo, "Cecilia Valdés: estudio critico," both in *Acerca de Cirilo Villaverde*, ed. Imeldo Alvarez (Havana: Editorial Letras Cubanas, 1982), 199–219 and 233–273, respectively. See Doris Sommer, *Foundational Fictions: The National Romances of Latin America* (Berkeley: University of California Press, 1991); and Norman Holland, "Fashioning Cuba," in *Nationalisms and Sexualities*, ed. A. Parker (New York: Routledge, 1992), 147–148, for critiques of such close readings.

3. For a broader view of sexual reproduction of class and race in Latin America see Muriel Nazzari, "Sex/Gender Arrangements and the Reproduction of Class in the Latin American Past," in *Gender Politics in Latin America, Debates in Theory and Practice*, ed. E. Dore (New York: Monthly Review Press, 1997), 134–148.

4. For discussion of colonial restrictions on the selection of marriage partners see Martinez-Alier, *Marriage, Class and Colour*; for elsewhere in Latin America see Asunción Lavrin, "Introduction: The Scenario, the Actors, and the Issues," in *Sexuality and Marriage in Colonial Latin America* (Lincoln: University of Nebraska Press, 1989), 1–43; Daisy Rípodas Ardanaz, *El matrimonio en Indias: realidad social y regulación jurídica* (Buenos Aires: Fundación para la Educación, la Ciencia y la Cultura, 1977); and Susan M. Socolow, "Acceptable Partners: Marriage Choice in Colonial Argentina, 1778–1810," in *Sexuality and Marriage in Colonial Latin America*, ed. A. Lavrin (Lincoln: University of Nebraska Press, 1989), 209–251.

5. Patricia Seed, *To Love, Honor, and Obey in Colonial Mexico: Conflicts over Marriage Choice, 1514–1821* (Stanford: Stanford University Press, 1988); Socolow, "Acceptable Partners"; and Ramón Gutiérrez, *When Jesus Came, the Corn Mothers Went Away:*

Marriage, Sexuality, and Power in New Mexico, 1500–1846 (Stanford: Stanford University Press, 1991), 284–292 and 317.

6. Martínez-Alier. *Marriage, Class and Colour.*

7. This study found inter-racial marriages allowed in the following petitions: ANC, Gobierno Superior Civil, leg. 888 no. 29871 (1813); leg. 888, no. 29913 (1813); leg. 888, no. 29969 (1814); leg. 890, no. 30044 (1815); leg. 891, no. 30091 (1816); leg. 893, no. 30297 (1818); leg. 895, no. 30472 (1820); leg. 895, no. 30487 (1820); leg. 895, no. 3052 (1821); leg. 897, no. 30698 (1822); leg. 897, no. 30724 (1822); leg. 899, no. 30829 (1826); leg. 900, no. 30881 (1827); leg. 912, no. 31671 (1849); leg. 913, no. 31731 (1850); leg. 935A, no. 32840 (1853); leg. 935B, no. 32963 (1858); leg. 921, no. 32129 (1859) (includes three approved petitions); leg. 924, no. 32284 (1862); and ANC, Gobierno General, leg. 348, no. 16760A (1868). However, this study admittedly did not review all the available records.

8. Konetzke, *Colección de documentos,* 3:2 n. 291, 594–597.

9. For a good description of this form of *gracias al sacar* see Twinam, *Public Lives, Private Secrets,* 43 and passim.

10. Konetzke, *Colección de documentos,* 3:2 n. 291, 594–597.

11. See Cope, *Limits of Racial Domination* for discussion of popular rejection of dominant forms of racial categorization.

12. Reconocimientos, leg. 11, exp. 5 (1865).

13. Ibid., leg. 25, exp. 6 (1868).

14. Ibid., leg. 36, exp. 56 (1875).

15. Ibid., leg. 2, exp. 6 (1851).

16. Ibid., leg. 81, exp. 68 (1885).

17. ANC, Gobierno Superior Civil, leg. 892, no. 30240 (1817). Another example is found in leg. 906, no. 31309 (1840). Examples from Church records include Reconocimientos, leg. 69, exp. 78 (1882), and leg. 7, exp. 97 (1864).

18. ANC, Superior, leg. 910, no. 31527 (1847).

19. Ibid., leg. 891, no. 30108 (1816).

20. Thomas, *Cuba,* 1541.

21. González, "Abandonment in Havana," 12–14.

22. Villaverde, *Cecilia Valdes.*

23. ANC, Gobierno Superior Civil, leg. 935A, no. 32823 (1851).

24. Recononcimientos, leg. 59, exp. 87 (1880).

25. Ibid., leg. 55, exp. 81 (1879).

26. Ibid., leg. 52, exp. 52 (1878); leg. 55, exp. 81 (1879); leg. 59, exp. 87 (1880); leg. 61, exp. 45 (1880); leg. 61, exp. 65 (1880); leg. 66, exp. 79 (1881); leg. 78, exp. 72 (1884); leg. 78, exp. 100 (1884); leg. 79, exp. 93 (1884); leg. 88, exp. 78 (1886); leg. 88, exp. 93 (1886); leg. 89, exp. 35 (1887); leg. 89, exp. 38 (1887); leg. 89, exp. 41 (1887); leg. 89, exp. 46 (1887); leg. 90, exp. 78 (1887); leg. 91, exp. 101 (1887); leg. 92, exp. 44 (1888); leg. 92, exp. 72 (1887); leg. 95, exp. 33 (1888); leg. 109, exp. 29 (1891); leg. 109, exp. 48 (1891); leg. 109, exp. 86 (1892); and leg. 110, exp. 14 (1892).

27. Ibid., leg. 4, exp. 57 (1860).

28. Ibid., leg. 4, exp. 83 (1861).

29. On the reproductive aspects of class see Chafetz, "Feminist Theory and Sociology," 121.

30. Reconocimientos, leg. 58, exp. 20 (1880).

31. Ibid., leg. 62, exp. 94 (1881).

32. Ibid., leg. 70, exp. 15 (1882).

33. Ibid., leg. 78, exp. 40 (1884).

34. Spain. Tribunal Supremo, *Sentencias del Tribunal Supremo en materia civil,* vol. 2 (Madrid: Impr. del Ministerio de Gracia y Justicia, 1883), 656.

35. Reconocimientos, leg. 71, exp. 95 (1882).

36. AES, *libros 55, 56, 57,* and *59 de bautismos de pardos y morenos* (hereafter *libro 55, libro 56, libro 57,* and *libro 59*).

37. Reconocimientos, leg. 19, exp. 80 (1870); leg. 46, exp. 2 (1878); leg. 68, exp. 61 (1882); leg. 79, exp. 54 (1884); and leg. 93, exp. 78 (1888).

38. ANC, Fondo Gobierno Superior Civil, leg. 906, no. 31309 (1840).

39. Interviews by the author, Havana, July–November 1999.

40. AES, *libros 55, 56, 57,* and *59.*

41. Francisco Calcagno, *Poetas de color* (Havana: Militar de la V. de Soler, 1878), 9–10.

42. ANC, Gobierno Superior Civil, leg. 914, no. 31756 (1850).

43. "Somos racistas de amor," *Previsión,* November 5, 1909, and "Baterías de rebote," *Prevision,* September 30, 1908, both cited in Helg, *Our Rightful Share,* 150.

44. ANC, Gobierno Superior Civil, leg. 954, no. 33752 (1862), cited in Garcia, ed., *La Esclavitud desde la esclavitud,* 182–184.

45. Moreno Fraginals, *El Ingenio,* 2:48–50, and Justo Germán Cantero, *Los ingenios: Colección de vistas de los principales ingenios de azúcar de la isla de Cuba,* ed. Luis Miguel García Mora and Antonio Santamaría García (Madrid: CSIC Press, 2005), 69 n. 165. The editors note that Don Esteban's "black" grandson Claudio, who managed the family's estate, became a member of the elite business association Círculo de Hacendados y Agricultores. In 1879, his father, Don Esteban's son Gabriel, joined others in establishing the elite Afro-Cuban civic club Casino Español de la Habana de Personas de Color, which initially had pro-monarchy leanings but later pro-abolitionist sentiments; see Joan Casanovas, *Bread or Bullets: Urban Labor and Spanish Colonialism in Cuba, 1850–1898* (Pittsburgh: University of Pittsburgh Press, 1998), 132.

46. *Pleito sobre filiación, incidente de al intestado de D. Esteban Santa Cruz de Oviedo, recurso de casación establecido á nombre de Enriqueta Sta. Cruz de Oviedo y compartes, sentencias dictadas por el Tribunal Supremo* (Havana: Editorial Mercantil, 1884).

47. Ibid., 18.

48. See Rafael Nieto y Cortadellas, *Dignidades Nobiliares en Cuba* (Madrid: Ediciones Cultura Hispánica, 1954), 222, for a brief biography of Pedro de Esteban y Gonzalez de Larrinaga. He was born in Havana on October 12, 1849, and graduated as doctor of civil and canon law from the University of Havana in 1879. He was granted the title of marquis by Pope Leon XII, which was confirmed by royal order in 1885. He became mayor of Havana in 1899.

49. AES, *libro 56,* entry 11 (1885).

50. For U.S. history, David Roediger's *The Wages of Whiteness: Race and the Making of the American Working Class* (New York: Verso, 1991) leads the way in the deconstruction of white identity. Also important is Theodore W. Allen, *The Invention of the White Race,* vol. 1, *Racial Oppression and Social Control* (London: Verso, 1994). For Latin American history see Elizabeth A. Kuznesof, "Ethnic and Gender Influences on 'Spanish' Creole Society in Colonial Spanish America," *Colonial Latin American Review* 4, no. 1 (1995): 153–176.

51. The presumption of an economic advantage enjoyed by people of notable mixed-race descent has been challenged by several authors; see Edward H. Telles, *Race in Another America: The Significance of Skin Color in Brazil* (Princeton: Princeton University Press, 2004); and Charles H. Wood and Peggy Lovell, "Skin Color, Racial Identity, and Life Chances in Brazil," *Latin American Perspectives* 25, no. 3 (May 1998): 90–109.

5. AFRO-CUBAN FAMILY EMANCIPATION

1. Reconocimientos, leg. 24, exp. 107 (1868).

2. ANC, Superior, leg. 938, no. 33092, quoted in García Rodríguez, *Esclavitud desde la esclavitud,* 108–109. The síndico procurador was the government official responsible for oversight of relations between enslaved people and their owners. They often assisted in negotiating the terms for obtaining freedom in individual cases. See Scott, *Slave Emancipation,* 75, and chapter 3.

3. ANC, Superior, leg. 938, no. 33092, quoted in García Rodríguez, *La eslavitud desde la eslavitud,* 108–109.

4. ANC, Superior, leg. 948, no. 33487, quoted in García Rodríguez, *La eslavitud desde la eslavitud,* 111.

5. Cowling, *Conceiving Freedom,* 13.

6. ANC, Superior, leg. 954, no. 33696, quoted in García Rodríguez, *La eslavitud desde la eslavitud,* 117.

7. ANC, Superior, leg. 968, no. 34211, quoted in Garcia Rodríquez, *La Esclavitud desde la esclavitud,* 124.

8. Ferrer, *Insurgent Cuba.*

9. Scott, *Slave Emancipation in Cuba,* 123, 124, and 127.

10. Ibid., 86–87.

11. Many northern states such as New York and Pennsylvania achieved abolition through gradual processes in the late eighteenth and early nineteenth centuries.

12. Malone, *Sweet Chariot,* chaps. 1 and 2; Robert Fogel, *Without Consent or Contract: The Rise and Fall of American Slavery* (New York: Norton, 1989), 150; and Deborah Gray White, *Ar'n't I a Woman?: Female Slaves in the Plantation South* (New York: Norton, 1985), 105. John W. Blassingame, *The Slave Community: Plantation Life in the Antebellum South* (New York: Oxford University Press, 1979), 86–87; and Jones, *Labor of Love, Labor of Sorrow,* 33–34, do not suggest the prevalence of nuclear families.

13. Gutman, *Black Family,* 141–162, 433; and Shepard Krech III, "Black Family Organization in the Nineteenth Century: An Ethnological Perspective," *Journal of Interdisciplinary History* 12 (Winter 1982): 429–452.

14. Gutman, *Black Family,* 9.

15. Joel Williamson, *New People: Miscegenation and Mulattoes in the United States* (New York: Free Press, 1980), 3, 82, 107–109; August Meier, *Negro Thought in America, 1880–1915: Racial Ideologies in the Age of Booker T. Washington* (Ann Arbor: University of Michigan Press, 1963), 161–255; and Willard B. Gatewood, *Aristocrats of Color: The Black Elite, 1880–1920* (Bloomington: Indiana University Press, 1990), 311–321.

16. Boris Fausto, *Crime e Cotidiano: A criminalidade em São Paulo (1880–1924)* (São Paolo: Brasiliense, 1984), 58, quoted from translation in George R. Andrews, *Blacks and Whites in São Paulo Brazil* (Madison: University of Wisconsin Press, 1991), 76.

17. João de Azevedo Carneiro Maia, *Notícias Históricas e Estatísticas do Município* (Rio de Janeiro, 1891), 253–254, cited in Stanely Stein, *Vassouras, A Brazilian Coffee County, 1850–1900: The Role of Planter and Slave in a Plantation Society*, 2nd ed. (Princeton: Princeton University Press, 1985), 292 n. 39.

18. Andrews, *Blacks and Whites in São Paulo*, 76–77.

19. Sandra Lauderdale Graham, *House and Street: The Domestic World of Servants and Masters in Nineteenth-Century Rio de Janeiro* (Cambridge: Cambridge University Press, 1988), 192.

20. Peter J. Wilson, "Reputation and Respectability: A Suggestion for Caribbean Ethnology," *Man* 4, no. 1 (1969): 70–84.

21. Beginning with John Hope Franklin, *From Slavery to Freedom: A History of American Negroes* (New York: A. A Knopf, 1947), the records of the Freedmen's Bureau have been essential sources for writing the post-emancipation African American experience.

22. For discussion of how slow American historians generally were to utilize these sources see Norman R. Yetman, "The Background of the Slave Narrative Collection," *American Quarterly* 19, no. 3 (Autumn 1967): 534–553.

23. For studies of missionary interest in the formerly enslaved peoples of the British Caribbean see for example Philip D. Curtin, *Two Jamaicas: The Role of Ideas in a Tropical Colony, 1830–1865* (Cambridge, Mass.: Harvard University Press, 1955), chap. 8; Patricia T. Rooke, "A Scramble for Souls: The Impact of the Negro Education Grant on Evangelical Missionaries in the British West Indies," *History of Education Quarterly* 21, no. 4 (Winter 1981): 429–447.

24. See for example, Walter Fraga Filho, *Encruzilhadas Da Liberdade: Histórias De Escravos E Libertos Na Bahia, 1870–1910* (Campinas, SP, Brazil: Editora UNICAMP, 2006).

25. The law is reprinted in Ortiz, *Los esclavos negros*, 317–320.

26. Reconocimientos, leg. 36, exp. 47 (1875).

27. Scott, *Slave Emancipation in Cuba*, 80.

28. Reconocimientos, leg. 49, exp. 84 (1878).

29. Aisnara Perera Díaz and Maria de los Angeles Meriño Fuentes, *Para librarse de lazos, antes buena familia que buenos brazos, Apuntes sobre la manumission en Cuba (1800–1881)* (Santiago de Cuba: Editorial Oriente, 2009), 259–263 and 300.

30. AES, *libro 48*, entries 793–868 (1847); *libro 49*, entries 1–268 (1847); *libro 52*, entries 184–400 (1857); and *libro 55*, entries 55–198 (1877).

31. Aisnara Perera Díaz and Maria de los Angeles Meriño Fuentes, *Nombrar las cosas, Aproximación a la onomástica de la familia negra en Cuba* (Guantánamo: El Mar y la Montaña, 2006), 56–57.

32. AES, *libro 55*, entries 55–198 (1877), excluding six baptisms of children with both parents listed as "Don" and "Doña" found within that range.

33. AES, *libro 56*, entries 199–348 (1887).

34. United States. War Department, Cuban Census Office, *Report on the Census of Cuba, 1899* (Washington, D.C.: Government Printing Office, 1900), 125, 137.

35. The Diocese of Havana was not raised to archdiocese level until 1925. Prior to an undetermined date in the middle of the nineteenth century, the majority of recertifications of ecclesiastic identity documents, of which paternal recognitions and legitimizations were sub-sets, were probably held in the island's archdiocese headquarters in Santiago.

36. Reconocimientos, leg. 1, exp. 2 (1804).

37. Ibid., leg. 4, exp. 5 (1859). This record provides few details and therefore it is not possible to determine under what situation this African couple achieved their freedom. They may have been emancipados or they may have purchased their own freedom.

38. Michael Zeuske, "Hidden Markers, Open Secrets: On Naming, Race-Marking, and Race-Making in Cuba," in *New West Indian Guide* 76 (2002): 211–241.

39. Reconocimientos, leg. 21, exps. 92 and 118; leg. 22 exps. 4, 11, 17, 28, 56, 65, 95, 97, 98, 99, and 102; leg. 23, exps. 18 and 27; leg. 25, exps. 93, 96, and 98; leg. 26, exps, 15, 34, 68, 74, and 81 (1871). All are from 1871.

40. Ibid., leg. 57, exp. 54 (1879).

41. Ibid., leg. 44, exp. 66 (1877).

42. Ibid., leg. 26, exp. 81 (1871).

43. Ibid., leg. 26, exp. 81 (1871).

44. Ibid., leg. 1, exp. 85 (1845); here a parish priest received clarification on how to annotate hijos naturales. The names of the parents were not to be excluded, as some priests had been in the habit of doing. See chapter 2.

45. Ibid., leg. 66, exp. 68 (1881)

46. Ibid., leg. 84, exp. 33 (1885).

47. Ramiro Guerra, *La Guerra de los 10 años* (Havana: Ciencias Sociales, 1972), 86–90.

48. AES, *libro 55*, entry 2 (1877).

49. Ibid., entry 743 (1881); and Reconocimientos, leg. 64, exp. 65 (1881).

50. AES, *libro 55*, entry 1175 (1884).

51. Reconocimientos, leg. 22, exp. 97 (1871).

52. Ibid., leg. 22, exp. 98 (1871).

53. Ibid., leg. 24, exp. 98 (1868).

54. Ibid., leg. 26, exp. 79 (1874).

55. Ibid., leg. 26, exp. 79 (1874).

56. Ibid., leg. 79, exp. 84 (1884).

57. AES, *libro 55*, entry 7 (1876).

58. One was baptized as a stillborn child and the other was baptized two months later; AES, *libro 55*, entry 246 (1878) and entry 308 (1878).

59. Ibid., entry 785 (1881) and 991 (1883).

60. Reconocimientos, leg.42, exp. 69 (1876).

61. AES, *libro 55*, entries 26 and 27 (1876), 417 (1879), 908 (1882) and *libro 56*, entry 132 (1886).

62. AES, *libro 55*, entry 65 (1876).

63. Ibid., entries 976 (1882) and 1160 (1884); and *libro 56*, entry 469 (1888).

64. AES, *libro 55*, entry 291 (1878).

65. Ibid., entry 302 (1878).

66. Reconocimientos, leg. 51, exp. 28 (1878).

67. AES, *libro 55*, entry 410 (1879).

68. Ibid., entry 410 (1882).

69. Ibid., entry 33 (1876).

70. Ibid., entries 249 (1878) and 779 (1881).

71. AES, *libro 56*, entry 266 (1887).

72. AES, *libro 52*, entry 255 (1857).

73. Reconocimientos, leg. 52, exp. 32 (1878).

74. AES, *libro 56*, entry 405 (1888).

75. AES, *libro 57*, entry 461 (1895).

76. AES, *libro 55*, entry 116 (1876).

77. "Acta de reconocimiento de hijo natural por el Meno [Moreno] Antonio Pérez," *Cienfuegos*, February 28, 1885, quoted from translation in Zeuske, "Hidden Markers," 220.

78. Reconocimientos, leg. 71, exp. 83 (1882).

79. AES, *libro 55*, entries 157 (1877) and 309 (1878).

80. Ibid., entry 436 (1879).

81. Ibid., entry 615 (1880).

82. Ibid., entry 1177 (1884); *libro 56*, entries 247 (1886); 329 (1887); and 493 (1889).

83. Reconocimientos, leg. 35, exp. 20 (1874) for Luis's petition for recognition of paternity, and leg. 71, exp. 83 (1882) for Melchor's petition.

84. Ibid., leg. 35, exp. 20 (1874).

85. Reconocimientos, leg. 41, exp. 94 (1876).

86. AES, *libro 55*, entry 195 (1877).

87. Ibid., entries 214 (1878) and 470 (1879).

88. Twinam, *Public Lives, Private Secrets*, 62–67.

89. AES, *libro 56*, entry 78 (1885).

90. Reconocimientos, leg. 78, exp. 40 (1884).

91. See the epilogue for additional evidence of these types of relationships.

92. For example, AES, *libro 55*, entries 56–60 (1876).

93. Ibid., entries 174 (1877) and 463 (1879).

94. AES, *libro 52*, entry 219 (1857); *libro 54*, entry 295 (1867); and *libro 55*, entry 518 (1880).

95. Reconocimientos, leg. 58, exp. 13 (1880).

6. "REGENERATING" FAMILY

1. Helg, "Race in Argentina and Cuba, 1880–1930"; and Christopher Schmidt-Nowara, "'Spanish' Cuba: Race and Class in Spanish and Cuban Antislavery Ideology, 1861–1868," *Cuban Studies* 25 (1995): 101–122.

2. For discussion of the concept of modernity in Latin America broadly see Charles Hale, "Political and Social Ideas in Latin America, 1870–1930," in *The Cambridge History*

of Latin America, vol. 4, ed. Leslie Bethell (Cambridge: Cambridge University Press, 1986); Richard Graham, "Introduction," in *The Idea of Race in Latin America*; and Walter Mignolo, *The Idea of Latin America* (Walton, Mass.: Blackwell, 2005).

3. Helg, "Race in Argentina and Cuba."

4. Martí's calls for multi-racial definition of Cuban and Hispanic American identity are well documented. This quote appears in the essay "Mi raza" (April 16, 1893) in *Obras completas* (Havana: Editorial Nacional de Cuba, 1963), 1:299.

5. José Martí, "Para las escenas" *Anuario del Centro de Estudios Martianos* no. 1 (1978): 33.

6. Gustavo Enrique Mustelier, *La extincion del negro: apuntes político sociales* (Havana: Impr. de Rambla, Bouza y ca., 1912), 4.

7. Kiple, *Blacks in Colonial Cuba*, 5–7.

8. Cuba, Dirección General del Censo, *Censo de la República de Cuba, año de 1919* (Havana: Maza, Arroyo y Caso, 1920).

9. F. Figueras, *Cuba y su evolucion colonial* (Havana: Avisador Comercial, 1907), 236, reprinted as "Agua Va," *La Prensa,* October 10, 1915, 6–8.

10. Alejandro de la Fuente, "Race and Inequality in Cuba, 1899–1981," *Journal of Contemporary History* 30 (1995): 136.

11. See note 9 in the preface.

12. K. Lynn Stoner, *From the House to the Streets: The Cuban Woman's Movement for Legal Reform, 1898–1940* (Durham, N.C.: Duke University Press, 1991), 10.

13. Paula Baker, "The Domestication of Politics: Women and American Political Society, 1780–1920," *American Historical Review* 89, no. 3 (June 1984): 620, studies a parallel development in the U.S. experience.

14. For discussion of the rise of the cult of *marianismo* as the veneration of the redemptive authority of female virtue and spirituality see Evelyn Stevens, "*Marianismo:* The Other Face of Machismo in Latin America," in *Male and Female in Latin America,* ed. A. Pescatello (Pittsburgh: University of Pittsburgh Press, 1973), 90–101.

15. Stoner, *From the House to the Streets,* 14.

16. Enid Logan, "Each Sheep with Its Mate: Marking Race and Legitimacy in Cuban Catholic Parish Archives, 1890–1940," *New West Indian Guide* 84, nos. 1–2 (2010): 32.

17. Centro de Estudios Demograficos, *La población de Cuba* (Havana: Editorial de Ciencias Sociales, 1976), 93. No statistics on the frequency of non-marital, inter-racial relationships are available for any period of Cuban history.

18. Robin Moore, *Nationalizing Blackness: Afrocubanismo and Artistic Revolution in Havana, 1920–1940* (Pittsburgh: University of Pittsburgh Press, 1997); Karen Y. Morrison, "Civilization and Citizenship in the Eyes of Afro-Cuban Intellectuals during the First Constitutional Period (1902–1940)," *Cuban Studies/Estudios Cubanos* 30 (1999): 76–99; Stephen Palmié, *Wizards and Scientists: Explorations in Afro-Cuban Modernity and Tradition* (Durham, N.C.: Duke University Press, 2002); and Bronfman, *Measures of Equality.*

19. For studies of the comparable sentiment expressed by African Americans in the United States see for example Harold Cruse, *The Crisis of the Negro Intellectual* (New York: Quill Publishers, 1984); and Kevin Gaines, *Uplifting the Race: Black Leadership, Politics, and Culture in the Twentieth Century* (Chapel Hill: University of North Carolina Press, 1996).

20. Carmen Montejo Arrechea, *"Minerva,* a Magazine for Women (and Men) of Color," in *Between Race and Empire: African-Americans and Cubans before the Cuban Revolution,* ed. Lisa Brock and Digna Castañeda Fuertes (Philadelphia: Temple University Press, 1998), 33–48.

21. de la Fuente, "Race and Inequality," 151, demonstrates the low level of secondary education achieved by Afro-Cubans in the early years of the republican era.

22. More details on this category are provided in chapters 4 and 5.

23. Reconocimientos, leg. 65, exp. 58 (1881).

24. AES, *libro* 55, entry 419 (1879).

25. Vasconcelos supplied a brief autobiographical sketch in T[ristán] [pseudo. Ramón Vasconcelos], "El que con niño se acuesta . . . ," *La Prensa,* September 16, 1915, 6–8.

26. Juan Joaquin Otero et al., *Libro de Cuba; una enciclopedia ilustrada que abarca las artes, las letras, las ciencias, la economía, la política, la historia, la docencia y el progreso general de la Nación Cubana. Edición conmemorativa del cincuentenario de la independencia, 1902–1952, y del centenario delnacimiento de José Martí, 1853–1953* (Havana: Publicaciones Unidas, 1954), 693; K. Lynn Stoner, personal communication, November 3, 2000.

27. Ana Hidalgo Vidal, "Dos palabras," *La Prensa,* September 9, 1915, 8.

28. Cecilia, "A la Señora Doña Pastora Ramírez de Calvo," *Minerva,* December 15, 1888, 3.

29. O. R. P, "¡Raza de Color Elevate!: La Familia," *Minerva,* December 30, 1888, 1–3.

30. Tristán, "Palpitaciones de la raza de color," *La Prensa,* August 3, 1915, 8.

31. Joaquín N. Aramburu, "Baturrillo," *La Prensa,* September 9, 1916, 8.

32. Indiana [pseudo.], "Reflecciones Femeninas," "Palpitaciones," *La Prensa,* August 31, 1915, 8.

33. Lucrecia Gonzalez, "La Instrucción," *Minerva,* January 26, 1889, 2.

34. "Como se piensa," "Palpitaciones," *La Prensa,* May 12, 1916, 4.

35. Indiana, "Reflecciones Femeninas."

36. Hidalgo Vidal, "Dos palabras."

37. Tristán, "Sociologia a la medida," *La Prensa,* August 30, 1915, 8.

38. "Como se piensa."

39. Ibid.

40. Ibid.

41. de la Fuente, "Race and Inequality," 152–153.

42. Helg, *Our Rightful Share,* 99 and 128; and de la Fuente, *A Nation for All,* 46–47.

43. Ada Ferrer, "Rustic Men, Civilized Nation: Race, Culture, and Contention on the Eve of Cuban Independence," *Hispanic American Historical Review* 78, no. 4 (1998): 663–687.

44. Cf. Pappademos, *Black Political Activism,* which highlights the more subtle political manifestations of Afro-Cuban organizations that publically presented themselves in social terms.

45. Helg, *Our Rightful Share,* 16 and passim.

46. de la Fuente, "Race and Inequality," 158.

47. Helg, *Our Rightful Share,* 102.

48. Vera Kutzinski, *Sugar's Secrets: Race and the Erotics of Cuban Nationalism* (Charlottesville: University Press of Virginia, 1993).

49. See Winthrop R. Wright, *Café con leche: Race, Class, and National Image in Venezuela* (Austin: University of Texas Press, 1990) for a study of early republican Venezuela.

50. Tristán, "Sociologia a la medida," *La Prensa,* August 30, 1915, 8.

51. Tristán, "Reflecciones Femeninas," *La Prensa,* August 31, 1915, 8.

52. Ibid.

53. Kutzinski, *Sugar's Secrets,* 143. For a thorough discussion of U.S. cultural influences in Cuba see Louis A. Pérez, *On Becoming Cuban: Identity, Nationality, and Culture* (Chapel Hill: University of North Carolina Press).

54. Interview by author, Havana, July 8, 1999.

55. Jeronimo A. Guerra, "¡A Cucharetear!," *La Prensa,* September 1, 1915, 7.

56. Cuba, Dirección General del Censo, *Censo de la República de Cuba,* 367.

57. Tristán, "Reflecciones Femeninas."

58. Felipa Basilio, "La Mujer Ante la Razon," *Minerva,* May 15, 1889, 1–2.

59. Knight, *Slave Society in Cuba;* and Klein, *Slavery in the Americas.*

60. See chapters 3 and 5.

61. Arturo González Dorticós, "Premisas: Del concepto de familia," *La Prensa,* November 5, 1915, 6.

62. Sergio Aguirre, "Seis actitudes de la burguesia cubana en el siglo XIX," *Dialéctica* 2 (1943): 153–177; Joan Casanovas Codina, "El movimiento obrero y la política colonial española en la Cuba de finales del xix," in *La nación soñada: Cuba, Puerto Rico y Filipinas ante el 98,* ed. Consuelo Naranjo Orovio, Miguel Angel Puig-Samper, and Luis Miguel García Mora (Madrid: Doce Calles, 1996), 363–375; Louis Pérez, "Identidad y nacionalidad: Las raices del separatismo cubano, 1868–1898," *Op. cit., Boletín del Centro de Investigaciones Históricas* (1997): 185–195.

63. On the Spanish liberal attack on the Catholic Church see Stanley G. Payne, *Spanish Catholicism: An Historical Overview* (Madison: University of Wisconsin Press, 1984), 80–96, and his "Spanish Conservatism 1834–1923," *Journal of Contemporary History* 13, no. 4 (1978): 265–289.

64. The implementation date of the civil registry varies across several sources. *Ley Provisional de Registro Civil Para las Islas de Cuba y Puerto Rico* (Havana: Imprenta del Gobierno y Captania General, por S. M., 1886), 23 lists 1884; José Guerra López, *Derecho de Familia* [manuscript] (Havana, 1936), 24–25, suggests 1888; and Decreto Presidencial 99 de 26 mayo de 1925, cited in José Machado, *Los Hijos Ilegitimos* (Havana: Cultural, S.A., 1941), 23, has 1895.

65. Ley provisional de registro civil, 13, indicates that no racial labels of either parents or children were required for the registration of birth. For Afro-Cuban political action on this point see Zeuske, "Hidden Markers," 224–225; and Logan, "Each Sheep with Its Mate," 18–19.

66. Baptismal registers at the parish of Espíritu Santo ended racial separation of baptismal records as of 1904; AES, *Libro de bautismos general 1* (1904).

67. Logan, "Each Sheep with Its Mate," 8.

68. José Portuondo y de Castro, *La filiación, examen de la jurisprudencia sentada por el Tribunal Supremo de Cuba sobre reconocimiento de hijos con vista de lo dispuesto en el art. 44 de la constitución y 135 del Código civil* (Havana, 1947), 7.

69. United States Army, Division of Cuba, *Civil Orders, Proclamations, and Circulars* (Havana, 1899–1901), order 66 (May 31, 1899); and Thomas, *Cuba or the Pursuit of Freedom*, 439.

70. For a useful analysis of the debates surrounding this decision see Enid Logan, "The 1899 Cuban Marriage Law Controversy: Church, State and Empire in the Crucible of Nation," *Journal of Social History* (2008): 469–550.

71. For average wage rates in the first two decades of the republic see Jorge Ibarra Cuesta, "La sociedad cubana en las tres primeras décadas del siglo XX," in Instituto de Historia de Cuba, *Historia de Cuba, La neocolonia: Organización y crisis, desde 1899 hasta 1940* (Havana: Editora Politica, 1998), 174.

72. United States Army, *Civil Orders*, orders 19, 140 and 307.

73. Stoner, *From the House to the Streets*, 46–52.

74. Ibid., 6.

75. One exception was the 1930 revocation of the Spanish colonial adultery law, which allowed a husband to murder an adulterous wife or her lover if he caught them in the act. Stoner, *From the House to the Streets*, 154–155.

76. For discussion of political goals of the anti-establishment movement of the early 1930s see Luis E. Aguilar, *Cuba 1933: Prologue to Revolution* (Ithaca, N.Y.: Cornell University Press, 1972), chap. 6 and passim; Fabio Grobart, "The Cuban Working Class Movement from 1925 to 1933," *Science and Society* 39 (1975): 73–103; José A. Tabares del Real, *La revolución del 30: sus dos últimos años*, 3rd ed. (Havana: Editorial de Ciencias Sociales, 1975), 67–82 and 97–116; and Lionel Soto, *La revolución del 33*, 3 vols. (Havana: Editorial de Ciencias Sociales, 1977), chap. 5 and passim.

77. de la Fuente, *Nation for All*.

78. Stoner, *From the House to the Streets*, 177–178.

79. For women's participation in various occupational categories see Stoner, *From the House to the Streets*, 167.

80. To date, scholarly analysis of the impact of the 1940 Cuban Constitution has been very limited by the view that Fulgencio Batista's control of government did not allow for meaningful reform. While this may be true in the domain of formal politics, the political value of social reforms remains an area in need of more research. For investigation of the events leading up to 1940 see Instituto de Historia de Cuba, *Historia de Cuba, La Neocolonia*, 336–381; and Robert Whitney, *State and Revolution in Cuba: Mass Mobilization and Political Change, 1920–1940* (Chapel Hill: University of North Carolina Press, 2001), 149–176.

81. Translated from *Constitución de la República de Cuba firmada en la ciudad de Guáimaro el día primero de julio de 1940* (Miami: Judicatura Cubana Democratica, 1963), 20–23.

82. Ibid., 23–24.

83. Marifeli Pérez-Stable, *The Cuban Revolution: Origins, Course, and Legacy* (New York: Oxford University Press), 42–44; Whitney, *State and Revolution*, 9 and passim; Robert Whitney, "The Architect of the Cuban State: Fulgencio Batista and Populism in Cuba, 1937–1940," *Journal of Latin American Studies* 32 (2000): 435–459.

84. de la Fuente, *Nation for All*, 249; Otero et al., *Libro de Cuba*, 693.

85. Carlos Moore, *Castro, the Blacks, and Africa* (Los Angeles: University of California Center for Afro-American Studies, 1988), x and 5; de la Fuente, *A Nation for All,* 17 and 135–136.

7. MESTIZAJE LITERARY VISIONS AND AFRO-CUBAN MEMORY

1. Saco quoted in Luis Duno Gottberg, *Solventando las diferencias: La ideología del mestizaje en Cuba* (Madrid: Iberoamericana, 2003), 31.

2. Ildefonso Pereda Váldes, *Lo negro y lo mulato en la poesía cubana* (Montevideo: Ediciones Ciudadela, 1970), 15–24.

3. Gaston Baquero, "Sobre la falsa poesia negra: tres notas polemicas," reprinted in *Dario, Cernuda, y otros temas poeticos* (Madrid: Editora Nacional, 1969), 209–217; Kutzinski, *Sugar's Secrets;* and Duno Gottberg, *Solventando las diferencias,* 89–94 and 111–112. For a general review of the cultural dimensions of Afrocubanismo see Robin Moore, *Nationalizing Blackness.*

4. Kutzinski, *Sugar's Secrets,* 143.

5. de la Fuente addresses this question at the level of political culture in *A Nation for All,* 185 and passim. Again, the present study demonstrates how the Cuban family and images of it were involved in this transformation.

6. The concept of *la raza cósmica* was popularized by José Vasconcelos in Mexico during the 1920s, with antecedents in the works of Andrés Molina Henríquez; see José Vaconcelos, *La raza cósmica* (Paris: Agencia mundial de librería, 1920); Alan Knight, "Racism, Revolution, and Indigenismo: Mexico, 1910–1940," in *The Idea of Race in Latin America, 1870–1940,* ed. Richard Graham (Austin: University of Texas Press, 1990), 71–113; and J. Jorge Klor de Alva, "The Postcolonization of the (Latin) American Experience: A Reconsideration of 'Colonialism,' 'Postcolonialism,' and 'Mestizaje,'" in *After Colonialism: Imperial Histories and Postcolonial Displacements,* ed. Gyan Prakash (Princeton: Princeton University Press, 1995), 241–277.

7. Kutzinski, *Sugar's Secrets,* 172.

8. Richard L. Jackson has long argued for recognition of a distinct Afro-Hispanic literary tradition created by black and mulatto authors. See his *Black Writers and the Hispanic Canon* (New York: Prentice Hall International, 1997) and *Black Writers in Latin America* (Albuquerque: University of New Mexico Press, 1979). The following critique applies his perspectives more specifically to Afrocubanismo writers.

9. Quoted in Kutzinski, *Sugar's Secrets,* 144 (her translation).

10. Jorge Luis Morales, ed., *Poesía afroantillana y negrista, Puerto Rico, Republica Dominicana y Cuba,* rev. ed. (Rio Piedras: Universidad de Puerto Rico, 1981), 377.

11. Kutzinski, *Sugar's Secrets,* 61–67, demonstrates these distinct representations. However, she does not discuss the re-interpretation of the black female by twentieth-century Afrocubanismo writers.

12. Morales, ed., *Poesía afroantillana y negrista,* Hernández Cata, "Rumba" (319); Ballagas, "El Baile de Del Papalote," (395); and Portuondo, "Rumba de la Negra Pancha," (396).

13. Agustín Acosta, *La zafra* (Havana: Editorial Minerva, 1926), 69–70.

14. Kutzinski, *Sugar's Secrets,* 141.

15. Ibid. (her translation).

16. Alejo Carpentier, "Problemática de la actual novela latinoamericana," in *Tientos y diferencias* (Montevideo: Editorial Arca, 1967), 11–12, cited in Lorna V. Williams, "The Emergence of an Afro-Cuban Aesthetic," *Afro-Hispanic Review* 14, no. 1 (Spring 1995): 54.

17. Fernando Ortiz, *Hampa afro-cubana: los negros brujos: apuntes para un estudio de etnología criminal* (Miami: Ediciones Universal, 1973[1906]), 19.

18. Fernando Ortiz, "Vocablos de la economía política afrocubana," *Cuba Contemporánea* 35, no. 138 (June 1924): 136–146, my emphasis.

19. For a more complete review of Ortiz's *Proyecto* see Bronfman, *Measures of Equality,* 127–128.

20. Both cited in de la Fuente, *Nation for All,* 183.

21. For discussion of the tensions between the criminalist and ethnographic approaches to study Afro-Cuban life, see Bronfman, *Measures of Equality.*

22. See for example Juan Luis Martín, "Yemayá tuvo trece hijo de una sola vez," *El Mundo,* March 29, 1931, 1–2; Romulo Lachatañeré, "El Sistema Religioso de los Lucumís y otras Influencias Africanas en Cuba," *Estudios Afrocubanos,* 3 (1939): 28–84 (pt. 1); 4 (1940): 27–38 (pt. 2); 5 (1946): 121–216 (pt. 3); and Lydia Cabrera, *Cuentos negros de Cuba* (Havana: La Verónica, 1940). Even Castellanos offered a small contribution in this area; Israel Castellanos, "Instrumentos musicales de los afrocubanos," *Archivos del folklore Cubano* 2, no. 3 (October 1926): 193–208.

23. Fernando Ortiz, *Cuban Counterpoint: Tobacco and Sugar* (Durham, NC: Duke University Press, 1995), 98. Originally published as *Contrapunteo cubano del tabaco y el azúcar* (Havana: Jesús Montero, 1940).

24. On this point, Ortiz demonstrates similarities with the work of his Brazilian contemporary, Gilberto Freyre. Both scholars accepted that their respective national cultures arose from the interaction of the European and African elements (and indigenous in the case of Brazil). They differed in that Freyre gave greater attention to the themes of the biological and sexual interaction. These themes appear only minimally in Ortiz's works. See for example his "Por la integración cubana de blancos y negros," *Estudios Afrocubanos* 5, nos. 945–946: 216–229. However, we will see below that other writers of the Afrocubanismo era explored these themes more directly.

25. Morales, *Poesía afroantillana y negrista,* 325–326.

26. Nancy Morejón, *Nación y Mestizaje en Nicolás Guillén* (Havana: Unión de Escritores y Artistas de Cuba, 1982), 43–57, discusses the close parallels between Guillén's and Ortiz's assessments of race mixture.

27. Nicolás Guillén, *Paginas vueltas, memorias* (Havana: Unión de Escritores y Artistas de Cuba, 1982), 48, my emphasis.

28. See for example "El blanco: he ahí el problema," *Diario de la Marina,* June 2, 1929, sect. 3:11, and "Racismo y cubanidad," *Mediodía,* January 15, 1937, reprinted in Ángel Augier, ed., *Nicolás Guillén, Prosa de Prisa 1929–1972* (Havana: Editorial Arte y Literatura, 1975), 65–67.

29. Ángel Augier, "Prologo," in *Nicolás Guillén: Obras Poeticas* (Havana: Editorial Letras Cubanas, 1995), xi.

30. An alternative reading of Guillen's *poemas mulatos* based on the infusion of Spanish literary styles with African rhythms instead of cultural or sociological concerns

is found in Gustavo Pérez Firmat, *The Cuban Condition: Translation and Identity in Modern Cuban Literature* (Cambridge: Cambridge University Press, 1989), 28.

31. Quoted in Kutzinski, *Sugar's Secrets,* 169.

32. Guillén, *Obras Poeticas,* 113–114.

33. *Nicolás Guillén: Obras Poeticas,* 117, originally published in his *West Indies, LTD* (1934).

34. Guillén, *Paginas vueltas,* 28–29.

35. Benjamin Muñoz Ginarte, "Comentos sin Comentarios: No, Primitivo, No! . . . ," *Diario de la Marina,* June 2, 1929, sect. 3:11.

36. B. Muñoz Ginarte, "¡Pobre Mama Inés!," "Ideales de la raza," *Diario de la Marina,* December 9, 1928, sect. 3:6.

37. Anon., "La Raza Cubana," *Diario de la Marina,* June 26, 1928, 8.

38. Gustavo E. Urrutia, "La raza cubana," "Ideales de la raza," *Diario de la Marina,* June 26, 1928, 8.

39. Urrutia, "Complejos de inferioridad," *Diario de la Marina* (Nov. 26, 1932) 14 and "La misión magistral del negro," *Diario de la Marina* (Nov. 10, 1932) 16, quoted in Bronfman, *Measure of Equality,* 152.

40. In 1999, the author conducted family history interviews with twenty-three Cuban seniors over the age of seventy-five. The participants were identified through three *casa de abuelos* (senior day centers) in Havana. The testimonies below are based on these interviews, unless otherwise noted. The names have been changed to protect their identities. The associated recordings and notes are in the author's possession. These original interviews are combined here with similar previously published testimonies.

41. Oscar Lewis, Ruth Lewis, and Susan Rigdon, *Four Men: Living the Revolution: An Oral History of Contemporary Cuba* (Urbana: University of Illinois Press, 1977), 167–349. "Alfred Barrera Bondi" is a pseudonym.

42. Montejo Arrechea, "Minerva," 33 and 41.

43. Oscar Lewis, Ruth Lewis, and Susan Rigdon, *Four Women: Living the Revolution: An Oral History of Contemporary Cuba* (Urbana: University of Illinois Press, 1977), 237–319. "Pilar" is a pseudonym.

44. Ibid., 254.

45. Ibid.

46. María de los Reyes Castillo Bueno, *Reyíta: The Life of a Black Cuban Woman in the Twentieth Century,* ed. Daisy Rubiera Castillo and trans. Anne McLean (Durham, N.C.: Duke University Press, 2000), 24–25.

47. Ibid., 25.

48. Ibid., 31–32 and 40.

49. Garveryism refers to the pan-African and Black Nationalist perspectives and practices of Jamaican-born Marcus Garvey (1887–1940) and his followers who were organized internationally through the Universal Negro Improvement Association and African Communities League (UNIA-ACL). Scholarly treatments of Garvey and UNIA abound, see for example, Edmund D. Cronon, *Black Moses: The Story of Marcus Garvey and the Universal Negro Improvement Association* (Madison: University of Wisconsin Press, 1955); and Tony Martin, *Race First: The Ideological and Organizational Struggle of Marcus Garvey and the Universal Negro Improvement Association* (Westport, Conn.: Greenwood

Press, 1976). For a discussion of Garveyism in Cuba, see for example, Tomás Fernández Robaina, "Marcus Garvey in Cuba: Urrutia, Cubans, and Black Nationalism," in *Between Race and Empire: African-Americans and Cubans before the Cuban Revolution,* eds. Lisa Brock and Digna Castañeda Fuertes (Philadelphia: Temple University Press, 1998), 120–128; and Marc C. McLeod, "'Sin dejar de ser cubanos': Cuban Blacks and the Challenges of Garveyism in Cuba," *Caribbean Studies* (2003): 75–105.

50. Lewis, *Four Men,* 59 and 166–167. "Argentina Bondi" is a pseudonym.

51. Ibid., 61 and 168–169.

52. See Brown, *Santería Enthroned*; and Tomás Fernández Robaina, *Hablen los paleros y santeros* (Havana: Editorial Ciencias Sociales, 1994).

53. See for example, Castellanos and Castellanos, *Cultura afrocubana,* 3:211–214; and Brown, *Santería Enthroned,* 71. For the 1882 white Abakuá society, see "Sociedad de los ñáñigos blancos. Instrucción y disposiciones reglamentarias para la Sociedad de los ñáñigos blancos" [Establecimiento Tipográfico de A.E., Havana, 1882] reprinted in *El Curioso Americano* (Havana) 1, no. 3 (January 1, 1893): 35–38; and 1, no. 4 (January 15, 1893): 56–58.

54. Murphy *Santería,* 33; and Brown, *Santería Enthroned,* 62–112.

55. Ibid, 63–65 and 71–73.

56. Palmié, *Wizards and Scientists,* 197.

EPILOGUE

1. Oficina Nacional de Estadísticas, *Cuba, Censo de población y viviendas 2012,* http://www.one.cu/resumenadelantadocenso2012.htm.

2. Central Intelligence Agency, "The World Factbook: Cuba," https://www.cia.gov/library/publications/the-world-factbook/geos/cu.html.

3. Barry Reckord, *Does Fidel Eat More Than Your Father?* (New York: Praeger, 1971), 126.

4. Reckord does not provide the son's name. "Miguel" is used here for readability.

5. Ibid., 126–127.

6. Ibid., 126.

7. Ibid., 127.

8. Ibid.

9. Ibid., 129.

10. Ibid., 135.

11. Ibid., 128.

12. Cf. Pierre Bourdieu, *The Logic of Practice* (Stanford: Stanford University Press, 1990[1980]), 148.

13. Fidel Castro, speech given on March 22, 1959, quoted in Moore, *Castro,* 20.

14. Cited in ibid., 3.

15. Ibid., 317, and de la Fuente, *Nation for All,* 270–272.

16. On the socio-economic gains of Cubans of color under the revolution see Marianne Masferrer and Carmelo Mesa-Lago, "The Gradual Integration of the Black in Cuba," in *Slavery and Race Relations in Latin America,* ed. Robert B. Toplin (Westport, Conn.: Greenwood Press, 1974), 348–384; and de la Fuente, "Race and Inequality," 131–167, and *Nation for All,* 307–316. These authors point to continued but decreasing

inequality while also noting the continuation of racism. On contemporary manifestations of Cuban racism also see for example Esteban Morales Dominguez, *Race in Cuba: Essays on the Revolution and Racial Inequality* (New York: Monthly Review Press, 2013); Pedro Pérez Sarduy and Jean Stubbs, *Afro-Cuban Voices: On Race and Identity in Contemporary Cuba* (Gainesville: University of Florida Press, 2000).

17. Benigno E. Aguirre, "Differential Migration of Cuban Social Races: A Review and Interpretation of the Problem," *Latin American Research Review* 11, no. 1 (1976): 103–124; and Silvia Pedraza-Bailey, "Cuba's Exiles: Portrait of a Refugee Migration," *International Migration Review* 19, no. 1 (Spring 1985): 4–34.

18. Helen Safa, *The Myth of the Male Breadwinner: Women and Industrialization in the Caribbean* (New York: Westview, 1995), 128.

19. Sonia Catasús Cervera, *Cuban Women: Changing Roles and Population Trends* (Geneva: International Labour Office, 1988), and her *La nupcialidad cubana en el siglo XX* (Havana: Editorial de Ciencias Sociales, 1994).

20. Lois Smith and Alfred Padula, *Sex and Revolution: Women in Socialist Cuba* (New York: Oxford University Press, 1996); Safa, *Myth of the Male Breadwinner*, 125–166; Sherly Lutjens, "Reading between the Lines: Women, the State, and Rectification in Cuba," *Latin American Perspectives* 22, no. 2 (Spring 1995): 100–124; Mariana Ravenet Ramirez, Niurka Pérez Rojas, and Marta Toledo Fraga, *La Mujer Rural y Urbana: Estudios De Casos* (Havana: Editorial de Ciencias Sociales, 1989); and Virginia Olesen, "Context and Posture: Notes on the Socio-Cultural Aspects of Women's Roles and Family Policy in Contemporary Cuba," *Journal of Marriage and Family* 33, no. 3 (August 1971): 548–560.

21. Pablo Rodríguez Ruiz, "La interracialidad y la intraracialidad en las estructuras familiares. Un estudio en barrios populares de La Habana," in Lázara Y. Carrazana Fuentes et al., *Las relaciones raciales en Cuba, estudios contemporáneos* (Havana: Fundación Fernando Ortiz, 2011), 229.

22. Logan, "Each Sheep with Its Mate," 32.

23. Rodrígez Ruiz, "La interracialidad," and Niurka Núñez González, Odalys Buscarón Ochoa, and Hernán Tirado Toirac, "La caracterización ethnocultural de los grupos raciales: El complejo habitacional, la religión, y las relaciones interraciales," in Carrazana Fuentes et al., *Las relaciones raciales en Cuba,* 125–172. Quote from the latter (167).

24. Nadine Fernández, *Revolutionizing Romance: Interracial Couples n Contemporary Cuba* (New Brunswick, N.J.: Rutgers University Press, 2011), 124–126 and 154–161.

25. Nadine Fernández, "Race, Romance, and Revolution: The Cultural Politics of Interracial Encounters in Cuba" (PhD diss., University of California Berkeley, 1996), 207.

26. Fernández, *Revolutionizing Romance,* 159. The bracketed insertions are hers.

27. Fernández, "Race, Romance, and Revolution," 210.

28. Fernández interviewed three additional couples composed of black male and white female partners; see "Race, Romance, and Revolution," 179–222.

29. Quoted in Pérez Sarduy and Stubbs, *Afro-Cuban Voices,* 71.

30. Ibid.

31. For brief discussion of the meaning of moyuba prayers see Christine Ayorinde, "Santeria in Cuba: Tradition and Transformation," in *Yoruba Diaspora in the Atlantic*

World, ed. Toyin Falola and Matt Childs (Bloomington: Indiana University Press, 2004), 209–230; Brown, *Santeria Enthroned*, 369.

32. In addition to the works of Ayorinde and Brown cited above, useful general introductions to Afro-Cuban religious philosophy can be found in Joseph Murphy, *Santería: African Spirits in the Americas* (Boston: Beacon Press, 1993); Lázara Menéndez Vázquez, "Un cake para Obatalá," *Temas* 4 (1995): 38–51; and Mercedes Cros Sandoval, *Worldview, the Orichas, and Santería: Africa to Cuba and Beyond* (Gainesville: University Press of Florida, 2006).

33. Quoted in Ivor Miller, "Religious Symbolism in Cuban Political Performance," *TDR: The Drama Review* 44, no. 2 (Summer 2000): 40.

34. Ibid., 30–55.

35. Jorge Duany, "After the Revolution: The Search for the Roots of Afro-Cuban Culture," *Latin American Research Review* 23, no. 1 (1988): 244–255. León was the first director of folkloric art at the Teátro Nacional. In 1960 and 1961 he offered a foundational seminar on Afro-Cuban cultures for a new cohort of revolutionary cultural specialists. Barnet and noted ethnographer Natalie Bolívar were among those in attendance who heard León's message of Afro-Cuban artistic beauty.

36. Miguel Barnet, *La fuente viva* (Havana: Editorial Letras Cubanas, 1983), 50.

37. Barreal quoted in Duany, "After the Revolution," 254.

38. Joseph Holbrook, "The Church in Cuba: Ambivalence between Regime and Revolution, 1952–1962" (paper presented at the International Congress of Latin American Studies Association, Rio de Janeiro, Brazil, June 11–14, 2009); and John Super, "Interpretations of Church and State in Cuba, 1959–1961," *Catholic Historical Review* 89, no. 3 (2003): 511–529.

39. Blas Roca, "La Lucha ideological contra las sectas religiosas," *Cuba socialista* 22 (June 1963): 34–41.

40. María Teresa Velez, *Drumming for the Gods: The Life and Times of Felipe García Villamil, Santero, Palero, and Abakuá* (Philadelphia: Temple University Press, 2000), 88.

41. Román Orozco and Natalia Bolívar, *Cuba Santa: Comunistas, Santeros y Cristianos de la Isla de Fidel Castro* (Madrid: El País Aguilar, 1998), 263.

42. Cited in Robin Moore, *Music and Revolution: Cultural Change in Socialist Cuba* (Berkeley: University of California Press, 2006), 211, and notes on p. 299.

43. Partido Comunista Cubano, *Tesis y Resoluciones* (Havana: Editorial Ciencias Sociales, 1981), 316–317.

44. Fidel Castro, speech delivered at Pinar del Rio on July 26, 1976, on the 23rd Anniversary of the Assault on the Moncada Barracks. *Fidel Castro Speech Database*, Latin American Network Information Center, University of Texas at Austin, http://lanic.utexas.edu/project/castro/db/1976/19760726.html.

45. Quoted in Tomás Fernández Robaina, *Hablen los santeros y paleros* (Havana: Editorial de Ciencias Sociales, 1994), 89–90.

46. Irene A. Wright, *Cuba* (New York: Macmillan, 1910), 147 and 149, cited in Brown, *Santeria Enthroned*, 68.

47. Quoted in Pérez Sarduy and Stubbs, *Afro-Cuban Voices*, 96.

REFERENCES

Abbot, Abiel. 1829. *Letters Written in the Interior of Cuba, between the Mountains of Arcana to the East, and of Cusco to the West: In the Months of February, March, April, and May, 1828.* Boston: Bowles and Dearborn.

Acosta, Agustín. 1926. *La zafra, poema de combate.* Havana: Editorial Minerva.

Aguilar, Luis E. 1972. *Cuba 1933: Prologue to Revolution.* Ithaca, N.Y.: Cornell University Press.

Aguirre, Benigno E. 1976. Differential Migration of Cuban Social Races: A Review and Interpretation of the Problem. *Latin American Research Review* 11 (1): 103–124.

Aguirre, Sergio. 1943. Seis actitudes de la burguesía cubana en el siglo XIX. *Dialéctica* 2: 153–177.

———. 1990. *Nacionalidad y nación: En el siglo XIX cubano.* Historia. Havana: Editorial de Ciencias Sociales.

Aimes, Hubert H. S. 1907. *A History of Slavery in Cuba, 1511 to 1868.* New York: G. P. Putnam's Sons.

Allen, Theodore. 1994. *The Invention of the White Race.* Haymarket Series. London: Verso.

Alvarez García, Imeldo, ed. 1982. *Acerca de Cirilo Villaverde.* Colección crítica. Havana: Editorial Letras Cubanas.

Amorós, Joaquín. 1777. *Discurso en que se manifiesta la necesidad y utilidad del consentimiento paterno para el matrimonio de los hijos y otros deudos, conforme á lo dispuesto en la real Pragmática de 23 de marzo de 1776.* Madrid: Por Blás Román.

Anderson, Benedict. 1991. *Imagined Communities: Reflections on the Origin and Spread of Nationalism.* Rev. ed. New York: Verso.

Andrews, George Reid. 1980. *The Afro-Argentines of Buenos Aires, 1800–1900.* Madison: University of Wisconsin Press.

———. 1991. *Blacks and Whites in São Paulo, Brazil, 1888–1988.* Madison: University of Wisconsin Press.

Appelbaum, Nancy P., Anne S. Macpherson, and Karin Alejandra Rosemblatt, eds. 2003. *Race and Nation in Modern Latin America.* Chapel Hill: University of North Carolina Press.

Arango y Parreño, Francisco. 2005. *Obras.* Biblioteca de clasicos cubanos. Vol. 1. Havana: Ciencias Sociales.

Ayorinde, Christine. 2004. Santería in Cuba: Tradition and Transformation. In *The Yoruba Diaspora in the Atlantic World*, ed. Toyin Falola and Matt D. Childs, 209–230. Bloomington: Indiana University Press.

Baker, Paula. 1984. The Domestication of Politics: Women and American Political Society, 1780–1920. *American Historical Review* 89 (3): 620–647.

Baquero, Gastón. 1969. *Darío, cernuda, y otros temas poéticos*. Colección ensayo. Madrid: Editora Nacional.

Barcia, María del Carmen. 2003. *La otra familia: Parientes, redes y descendencia de los esclavos en cuba*. Ensayo histórico-social. Havana: Casa de las Américas.

———. 2009. *Los ilustres apellidos: Negros en la habana colonial*. Colección raices/ ediciones boloña. Havana: Ediciones Boloña.

Barnet, Miguel. 1983. *La fuente viva*. Colección crítica. Havana: Editorial Letras Cubanas.

Bergad, Laird W., Fe Iglesias García, and María del Carmen Barcia. 1995. *The Cuban Slave Market, 1790–1880*. Cambridge Latin American Studies. Vol. 79. New York: Cambridge University Press.

Berlin, Ira. 1998. *Many Thousands Gone: The First Two Centuries of Slavery in North America*. Cambridge, Mass.: Belknap Press of Harvard University Press.

Blassingame, John W. 1979. *The Slave Community: Plantation Life in the Antebellum South*. Rev. and enl. ed. New York: Oxford University Press.

Bourdé, Guy. Fuentes y métodos de la historia demográfica en Cuba, siglos XVIII y XIX. *Revista de la Biblioteca Nacional José Martí* 65 (1): 21–68.

Bourdieu, Pierre. 1976. Marriage Strategies as Strategies of Social Reproduction. In *Family and Society: Selections from the Annales: Économies, Sociétés, Civilisations*, ed. R. Forster and O. Ranum, 117–144. Baltimore: Johns Hopkins University Press.

———. 1977. *Outline of a Theory of Practice* [Esquisse d'une théorie de la pratique]. Trans. Richard Nice. Cambridge, Mass.: Harvard University Press.

———. 1984. *Distinction: A Social Critique of the Judgement of Taste* [La distinction, critique sociale du jugement]. Trans. Richard Nice. Cambridge, Mass.: Harvard University Press.

———. 1990. *The Logic of Practice* [Le Sens pratique]. Trans. Richard Nice. Stanford, Calif.: Stanford University Press.

Brading, David A. 1993. *First Americas: The Spanish Monarchy, Creole Patriots and the Liberal State 1492–1866*. New York: Cambridge University Press.

Brana-Shute, Rosemary. 1998. Manumission. In *A Historical Guide to World Slavery*, ed. Seymour Drescher and Stanley Engerman. Oxford: Oxford University Press.

Bremer, Fredrika. 1853. *The Homes of the New World: Impressions of America*. Trans. Mary Botham Howitt. New York: Harper and Bros.

Bronfman, Alejandra. 2004. *Measures of Equality: Social Science, Citizenship, and Race in Cuba, 1902–1940*. Envisioning Cuba. Chapel Hill: University of North Carolina Press.

Brown, David H. 2003. *Santería Enthroned: Art, Ritual, and Innovation in an Afro-Cuban Religion*. Chicago: University of Chicago Press.

Brown, Kathleen M. 1996. *Good Wives, Nasty Wenches, and Anxious Patriarchs: Gender, Race, and Power in Colonial Virginia*. Chapel Hill: Institute of Early American History and Culture/University of North Carolina Press.

Burns, Kathryn. 1998. Gender and the Politics of Mestizaje: The Convent of Santa Clara in Cuzco, Peru. *Hispanic American Historical Review* 78 (1): 5–44.

Bush, Barbara. 1990. *Slave Women in Caribbean Society, 1650–1838*. Kingston, Jamaica: Heinemann Publishers Caribbean.

Caballero, José Agustín. 1999. *Obras*. Havana: Editorial Ciencias Sociales.

Cabrera, Lydia. 1940. *Cuentos negros de cuba*. Havana: La Verónica.

Calcagno, Francisco. 1878. *Poetas de color*. Havana: Militar de la V. de Soler.

Cantero, J. G., and E. Laplante. 2005. *Los ingenios: Colección de vistas de los principales ingenios de azúcar de la isla de cuba*. Ed. Luis Miguel García Mora and Antonio Santamaría García. Madrid: Centro Estudios y Experimentación de Obras Públicas.

Carrazana Fuentes, Lázara Yolanda. 2011. *Las relaciones raciales en Cuba: estudios contemporáneos*. Ciudad de La Habana: Fundación Fernando Ortiz.

Casanovas, Joan. 1998. *Bread or Bullets!: Urban Labor and Spanish Colonialism in Cuba, 1850–1898*. Pitt Latin American Series. Pittsburgh: University of Pittsburgh Press.

Casanovas Codina, Joan. 1996. El movimiento obrero y la política colonial española en la cuba de finales del XIX. In *La nación soñada, cuba, puerto rico y filipinas ante el 98: Actas del congreso internacional celebrado en aranjuez del 2 al 28 de abril de 1995*, ed. Consuelo Naranjo Orovio, Miguel Angel Puig-Samper, and Luis Miguel García Mora, 363–376. Madrid: Ediciones Doce Calles.

Castellanos, Israel. 1926. Instrumentos musicales de los afrocubanos. *Archivos Del Folklore Cubano* 2 (3): 193–208.

Castellanos, Jorge, and Isabel Castellanos. 1988–1994. *Cultura afrocubana*. 4 vols. Colección ebano y canela. Miami: Ediciones Universal.

Castillo Bueno, María de los Reyes, and Daisy Rubiera Castillo. 2000. *Reyita: The Life of a Black Cuban Woman in the Twentieth Century* [Reyita, sencillamente]. Durham, N.C.: Duke University Press.

Catasús Cervera, Sonia. 1988. *Cuban Women: Changing Roles and Population Trends*. Women, Work, and Development. Vol. 17. Geneva: International Labour Office.

———. 1994. *La nupcialidad cubana en el siglo XX*. Demografía. Havana: Editorial de Ciencias Sociales.

Chacón Jiménez, Francisco, and Josefina Méndez Vázquez. 2007. Miradas sobre el matrimonio en la España del último tercio del siglo XVIII. *Cuadernos De Historia Moderna* 32: 61–85.

Chafetz, Janet Saltzman. 1997. Feminist Theory and Sociology: Underutilized Contributions for Mainstream Theory. *Annual Review of Sociology*: 97–120.

Chaves, María Eugenia. 1999. *La estrategia de libertad de una esclava del siglo XVIII las identidades de amo y esclavo en un puerto colonial*. 2nd ed. Vol. 1. Serie estudios históricos. Quito, Ecuador: Ediciones Abya-Yala.

Childs, Matt D. 2006. *The 1812 Aponte Rebellion in Cuba and the Struggle against Atlantic Slavery*. Envisioning Cuba. Chapel Hill: University of North Carolina Press.

Childs, Matt D., and Manuel Barcia. 2010. Cuba. In *The Oxford Handbook of Slavery in the Americas*, ed. Robert L. Paquette and Mark M. Smith, 90–110. Oxford: Oxford University Press.

China Cuba Commission. 1993. *The Cuba Commission Report: A Hidden History of the Chinese in Cuba: The Original English-Language Text of 1876.* Johns Hopkins Studies in Atlantic History and Culture. Baltimore: Johns Hopkins University Press.

Collins, Patricia Hill. 1990. *Black Feminist Thought: Knowledge, Consciousness, and the Politics of Empowerment.* Perspectives on Gender. Vol. 2. Boston: Unwin Hyman.

———. 1998. It's All in the Family: Intersections of Gender, Race, and Nation. *Hypatia* 13 (3): 62–82.

Collins, Randall, Janet Saltzman Chafetz, Rae Lesser Blumberg, Scott Coltrane, and Jonathan H. Turner. 1993. Toward an Integrated Theory of Gender Stratification. *Sociological Perspectives* 36 (3): 185–216.

Cooper, Sheila McIsaac. 1999. Historical Analysis of the Family. In *Handbook of Marriage and the Family,* ed. Marvin B. Sussman, Suzanne K. Steinmetz, and Gary W. Peterson, 13–37. New York: Plenum Press.

Cope, R. Douglas. 1994. *The Limits of Racial Domination: Plebeian Society in Colonial Mexico City, 1660–1720.* Madison: University of Wisconsin Press.

Corwin, Arthur F. 1967. *Spain and the Abolition of Slavery in Cuba, 1817–1886.* Latin American Monographs. Vol. 9. Austin: Institute of Latin American Studies/ University of Texas Press.

Cosner, Charlotte A. 2008. Rich and Poor, White and Black, Free and Slave: The Social History of Cuba's Tobacco Farmers, 1763–1817. PhD dissertation, Florida International University.

Cottrol, Robert J. 2013. *The Long, Lingering Shadow: Slavery, Race, and Law in the American Hemisphere.* Studies in the Legal History of the South. Athens: University of Georgia Press.

Cowling, Camillia, 2013. *Conceiving Freedom: Women of Color, Gender, and the Abolition of Slavery in Havana and Rio de Janeiro.* Chapel Hill: University of North Carolina Press.

Craton, Michael. 1978. *Searching for the Invisible Man: Slaves and Plantation Life in Jamaica.* Cambridge, Mass.: Harvard University Press.

———. 1979. Changing Patterns of Slave Families in the British West Indies. *Journal of Interdisciplinary History* 10 (1): 1–35.

Cronon, Edmund. 1955 *Black Moses: The Story of Marcus Garvey and the Universal Negro Improvement Association.* Madison: University of Wisconsin Press.

Cros Sandoval, Mercedes. 2006. *Worldview, the Orichas, and Santería: Africa to Cuba and Beyond.* Gainesville: University Press of Florida.

Cruse, Harold. 1984[1967]. *The Crisis of the Negro Intellectual.* New York: Quill.

Cuadrado Melo, Manuel. 1970. *Obispado de la Habana, su historia a traves de los siglos.* 5 vols. Havana.

Cuba. Centro de estadistica and José D. Frías. 1864. *Noticias estadisticas de la isla de Cuba, en 1862.* Havana: Imprenta del gobierno.

Cuba. Comisión de estadistica. 1829. *Cuadro estandistico de la siempre fiel isla de Cuba, correspondiente al año de 1827.* Havana: Oficina de las Viudas de Arazoza y Soler, Impresoras del Gobierno y Capitaná General.

Cuba. Comision encargada del censo de poblacion. 1842. *Resumen del censo de poblacion de la isla de Cuba a fin del año de 1841.* Havana: Imprenta del Gobierno por S.M.

Cuba. Constitution. Judicatura Cubana Democratica. 1963. *Constitución de la República de cuba firmada en la ciudad de Guáimaro el día primero de julio de 1940.* Miami: Judicatura Cubana Democrática.

Cuba. Dirección general del censo. 1920. *Censo de la república de Cuba, año de 1919.* Havana: Maza, Arroyo y Caso, s. en c., impresores.

Cuba. Oficina Nacional de Estadísticas. 2005. *Cuba, censo de población y viviendas 2002.* Available from http://www.cubagob.cu/otras_info/censo/index.htm.

Cuba. Spain. 1884. *Ley provisional del registro civil para las islas de Cuba y Puerto-Rico.* Havana: Impr. del gobierno y capitania general por S. M.

Curtin, Philip D. 1955. *Two Jamaicas; The Role of Ideas in a Tropical Colony, 1830–1865.* Cambridge, Mass.: Harvard University Press.

———. 1969. *The Atlantic Slave Trade: A Census.* Madison: University of Wisconsin Press.

Davis, Angela. 1971. Reflections on the Black Woman's Role in the Community of Slaves. *Black Scholar* 3 (4): 2–15.

de la Fuente, Alejandro. 1995. Race and Inequality in Cuba, 1899–1981. *Journal of Contemporary History* 30 (1): 131–168.

———. 2001. *A Nation for All: Race, Inequality, and Politics in Twentieth-Century Cuba.* Envisioning Cuba. Chapel Hill: University of North Carolina Press.

———. 2004. Slave Law and Claims-Making in Cuba: The Tannenbaum Debate Revisited. *Law and History Review* 22 (2): 339–369.

———. 2010. From Slaves to Citizens? Tannenbaum and the Debates on Slavery, Emancipation, and Race Relations in Latin America. *International Labor and Working-Class History* (77): 154–173.

de la Sagra, Ramón. 1831. *Historia economico-politica y estadistica de la isla de Cuba; ó sea de sus progresos en la poblacion, la agricultura, el comercio y las rentas.* Havana: Impr. de las viudas de Arazoza y Soler.

de la Torre, José Marie. 1857. *Lo que fuimos y lo que somos o La Habana antigua y moderna.* Havana: Spencer y Co.

Deschamps Chapeaux, Pedro. 1976. *Los batallones de pardos y morenos libres.* Havana: Editorial Arte y Literatura, Instituto Cubano del Libro.

Díaz, María Elena. 2000. *The Virgin, the King, and the Royal Slaves of El Cobre: Negotiating Freedom in Colonial Cuba, 1670–1780.* Cultural Sitings. Stanford, Calif.: Stanford University Press.

Dore, Elizabeth. 2000. Introduction. In *Reyíta: The Life of a Black Cuban Woman in the Twentieth Century,* ed. Daisy Rubiera Castillo. Durham, N.C.: Duke University Press.

Dorsey, Joseph C. 1994. Women without History: Slavery and the International Politics of *partus-sequitur-ventrem* in the Spanish Caribbean. *Journal of Caribbean History* 28 (2): 165–207.

Duany, Jorge. 1985. Ethnicity in the Spanish Caribbean: Notes on the Consolidation of Creole Identity in Cuba and Puerto Rico, 1762–1868. In *Caribbean Ethnicity Revisited,* ed. Stephen Glazier, 15–39. New York: Gordon and Breach.

———. 1988. After the Revolution: The Search for Roots in Afro-Cuban Culture. *Latin American Research Review* 23 (1): 244–255.

Dumoulin, John. 2002. Los matrimonios santiagueros en el siglo XIX: Apuntes para un debate sobre esclavitud y ciudadanía en Las Américas. In *Ciudadanos en la nación,* ed. Olga Portuondo Zúñiga and Michael Zeuske. Santiago de Cuba: BPR Publishers.

Dunn, Richard S. 1972. *Sugar and Slaves: The Rise of the Planter Class in the English West Indies.* Chapel Hill: University of North Carolina Press.

Duno Gottberg, Luis. 2003. *Solventando las diferencias: La ideología del mestizaje en Cuba.* Colección nexos y diferencias. Vol. 9. Madrid: Iberoamericana.

Duque de Estrada, Nicolás. 1818. *Explicación de la doctrina cristiana acomodada a la capacidad de los negros bozales.* Havana: Arazoza y Soler.

Eblen, Jack Ericson. 1975. On the Natural Increase of Slave Populations: The Example of the Cuban Black Population, 1775–1900. In *Race and Slavery in the Western Hemisphere: Quantitative Studies,* ed. S. L. Engerman and E. D. Genovese, 211–248. Princeton, N.J.: Princeton University Press.

Ekelund, Jr., Robert B., Donald R. Street, and Audrey B. Davidson. 1996. Marriage, Divorce and Prostitution: Economic Sociology in Medieval England and Enlightenment Spain. *Journal of the History of Economic Thought* 3 (2): 183–199.

Eltis, David. 1987a. *Economic Growth and the Ending of the Transatlantic Slave Trade.* New York: Oxford University Press.

———. 1987b. The Nineteenth-Century Transatlantic Slave Trade: An Annual Time-Series of Imports into the Americas Broken Down by Region. *The Hispanic American Historical Review* 67 (1): 109–138.

Eltis, David, and Stanley L. Engerman. 1992. Was the Slave Trade Dominated by Men? *Journal of Interdisciplinary History* 23 (2): 237–257.

Fanon, Frantz. 1967. *Black Skin, White Masks* [Peau noire, masques blancs]. Trans. Charles Lam Markmann. New York: Grove Press.

Fernandez, Nadine T. 2010. *Revolutionizing Romance: Interracial Couples in Contemporary Cuba.* New Brunswick, N.J.: Rutgers University Press.

Fernandez, Nadine Therese. 1996. Race, Romance, and Revolution: The Cultural Politics of Interracial Encounters in Cuba. PhD dissertation, University of California Berkeley.

Fernández Robaina, Tomás. 1994. *Hablen paleros y santeros.* Colección echú bi. Havana: Editorial de Ciencias Sociales.

———. 1998. Marcus Garvey in Cuba: Urrutia, Cubans, and Black Nationalism. In *Between Race and Empire: African-Americans and Cubans before the Cuban Revolution,* eds. Lisa Brock and Digna Castañeda Fuertes, 120–128. Philadelphia: Temple University Press.

Ferrer, Ada. 1998. Rustic Men, Civilized Nation: Race, Culture, and Contention on the Eve of Cuban Independence. *Hispanic American Historical Review* 78 (4): 663–686.

———. 1999. *Insurgent Cuba: Race, Nation, and Revolution, 1868–1898.* Chapel Hill: University of North Carolina Press.

Fogel, Robert William. 1989. *Without Consent or Contract: The Rise and Fall of American Slavery.* New York: Norton.

Foucault, Michel. 1978. *The History of Sexuality* [Histoire de la sexualité]. Trans. Robert Hurley. Vol. 1. New York: Pantheon Books.

Fraga Filho, Walter. 2006 *Encruzilhadas da liberdade: Histórias de escravos e libertos na Bahia, 1870–1910.* Campinas, SP, Brazil: Editora UNICAMP.

Franco, José Luciano. 1975. *Las minas de Santiago del Prado y la rebelión de los cobreros, 1530–1800.* Nuestra historia. Havana: Editorial de Ciencias Sociales.

———. 1980. *Comercio clandestino de esclavos.* Nuestra historia. Havana: Editorial de Ciencias Sociales.

Franklin, John Hope. 1947. *From Slavery to Freedom: A History of American Negroes.* New York: A. A. Knopf.

Gacto Fernández, Enrique. 1969. *La filiación no legítima en el derecho histórico español.* Serie derecho. Vol. 5. Sevilla: Universidad de Sevilla.

Gaines, Kevin Kelly. 1996. *Uplifting the Race: Black Leadership, Politics, and Culture in the Twentieth Century.* Chapel Hill: University of North Carolina Press.

Gallego, José María Laina. 1991. *Libertad y consentimiento paterno para el matrimonio en la legislación española (de la pragmática de Carlos III al proyecto de código civil de 1851).* Madrid: Universidad Complutense de Madrid, Servicio de Publicaciones.

García, Gloria. 1994. El auge de la sociedad esclavista en Cuba. In Instituto de Historia de Cuba, *La colonia: Evolucíon socioeconomica y fomacion national desde los orígines hasta 1867.* Vol. 1, 225–264. Havana: Editora Política.

García González, Armando. 1994. En torno a la antropología y el racismo en Cuba en el siglo XIX. In *Cuba: La perla de las Antillas,* ed. Consuelo Naranjo Orovio and Tomas Mallo Gutierrez, 45–64. Madrid: CSIC.

García Rodríguez, Gloria. 1996. *La esclavitud desde la esclavitud: La visión de los siervos.* México: Centro de Investigacíon Científica "Ing. Jorge L Tamayo."

García Rodríguez, Mercedes. 1999. Presencia jesuita en la economía de cuba. PhD dissertation, Universidad of Havana.

———. 2009. De productores empíricos a hacendados ilustrados: El mundo del azúcar que precedió a Francisco de Arango y Parreño. In *Francisco Arango y la invención de la Cuba azucarera,* ed. María Dolores González-Ripoll Navarro, Izaskun Álvarez Cuartero, 85–104. Salamanca: Ediciones Universidad de Salamanca.

Gatewood, Willard B. 1990. *Aristocrats of Color: The Black Elite, 1880–1920.* Bloomington: Indiana University Press.

Genovese, Eugene D. 1968. Materialism and Idealism in the History of Negro Slavery in the Americas. *Journal of Social History* 1 (4): 371–394.

Gómez Abreu, Nery, and Manuel Martínez Casanova. 1986. Contribución al estudio de la presencia de las diferentes etnias y culturas africanas en la región central de Cuba: Zona de Placetas (1817–1886). *Isla* 85.

González, Ondina. "Abandonment in Havana: The Response of the State and the Church, 1700–1750" (paper presented at the International Congress of the Latin American Studies Association, Miami, Florida, 2000).

González, Reynaldo. 1983. *Contradanzas y latigazos.* Havana: Editorial Letras Cubanas.

González-Ripoll Navarro, Ma Dolores, and Izaskun Alvarez Cuartero. 2009. *Francisco Arango y la invención de la Cuba azucarera.* Aquilafuente. Vol. 158. Salamanca: Ediciones Universidad Salamanca.

Good, Anthony. 1996. Kinship. In *Encyclopedia of Social and Cultural Anthropology,* ed. Alan Bernard and Jonathan Spenser, 311–318. New York: Routledge.

Gordon, Lewis, R. 2000. *Existentia Africana: Understanding Africana Existential Thought.* New York: Routledge.

Graham, Richard. Introduction. In *The Idea of Race in Latin America,* ed. Richard Graham. Austin: University of Texas Press.

Guerra, Ramiro. 1927. *Azúcar y población en las antillas.* Havana: Cultural.

———. 1972. *Guerra de los 10 años.* 2 vols. Havana: Editorial de Ciencias Sociales.

Guillén, Nicolás. 1931. *Sóngoro cosongo: Poemas mulatos.* Havana: Úcar, García y Cía.

———. 1975–1976. *Prosa de prisa, 1929–1972.* Letras cubanas. Havana: Editorial Arte y Literatura.

———. 1980. *Obra poética.* Ed. Ángel Augier. Havana: Editorial Letras Cubanas.

———. 1982. *Páginas vueltas: Memorias.* Havana: Unión de Escritores y Artistas de Cuba.

Guirao, Ramón. 1938. *Orbita de la poesía afrocubana, 1928–37 (antología).* Havana: Talleres de Ucar, García y cía.

Gutiérrez, Ramón A. 1991. *When Jesus Came, the Corn Mothers Went Away: Marriage, Sexuality, and Power in New Mexico, 1500–1846.* Stanford, Calif.: Stanford University Press.

Gutman, Herbert George. 1976. *The Black Family in Slavery and Freedom, 1750–1925.* New York: Vintage Books.

Gyekye, Kwame. 1995. *An Essay on African Philosophical Thought: The Akan Conceptual Scheme.* Rev. ed. Philadelphia: Temple University Press.

Hale, Charles. 1986. Political and Social Ideas in Latin America, 1870–1930. In *The Cambridge History of Latin America.* Vol. 4, ed. Leslie Bethell, 367–441. Cambridge: Cambridge University Press.

Hall, Gwendolyn Midlo. 1971. *Social Control in Slave Plantation Societies: A Comparison of St. Domingue and Cuba.* Johns Hopkins University Studies in Historical and Political Science. Ser. 89, no. 1. Baltimore: Johns Hopkins University Press.

Hareven, Tamara. 1987. Family History at the Crossroads. *Journal of Family History* 12 (1–3): ix–xxiii.

Hartman, Saidiya. 1997. *Scenes of Subjection: Terror, Slavery and Self-Making in Nineteenth-Century America.* New York: Oxford University Press.

Havana (Cuba), Ayuntamiento. 1890. *Exposición del ayuntamiento de La Habana el exemo. Señor ministro de ultramar, acerca del caracter de establecimiento municipal de las reales casas de beneficencia y maternidad.* Havana: Impr. de P. Fernñdez y compañia.

Helg, Aline. 1990. Race in Argentina and Cuba, 1880–1930: Theory, Policies, and Popular Reaction. In *The Idea of Race in Latin America, 1870–1940,* ed. Richard Graham, 37–70. Austin: University of Texas Press.

———. 1995. *Our Rightful Share: The Afro-Cuban Struggle for Equality, 1886–1912.* Chapel Hill: University of North Carolina Press.

Heredia, José María. 1892. *Poesías líricas con prólogo de Elías Zerolo.* Paris: Garnier Hermanos.

Higginbotham, Evelyn Brooks. 1992. African-American Women's History and the Metalanguage of Race. *Signs* 17 (2): 251–274.

Higman, B. W. 1995. *Slave Populations of the British Caribbean, 1807–1834.* Kingston, Jamaica: University of the West Indies Press.

Holbrook, Joseph. 2009. The Church in Cuba: Ambivalence between Regime and Revolution, 1952–1962. Paper presented at the International Congress of Latin American Studies Association, Rio de Janeiro, Brazil, June 11–14.

Hurlbert, William Henry. 1854. *Gan-Eden, or, Pictures of Cuba.* Boston: John P. Jewett.

Ibarra Cuesta, Jorge. 1998. La sociedad cubana en las tres primeras décadas del siglo XX. In Instituto de Historia de Cuba, *La neocolonia: Organización y crisis, desde 1899 hasta 1940.* Havana: Editora Politica.

Idowu, E. Bolaji. 1973. *African Traditional Religion: A Definition.* Maryknoll, N.Y.: Orbis Books.

Iliffe, John. 1989. The Origins of African Population Growth. *Journal of African History* 30 (1): 165–169.

Instituto de Historia de Cuba. 1994. *La colonia: Evolución socioeconómica y formación nacional de los orígenes hasta 1867.* Havana: Editora Política.

———. 1998. *La neocolonia: Organización y crisis, desde 1899 hasta 1940.* Vol. 3. Havana: Editora Política.

Irisarri Aguirre, Ana. 2002. Joaquín de Osés y Alzúa, un obispo ilustrado (1755–1823). Paper presented at Grupos sociales en la historia de Navarra, relaciones y derechos: actas del V Congreso de Historia de Navarra. September, Pamplona.

Jackson, Richard L. 1979. *Black Writers in Latin America.* Albuquerque: University of New Mexico Press.

———. 1997. *Black Writers and the Hispanic Canon.* Twayne's World Authors Series. Vol. 867. New York: Prentice Hall International.

Johnson, Ralph. 2001. Freedom's Trail: The Florida Cuba Connection. Paper presented at the U.S. National Park Service "Places of Cultural Memory: African Reflections on the American Landscape" Conference, Atlanta, Georgia, May 9–12.

Johnson, Sherry. 2001. *The Social Transformation of Eighteenth-Century Cuba.* Gainesville: University Press of Florida.

Jones, Jacqueline. 1985. *Labor of Love, Labor of Sorrow: Black Women, Work, and the Family from Slavery to the Present.* New York: Basic Books.

Kiple, Kenneth F. 1976. *Blacks in Colonial Cuba, 1774–1899.* Latin American Monographs. 2nd ser., no. 17. Gainesville: University Press of Florida.

Klein, Herbert S. 1966. The Colored Militia of Cuba: 1568–1868. *Caribbean Studies* 6 (2): 17–27.

———. 1967. *Slavery in the Americas: A Comparative Study of Virginia and Cuba.* London: Institute of Race Relations/Oxford University Press.

———. 1978. *The Middle Passage: Comparative Studies in the Atlantic Slave Trade.* Princeton, N.J.: Princeton University Press.

———. 1983. African Women in the Atlantic Slave Trade. In *Women and Slavery in Africa,* ed. C. C. Robertson and M. A. Klein, 29–38. Madison: University of Wisconsin Press.

———. 1986. *African Slavery in Latin America and the Caribbean.* New York: Oxford University Press.

Klein, Herbert S., and Stanley L. Engerman. 1978. Fertility Differentials between Slaves in the United States and the British West Indies: A Note on Lactation Practices and Their Possible Implications. *William and Mary Quarterly* 35 (2): 357–374.

Klor de Alva, Jorge. 1995. The Postcolonization of the (Latin) American Experience: A Reconsideration of "Colonialism," "Postcolonialism," and "Mestizaje." In *After*

Colonialism: Imperial Histories and Postcolonial Displacements, ed. Gyan Prakash, 241–277. Princeton, N.J.: Princeton University Press.

Knight, Alan. 1990. Racism, Revolution, and Indigenismo: Mexico, 1910–1940. In *The Idea of Race in Latin America, 1870–1940*, ed. Richard Graham, 71–113. Austin: University of Texas Press.

Knight, Franklin W. 1970. *Slave Society in Cuba during the Nineteenth Century*. Madison: University of Wisconsin Press.

———. 1972. Cuba. In *Neither Slave nor Free: The Freeman of African Descent in Slave Societies of the New World*, ed. David W. Cohen and Jack P. Greene, 278–308. Baltimore: Johns Hopkins University Press.

Konetzke, Richard. 1953. *Colección de documentos para la historia de la formación social de Hispanoamerica*. Madrid: Consejo Superior de Investigaciones Científicas.

Krech, Shepard. 1982. Black Family Organization in the Nineteenth Century: An Ethnological Perspective. *Journal of Interdisciplinary History* 12 (3): 429–452.

Kuethe, Allan J. 1986. *Cuba, 1753–1815: Crown, Military, and Society*. Knoxville: University of Tennessee Press.

Kutzinski, Vera M. 1993. *Sugar's Secrets: Race and the Erotics of Cuban Nationalism*. New World Studies. Charlottesville: University Press of Virginia.

Kuznesof, Elizabeth, and Robert Oppenheimer. 1985. The Family and Society in Nineteenth-Century Latin America: An Historiographical Introduction. *Journal of Family History* 10 (3): 215–234.

Kuznesof, Elizabeth Anne. 1995. Ethnic and Gender Influences on "Spanish" Creole Society in Colonial Spanish America. *Colonial Latin American Review* 4 (1): 153–176.

Labinjoh, Justin. 1974. The Sexual Life of the Oppressed: An Examination of the Family Life of Ante-Bellum Slaves. *Phylon* 35 (4): 375–397.

Lachatañeré, Romulo. 1939. El sistema religioso de los lucumís y otras influencias africanas en cuba. *Estudios Afrocubanos* 3: 28–84.

Landers, Jane. 1999. *Black Society in Spanish Florida*. Urbana: University of Illinois Press.

———. 2006. Cimarrón and Citizen: African Ethnicity, Corporate Identity, and the Evolution of Free Black Towns in the Spanish Circum-Caribbean. In *Slaves, Subjects, and Subversives: Blacks in Colonial Latin America*, eds. Jane Landers and Barry Robinson, 111–147. Albuquerque: University of New Mexico Press.

Lantz, Herman. 1980. Family and Kin as Revealed in the Narratives of Ex-Slaves. *Social Science Quarterly* 60 (4): 667–674.

Lauderdale Graham, Sandra. 1988. *House and Street: The Domestic World of Servants and Masters in Nineteenth-Century Rio de Janeiro*. Cambridge Latin American Studies. Vol. 68. Cambridge: Cambridge University Press.

Lavrin, Asunción. 1989. Introduction: The Scenario, the Actors, and the Issues. *Sexuality and Marriage in Colonial Latin America*, 1–46. Lincoln: University of Nebraska Press.

Lazo, Raimundo. 1982. Cecilia Valdés: estudio critico. In *Acera de Cirilo Villaverde*, ed. Imeldo Alvárez. Havana: Editorial Letras Cubanas.

Le Riverend, Julio. 1967. *Historia económica de Cuba*. Havana: Ensayo.

Leacock, Eleanor Burke. 1972. Introduction. In Friedrich Engels, *The Origin of the Family, Private Property, and the State*, 7–67. New York: International Publishers.

Lewis, Oscar, Ruth M. Lewis, and Susan M. Rigdon. 1977–1978. *Living the Revolution: An Oral History of Contemporary Cuba.* 3 vols. Urbana: University of Illinois Press.

Logan, Enid Lynette. 2008. The 1899 Cuban Marriage Law Controversy: Church, State and Empire in the Crucible of Nation. *Journal of Social History* 42 (2): 469–494.

———. 2010. Each Sheep with Its Mate: Marking Race and Legitimacy in Cuban Catholic Parish Archives, 1890–1940. *New West Indian Guide/Nieuwe West-Indische Gids* 84 (1–2): 5–39.

López Valdés, Rafael L. 2002. *Los africanos de Cuba.* Biblioteca del centro. San Juan, P.R.: Centro de Estudios Avanzados de Puerto Rico y el Caribe.

Lovell, Peggy A., Wood, and Charles Howard. 1998. Skin Color, Racial Identity, and Life Chances in Brazil. *Latin American Perspectives* 25 (3): 90–109.

Lucena Salmoral, Manuel. 1996. El reglamento de esclavos de Cuba. *Del Caribe* 25: 88–99.

Lutjens, Sheryl L. 1995. Reading between the Lines: Women, the State, and Rectification in Cuba. *Latin American Perspectives* 22 (2): 100–124.

Machado, José. 1941. *Los hijos ilegítimos.* Havana: Cultural, s.a.

Mair, Lucy. 1974. *African Societies.* London: Cambridge University Press.

Malone, Ann Patton. 1992. *Sweet Chariot: Slave Family and Household Structure in Nineteenth-Century Louisiana.* Fred W. Morrison Series in Southern Studies. Chapel Hill: University of North Carolina Press.

Manzano, Juan Francisco. 1975. *Poems by a Slave in the Island of Cuba, Recently Liberated,* ed. Richard Robert Madden. London: T. Ward and Co.

———. 1996. *The Autobiography of a Slave.* Latin American Literature and Culture Series. Bilingual ed. Detroit: Wayne State University Press.

Marrero, Leví. 1972–1992. *Cuba, economía y sociedad.* 15 vols. Río Piedras, P.R.: Editorial San Juan.

Martí, José. 1963–1973. *Obras completas.* 27 vols. Havana: Editorial Nacional de Cuba.

———. 1978. Para las escenas. *Anuario del Centro de Estudios Martianos* (1): 31–33.

Martin, Tony. 1976. *Race First: The Ideological and Organizational Struggle of Marcus Garvey and the Universal Negro Improvement Association.* Westport, Conn.: Greenwood Press.

Martínez, María Elena. 2008. *Genealogical Fictions: Limpieza de Sangre, Religion, and Gender in Colonial Mexico.* Stanford, Calif.: Stanford University Press.

Martinez-Alier, Verena. 1974. *Marriage, Class and Colour in Nineteenth-Century Cuba: A Study of Racial Attitudes and Sexual Values in a Slave Society.* Cambridge: Cambridge University Press.

Masferrer, Marianne, and Carmelo Mesa-Lago. 1974. The Gradual Integration of the Black in Cuba: Under the Colony, the Republic, and the Revolution. In *Slavery and Race Relations in Latin America,* ed. Robert B. Topline, 348–384. Westport, Conn.: Greenwood Press.

Mbiti, John S. 1991. *Introduction to African Religion.* 2nd rev. ed. Portsmouth, N.H.: Heinemann Educational Books.

McCaa, Robert. 1991. Introduction [special issue on Latin America]. *Journal of Family History* 16 (3).

McClintock, Anne. 1995. *Imperial Leather: Race, Gender, and Sexuality in the Colonial Contest.* New York: Routledge.

————. 1996. No Longer in a Future Heaven: Nationalism, Gender, and Race. *Becoming National: A Reader,* ed. Geoff Eley and Ronald Grigor Suny, 260–284. Oxford: Oxford University Press.

McLeod, Marc C. "Sin dejar de ser cubanos": Cuban Blacks and the Challenges of Garveyism in Cuba. *Caribbean Studies* (2003): 75–105.

Meier, August. 1963. *Negro Thought in America, 1880–1915; Racial Ideologies in the Age of Booker T. Washington.* Ann Arbor: University of Michigan Press.

Mendizabal, Isabel, Karla Sandoval, Gemma Berniell-Lee, Francesc Calafell, Antonio Salas, Antonio Martínez-Fuentes, and David Comas. 2008. Genetic Origin, Admixture, and Asymmetry in Maternal and Paternal Human Lineages in Cuba. *BMC Evolutionary Biology* 8 (1): 213.

Menéndez Vázquez, Lázara. 1995. ¡¿ Un cake para obatalá?! *Temas* 4: 38–51.

Meriño Fuentes, María de los Ángeles, and Aisnara Perera Díaz. 2007. *Matrimonio y familia en el ingenio: Una utopía posible: La habana (1825–1886).* Senderos. Havana: Editorial Unicornio.

————. 2008. *Un café para la microhistoria: Estructura de posesión de esclavos y ciclo de vida en la llanura habanera, 1800–1886.* Historia. Havana: Editorial de Ciencias Sociales.

Metcalf, Alida C. 1992. *Family and Frontier in Colonial Brazil: Santana de Parnaíba, 1580–1822.* Berkeley: University of California Press.

Mignolo, Walter. 2005. *The Idea of Latin America.* Blackwell Manifestos. Malden, Mass.: Blackwell.

Milanich, Nara. Whither Family History: A Road Map from Latin America. *American Historical Review* 112 (2): 439–458.

Miller, Gary M. 1990. Bourbon Social Engineering: Women and Conditions of Marriage in Eighteenth-Century Venezuela. *Americas* 46 (3): 261–290.

Miller, Ivor L. 2000. Religious Symbolism in Cuban Political Performance. *TDR/The Drama Review* 44 (2): 30–55.

Miller, Joseph C. 1984. Demographic History Revisited. *Journal of African History* 25 (1): 93–96.

Montejo, Esteban. 2003. *Biography of a Runaway Slave* [Biografía de un cimarrón]. Rev. ed. Ed. Miguel Barnet. Trans. W. Nick Hill. Willimantic, Conn.: Curbstone Press.

Montejo Arrechea, Carmen. 1993. *Sociedades de instrucción y recreo de pardos y morenos que existeron en Cuba colonial.* Veracruz: Instituto Veracruzano de Cultura.

————. 1998. Minerva: A Magazine for Women (and Men) of Color. In *Between Race and Empire: African-Americans and Cubans before the Cuban Revolution.* Vol. 36, ed. Lisa Brock and Digna Castañeda Fuentes, 33–48. Philadelphia: Temple University Press.

Moore, Carlos. 1988. *Castro, the Blacks, and Africa.* Afro-American Culture and Society. Vol. 8. Los Angeles: Center for Afro-American Studies, University of California.

Moore, Robin. 1997. *Nationalizing Blackness: Afrocubanismo and Artistic Revolution in Havana, 1920–1940.* Pitt Latin American Series. Pittsburgh: University of Pittsburgh Press.

————. 2006. *Music and Revolution: Cultural Change in Socialist Cuba.* Music of the African Diaspora. Vol. 9. Berkeley: University of California Press.

Morales, Jorge Luis, ed. 1981. *Poesía afroantillana y negrista (Puerto Rico, República Dominicana, Cuba)*. Rev. and enl. ed. Río Piedras P.R.: Editorial Universitaria, Universidad de Puerto Rico.

Morales Domínguez, Esteban. 2013. *Race in Cuba: Essays on the Revolution and Racial Inequality*, ed. Gary Prevost and August H. Nimtz. New York: Monthly Review Press.

Morejón, Nancy. 1982. *Nación y mestizaje en Nicolás Guillén*. Havana: Unión de Escritores y Artistas de Cuba.

Moreno Fraginals, Manuel. 1977. Africa in Cuba: A Quantitative Analysis of the African Population in the Island of Cuba. *Annals of the New York Academy of Sciences* 292 (1): 187–201.

———. 1978. *El ingenio: Complejo económico social cubano del azúcar*. 3 vols. Nuestra historia. Havana: Editorial de Ciencias Sociales.

Morgan, Jennifer L. 2004. *Laboring Women: Reproduction and Gender in New World Slavery*. Philadelphia: University of Pennsylvania Press.

Mörner, Magnus. 1967. *Race Mixture in the History of Latin America*. Boston: Little, Brown.

Morrison, Karen Y. 1999. Civilization and Citizenship in the Eyes of Afro-Cuban Intellectuals during the First Constitutional Period (1902–1940). *Cuban Studies/ Estudios Cubanos* 30: 76–99.

———. 2012. "Whitening" Revisited: Nineteenth-Century Cuban Counterpoints. In *Africans into Spanish America: Expanding the Diaspora*, ed. Sherwin Bryant, Rachel O'Toole, and Ben Vinson III, 163–185. Urbana: University of Illinois Press.

Morrissey, Marietta. 1989. *Slave Women in the New World: Gender Stratification in the Caribbean*. Studies in Historical Social Change. Lawrence: University Press of Kansas.

Mosse, George L. 1985. *Nationalism and Sexuality: Middle-Class Morality and Sexual Norms in Modern Europe*. Madison: University of Wisconsin Press.

Murphy, Joseph M. 1993. *Santería: African Spirits in America*. Rev. ed. Boston: Beacon Press.

Murray, David R. 1980. *Odious Commerce: Britain, Spain, and the Abolition of the Cuban Slave Trade*. Cambridge Latin American Studies. Vol. 37. New York: Cambridge University Press.

Mustelier, Gustavo Enrique. 1912. *La extincion del negro*. Havana: Impr. de Rambla, Bouza y ca.

Nazzari, Muriel. 1997. Sex/Gender Arrangements and the Reproduction of Class in the Latin American Past. In *Gender Politics in Latin America, Debates in Theory and Practice*, ed. Elizabeth Dore, 134–148. New York: Monthly Review Press.

Nieto y Cortadellas, Rafael. 1954. *Dignidades nobiliarias en cuba*. Madrid: Ediciones Cultura Hispánica.

Núñez González, Niurka, Odalys Buscarón Ochoa, and Hernán Tirado Toirac. 2011. La caracterización ethnocultural de los grupos raciales: El complejo habitacional, la religión, y las relaciones interraciales. In Lázara Y. Carrazana Fuentes et al., *Las relaciones raciales en Cuba, estudios contemporáneos*, 125–172. Havana: Fundación Fernando Ortiz.

O'Brien, Mary. 1989. *Reproducing the World: Essays in Feminist Theory*. Boulder, Colo.: Westview Press.

Olesen, Virginia. 1971. Context and Posture: Notes on Socio-Cultural Aspects of Women's Roles and Family Policy in Contemporary Cuba. *Journal of Marriage and Family* 33 (3): 548–560.

Omi, Michael, and Howard Winant. 1994. *Racial Formation in the United States: From the 1960s to the 1990s*. New York: Routledge.

Orozco, Román, and Natalia Bolívar Aróstegui. 1998. *Cuba santa: Comunistas, santeros y cristianos en la isla de Fidel Castro*. Madrid: El País Aguilar.

Ortiz, Fernando. 1924. Vocablos de la economía política afrocubana. *Cuba Contemporánea* 35 (138): 136–146.

———. 1947. *Cuban Counterpoint: Tobacco and Sugar* [Contra punteo cubano del tabaco y el azúcar]. Trans. Harriet De Onís. New York: A. A. Knopf.

———. 1973. *Hampa afro-cubana: Los negros brujos: Apuntes para un estudio de etnología criminal*. Colección ebano y canela. Vol. 2. Miami: Ediciones Universal.

———. 1984. *Ensayos etnográficos*. Pensamiento cubano. Ed. Miguel Barnet and Angel Luis Fernández. Havana: Editorial de Ciencias Sociales.

———. 1996[1916]. *Los negros esclavos*. Havana: Editorial de Ciencias Sociales.

Otero, Juan Joaquin, et al. 1954 *Libro de Cuba. una enciclopedia ilustrada que abarca las artes, las letras, las ciencias, la economía, la política, la historia, la docencia y el progreso general de la nación cubana. Edición conmemorativa del cincuentenario de la independencia, 1902–1952, y del centenario del nacimiento de José Martí, 1853–1953*. Havana: Publicaciones Unidas.

O'Toole, Rachel Sarah. 2012. *Bound Lives: Africans, Indians, and the Making of Race in Colonial Peru*. Pitt Latin American Series. Pittsburgh: University of Pittsburgh Press.

Palmié, Stephan. 2002. *Wizards and Scientists: Explorations in Afro-Cuban Modernity and Tradition*. Durham, N.C.: Duke University Press.

———. 2006. Creolization and Its Discontents. *Annual Review of Anthropology* 35: 433–456.

Pappademos, Melina. 2011. *Black Political Activism and the Cuban Republic*. Envisioning Cuba. Chapel Hill: University of North Carolina Press.

Paquette, Gabriel. 2008. *Enlightenment, Governance and Reform in Spain and its Empire 1759–1808*. Basingstoke, UK: Palgrave Macmillan.

Paquette, Gabriel B., ed. 2009. *Enlightened Reform in Southern Europe and Its Atlantic Colonies, c. 1750–1830*. Empires and the Making of the Modern World, 1650–2000. Farnham, UK. Burlington, Vt.: Ashgate.

Paquette, Robert L. 1988. *Sugar Is Made with Blood: The Conspiracy of La Escalera and the Conflict between Empires over Slavery in Cuba*. Middletown, Conn.: Wesleyan University Press.

Parker, Andrew. 1992. *Nationalisms and Sexualities*. New York: Routledge.

Partido Comunista de Cuba. Congreso. 1981. *Tesis y resoluciones*. Havana: Editorial de Ciencias Sociales.

Pastor, Manuel. 1829. *Año de 1828. Censo de la siempre fidelisima ciudad de la Habana* . . . Havana: Imprenta del gobierno y capitania general por S. M.

Payne, Stanley G. 1978. Spanish Conservatism 1834–1923. *Journal of Contemporary History* 13 (4): 765–789.

———. 1984. *Spanish Catholicism: An Historical Overview*. Madison: University of Wisconsin Press.

Pedraza-Bailey, Silvia. 1985. Cuba's Exiles: Portrait of a Refugee Migration. *International Migration Review* 19: 4–34.

Pereda Valdés, Ildefonso. 1970. *Lo negro y lo mulato en la poesía cubana*. Montevideo: Ediciones Ciudadela.

Perera Díaz, Aisnara, and Meriño Fuentes, María de los Ángeles. 2006. *Esclavitud, familia y parroquia en Cuba: Otra mirada desde la microhistoria*. Santiago de Cuba: Instituto Cubano del Libro, Editorial Oriente.

———. 2006. *Nombrar las cosas: Aproximación a la onomástica de la familia negra en Cuba*. Colección la fama. Guantánamo: El Mar y la Montaña.

———. 2009. *Para librarse de lazos, antes buena familia que buenos brazos: Apuntes sobre la manumisión en Cuba (1800–1881)*. Bronce. Santiago de Cuba: Editorial Oriente.

Pérez, Louis A. 1992. *Slaves, Sugar and Colonial Society: Travel Accounts of Cuba, 1801–1899*. Latin American Silhouettes. Wilmington, Del.: Scholarly Resources.

———1997. Identidad y nacionalidad: las raíces del separatismo cubano, 1868–1898. *Op.Cit., Boletín del Centro de Investigaciones Históricas* 23 (9): 185–199.

———. 1999. *On Becoming Cuban: Identity, Nationality, and Culture*. H. Eugene and Lillian Youngs Lehman Series. Chapel Hill: University of North Carolina Press.

Pérez de la Riva, Juan. 1974. El monto de la inmigración forzada en el siglo XIX. *Revista de la Biblioteca Nacional José Martí, 3ra Epoca* 16 (1): 77–110.

———. 1977. *Cuántos africanos fueron traídos a Cuba?* Havana: Editorial de Ciencias Sociales.

Pérez Firmat, Gustavo. 1989. *The Cuban Condition: Translation and Identity in Modern Cuban Literature*. Cambridge Studies in Latin American and Iberian Literature. Vol. 1. New York: Cambridge University Press.

Pérez Murillo, María Dolores. 1988. *Aspectos demográficos y sociales de la isla de Cuba en la primera mitad del siglo XIX*. Cádiz: Servicio de Publicaciones, Universidad de Cádiz.

Pérez Sarduy, Pedro, and Jean Stubbs, eds. 2000. *Afro-Cuban Voices: On Race and Identity in Contemporary Cuba*. Contemporary Cuba. Gainesville: University Press of Florida. Pérez-Stable, Marifeli. 1993. *The Cuban Revolution: Origins, Course, and Legacy*. New York: Oxford University Press.

Pezuela, Jacobo de la. 1863. *Diccionario geografico, estadístico, historico, de la isla de Cuba*. Madrid: Impr. del estab. de Mellado.

Pichardo Viñals, Hortensia. 2000. *Documentos para la historia de Cuba*. 5 vols. Editorial Pueblo y Educación.

Pleito sobre filiación, incidente de al intestado de D. Esteban Santa Cruz de Oviedo, recurso de casación establecido á nombre de Enriqueta Sta. Cruz de Oviedo y compartes, sentencias dictadas por el Tribunal Supremo. Editorial Mercantil: Havana, 1884. .

Portuondo y de Castro, José. 1947. *La filiación, examen de la jurisprudencia sentada por el Tribunal Supremo de Cuba sobre reconocimiento de hijos con vista de lo dispuesto en el art. 44 de la constitución y 135 del código civil*. Havana: Seoane, Fernandez y Cia.

Portuondo Zúñiga, Olga, ed,. 1986. *Nicolás Joseph de Ribera*. Havana: Editorial de Ciencias Sociales.

Postma, Johannes. 1990. *The Dutch in the Atlantic Slave Trade, 1600–1815*. New York: Cambridge University Press.

Premo, Bianca. 2013. Familiar: Thinking beyond Lineage and across Race in Spanish Atlantic Family History. *William and Mary Quarterly* 70 (2): 295–316.

Pruna Goodgall, Pedro M. 1991. *Los jesuitas en Cuba hasta 1767*. Havana: Editorial de Ciencias Sociales.

Puig Peña, Federico. 1962. Hijos de padres desconocidos. In *Nueva enciclopedia juridical*. Vol. 10, 9–10. Barcelona: Editorial Francisco Seix.

Quarles, Benjamin. 1969. *Black Abolitionists*. New York: Oxford University Press.

Quintana, Hilda E., María Cristina Rodríguez, and Gladys Vila Barnés, eds. 1996. *Personalidad y literatura puertorriqueñas*. Río Piedras, P.R.: Editorial Plaza Mayor.

Quiroz, Alfonso W. 2011. Free Association and Civil Society in Cuba, 1787–1895. *Journal of Latin American Studies* 43: 33–64.

Rael, Patrick. 2002. *Black Identity and Black Protest in the Antebellum North*. Chapel Hill: University of North Carolina Press.

Ravenet Ramírez, Mariana, Niurka Pérez Rojas, and Marta Toledo Fraga, eds. 1989. *La mujer rural y urbana: Estudios de casos*. Sociología. Havana: Editorial de Ciencias Sociales.

Real cédula de 21 de octubre de 1817 sobre aumentar la población blanca de la isla de Cuba. Imprenta del Gobierno y Capitania General. Havana, 1828.

Reckord, Barry. 1971. *Does Fidel Eat More Than Your Father? Conversations in Cuba*. New York: Praeger Publishers.

Reglamento para las milicias de infanteria y caballeria de la isla de Cuba aprobado por S. M. 1769. n.p.: Madrid.

Reid, Michele. 2004. Negotiating a Slave Regime: Free People of Color in Cuba, 1844–1868. PhD dissertation, University of Texas Austin.

Reid-Vazquez, Michele. 2011. *The Year of the Lash: Free People of Color in Cuba and the Nineteenth-Century Atlantic World*. Athens: University of Georgia Press.

Rípodas Ardanaz, Daisy. 1977. *El matrimonio en Indias: Realidad social y regulación jurídica*. Buenos Aires: Fundación para la Educación, la Ciencia y la Cultura.

Roca, Blas. 1963. La lucha ideological contra las sectas religiosas. *Cuba Socialista* 22: 34–41.

Rodríguez Reyes, Andrés. El cabildo Lucumí de Santa Teresa en la ciudad de Matanzas. Unpublished manuscript. Centro Provincial de Superación para la Cultura, Matanzas, Cuba.

Rodríguez Ruiz, Pablo. 2011. La interracialidad y la intraracialidad en las estructuras familiars. Un estudio en barrios populares de la Habana. In Lázara Y. Carrazana Fuentes et al., *Las relaciones raciales en Cuba, estudios contemporaneous*. 217–282. Havana: Fundación Fernando Ortiz.

Roediger, David R. 1991. *The Wages of Whiteness: Race and the Making of the American Working Class*. Haymarket Series. New York: Verso.

Roldan de Montaud, Ines. 1982. Origen, evolución y supresión del grupo de negros, emancipados en Cuba (1871–1870). *Revista de Indias* 42 (169–170): 560–641.

Rooke, Patricia T. 1981. A Scramble for Souls: The Impact of the Negro Education Grant on Evangelical Missionaries in the British West Indies. *History of Education Quarterly* 21 (4): 429–447.

Rout, Leslie B. 1976. *The African Experience in Spanish America, 1502 to the Present Day.* Cambridge Latin American Studies. Vol. 23. Cambridge: Cambridge University Press.

Saco, José Antonio. 1879. *Historia de la esclavitud de la raza africana en el nuevo mundo y en especial en los paises américo-hispanos.* Barcelona: Impr. de J. Jepús.

Safa, Helen Icken. 1995. *The Myth of the Male Breadwinner: Women and Industrialization in the Caribbean.* Conflict and Social Change Series. Boulder, Colo.: Westview Press.

Schmidt-Nowara, Christopher. 1995. "Spanish" Cuba: Race and Class in Spanish and Cuban Anti-slavery Ideology, 1861–1868. *Cuban Studies* (25): 101–122.

Schwartz, Stuart. 1992. Rethinking Palmares: Slave Resistance in Colonial Brazil. In *Slaves, Peasants, and Rebels: Reconsidering Brazilian Slavery,* 103–136. Urbana: University of Illinois Press.

Schwartz, Stuart B. 1985. *Sugar Plantations in the Formation of Brazilian Society: Bahia, 1550–1835.* Cambridge Latin American Studies. Vol. 52. New York: Cambridge University Press.

Scott, Rebecca J. 1985. *Slave Emancipation in Cuba: The Transition to Free Labor, 1860–1899.* Princeton, N.J.: Princeton University Press.

Seed, Patricia. 1988. *To Love, Honor, and Obey in Colonial Mexico: Conflicts over Marriage Choice, 1574–1821.* Stanford, Calif.: Stanford University Press.

Sexton, Jared. 2010. People-of-Color-Blindness: Notes on the Afterlife of Slavery. *Social Text* 28 (Summer): 31–56.

Smith, Lois M., and Alfred Padula. 1996. *Sex and Revolution: Women in Socialist Cuba.* New York: Oxford University Press.

Socolow, Susan M. 1989. Acceptable Partners: Marriage Choice in Colonial Argentina, 1778–1810. In *Sexuality and Marriage in Colonial Latin America,* ed. Asunción Lavrin, 209–251. Lincoln: University of Nebraska Press.

Sommer, Doris. 1991. *Foundational Fictions: The National Romances of Latin America.* Latin American Literature and Culture. Vol. 8. Berkeley: University of California Press.

Soto, Lionel. 1977–1978. *La revolución del 33.* 3 vols. Nuestra historia. Havana: Editorial de Ciencias Sociales.

Spain. Ejército. 1769. *Reglamento para las milicias de infanteria y caballeria de la isla de Cuba, aprobado por S. M., y mandado que se observen inviolablemente todos sus articulos, por real cedula expedida en el Prado à 19 de enero . . . 1769.* Madrid.

Spain. Tribunal Supremo. 1883. *Sentencias del Tribunal Supremo en materia civil.* Colección legislativa de España. Vol. 2. Madrid: Imprenta del Ministerio de Gracia y Justicia.

Spillers, Hortense J. 1987. Mama's Baby, Papa's Maybe: An American Grammar Book. *Diacritics* 17 (2): 65–81.

Stark, David M. 1996. Discovering the Invisible Puerto Rican Slave Family: Demographic Evidence from the Eighteenth Century. *Journal of Family History* 21 (4): 395–418.

Stein, Stanley J. 1985[1957]. *Vassouras, a Brazilian Coffee County, 1850–1900: The Roles of Planter and Slave in a Plantation Society.* Princeton, N.J.: Princeton University Press.

Stevens, Evelyn. 1973. *Marianismo:* The Other Face of Machismo in Latin America. In *Male and Female in Latin America,* ed. Anne Pescatello, 90–101. Pittsburgh: University of Pittsburgh.

Stoler, Ann L. 1995. *Race and the Education of Desire: Foucault's History of Sexuality and the Colonial Order of Things.* Durham, N.C.: Duke University Press.

———. 2002. *Carnal Knowledge and Imperial Power: Race and the Intimate in Colonial Rule*. Berkeley: University of California Press.

Stoner, K. Lynn. 1991. *From the House to the Streets: The Cuban Woman's Movement for Legal Reform, 1898–1940*. Durham, N.C.: Duke University Press.

Suárez Polcari, Ramón. 2002. *Historia de la iglesia católica en Cuba*. Colección Félix Varela. Vol. 17. Miami: Ediciones Universal.

Super, John C. 2003. Interpretations of Church and State in Cuba, 1959–1961. *Catholic Historical Review* 89 (3): 511–529.

Tabares del Real, José A. 1975. *La revolución del 30: Sus dos últimos años*. Nuestra historia. 3rd ed. Havana: Editorial de Ciencias Sociales, Instituto Cubano del Libro.

Tannenbaum, Frank. 1946. *Slave and Citizen*. New York: A. A. Knopf.

Tardieu, Jean-Pierre. 2003. *"Morir o dominar," En torno al reglamento de esclavos de Cuba (1841–1866)*. Madrid: Iberoamericana.

Telles, Edward E. 2004. *Race in Another America: The Significance of Skin Color in Brazil*. Princeton, N.J.: Princeton University Press.

Telles, Edward E., and Tianna Pascal. 2012. Beyond Fixed or Fluid: Degrees of Fluidity in Racial Identification in Latin America. Paper presented at the International Congress of the Latin American Studies Association, San Francisco, California, May 23–26.

Thomas, Hugh. 1997. *The Slave Trade: The Story of the Atlantic Slave Trade, 1440–1870*. New York: Simon and Schuster.

———. 1998. *Cuba, or the Pursuit of Freedom*. Updated ed. New York: Da Capo Press.

Tornero Tinajero, Pablo. 1996. *Crecimiento ecónomico y transformaciones sociales: Esclavos, hacendados y comerciantes en la Cuba colonial (1760–1840)*. Madrid: Ministerio de Trabajo y Seguridad Social.

Torres-Cuevas, Eduardo. 1999. Ensayo introductorio: Hacia una interpretación del Obispo de Espada y su influencia en la sociedad y el pensamiento cubanos. In *Obispado de espada, papeles*, 1–163. Havana: Casa de Altos Estudios Don Fernando Ortiz.

Torres-Cuevas, Eduardo, and Edelberto Leiva Lajara. 2005. *Presencia y ausencia de la Compañía de Jesús en Cuba*. Madrid: Fundación Ignacio Larramendi.

———. 2008. *Historia de la iglesia católica en Cuba: La iglesia en las patrias de los criollos (1516–1789)*. Havana: Editorial de Ciencias Sociales.

Twinam, Ann. 1999. *Public Lives, Private Secrets: Gender, Honor, Sexuality, and Illegitimacy in Colonial Spanish America*. Stanford, Calif.: Stanford University Press.

United States Army. Division of Cuba. 1899–1901. *Civil Orders, Proclamations, and Circulars*. Havana.

United States War Department. Cuban Census Office. 1900. *Report on the Census of Cuba, 1899*. Washington, D.C.: Government Printing Office.

Universidad de La Habana. Centro de Estudios Demográficos, and Ernesto Chávez Alvarez. 1976. *La población de Cuba*. CICRED series. Havana: Editorial de Ciencias Sociales, Instituto Cubano del Libro.

Vasconcelos, José. 1920. *La raza cósmica*. Paris: Agencia mundial de librería.

Vélez, María Teresa. 2000. *Drumming for the Gods: The Life and Times of Felipe García Villamil, Santero, Palero, and Abakuá*. Studies in Latin American and Caribbean Music. Philadelphia: Temple University Press.

Villaverde, Cirilo. 1977. *Cecilia Valdés*. Havana: Editorial de Arte y Literatura.

von Humboldt, Alexander. 1840. *Ensayo político sobre la isla de Cuba*. Ed. José López de Bustamante. Nueva ed. Paris: Lecointe y Lasserre.

Wade, Peter. 2003. Afterword, Race and Nation in Latin America: An Anthropological View. In *Race and Nation in Modern Latin America*, ed. Nancy Appelbaum, Anne S. Macpherson, and Karin Alejandra Rosemblatt, 263–281. Chapel Hill: University of North Carolina Press.

———. 2006. Afro-Latin Studies: Reflections on the Field. *Latin American and Caribbean Ethnic Studies* 1 (1): 105–124.

———. 2009. *Race and Sex in Latin America*. New York: Pluto Press.

Weir, David R. 1984. Life under Pressure: France and England, 1670–1870. *Journal of Economic History* 44 (1): 27–47.

White, Deborah G. 1985. *Ar'n't I a Woman?: Female Slaves in the Plantation South*. New York: Norton.

Whitney, Robert. 2000. The Architect of the Cuban State: Fulgencio Batista and Populism in Cuba. *Journal of Latin American Studies* 32 (2): 435–460.

———. 2001. *State and Revolution in Cuba: Mass Mobilization and Political Change, 1920–1940*. Envisioning Cuba. Chapel Hill: University of North Carolina Press.

Wilderson, Frank. 2008. *Red, White, and Black: Cinema and the Structure of U.S. Antagonisms*. Durham, N.C.: Duke University Press.

Williams, Brackette F. 1995. Classification Systems Revisited: Kinship, Caste, Race, and Nationality as the Flow of Blood and the Spread of Rights. In *Naturalizing Power: Essays in Feminist Cultural Analysis*, ed. Sylvia Yanagisako and Carol Delaney, 201–236. New York: Routledge.

Williams, Lorna V. 1995. The Emergence of an Afro-Cuban Aesthetic. *Afro-Hispanic Review*: 48–57.

Williamson, Joel. 1980. *New People: Miscegenation and Mulattoes in the United States*. New York: Free Press.

Wilson, Peter J. 1969. Reputation and Respectability: A Suggestion for Caribbean Ethnology. *Man* 4 (1): 70–84.

Wood, Charles H., and Peggy Lovell. Skin Color, Racial Identity, and Life Chances in Brazil. *Latin American Perspectives* 25 (3): 90–109.

Wright, Winthrop R. 1990. *Café con Leche: Race, Class, and National Image in Venezuela*. Austin: University of Texas Press.

Yetman, Norman R. 1967. The Background of the Slave Narrative Collection. *American Quarterly* 19 (3): 534–553.

Young, Robert J. 1995. *Colonial Desire: Hybridity in Theory, Culture, and Race*. London: Routledge.

Zeuske, M. 2002. Hidden Markers, Open Secrets: On Naming, Race-Marking, and Race-Making in Cuba. *Nieuwe West-Indische Gids/New West Indian Guide* 76 (3–4): 211–241.

Zeuske, Michael. 2002. Novedades de Estaban Montejo. *Del Caribe* 38: 95–101.

INDEX

Page numbers in *italic* refer to illustrations. Tables are indicated by t following the page number, and endnotes by n and the note number, e.g., 299n75. Initial articles (e.g., The, El, La) are ignored in sorting.

KAREN Y. MORRISON, "Kym," was born in Kingston, Jamaica, and raised in suburban Washington, DC. She is an assistant professor in the W. E. B. Du Bois Department of Afro-American Studies at the University of Massachusetts Amherst, and a social historian of the African diaspora. She earned a Bachelor of Science in electrical engineering from Duke University and then worked for a few years in military weapons-systems development. She subsequently completed graduate studies in Latin American and African histories at the University of Florida. Her research explores the interactions between global and local racial-formation processes, especially as they were manifested in nineteenth- and twentieth-century Cuba. She has published in *Cuban Studies/Estudios Cubanos*, the *Journal of Social History, Abolition and Slavery, The Encyclopedia of the Modern World*, and contributed to *Africans to Spanish America: Expanding the Diaspora* (2014), edited by Sherwin K. Bryant, Rachel Sarah O'Toole, and Ben Vinson III.

BLACKS IN THE DIASPORA

Herman L. Bennett, Kim D. Butler, Judith A. Byfield, and
Tracy Sharpley-Whiting, editors

FOUNDING EDITORS:
Darlene Clark Hine, John McCluskey, Jr., and
David Barry Gaspar

Nation of Cowards: Black Activism in Barack Obama's Post-Racial America. David H. Ikard and Martell Lee Teasley

"New Negroes from Africa": Slave Trade Abolition and Free African Settlement in the Nineteenth-Century Caribbean. Rosanne Marion Adderley

The Other Black Bostonians: West Indians in Boston, 1900–1950. Violet Showers Johnson

Our Mothers, Our Powers, Our Texts: Manifestations of Àjé in Africana Literature. Teresa N. Washington

Private Politics and Public Voices: Black Women's Activism from World War I to the New Deal. Nikki Brown

Race for Sanctions: African Americans against Apartheid, 1946–1994. Francis Njubi Nesbitt

Richard B. Moore, Caribbean Militant in Harlem: Collected Writings, 1920–1972. Edited by W. Burghardt Turner and Joyce Moore Turner

Rumba: Dance and Social Change in Contemporary Cuba. Yvonne Daniel

Santería from Africa to the New World: The Dead Sell Memories. George Brandon

Screenplays of the African American Experience. Edited by Phyllis Rauch Klotman

"Seeing Red": Federal Campaigns against Black Militancy, 1919–1925. Theodore Kornweibel

Seizing the New Day: African Americans in Post-Civil War Charleston. Wilbert L. Jenkins

Simple Decency and Common Sense: The Southern Conference Movement, 1938–1963. Linda Reed

The Slave's Rebellion: Literature, History, Orature. Adélékè Adéèkó

Slavery and Identity: Ethnicity, Gender, and Race Relations in Salvador, Brazil, 1808–1888. Mieko Nishida

Stolen Childhood: Slave Youth in Nineteenth-Century America. Wilma King

Stolen Childhood: Slave Youth in Nineteenth-Century America, Second Edition. Wilma King

Strangers in the Land of Paradise: Creation of an African American Community in Buffalo, New York, 1900–1940. Lillian Serece Williams

That the Blood Stay Pure: African Americans, Native Americans, and the Predicament of Race and Identity in Virginia. Arica L. Coleman

Unequal Justice: A Question of Color. Coramae Richey Mann

Women in the Civil Rights Movement: Trailblazers and Torchbearers, 1941–1965. Edited by Vicki L. Crawford, Jacqueline Anne Rouse, and Barbara Woods

Word, Image, and the New Negro: Representation and Identity in the Harlem Renaissance. Anne Elizabeth Carroll

The World of the Haitian Revolution. Edited by David Patrick Geggus and Norman Fiering

Writing the Black Revolutionary Diva: Women's Subjectivity and the Decolonizing Text. Kimberly Nichele Brown

Written by Herself: Literary Production by African American Women, 1746–1892. Frances Smith Foster

The Yoruba Diaspora in the Atlantic World. Edited by Toyin Falola and Matt D. Childs